performing women
and modern literary culture
in latin america

T0324029

intervening acts

PERFORMING WOMEN AND MODERN LITERARY CULTURE IN LATIN AMERICA

VICKY UNRUH

University of Texas Press AUSTIN

Copyright © 2006 by the University of Texas Press
All rights reserved
Printed in the United States of America
First edition, 2006

Requests for permission to reproduce material from this work
should be sent to:
  Permissions
  University of Texas Press
  P.O. Box 7819
  Austin, TX 78713-7819
  www.utexas.edu/utpress/about/bpermission.html

♾ The paper used in this book meets the minimum requirements of
ANSI/NISO Z39.48-1992 (R1997) (Permanence of Paper).

LIBRARY OF CONGRESS CATALOGING-IN-PUBLICATION DATA

Unruh, Vicky.
  Performing women and modern literary culture in Latin
America : intervening acts / Vicky Unruh.
     p.   cm.
  Includes bibliographical references and index.
  ISBN 978-0-292-73935-2
  1. Latin American literature—Women authors—History and
criticism.   2. Latin American literature—20th century—History
and criticism.   I. Title.
  PQ7081.5.U67 2006
  860.9′9287′0980904--dc22
                                        2005011121

In loving memory of Elsie, Maria, and Til,

and for Virginia and Norma,
Jennifer and Rachel,
strong women all.

And now, of course,
for Sam.

contents

Unless otherwise indicated, all translations from Spanish and Portuguese are my own. When citing published translations of works in the text, I provide two parenthetical page sources: the first for the original, the second for the translation. Throughout the text I cite these translations of works using the following abbreviations.

DM   Doris Meyer translation of *Cartucho* by Nellie Campobello

EKDJ   Elizabeth Jackson and K. David Jackson translation of *Parque industrial* by Patrícia Galvão

HOFHF   Harriet de Onís and Frederick H. Fornoff translation of *Las memorias de Mamá Blanca* by Teresa de la Parra

IM   Irene Matthews translation of *Las manos de mamá* by Nellie Campobello

acknowledgments

Support for this book from the University of Kansas included a Hall Center for the Humanities Fellowship, a semester's sabbatical, a General Research Fund summer grant, and release time from the College of Liberal Arts and Sciences and the Department of Spanish and Portuguese. A National Endowment for the Humanities University Fellowship, coupled with a bridge grant from the College of Liberal Arts and Sciences, supported the writing stage. Several people assisted primary research: at the University of Texas, Ann Hartness, Director of the Benson Latin American Collection, and Nicolas Shumway, Director of the Teresa Lozano Long Institute for Latin American Studies; at the University of Florida, Richard Phillips, Director of the Latin American Collection at the Smathers Library; and, as research assistants, Rachel Unruh, Dan Rogers, and Ariel Strichartz. In 1998, I codirected with Iris Smith Fischer a multidisciplinary, semester-long faculty seminar on Performance and Performativity at the University of Kansas Hall Center for the Humanities. The dialogue with seminar participants and with Iris, who also provided inspired feedback on proposals and manuscript sections, nurtured the book's theoretical approach. The dynamic Tertulia Paradiso study group in Lawrence provided a matchless exchange on women and modernism, and fellow *tertulianas* Roberta Johnson and Janet Sharistanian offered incisive comments on proposals or manuscript segments. I have a special debt to Danny Anderson, ever generous with materials, who first suggested the pertinence of Pierre Bourdieu's "art of living" to my work and who, as exemplary department chairman and colleague, moved mountains to facilitate the book's completion. Theresa J. May's interest in the project for the University of Texas Press propelled it to fruition, and Lynne Chapman, Leslie Tingle, and Tana Silva provided invaluable assistance during the editorial process. As readers for the Press, Jean Franco and Francine Masiello made excellent suggestions, some of which I incorporated. Others (in alphabetical order) provided manuscript feedback or material, information, comments, or support for proposals: Leslie Cardone, Resha Cardone, Sara Castro-Klarén, Andrew Debicki,

David Jackson, Roberta Johnson, Elena M. de Jongh, Gwen Kirkpatrick, Jill Kuhnheim, Sandra Messinger Cypess, Gustavo Pérez Firmat, Charles Perrone, Nicolas Shumway, and Ben Sifuentes-Jáuregui. Jennifer Unruh, Pam Rowe, Paula Courtney, and the late Lynn Porter provided technical support. Ann Dosch generously housed me in Austin, and Charles Perrone and Regina Rheda did the same in Gainesville. I am thankful beyond measure to David Unruh for his unflagging help with every aspect of this project and for encouraging me *always* and in ways that I can never repay. All these people helped make this a better book. Its flaws are singularly my own.

Some material appeared in earlier forms and is reprinted with permission. The section on Teresa de la Parra in the introduction is a revised version of "Teresa de la Parra and the Avant-Gardes: An Equivocal Encounter with Literary Culture," in *Todo ese fuego: Homenaje a Merlin Forster,* edited by Mara García and Douglas Weatherford (Universidad Autónoma de Tlaxcala, 1999, 65–79). Parts of Chapters 3 and 8 are revised versions of "Las ágiles musas de la modernidad: Patrícia Galvão y Norah Lange," in *Revista iberoamericana* 64, no. 182–183 (1998): 271–286; and part of Chapter 8 is a revised version of "¿De quién es esta historia? La narrativa de vanguardias en Latinoamérica," in *Naciendo el hombre nuevo . . . Fundir la literatura, artes y vida como práctica de vanguardias en el Mundo Ibérico,* edited by Hans Wentzlaff Eggebert (Frankfurt am Main, Germany: Vervuert Verlag, 1999) 249–265. Part of Chapter 5 is revised from "Una reacia Eva moderna: Performance y pesquisa en el proyecto cultural de Antonieta Rivas Mercado," *Revista de Crítica Literaria Latinoamericana* 24, no. 28 (1998): 61–84. Part of Chapter 7 is revised from "Las rearticulaciones inesperadas de las mujeres de *Amauta:* Magda Portal y María Wiesse," in *Narrativa femenina en América Latina: Prácticas y perspectivas teóricas,* edited by Sara Castro-Klarén (Frankfurt am Main, Germany: Vervuert Verlag, 2003) 93–110.

THE "FATAL FACT" OF THE NEW WOMAN WRITER IN LATIN AMERICA, 1920S–1930S

introduction

In a memoir of Buenos Aires literary activity in the 1920s and 1930s, Alberto Pineta described his nervous, stammering debut in 1929 as a young lecturer for the prestigious cultural institution Amigos del Arte. Highlighting his recollection of the event is the intimidating impact on his demeanor every time he glanced up at the audience and encountered the imposing figure of Victoria Ocampo. Pineta also detailed a gathering of the vanguard Martín Fierro group and the arresting presence of Norah Lange. Her "grace, sensibility, and creative talent," he noted, caused those present to accept "*without protest* the *fatal fact* of the woman writer." Succumbing to this fate, Pineta reported having been flattered by the bestowal of her "personal poetry" when she accepted his invitation to dance (69, 89–90; my emphasis). Weaving through an account of the cultural activity of male writers, these anecdotes showcase the eclectic character of a literary world remapping its boundaries. A small but increasing number of women writers inhabited the Latin American literary landscape, but as these stories reveal, their presence was still sufficiently novel to provoke mixed reviews.

Pineta was not alone. In their equation of a woman's talent with her performative presence, his remarks typify their time. Contemporary accounts, literary memoirs, and reviews of women's writing in Buenos Aires, Mexico City, Havana, Lima, São Paulo, and other Latin American cities highlight the growing but still anomalous participation of women writers, artists, and journalists in artistic circles of the 1920s and 1930s. This tumultuous era represents a key period in Latin America's social and cultural history. Literary groups aimed to revolutionize artistic expression, while nascent feminist movements sought civic reforms that paralleled women's increased presence in the workplace and public sphere. Although the rhetoric of cultural modernization and political feminism periodically intertwined in the public conversation, women received radically mixed messages about their changing roles. Popular middlebrow periodicals—*Caras y caretas* in Buenos Aires, Mexico City's *El universal ilustrado,* Havana's *Carteles* and *Bohemia,* Lima's *Variedades,* and Brazil's *Para todos* or *Kosmos*—celebrated flappers, movie stars, women athletes and aviators, and the New Woman as consumer of modern goods, leisure activities, and incipient media culture. At the same time, Latin America's reformist upper- and middle-class feminists lobbied for civil rights and imagined a useful woman citizen as the guardian of national family values through the concept of social motherhood.[1] For their part, young male writers celebrated a dynamic new Eve as the muse for their artistic modernity: to name a few, the chronometric *Señorita Etc.* of Arqueles Vela's *estridentista* novel in Mexico, Oliverio Girondo's flying woman in *Espantapájaros (al alcance de todos),* Paulo Menotti del Picchia's active and tango-dancing new Brazilian Eve, "useful at home and on the streets" (291), or the Peruvian journal *Amauta*'s New Woman of the barricades who would incite Peru's new men to action (Delafuente, 102).

But where did women who wanted to be writers rather than muses build their intellectual homes? In a cultural arena that still regarded their presence as uncommon or even forbidding, how did they fashion their writing personas, and what did they understand their artistic missions to be? For the women in this book, one answer lies in the striking fact that their access to the artistic world derived in part from public performance: theatre, poetry declamation, song, dance, oration, witty display, or bold journalistic self-portraiture. This performance experience provides decisive common ground in the dissimilar intellectual odysseys of women from remarkably different backgrounds: Venezuela's Teresa de la Parra; Argentina's Alfonsina Storni, Victoria Ocampo, and Norah Lange; Mexico's Nellie Campobello and Antonieta Rivas Mercado; Cuba's Mariblanca Sabas Alomá and Ofelia Rodríguez Acosta; Peru's Magda Portal and María Wiesse; and Brazil's Patrícia Galvão. Moreover, an encounter with the modern literary culture of the artistic avant-gardes, through a literary circle, a prominent male figure, or the adoption of an innovative style, constituted a pivotal moment in these women's development as writers. As self-construed modern women, they channeled their experience with performance into their own intellectual undertakings. Thus their performance training or experience not only provided an avenue to negotiate their public identity as writers but also shaped their distinct conceptions of writing and its purpose. Not surprisingly, images of dislocation pepper the self-portraits of Latin American literary women of the early twentieth century. But notwithstanding their frustrated search for an intellectual home, the women in this book in fact viewed themselves as part of the action and their writing as an assertive intervention in public cultural life. Many undertook a critical dialogue with modern male writers or embraced a vanguard conception of artistic work as a dynamic cultural engagement. But as these women imagined themselves as instigators for change rather than its muses, they unleashed penetrating critiques of projects for social or artistic modernization, including—but by no means exclusively—their casting of women.

PERFORMANCE, INQUIRY, AND THE "ART OF LIVING" AS A WRITER

A multilayered concept of performance shapes my readings of these women's intellectual careers in the 1920s and 1930s. In 1996, Bert States made the timely observation that the word *performance* had assumed a life of its own in critical discourse and become a "keyword," in Raymond Williams's sense of the term (Williams, 11–26), or as States put it, a word that suddenly moves from "normal semantic practice" and takes rhetorical flight: "a word you are hearing, say, a dozen times a week, and you can bet . . . is a proto-keyword spreading on the wings of metaphor" (1). As diverse disciplinary approaches converged in a theoretical fascination with performance, they produced what Andrew Parker and Eve Kosofsky Sedgwick aptly term "a carnivalesque echolalia of . . . extraordinarily productive cross-purposes" (1).[2] While many scholars (I include myself) find such mixing it up fruitful, a well-founded complaint that accompanies such keywords in their transdisciplinary chain reactions is that they can mean just about anything. In a constructive response to this problem, in *Performance: A Critical Introduction* (also from 1996 and now in its second edition), Marvin Carlson executed a masterful mapping of the term's disciplinary roots and evolution in theatre, anthropology, sociology, psychology, and linguistics, as well as its historical and contemporary reinterpretations through various types of performance art. Carlson's work reminds us that, even if we tap into the productive cross-purposes of a word's diverse disciplinary connotations, our critical practice is grounded in our specific deployment of the concepts we choose.

Although I have noted convergences, States on the one hand and Parker and Sedgwick on the other actually come to performance theory from different conceptual lines that are related but not always harmonious: one that sees theatrical activity itself as the primary source for ideas about performance and another that draws on J. L. Austin's concept of "performatives," that is, speech acts that "perform" by actually *doing* what they embody as they are emitted, to focus on the "performativity" of discourse itself and its consequent (re)iteration. Judith Butler's work is among the most widely disseminated in this line. But Austin's oft-cited prototype of a "performative sentence"—the "I do" of a wedding (4–11)—constitutes a ceremonial exchange that is both profoundly theatrical in the aesthetic sense and shot through with cultural hierarchies and thus highlights the actual close ties between the dramatic and the discursive veins of performance theory. Richard Schechner's work exemplifies a third major line of performance theory focused on performance and culture. In dialogue with the late anthropologist Victor Turner, Schechner showcases the correspondences between certain features of aesthetic theatre—the dynamic between actors and roles, the rehearsal, the repetitions of things done before, and the search for transformation—and community-based, cultural rituals. Schechner's definition of performance as "restored behavior" underlies this analogy between aesthetic theatre and ritual, a comparison that foregrounds the choices among available options that theatre practitioners or cultural communities make in executing their performances, as well as the common ground of these two types of activity as sites of repetition or "restoration" and of potential change (*Between Theater and Anthropology*, 36–37).

My own approach to performance brings together these three theoretical lines—the theatrical, the cultural, and the discursive—to argue that the women in this book transformed their concrete experience with performance not only into self-castings as participants in a literary culture that did not welcome them with open arms, but also, and most important, into an analytical tool in the subject matter and the singular literary qualities of their own writing. As a point of departure, I highlight the fact that cultural expectations for women or their actual formal training led the writers I study to perform in the most basic, theatrical sense of the word: reiterating specific scripts, written or implicit, they executed before an audience self-conscious bodily, musical, or verbal acts. Drawing first of all on theatre-based theories of performance, I also argue that these women's writing exhibits a heightened alertness to the epistemological power of performance itself, a more theoretical kind of knowledge and a tool for their analysis that derives from their concrete experience either through actual performing or as women named by their culture—"hailed" or "interpellated," in Althusser's sense (173–174)—as performers.

Although I tease out these women's reflective inclination to theorize their own experience through writing, I am far from proposing that they were poststructuralist performance theorists. For one thing, their subscription to gender or race essentialism—occasional but startling—precludes such anachronistic readings, even though their work was markedly investigative. Rather I hold that performing in the theatrical sense is a practice that generates critical thought in the *performer*. Contemporary theatre practitioners who are also performance theorists share this view. In conceiving performance as a cognitive process—a way of figuring things out—these theorists privilege the rehearsal phase of performance activity rather than finished products. Thus Herbert Blau, who has long showcased the "doing" substance of performance, casts it as a "speculative procedure" and a "taking on and putting off of ideas" (*To All Appearances*, 41). Blau draws here on Harold Pinter's description of the dramatic rehearsal as an undertaking whereby "facts are lost, collided with, found again" (quoted in Blau, *To All Appearances*, 43). On the interface of theatre and anthropology, Schechner theorizes performance through the group-based, dramatic rehearsal, conceived as a "hunt" or a series of actions with "high information potential" (*Performance Theory*, 182). Drawing on both Schechner and Blau, and showcasing the bodily aspect of performance, Joseph Roach uses the concept of the "kinesthetic imagination" as a rich location for cultural memory, transmission, and change (26).

Drawing on the theatre-based concept of performance as cognitive inquiry, then, this book highlights the arresting role of theatre or performance strategies and metaphors in these women's singular intellectual mode as manifested in their literary investigations into art, politics, gender, and social experience. Although some—Storni, Ocampo, Rivas Mercado, Wiesse, Campobello—did actually compose plays or performance pieces (such as ballets), moreover, underlying my analysis is the premise that theatricality—and its propensity for performative inquiry—can mark *any* literary genre. This emerges not simply in the thematic focus on performance that characterized many of these women's writing—they sometimes talked directly about performance—but also in their strategic literary-technical choices or in the intricate construction in their work of a speaking or perceiving persona whose performative identity is not always straightforward. Bakhtin highlighted the performative qualities of narrative through the interactive speech acts of dialogism (*Dialogic Imagination*), a quality that can also mark poetry.[3] Bakhtin also brought into view the theatrical substance of narrative constructions of subjectivity whereby an authorial persona invents itself through sometimes subtle, reciprocal acts of seeing and being seen by an other (*Art and Answerability*, 27–61).

In this vein, my analysis of these women's work draws not just on the performance pieces some of them composed for theatre or dance but also on their investment of stories, novels, essays, or poems with the critical malleability—the *movement*—of theatre-based performance. On the most obvious level, narrative can shift toward the theatrical, for example, in a studied preponderance of scene over summary or in descriptions marked by a clipped stage-direction style, features we find in prose by Ocampo, Lange, Campobello, Rivas Mercado, Rodríguez Acosta, Wiesse, and Galvão. More interesting is the frequent deployment of synecdoche—the embodied replacement of one figure or part by another, which calls to mind Roach's definition of performance as "surrogation" (2). Lange, Campobello, and Galvão in particular bring out the performative quality of synecdoche, especially when used for body parts or fashion. This verbal strategy resembles the visual caricaturist's exaggeration of a key element of a face or body, as well as the more malleable ostension of a single feature through posing, gesture, and movement in theatrical performance. As in theatre, such synecdoche-based choices in narrative or poetry underscore the interplay of what will be shown and what will not and the movement between the two. Similar to theatre, the narrative, lyrical, or essayistic construction of subjectivity undertaken by all of the women in this book, moreover, offers a performative dynamic between seeing and being seen, between the flow of movement and the stylization of a pose, between what will be shown off and what will be hidden. In the chapters that follow, for example, Storni's frenetically declaiming *poetisas* or Sabas Alomá's hyperbolic femininity as the woman intellectual's defense maximize the showing-off, whereas the spying artists created by Lange, Rivas Mercado, and Galvão or the multiple masks of authorial persona assumed by Rivas Mercado, Portal, Rodríguez Acosta, or Galvão all lay claim to concealment.

The performative quality of Latin America's early twentieth-century literary culture offers a conceptual bridge between these women's public activity and the investigative itineraries of their writing. Thus I draw also on the cultural dimensions of performance. I consider the literary world itself as a kind of culture marked not only by evolving habits of the mind but also by shared repertoires of activity, both in art and in everyday life. Closely akin to my own larger view of culture here is the performance-based definition crafted by the social historian Robert Hymes, who proposes that culture is a *repertoire* from which people choose to "show themselves as cultural *actors,* as constant makers and remakers of culture, not simply as middlemen through whom culture somehow does its inexorable work" (5; emphasis in original). This "repertoire," Hymes elaborates, is "not a smoothly coherent system but a lumpy and varied historical accumulation of models, systems, rules, and other symbolic *resources,* differing and unevenly distributed, upon which people draw and through which they negotiate life with one another" (5; emphasis in original). As I consider the early twentieth-century literary or artistic world as a kind of culture in which women writers made use of unevenly distributed repertoires to negotiate their roles as writers, moreover, Pierre Bourdieu's performative conception of modern literary groups is especially germane. Grounded in a conception of cultural practice as both embodied and improvisational—a way of learning by doing[4]—Bourdieu coined the term "the art of living" to describe the intricate, group-based forging of new artistic personae in late-nineteenth-century European literary culture. A "fundamental dimension of the enterprise of artistic creation," Bourdieu argued, was the invention of the *"style of an artist's life."* Thus writers introduced audacities or innovations not only into their written works "but *also into their existence,"* which, Bourdieu argued, was itself conceived as a work of art (58; my emphasis). Similarly, I myself have argued elsewhere that the early-twentieth-century avant-gardes in Latin America are best understood not as a series of canonical works or experiments in a single genre, but rather as a form of multifaceted activity that coalesced around the quest for a particular, if varied, style.[5] Modern literary artists, in Europe and the Americas, sought a style of *acting* in the public sphere as much as of writing, and thus I make repeated reference in this book to women's "art of living" in relationship to literary culture.

Given the intricate ties between cultures and their languages, I also often allude to cultural dialogues, debates, or conversations within the literary or intellectual field. Although numerous theorists have explored the social or philosophical aspects of dialogue, my own use of this terminology is grounded specifically in Danny Anderson's formulation, drawing on Steven Mailloux and Kenneth Burke, that literary works (and by extension, multifaceted literary or artistic activity, I would argue) constitute "acts" of participation in a "cultural conversation" and that "the appearance of a text is like a person's entrance into a room where a conversation was already in progress before the text entered . . . and . . . remains unfinished after the text has left the scene, much like the boundless quality of context" (Anderson, 15). But Anderson, like Hymes, emphasizes the uneven distribution of resources in such conversations, noting that Mailloux highlights the "variety of positions or voices" and "rhetorical struggles for power" that constitute them (Anderson, 15). That the women studied here actively chose to intervene in such conversations with their writing—and this book showcases choice—does not imply, then, that their entries were smooth or that all participants (human or textual) joined on anything approximating equal footing. The notion of a textual intervention in a cultural conversation also emphasizes that beyond whatever theatrical qualities they may possess, literary works (not only their authors) "perform" as actors in that exchange.[6]

For investigating women writers' work in particular, the concept of a multifaceted, performative art of living—within a contextually specific literary-cultural world and marked by historically specific cultural conversations, dialogues, or debates—offers an alternative to readings that highlight strategies of oppositional resistance or that characterize women's work as the embodiment of polarized margin-center relations. Such models can impoverish how we read women's writing and obscure their de facto intellectual mobility—again, their *choices*—in the cultural conversations they join. The art-of-living concept, by contrast, brings into focus the degree to which literary activity and the enactment of an artistic persona constitute not a preconceived project but rather, to use Bourdieu's words, the "taking up" of a "*position to be made*" (76; emphasis in original). In reading these women's writing and self-portraits, then, I trace the multiple cultural sites and genres through which they moved in taking up specific artistic or intellectual positions in the making.

At the same time, grounding this improvisational art of living in a specific time and place necessarily underscores the qualified autonomy that it embodied, and here I draw on the discursive vein of performance theory. For all its capacity for cognitive discovery, a rehearsal-based notion of performance as individual or collective speculation through practice must also contend with the inseparability of experience from the discourse that frames it, to recall Joan Scott's work (33). Here I draw on Judith Butler's concept of the "compulsory citationality" of cultural discourse that forces one to "quote" or repeat it, even as these reiterations can generate change through new, unexpected meanings, or what she calls the "unanticipated resignifications" of "highly contested terms" ("Critically Queer," 23, 28). Although unlike Butler I underscore the active choices women writers made and the periodic new meanings with which they invested the discourses framing their experience, like Butler I show that their options were not unencumbered as to which public identity from the available repertoire they might perform in any given setting. Rather I locate them in a web of competing debates about literature, politics, and gender, cultural scripts with which they could negotiate but that they could not fully escape. The women in this book executed their intellectual choices, for example, in the heart of a literary culture whose gendered discourse of modernity conceptualized them either outside of the modern or as its muses rather than its agents. That the collective art of living and cultural conversations marking early-twentieth-century literary culture in Latin America were enacted primarily by groups of creative young men underscores the challenges women writers faced. If literary culture was the ostensible habitat of men, women were allocated their dwelling place in what I often refer to as a performance culture, a multifaceted conglomerate of media imagery and performative leisure activity, upon which the women in this book invariably cast a discerning, critical eye, even as they embraced their roles as performers. Thus, although they were in no way immune to gender scripting of their time, these women's writing and public personae reveal their razor-sharp awareness of themselves, their defining contexts, and their own historicity. Moreover, their simultaneous negotiation of a supposedly male literary world and an ostensibly female cultural world of performance and modern consumption enacted a more androgynous conception of art, social roles, and culture itself. This androgyny—a repeated motif in the chapters that follow—reverberates throughout these women's serial enactments of mobile artistic personae and in the multiple critical moves of their writing.

A HABITAT FOR FRATERNITY AND THE WOMEN WHO WROTE THERE

In the realm of feminist civic movements in Latin America, a network of women activists emerged by the 1920s. But although some women in this book actually met one another and some forged real or imagined liaisons with other women, all negotiated their intellectual lives among men. Even as women's presence in public life grew, literary culture throughout Latin America, irrespective of aesthetic or political orientation, conceived itself as a habitat for fraternity. Thus aestheticist Florida and politicized Boedo writers alike embraced the Argentine novel *Don Segundo Sombra* (1926), and writers as diverse as Borges and Roberto Arlt regarded its author, Ricardo Güiraldes, as their mentor. In this nationalist epic, published the same year that the new Argentine Civil Code granted limited civil rights to women, masculine plenitude derives from bodily feats executed in a world without them. Fabio Cáceres, a gentleman-writer-to-be whose mixed origins pose a fusion of old money with populist autochthony, advances toward manhood, reclaims his patrimony, and assumes his lettered avocation only when he flees immigrants, bourgeois values, and, above all, authoritarian women to join a band of pampa-wandering men.[7] Comparable homosocial male bonding and rites of passage mark novels pivotal for other artistic projects. Alejo Carpentier's vanguard novel *¡Ecué-Yamba-O!*

(written in 1927 and published in 1933) locates the emergent Afro-Cuban aesthetic of the Havana vanguard in its black protagonist's initiations, first into a mostly male *ñáñigo* subculture and then into a gang in Havana. Most notoriously, Mariano Azuela's *Los de abajo* (1916), whose roving band of revolutionaries forms the novel's collective protagonist, became the centerpiece in the mid-1920s for an acrimonious, gendered Mexican debate about nationalist (masculine) or Europeanized (effeminate) writing modes.

As Robert Irwin has detailed for Mexico, such male bonding abounded in nineteenth-century Latin American fiction.[8] Literary culture of the 1920s and 1930s, however, linked such imagery not only to national projects but also to innovative artistic "positions to be made." Self-consciously modern writers constituted their art of living in their fiction, first-person-plural manifestos, staged polemics, performance events, group nocturnal wanderings, or gatherings at favorite watering holes. Vanguard literary culture in particular was profoundly performative, as writers openly courted or rejected audiences, real or imagined.[9] Graciela Montaldo ties such activity to the democratization of the cultural field, particularly to writers' keen awareness of a growing readership addressed by journalism and a consequent autobiographical impulse to constitute themselves as public figures (26, 53–56). Similarly, Francine Masiello notes that the vanguard writing persona of the 1920s forged a "coherent ego" through a "complex countenance of extra-literary activities" (*Lenguaje e ideología,* 52). But this pursuit of coherence often assumed the collective countenance of an "everlasting club," to borrow Roach's term for the serial performance of group identity (17–25). Anchoring the self-stories of these literary assemblages was their fraternal group habitat, as in the "Cafe de Nadie" for Mexico's *estridentistas,* the Mariátegui house on Lima's Washington Street for the *Amauta* circle, Emilio Roig de Leuchsenring's Havana office for the Grupo Minorista's "sabbatical luncheons," or the oft-named Lange house on Calle Tronador for the emergent Martín Fierro group.

The tropes of cultural modernism were as gendered as its group affiliations. In European modernist writing, as Rita Felski observes, the modernity of the New Woman provided the "bold imagining of an alternative future," but the "modern" also often embodied "crisis" (14). Thus, she argues, the prostitute, the actress, the mechanical woman, the nostalgia-ridden prehistoric woman, and the voracious modern consumer woman all manifested art's ambivalent response to capitalism, technology, and social change.[10] In Latin America, where more uneven, frustrated modernization marked neocolonialist national projects, or where, as Carlos Alonso has argued, modernity itself was often as much trope as reality, gender anxiety flourished. Linking an embodied art of living—say competitions in physical dexterity at a Palermo sweets shop[11]—to their writing, Argentine vanguard writers, for example, aggressively affirmed the masculinity of their modern experiments. In the preface to his prose collection *Aquelarre,* Florida group writer Eduardo González Lanuza proclaimed that his was a "masculine book" of "vigorous" art without the "affectations" of the "confectionery" (8). Today's reader is struck not by the vigor of his prose but rather by its ephemeral language. But González Lanuza's preface betrays qualms that the studied lyricism of his modern prose—a quality ascribed at the time to the work of (women) *poetisas*—might impugn his masculinity (7). Similarly, ironic play notwithstanding, a *Martín Fierro* review of Girondo's experimental verse portrays these lyric, urban snapshots as manly exploits of "gaucho frankness" that "hurl words" like hunting slings (Sarlo, *Martín Fierro,* 21). In postrevolutionary Mexico, on the other hand, the defenders of *mexicanidad* claimed masculinity for realist art with nationalist themes such as *Los de abajo* and dismissed the lyricism of the Contemporáneos writers, and the writers themselves, as effeminate. Always gendered, then, comparable experimental writing was masculine for its creators in Argentina and effeminate for its detractors in Mexico.

As male writers celebrated the modern Eve as an artistic muse, an intricate public dialogue evinced the unwritten rules for real women's writing. Like the modern civic woman imagined by emergent feminist political reformers, the woman writer was to forge her artistic identity through the "special" qualities of her sex. Just as civic feminists argued that a woman's ostensible moral superiority guaranteed her public usefulness, particularly the creation of healthy (national) families, so did the public conversation about writing affirm that women should be more chaste than men in art as in life. Numerous reviews of women's poetry and prose in mass media and forums self-identified as more literary reinforced them for writing in self-abnegating modes and chastised those who did otherwise for writing like men. A favorable review in a March 1926 *Caras y caretas* of the poetry collection *Rama frágil* by María Luisa Carnelli exemplifies these standards: "The verses of this distinguished poetess possess the eminent quality that all poetry should have, and *especially those by women:* they create emotion softly and deeply. They have *no passionate violence whatsoever;* rather a *sweet resignation* translated in always harmonious, well made, and diaphanous verse. Not even love itself can take the poetess out of the atmosphere of *tender serenity* to which her select spirit has risen" ("Rama frágil," n.pag.; my emphasis). The response to a Carnelli contemporary who did otherwise is instructive. Four years after *Don Segundo Sombra* appeared, Victoria Gukovsky, a founding member of the Argentine socialist party and an educational reformer, published *El santo de la higuera,* a collection of gaucho tales. While applauding her continuation of the gauchesque tradition, a review in the prestigious journal *Nosotros* took Gucovsky to task for giving short shrift to female characters, for using "manly motifs," and above all for writing like a man. "Even the form is masculine," the reviewer complained, adding that had he not known the author, he would have suspected the "indirect hand of a man" in the exacting descriptions of scenes among men; the collection's stories about proletarian children, by contrast, manifested the author's "exquisite feminine soul" (Montesano Delchi, 92–93). This gendered conversation about writing permeated artistic culture throughout Latin America, and the women in this book negotiated their literary personae and writing projects through intricate rejoinders.

SEE BEBA BUY BOOKS:
THE NEW WOMAN CONSUMES AND PERFORMS

Clearly these debates on the gender of writing were "about" many things. In Mexico, for one, they signaled the presence of openly gay men in post-revolutionary cultural institutions.[12] Although change was less extensive in some countries (Peru, for example) than others (Argentina or Brazil), historians document the expanded presence of working- and middle-class women in the workforces of Latin American cities, and, as Beatriz Sarlo points out, modern urban leisure activities incorporated upper- and middle-class women into public life in new ways (*Una modernidad periférica,* 21–25). But efforts to reconstitute traditional roles through the gendered division of literary labor manifested not only anxiety about real social change but also the diversification of the cultural field in which closed clubs were actually more open than they appeared at first glance. Membership in literary groups of the period was a moving target and ideological mix. Rarely was there a single leader or authorial group voice. As the Contemporáneos gathering's designation by one member as the "group without a group" exemplifies (Irwin, 160), determining just who was in or out of any of these groups has generated endless accounting by participant-memoirists and vanguard scholarship. While men were certainly more "in" than women and the latter's presence more vulnerable to historical amnesia, a few women—not only those in this book—participated in or moved through most of the major literary groups in Latin America of this period. Women's vanishing presence in *Don Segundo Sombra* notwithstanding, moreover, Latin American fiction of the period was deeply engaged with—if often corrective toward—the subject of women's changing social roles, as in Manuel Gálvez's flighty Argentine protagonist of *Una mujer muy moderna,* the trendy Miss Annie Doll of Martín Adán's *La casa de cartón* in Lima, the cinematographic women of Jaime Torres Bodet's vanguard novellas, the feminist Isabel Machado of Cuban novelist Carlos Loveira's *La última lección,* and the cosmopolitan prostitutes who initiate the eponymous hero, Macunaíma, into modern São Paulo in Mário de Andrade's classic. Notably absent from much fiction by men was the new woman writer or intellectual, notwithstanding her growing presence in actual literary culture.

Debates about literature and gender intersected most palpably in the eclectic, high-circulation journalism in which literary writers throughout Latin America collaborated. Ángel Rama highlighted the role of Latin American journalism in creating the professional writer, and Aníbal González illuminates the ambivalent liaison between journalism and self-conscious literary practice in the 1920s and 1930s, as writers embraced this source of livelihood and access to audiences while simultaneously distancing themselves from media culture through more rarified concepts of the literary. During this time, in fact, *two* new social actors—the professional writer and the performing modern woman—cohabited in the cultural imaginary of widely read journalism. The cautionary tale of the fictional Beba, signed by "Roxana" and serialized from October 1927 until March 1928 in *Caras y caretas,* dramatizes this encounter. Here in narrative and sketches, the short-haired, flapper-styled Beba shops, smokes, attends theatre and films, dances, sings tangos, performs in a *tableau vivant* for a charity ball, disguises herself for carnival, models a risqué bathing suit at Mar de Plata, and eventually marries upward into affluent *porteño* society. Although the fun-loving Beba throws herself into this social masquerade, the final installment forecasts the disintegration of her marriage and dire consequences for national life generated by the unfettered freedom and ambiguous moral code she practices. Beba's counterparts populate comparable media in Brazil, Cuba, Mexico, and Peru, in fictional offerings and a plethora of photographic images in the society pages. Women, too, including all of the writers in this book, wrote for popular periodicals. But the popular weeklies devoted far more space to modern women as performers than to commentary on their writing.[13] Beyond numerous features on movie stars and actresses from Latin America, Hollywood, and Europe, these magazines also depicted ordinary middle- and upper-class women—in stances from decorative to seductive—declaiming poetry, posing in *tableaux vivants,* or representing Greek muses, flappers, Mexican folkloric dancers, Hawaiian hula girls, gypsies, eighteenth-century Parisians, or veiled, quasi-Asian figures.

A defining trait of the modern Latin American woman portrayed by Beba is her equivocal relationship to literary culture. Thus in the first installment, Beba goes to buy books. Although romance novels are her favorites, she also purchases poetry by Mexico's sentimental *modernista* Amado Nervo, the prescribed model of the day for aspiring *poetisas.* This portrayal of the New Woman as a reader whose choices warrant regulation juxtaposes an anxiety toward women's changing roles with the literary world's ambivalent relationship to media culture. As Andreas Huyssen argues, European modernists projected such an equivocal stance through portraits of women (say, Madame Bovary) as readers of modernity's mass-produced fare and cast their male counterparts as more reflective readers of artistically superior writing (46). Similarly, Felski highlights the modernist representational link between a woman's indiscriminate appetites as a middlebrow reader and her portrayal as a voracious consumer through shopping (61–63). Gustavo Pérez Firmat notes the gendering of reading itself—"masculine readers and feminine texts"—posed by the fictions of the Hispanic vanguards (59). Within a nascent culture industry, Beba's story stages a virtual encounter between the new professional writer and the New Woman in a bookstore, a locale of growing social importance. Those who write books, the series intimates, might imagine performing New Women like Beba among their readers, as her eclectic tastes test the boundaries of elite literary culture. The Beba bookstore episode manifests a lack of consensus on what kind of material contemporary writers should produce and for whom. But it also showcases related mixed views on modern women's role in cultural life. Given that women poets of the 1920s were sometimes aficionados of Nervo's work, Beba's key reading choice, the series also implicitly casts the new *porteña* as a potential writer herself.

Most important, Beba's story signals the dynamics between liberation and regulation encompassed in the idea that the role of modern Latin American women in artistic culture was to perform. Neither the designation of women as performers nor the acting-out of societal gender tensions and regulations through theatrical modes (whether on traditional stages or in the alternative public spheres of growing cities) were new phenomena in Latin America or in international Western culture. In late-nineteenth-century Latin America, private performances by upper-class Latin American women for select, family-based audiences displayed a limited education in literature, poetry declamation, music, and the plastic arts. But in the twentieth century's early decades, expanding leisure activities increased the more public venues where upper- or middle-class women could perform—chaperoned social events or clubs, charity functions, or service organization fund-raisers—and still maintain the respectability denied women who did so for a living. In the context of these events' social usefulness, moreover, journalistic images of the modern woman as a performer synthesized the concept of women's "special" social role embodied in feminist campaigns for the new civic woman with the mobility implicit in the New Woman as a dynamic consumer of leisure activities.

This imagery of constant body *movement* and urban mobility through multiple cultural sites—Beba, we should recall, is everywhere—evokes the futuristic dynamism of the avant-gardes. It also encapsulates the difference between the performing woman as object of contemplation or inspiration that populated late-nineteenth-century Spanish American *modernismo* (or Brazilian symbolism) and her New Woman heir of the 1920s and 1930s. If the static *tableau vivant,* which persisted in the Latin America's middle-brow print media of the 1920s, reiterated earlier gender scripts, photojournalism on Isadora Duncan, Josephine Baker, Amelia Earhart, and on local and international women dancers and athletes advanced more porous, androgynous notions of gender and striking imagery of bodies in motion as a signifier of change. But this media iconography of the New Woman appeared side by side with cautionary pieces that plumbed in sensationalist or satirical modes the potential nefarious consequences of too much public mobility—and resulting androgyny—for women and in reaction to more hybrid social gatherings, for example chaperoned dance clubs or *días de recibo* (open-house days) in Mexico City (Collado, 111) or the growing multiclass practice in Rio de Janeiro of *fazendo a avenida,* in Portuguese literally "making the avenue," making the scene (Hahner, 80).

That women's performances provoked the regulatory impulse underlying Beba's story and comparable fare throughout Latin America testifies to the recognition of their (potentially threatening) transformational power. In 1923 Enrique García Velloso, an Argentine playwright and author of popular fiction that cast women's changing mores as a problem, published *Piedras preciosas,* a manual of poetry declamation dedicated to his daughter. The contrast between the guide's normative dictionary of gestures and intonations and its cover art of a declaiming woman—a cross between a genie and a flapper—signals the era's deep-seated ambivalence toward women's performances. Their potential for upending gender norms and for autonomous creative expression unfolded in the rising star of Argentina's Berta Singerman, which also underscored the renewed penchant for modern male writers to recast performing women as their muses. Singerman, who synthesized a songlike declamation mode and gestures into a personal performance style, recited in packed halls throughout Latin America and Europe and elicited hyperbolic praise from male writers as diverse as Mexico's Salvador Novo and Spain's Unamuno or Valle Inclán. Journalistic accounts throughout Latin America underscored the power of her voice and body in motion and her transfiguration of a lyrical repertoire by others into her own aesthetic form.

Casting a woman on display as the muse for male creativity was nothing new. But as a more dynamic and independent figure than her immediate predecessor—the decorative, often immobile *femme fatal* of Spanish America's literary *modernistas*[14]—the New Woman model of musedom signaled change. Much as the classical muses synthesized the capacity for inspiration with their own artistic talent, the performing woman as portrayed in Latin American literary culture of the time offered a bridge from representations of women as art objects or catalysts to their conception as cultural actors. The women in this book all underwent, to varying degrees, the performance training that marked the education of Latin American women. They all also performed before an artistic or intellectual audience at some moment in their careers and in a specific cultural circle. Several— Ocampo, Lange, Campobello, Rivas Mercado, Portal, and Galvão—were at some point explicitly invoked as sources of artistic inspiration. Most of these writers evidenced acute insight into the role of contemporary performance culture in women's experience or into a penchant to render women as performers. Most also criticized what they saw. Thus Singerman as a performing New Woman more often served as their target than as their role model. But to expand on a central proposition of this book, performance activity—even when it shored up gender norms in the face of change— provided these women a far richer repertoire and more malleable site for negotiating their art of living as intellectuals than did reigning models of women's writing, embodied for example in the *poetisa*. These women's experience with performance was pivotal for their choices as writers and their conception of writing as a critical move in cultural life.

THE ART OF THE GETAWAY: TERESA DE LA PARRA'S WARNING

In her fiction and essays, Venezuela's Teresa de la Parra (1889–1936) identified the challenges facing women writers in literary culture, particularly of the vanguards, and she highlighted key issues also explored by the ten women in the following eight chapters. But she ultimately imagined her own intellectual home outside the dominant literary culture that surrounded her. Her work, therefore, in particular her 1928 novel *Las memorias de Mamá Blanca* (translated as *Mamá Blanca's Memoirs,* 1993), provides an illuminating counterexample to the acts of cultural intervention undertaken by the women in the eight chapters that follow. The novel opens with an *advertencia* or warning.[15] Here an editor-narrator invokes the Cervantine device of an inherited manuscript to introduce an old woman's memoirs into the literary world of the 1920s. Praising the manuscript's style, she contrasts it with the vanguards' "hermetic school" and notes that although she has always approached cubist expositions and dada anthologies with a will to believe, they have offered only "darkness and silence" (12–13; HOFHF, 13). The editor claims Mamá Blanca as her mentor, and the old woman in turn praises her own mother's verbal talent, contrasting it with the vanguards' "futuristic flashiness" and "esotericism" (24).[16] It is tempting to take these fictional voices at their word when we consider that in 1926 Parra claimed that she herself was almost impermeable to the "pseudo-new sensibilities" of the new art (*Obra escogida,* 3:219).

Parra, however, repeatedly cautioned critics against mistaking her characters' views for her own, and the innovations of her own fiction are unquestionable. Nelson Osorio credits her with rejuvenating Venezuelan prose (143); Louis Lemaître notes the "vanguard tendency" (83) of her 1924 novel, *Ifigenia: Diario de una señorita que escribió porque se fastidiaba* (translated as *Iphigenia: The diary of a young lady who wrote because she was bored*); Doris Sommer notes the "representational disencounters" and "verbal misfires" that characterize *Memorias* ("Mirror, Mirror," 166–172); and I have argued that *Memorias* is, in fact, a vanguard novel.[17] But as a *Küntslerroman* or portrait of the artist, the work also illuminates Parra's search for a public identity as a woman writer. The resulting tensions suggest that Parra found the available role models deficient and that in contrast to the other women in this book, she ultimately chose to turn away from public literary culture. The prefatory remarks of the novel's adult editor-narrator recount clandestine childhood meetings with the elderly Mamá Blanca that served as an apprenticeship in life and art. Now the editor has inherited the five hundred handwritten pages of the old woman's memoirs and, counter to her wish that they remain secret, has decided to edit and publish the first one hundred pages. In the memoir itself, Mamá Blanca offers sketches of her mid-nineteenth-century childhood on the family hacienda, Piedra Azul. In this predominantly female community, Blanca Nieves (Snow White, the young Mamá Blanca), her mother, five sisters, and governess live an apparently idyllic existence of freedom and proximity to nature, because the hacienda's supreme authority, the father, is seldom there. Other men inhabit this women's world—the displaced intellectual and failed politician Primo Juancho, the mulatto laborer Vicente Cochocho, and the mestizo cowhand Daniel. But they, too, function outside the hacienda's center of power with, Mamá Blanca would have us believe, significant room for maneuver. The idyll ends abruptly with the family's move to Caracas, where schools, class conventions for women's behavior, and physical restrictions of urban life radically curtail the autonomy the sisters have enjoyed in the vanishing world of Piedra Azul.

In Parra's first novel, *Ifigenia,* the young protagonist rails against the oppression of women but for economic reasons succumbs to a loveless marriage. This work's critique of women's situation has always seemed clear. By contrast, *Memorias* has provoked critical indecision. While Masiello ("Women, State, and Family") and Doris Sommer ("Mirror, Mirror") argue for its feminist critique through narrative subversions, Elizabeth Garrels calls it an "anachronistic colonial fantasy" (*"Piedra Azul,"* 136), and Juan Liscano describes it as a reaction against modernity ("Testimony," 125). Through its vanguard construction of an ostensibly outmoded women's world, the work in fact addresses profoundly modern artistic concerns and—through the very strategies she ostensibly rejected—enacts Parra's own search for viability as a woman writer. *Memorias* possesses the genre indeterminacy that characterized stylistically diverse Latin American vanguard fiction of the period.[18] Parra herself observed this feature of *Memorias,* as not quite a novel because of its disconnected sketches (*Obra escogida,* 2:234). The work is vanguard as well in the impious appropriation by its storytelling characters of a hodgepodge of literary traditions. Thus Mamá Blanca reveals that her mother embodied a hyperbolic romanticism bordering on kitsch, and the stories she told while curling her daughter's hair formed a mélange from other sources. And although Mamá Blanca explains that it was her job to bestow unity on her mother's tales, the child was equally irreverent in her juxtapositions of heroes of chivalric, romantic, and biblical sources. Another role model, Primo Juancho, is a "man of the Enlightenment" possessed of encyclopedic knowledge and from whom we might expect a classical style. But as in a vanguard experiment, his discourse is marked by "the lightning-like transitions" and the "delightful incoherence" of a dictionary's illogical sequencing or an "unbound Larousse" (*Memorias,* 51; HOFHF, 46).

The novel's nostalgic tone, if one ignores lurking ironies, gives Piedra Azul the air of a *beatus ille*. Thus in her opening description of Mamá Blanca, the editor forges metonymies between the old woman and nature, orality, authenticity, and the roots of tradition, all of which she contrasts with urban culture, the artifice of writing, and modern life's frivolity. But the characters' nonchalance toward their literary ancestors links the editor's modern world of enigmatic cubist expositions and Mamá Blanca's child-hood utopia.

The work records not one but two artistic apprenticeships, and we must ask what the connections between them might be. The first is the story of Blanca Nieves, who grows into the memoir-writer Mamá Blanca with the tutelage of her Piedra Azul mentors. The second, which in the novel frames the first, is the tale of the *advertencia*'s narrator-editor and the elderly Mamá Blanca, a tie also rooted in childhood that culminates when the narrator edits her mentor's private memoirs for public consumption. The *advertencia* casts these two women as opposites, as the editor denigrates herself as somebody who exercises "the profession of letters" (*Memorias,* 12; HOFHF, 13) and praises Mamá Blanca as an "artist without a profession" (8). Thus Parra's novel paints a composite portrait of the artist as both a cosmopolitan woman immersed in the public world of professional writing and an eccentric grandmother who lives alone, talks to children, animals, and flowers, and writes a private memoir for an audience of one: her editor-protégé. But the work blurs the boundaries between the two figures as the grandmother produces a text as modern as the editor's public life. The editor tells us, moreover, that she has altered Mamá Blanca's manuscript, and the shared style and irony of the *advertencia* and the memoir elide the novel's opposition between the two women. Their most striking similarity is the emphatic attack on modern literary culture from two artists portrayed—each in her domain—as aesthetically modern.[19]

To understand the apparent contradiction, one must distinguish—as Parra evidently did—between innovative aesthetic strategies that challenged literary conventions and the public literary culture in which individual women negotiated their place among groups of men. The tensions mobilized by *Memorias* encapsulate the complex relationship of women writers to Latin American literary culture that constitutes a central focus of this book, and Parra spelled out the same ambivalence enacted by the women in this study toward the culture of performance that they alternately embraced and challenged. The adult Parra spent as much time in Europe as in Caracas, but although she was older than the vanguard generation, she maintained contact with innovative circles on both sides of the Atlantic. She was a professional writer by the terms of the times, as she published early stories and parts of *Ifigenia* in the Caracas periodical *La lectura semanal,* and the *Memorias* appeared in the Parisian *Revue de l'Amerique Latine.* But beyond the material details of publishing a work, a process to which the *Memorias* editor alludes, Parra clearly saw writing as a public role, an identity assumed, she said, through the "miracle of doubling" (*Obra escogida,* 2:196). She reflected on this role in opening her 1930 Bogota lectures on women's influence in a Latin American "spirit," events to which she was welcomed as a public celebrity: "How to assume the role of an author present before an audience?" she wondered (*Obra,* 472).

This question underlies the dynamic in the *advertencia* of *Memorias* between the professional editor and the grandmother without an artistic profession. Parra made clear in assuming the role of "an author present before an audience" that she found the personae of professional writer and New Woman deficient because of their common frivolity and artifice. She was known for her stylish, modern persona (complete on occasion with silk pajamas and cigarette holder), her love of the Charleston, her ease in the world of Parisian fashion, and the linguistic and musical talents acquired through the training typical for a woman of her class. But she also cast aspersions on the "happy vanity" of fashion, the "avalanche of momentary pleasures" (*Obra escogida,* 2:202, 2:119), and "empty mundane flitting about" (*Obra,* 474). She argued that for Latin American women of the privileged classes, cloistered by overprotected childhoods and repressive educations, this role combined false promises of liberation and inadequate preparation for real autonomy. Parra's critique of the New Woman weaves through all her work. She assumed the pseudonym "Fru-Fru" in early journalism, ironically embracing the designation "la señorita Frivolidad" ascribed to Caracas society types (Lemaître, 60–62). Parra's version of such a woman, María Eugenia Alonso, the protagonist of *Ifigenia,* possessed cultured refinement that was as much clothing-based as intellectual, Parra argued, her vast reading notwithstanding (*Obra escogida,* 2:212). Similarly, we learn in *Memorias* that Mamá Blanca's daughters-in-law, whom the old woman rejects as heirs to her memoirs, are kindred in New Woman façades and vacuous spirit to their predecessor in *Ifigenia.*

For Parra, then, public literary culture, or "the printing carnival," as she called it in 1930 (*Obras completas,* 787), and the role of professional writer—"that very intermittent and fragile literary vocation" (*Obra,* 472)—were of a piece with the "happy vanity" of the New Woman role. Gabriela Mistral's depiction of Parra as a Parisian *tertulia* participant documents her performance as a modern woman in the literary milieu. Mistral portrays her as elegant and cosmopolitan, with the verbal agility to change the subject in these gatherings primarily of men (Mistral, 40). But in 1926 Parra summarily dismissed both her "noisy and oblivious" female contemporaries and the literary culture of the *tertulia*: "the masculine groups, congregated in clubs or scattered on the corners" that, she argued, destroyed audience interest in their monotonous stories (*Obra escogida*, 2:209). The focus of Parra's 1930 Bogota lectures on the historical influence of Latin American women provides a context for the alliance in *Memorias* between a modern literary woman and a grandmotherly "artist without a profession" as an antidote to a public literary culture in which Parra ultimately declined to locate her intellectual home. Just as the narrating editor in *Memorias* aligns herself with her artistic foremother, so does Parra trace a genealogy of influential women that begins in the colonial era.

Some see *Memorias* as a reactionary retreat from modernization, and a patronizing nostalgia and racialist stereotyping do pepper the idealized portrayals of people of color or from lower classes inhabiting Piedra Azul. But these markers of her class elitism notwithstanding, Parra searched through Mamá Blanca's mentors in Piedra Azul and through the women of Latin America's past for "modern" strategies of "disorder" as tools for negotiation within oppressive situations. As did the other writers in this book, Parra worried about the consequences specifically for women of state modernization, as when the novel admonishes that, as Doris Sommer has put it, "the marches of progress might take note of where and on whom they step" ("Mirror, Mirror," 180). But as a self-described "moderate feminist," Parra unequivocally supported the modernization of women's roles. For woman to be strong, she argued, she should not be "subjugated" by the changing ways of life but instead should be "free before herself, conscious of the dangers and responsibilities, useful in society even if she is not a mother, and financially independent through her work and her collaboration with man," who would not be "her owner, enemy, or candidate for exploitation, but rather a comrade and friend" (*Obra*, 474). This change, she implied in proposing a new history of Latin American women, could be accelerated by drawing on the forces of the past, that is, by enacting a "genealogy" of "counter-memory" to borrow Roach's term (26).[20] Parra, like countless women writers internationally, sought literary foremothers in the past, but we must not mistake art for life, as she warned, and believe that she actually imagined returning to a colonized world. Thus, although the city of Tunja, Colombia, "a city that [had] not budged from the 19th century," enchanted her, she was unimpressed by the state of its cloistered women, who possessed the sadness of those "who have not lived nor suspect what life is" (*Obra escogida,* 2:262). Change, then, Parra argued, did not respect hermetic worlds like Piedra Azul: The crisis of change lived by modern women, she observed, could not be "cured by preaching submission," as when women lived "behind house doors." Rather, she continued, the modern life of travel and technology did not "respect closed doors" and could "pass through walls" (*Obra,* 474).

Even as Parra herself defied convention, though, evasion persists as an enduring motif of her literary persona, not only in the nostalgic alliance between the modern literary woman and Mamá Blanca in a bygone community of marginalized women and eccentric men, but also in Parra's self-imposed exile from the literary fray and Latin America itself. Countless critics have cited the "homelessness" of the woman intellectual, and Francine Masiello uses the term specifically in reference to Parra and other women of the avant-gardes ("Women, State, and Family," 37). Sylvia Molloy argues that a *"dislocation in order to be"* marks women's writing in Latin America (Introduction, 107–108; emphasis in original) and argues that for Parra textual relocations and the choice to live abroad provided a "place to write (however obliquely) one's difference" ("Disappearing Acts," 248).[21] The ten women whose work of the 1920s and 1930s I examine in the following chapters experienced challenges comparable to those articulated by Parra. They, too, criticized the literary culture through which they moved, the representations of women grounding the discourse of modernity, and the consequences for ordinary women of the continent's fits and starts of modernization. With the possible exception of Ocampo, whose elite background provided the economic and cultural capital to build her own, none found an enduring intellectual home. But even as they shared Parra's frustration, the women in this book immersed themselves in the cultural world that she ultimately rejected. Thus are their stories—as I tell them—tales less of escape than of artful arbitration and willful intervention.

THE TANGLED PATHS TO A WOMAN WRITER'S PLACE

A challenge for a feminist weaned in the late twentieth century is the inescapable fact that the women in this book all negotiated their intellectual identities in the cultural worlds of artistic or political men. Although some crossed paths, corresponded, or read one another's work, they did not constitute the kind of sisterhood of intellectual women that Parra imagined constructing a women's genealogy. Storni, Sabas Alomá, Rodríguez Acosta, and Portal participated in women's groups of various kinds, but these did not constitute the primary sites of their art of living as writers. Those who did interact more extensively with other women, moreover, sometimes assumed a tutorial stance, a role consistent with the ties between early Latin American feminism and the rise of Normal Schools to train women teachers and with the commitment to social usefulness that typified feminist projects. The women in this book also sometimes reinforced gender stereotypes as they criticized other women, and even when they assumed a clearly feminist political stance, they periodically reiterated prejudices of class, race, and sexual orientation typical for their milieu.

Irrespective of their relationship to women's movements, all of these women manifested an emergent feminism for its time: a distinct self-consciousness about gender, a recognition that the rhetoric or realities of modernity posed singular challenges for women, and keen attention to their own anomalous status as women writers. With the exception of Storni, Sabas Alomá, and Rodríguez Acosta (whom historians of political feminism include in their work), during the 1920s and 1930s, these women did not explicitly or fully embrace political feminism. The fact that historians describe Galvão as an alternative or non-mainstream feminist and Portal as an antifeminist underscores the term's instability and historicity.[22] In her studies of Brazilian women's movements, Susan Besse highlights this semantic porosity. As Besse, Francesca Miller, Asunción Lavrin, June Hahner, Anna Macías, and Lynn Stoner demonstrate, moreover, the women's movements of the period were predominantly reformist and sought to integrate women into civic life without profoundly challenging patriarchal structures. The title of Besse's book, *Restructuring Patriarchy: The Modernization of Gender Inequality in Brazil, 1914–1940,* captures this quality of early political feminism in Latin America. Similarly, the title of Kathleen Newman's "The Modernization of *Femininity:* Argentina, 1916–1926" (my emphasis) underscores the comparable "patriarchal reconfiguration" she documents in Buenos Aires in response to the threat of changing women's roles (79). Writing from the left, in fact, Portal and Galvão, respectively, attacked official feminism in Peru and Brazil as too conservative.

The women in this book inhabited a range of locations on the spectrum of political feminism, and some had little contact with women's movements at all. Some drew on the work of such international feminists as the Soviet Union's Alexandra Kollontai or Spain's María de Maeztu and Margarita Nelken. They also varied significantly in their social origins and contact or identification with women from other backgrounds. But irrespective of their politics, these writers shared with political feminists their negotiation of an active role in public life. As Lavrin documents for the Southern Cone, women's movements manifested the "rise of women's self-consciousness as *actors* in the body politic" (13; my emphasis). The public artistic careers of the women I study here aligned them with political feminists who enacted this awareness through public performances, as skillful orators or even in direct theatrical incursions. Susan Glenn argues persuasively that the enactment of new women's roles constituted the "theatrical roots" of modern European and U.S. feminism and links the diverse careers of Sarah Bernhardt, Emma Goldman, and modern chorus girls. In Latin America, too, theatricality often constituted the common terrain for women's political and artistic activism. Political feminists in Havana created the Lyceum, a cultural institution where women were as apt to declaim or lecture as men, and some of Mexico's notable feminists also gained renown as performers. The playwright, actress, and drama critic Catalina D'Erzell, for example, executed her feminist politics through plays that were widely performed in Mexico, Buenos Aires, and Los Angeles and a regular column for the newspaper *Excelsior,* "Digo yo como mujer" (I speak as a woman).

The circuitous roads followed by the women in this book to participate in literary culture manifest not only their range of responses to mainstream feminism but also the specific circumstances shaping public life in the cities where their careers unfolded. The central role of performance in their intellectual inquiry, pivotal encounters with modern male literary culture embodied in the avant-gardes, and self-conscious fashioning of an intellectual persona constitute key selection criteria for inclusion in this book. As I explain below, geographical region is an important organizing principle, but not the only one. Grouping the women by region underscores defining local, historical contexts and differences in their public lives and individual trajectories. Argentina's literary culture of the 1920s and 1930s, where Storni, Ocampo, and Lange mapped out strikingly distinct roles from one another, for example, was the most extensive, institutionalized, and heterogeneous among the regions represented in this book, a diversity that marked the country's feminism as well. Buenos Aires had experienced dramatic urban growth, technological development, and changing class and ethnic demographics resulting from massive immigration. In response to that change, vanguard literary culture, in particular the somewhat conservative Martín Fierro group associated with a journal of the same name (1924–1927), manifested what Sarlo aptly terms the "urban *criollismo*" of a "peripheral modernity" (*Una modernidad periférica,* 27). Male writers in this milieu displayed a simultaneous impulse to be as European as possible and to reinvent a "real" Argentina in the face of such enormous change.

In Mexico the careers of Campobello and Rivas Mercado, on the other hand, dramatize the profound impact of postrevolutionary politics on proliferating cultural institutions and artistic life. Here literary alliances grew polemical, with a self-claimed loyalty to *mexicanidad* cultivated by state-affiliated cultural leaders and the vanguard *estridentistas* (with whom Campobello enjoyed significant ties) on one side and a stronger interest in European and U.S. artistic developments pursued by the Contemporáneos writers, among whom Rivas Mercado carried out much of her cultural activity. Although the presence of women in Mexico City public life had increased to some degree and although accounts of *soldaderas* who had fought in the revolution forged a growing cultural iconography, real change for Mexican women was less extensive than in Buenos Aires or São Paulo, and Mexican political feminism was less developed. In part because of the ties between many Mexican women and the Catholic Church and their consequent supportive stance toward the Cristero rebellion, postrevolutionary leadership saw women as a potential counterrevolutionary force (Miller, 91). But women painters, journalists, photographers, dancers, and writers participated actively in the rich cultural and artistic life of Mexico City in the 1920s and 1930s. The proximity of the United States, moreover, manifested itself strongly in Mexico's media culture and intensified the love-hate ambivalence of Mexican women writers and intellectuals toward U.S. models of the New Woman.

As the careers of Sabas Alomá and Rodríguez Acosta embody, the ties between vanguard literary culture and feminism of the left were strongest in Havana, where women obtained the vote in 1934, as compared to 1947 in Buenos Aires, 1953 in Mexico City, and 1955 in Lima. Among the countries represented in this study, only Brazil, in 1932, preceded Cuba in letting women vote. Active political feminists, Sabas Alomá and Rodríguez Acosta participated energetically in Havana's literary world. A central factor in this distinctive alliance was the heterogeneous coalition of intellectuals and artists who rallied to support cultural and political reform and to challenge the repressive governments of Alfredo Zayas (1921–1925) and especially Gerardo Machado (1925–1933). Havana's cultural innovators—the Grupo Minorista (roughly 1923 to 1928–1929) and those from its ranks who constituted the smaller but more literary *Revista de avance* circle (1927–1930)—were among the most eclectic vanguard groups of Latin America. Here, as in Mexico, proximity to the United States was key both in political reaction and in literary and media culture. In addition, due to geography and political alliances, Havana sometimes served as a cultural way station not only for such notables as Lorca or Langston Hughes, but also for Campobello, Parra, Portal, and Wiesse among the non-Cubans in this book.

As in Havana, in Lima a political regime—the reformist dictatorship of Augusto B. Leguía (1919–1930)—generated strong reaction among intellectuals. But the status of women in Lima had changed the least compared to what we find in the other four cities, and Lima's official feminists, who generally supported Leguía, were among the most conservative on the continent. Women joining anti-oligarchic movements, including the nascent Peruvian communist party and the emerging populist APRA (Alianza Popular Revolucionaria Americana), of which Portal was a founder, were pressured to subsume gender concerns to remedying class inequities. Moreover, ethnicity and class—not gender—dominated the revolutionary cultural politics of the intellectual circle coalescing around Latin America's first major Marxist thinker, José Carlos Mariátegui, and his influential avant-garde journal, *Amauta* (1926–1930). But over time Mariátegui grew more interested in the revolutionary potential of feminism, his own views of women became less stereotypical, and the *Amauta* circle offered a provisional, if not ideal, intellectual home for a few literary women, most notably Portal and Wiesse.

During these years, São Paulo as well as Rio de Janeiro witnessed marked changes in women's lives and active, diverse political feminism. The innovative artistic culture of the Brazilian avant-gardes known as *modernismo,* moreover, particularly in São Paulo but also in Rio and other cities, was as dynamic and productive as any vanguard movement in Latin America and, some would argue, more enduring in its impact on the nation's twentieth-century literature. Although historians consistently incorporate Galvão into the history of Brazilian feminism, and contemporary Brazilian feminist scholars regard her as a foremother, the two movements did not generally intersect, and Galvão herself attacked official Brazilian feminism as elitist and frivolous. As in Mexico, however, artistic and literary women played central roles in the public cultural activities of São Paulo-based Brazilian modernism, as salon catalysts, artistic innovators, or muses for particular artistic agendas. As in Mexico City and Buenos Aires, innovative literary activity bore the strong mark of cultural nationalism, as vanguard writers forged strong ties with the European avant-gardes while constructing an explicitly Brazilian cultural imaginary and rendition of international vanguard primitivism. The radical circle of the *Revista de antropofagia* (1928–1929) embraced Galvão as the primitivist

New Woman muse of this project, a role that she by turns embraced and jettisoned with disdain.

INTERVENING ACTS: THE MOVEMENT OF WRITING

Beyond regional contexts, the following chapters reveal shifting facets in the impact of performance on women writers' arbitration of literary culture and on their writing. With the exception of María Wiesse (b. 1892), I begin with those born first—Ocampo (1890) and Storni (1892)—and end with Galvão (1910), born last. In between I treat the women whose turn-of-the-century dates of birth align them most closely with Latin America's male vanguard generation and who, adding Wiesse, had closer or longer-lasting ties with male vanguard groups or writers: Lange (1906), Campobello (1900), Rivas Mercado (1900), Sabas Alomá (1901), Rodríguez Acosta (1902), and Portal (1903). Roughly paralleling these mid-generational shifts we find an increasingly intricate critique of performance culture, paralleled by more inventive stylizations, exaggerations, and perversions of the performing woman role. Already in Storni we find criticism of fashion practices and lightweight cultural fare for women, but Sabas Alomá, Rodríguez Acosta, Portal, and Wiesse subjected performance culture to more extensive or rigorous scrutiny, and Wiesse and Galvão dedicated scathing novels to the subject.

The unfolding chapters also present more intricate, sometimes unresolved, rejoinders to the gender trouble in the air. In response to the cultural conversation that allocated distinct habitats, genres, or writing styles to women and men, androgyny constitutes a recurrent motif. Already in Storni and Ocampo we find the assumption of an androgynous position as an imagined more fluid, in-between locale, free of what Ocampo called the "most bothersome discipline" of gender (*Obras escogidas: Teatro,* 2:30). But in the younger women, this embrace of androgyny grows both more intense and more complex. At times ostending an explicitly androgynous authorial persona, Campobello, Rivas Mercado, Rodríguez Acosta, Portal, and Galvão also executed temporary identity shifts in masked or ventriloquist enactments of male characters, narrators, or poetic speakers. Rodríguez Acosta and, with ambivalence, Galvão also staged homosexual characters or encounters in their work, while Sabas Alomá crafted an overblown femininity and displayed intermittent homophobia as defenses against the denigration of women intellectuals as masculine.

Throughout the book we also witness—in fits and starts, indecisions and revisions—a gathering refusal to perform. Interestingly, Parra and

Galvão, twenty-one years apart in age and the bookends for this account, executed the most adamant negations, though different in kind. Parra walked away from modern, certainly vanguard, literary culture itself, signaling the pitfalls for women of its frivolity, and assumed a more reclusive intellectual life than undertaken by the ten women in the following chapters. The writers closest to Parra's age here engaged performance directly, through theatre. Ocampo trained to be an actor; Storni worked as an actor, taught drama, and wrote and declaimed her own plays; and Wiesse launched her literary career writing plays about women. Their younger contemporaries alternately assumed and critically deformed conventional performance modes. Thus Lange's uncanny rendition of the performing woman, like her prose, turned a dissecting stare onto her audience, while Campobello challenged the cultural correctness of her successful dance career in the choreographies of her experimental prose and alternations in her narrative persona between reclusive poses and the mobile precision of bullets. Galvão, who, along with Lange, unleashed the most extravagant performance, also executed the most intricate refusal. Through the complex fictive personae of her prose, she effectively repudiated the performing woman mode of her adolescent initiation and claimed a critical zone of reserve, radical in its privacy.

Whether by active choice or, as in Ocampo's case some would argue, compensatory default, all the women in this book at some point privileged writing—particularly literature—over more literal performance, even as they mined repertoires of performance culture to assert their status as cultural actors. Thus Campobello affirmed that literature provided an intellectual refuge from her dance career; Sabas Alomá, while contesting its boundaries with mass culture, argued that literature constituted a form of mental calisthenics for women; and Portal chose poetry over political oratory to cultivate a more autonomous, labile voice. At the same time, as literary practitioners, many imbued their writing and their artistic personae with the movement and plasticity of performance. A striking feature of their intellectual careers is, in fact, their dynamic mobility through multiple cultural sites, even countries: like the mythical Beba, these women were everywhere. Similarly, their deployment of multiple genres and irreverence toward genre boundaries and their stylistic strategies—mercurial lyric or narrative voices that refuse fixed positions or mine gaps between them, narrative or lyrical fragments, distorting ostensions through synecdoche, hyperbolized accumulations of imagery, essays vacillating between conversational flow and interruptions—channel into their writing the critical power of movement gleaned from their performative turns. None of these strategies is exclusive to women, but their cumulative deployment by women writers in the literary culture of the 1920s and 1930s constitutes a potent, imaginative recasting of the repertoires available to women as interventionist players in a gendered literary field.

While this book encompasses five regions and the cultural projects of ten women, it does not pretend to be exhaustive. Others might have been included from the countries represented here—Argentina's Nydia Lamarque or Sara de Etcheverts; Mexico's Lupe Marín, Catalina D'Erzell, or Amalia de Castillo Ledón; Cuba's Lydia Cabrera or Dulce María Loynaz; Peru's Angela Ramos; or Brazil's Cecília Meireles, Ercília Nogueira Cobra, or Aldazira Bittencourt—or from other countries: Blanca Luz Brum (Uruguay), María Luisa Bombal (Chile), Clementina Suárez (Honduras), or Clara Lair (Puerto Rico).[23] Performance experience, motifs, or critiques also figured in many of these women's negotiations with literary culture and artistic experiments. But the chapters that follow demonstrate through an exemplary rather than exhaustive selection the rich variety of circuitous paths chosen by Latin American women writers of the 1920s and 1930s as they faced the considerable challenge of finding a viable place from which to write.

In May 1919, as her regular contribution to the Buenos Aires periodical *La nota,* Alfonsina Storni (1892–1938) crafted the whimsical tale "Historia sintética de un traje tailleur" (The concise story of a tailored dress). In this brief memoir, the garment traces its metamorphosis from the sheep that provided its wool to the tailored suit of a bourgeois *porteña* to the mended attire of a widowed mother who rides the streetcar to work and, finally, to the refashioned dress of a lively young girl. Now outgrown and discarded in the trash, which also includes scraps of writing, the dress reflects on its embodied education through the lives of the women it has clothed (*Nosotras,* 44–48). Storni wrote this piece when she was twenty-seven, the year she published her third poetry collection, *Irremediablemente.* Its story raises key issues that marked Storni's lifelong inquiry into the gender inequities of Argentine modernity and the role of women as writers and intellectuals. Storni's creative activity culminated with her innovative poetry in *Ocre* (1925), *Mundo de siete pozos* (1934), and *Mascarilla y trébol* (1938), as well as in the groundbreaking "pyrotechnic farces" *Cimbelina en 1900 y pico* and *Polixena y la cocinerita* (1931). While critics accurately situate her achievements in the experimentalism of this later writing, Storni pursued the questions invoked by the memoir of a tailored dress in the seven poetry collections, four plays, six children's plays, and countless journalistic chronicles, short stories, and essays that constitute her work. Fashion, as summoned by the mercurial *traje tailleur* provided a central metaphor for her inquiry into the embodied constitution of the self in the world. In this tale, the shifting semiotics of the garment through the human actors it clothes for diverse social roles point to the cardinal position of performance in Storni's artistic formation, initiation into public literary life, and mode of cognitive inquiry. The dress's hand-me-down identity provides an apt metaphor for Storni's poetic, journalistic, and dramatic investigation into the power of inherited cultural scripts in human interaction. At the same time, the garment's reincarnations through the bodies that wear it intimate the susceptibility of those librettos, even as they are repeated, to change.

The concluding metonymy of the dress's remains with scraps of writing typifies Storni's frequent juxtaposition of fashion and books, two powerful transmitters and challengers of cultural norms, to speak about women's conflictive relationship to intellectual life. It also connects this process of reenactment and change to Storni's ongoing struggle, as Argentina's most renowned *poetisa* of her time, to refashion this public role and its pre-scribed expressive modes for women, not only into a more comfortable fit but also into a full-blown critique of its own terms. Critics have argued that Storni's abandonment of the clichéd love poetry of her youth for ma-ture experimental writing signaled artistic liberation. But my focus here is her embrace of the *poetisa* identity as the available role for a woman seeking to write and her redirection of the knowledge thus gleaned into an analysis of the gender dynamics of Argentine intellectual life. Storni was of two minds about the *poetisa* role right from the start, and over time this ambivalence produced her unique conception of women intellectuals. On the surface the *poetisa* lyrical mode consolidated gender stereotypes of a confessional, self-abnegating femininity. But declaiming one's work before an audience, with embellishments of gesture and tone, constituted a funda-mental element of the *poetisa* role, and Storni repeatedly mined the critical and analytical power of this performative malleability.

Fraught with contradictions, the high-profile position Storni secured in Buenos Aires cultural life, from her arrival in the city in 1911 until her untimely death in 1938, was unprecedented. While she gained popularity as a *poetisa* enacting the designated themes of love and loss, she was also the first modern Latin American poet to write widely read feminist poems, including the mordant "Hombre pequeñito" or the more reflective but still polemical "Tu me quieres blanca." Storni became the first Argentine woman to participate as a writer, rather than as somebody's significant other, in the lively literary gatherings of Buenos Aires. She was a popular lecturer and poetry declaimer for women's groups, ranging from socialist gatherings in neighborhood libraries or meetings of the Lavanderas Unidas (Delgado, 93–94) to the more middle-class Club Argentino de Mujeres.[1] But Storni's biographers also underscore her high visibility at male liter-ary banquets and *tertulias,* with the influential *Nosotros* group in the late teens and early 1920s, the Grupo Anaconda in the early 1920s (along with Horacio Quiroga), the La Peña group that began meeting in 1926 and hosted such notables as Pirandello and Josephine Baker, and in the late

1920s and 1930s the Signo group that enjoyed visits from Spanish vanguardist Ramón Gómez de la Serna, Italian futurist Massimo Bontempelli, and Lorca. Although Leopoldo Lugones saw to it that Storni was initially excluded from the more formal Sociedad Argentina de Escritores when it was founded in 1928, she gradually assumed a role in this organization as well.

Storni's versatile movement through multiple cultural sites constituted a signature quality of her career. She crossed paths with the Argentine vanguards, with Martín Fierro writers at their gatherings at Norah Lange's home in the 1920s, and with Roberto Arlt at the Signo *tertulia* in the early 1930s. But even as her own experimentalism increased, Storni's relationship to vanguard groups was awkward. Born in 1892, she was seven or eight years older than the typical Florida or Boedo writer and found her first provisional intellectual home among the writers gathered around the prestigious journal *Nosotros,* who in a 1923 survey of new literary trends designated themselves the predecessors of the vanguard generation. But critics have noted that Storni's most experimental artistic achievements actually paralleled in time those of the vanguards,[2] even though young male vanguard writers of Buenos Aires denied her work serious attention. Too old to serve as a resident New Woman muse like Norah Lange, Storni possessed less distinguished social credentials. By the time Florida and Boedo writers dominated the literary scene, moreover, Storni had already forged her public persona as a professional writer who, like Quiroga, gave interviews as a local celebrity to middlebrow periodicals. Moreover, her candid attacks on gender inequities ran counter in spirit to the habitat for fraternity forged by male vanguardists in response to growing gender, class, and ethnic challenges to Argentine identity. While vanguard writers consolidated their literary personae in contrast to the mass culture in which they sometimes participated through journalism, Storni forged her public persona in that popular milieu.

Storni's verse of the 1930s turned away from the popular audience for her more accessible early poetry. But through the multiple genres of her work, including the didactic facet of her journalism, Storni enacted a more socially variegated art of living as a writer than that executed by her vanguard contemporaries. Through her popular success, Storni embodied much of what vanguard writers ostensibly sought to avoid. For all their bravado against the literary institutionalism of a previous generation and notwithstanding their vacillating courtship of a wider audience, the Martín Fierro writers in particular enacted autonomous models of the literary as a shield from the mass culture that sometimes supplemented their incomes. Storni, by contrast, came to literature through the middlebrow path of theatre and performance, the locus of her artistic education. In her theatrical experience, moreover, art was implicitly democratic, an impulse that wove through Storni's art of living, even as her poetry grew more hermetic. This training, along with Storni's work as a drama teacher and role as a performing woman in Buenos Aires literary life, lay at the core of her gendered critique of Argentine modernity and her transmutation from *poetisa* to writer and intellectual.

Storni's vast performance experience began in childhood in Rosario, where recitation and dance comprised part of her early education in the immigrant, working-middle-class family into which she was born.[3] Beyond homemade scenarios of her own invention, her first public performance in the male role of Saint John the Baptist provided an early crossover experience with the performativity of gender. At thirteen, Storni traveled with the theatre company of José Tallavi, crossing paths with the renowned actress Camilla Quiroga, and she performed minor roles in works by Ibsen, Galdós, and Uruguayan playwright Florencio Sánchez.[4] Later, as a Normal School student in Coronda, she declaimed poetry and sang opera arias and romanzas at public events while supplementing her income singing at bars in Rosario. Following the peripatetic job history of her early Buenos Aires years, in 1919 Storni began teaching declamation and theatre and eventually held secure positions at the Teatro Infantil Labardén and the Conservatorio de Música y Declamación. At the Labardén she directed children's performances, sometimes of her own plays. But even before dramatic pedagogy became a source of her livelihood, supplemented by the journalistic vocation she initiated in 1916, performance shaped her assumption of the *poetisa* role and her debut into *porteña* literary society. At *Nosotros* banquets she recited verse with what male observers described as "extraordinary vigor and vibration" (quoted in Delgado, 149). She declaimed frequently for women's groups and, along with the popular Berta Singerman, provided countless aspiring Buenos Aires *poetisas* with a role model, while in male literary circles she sometimes supplemented poetic performances with singing and dancing tango. By all accounts, Storni loved performing for an audience, particularly in an impromptu mode. Gwen Kirkpatrick has argued that, on stage or not, Storni consciously crafted her own public image.[5] Contemporary witnesses underscored Storni's studied gestures, her memorable voice, and her theatricality, for example in the artful dispersal of white rose petals to accentuate a recitation of "Una rosa" (Félix Visillac quoted in Delgado, 84). But these accounts also intimate that Storni rarely adhered to the tight script for declaimers found in recitation manuals for young women,[6] that she sometimes peppered these performances with irony, and that she enjoyed parodying others, including Singerman, who in turn relished these impersonations.

These anecdotal manifestations of self-reflexive performance suggest that Storni exploited the theatrical as an analytical tool. Although her theatre, particularly the metatheatrical farces, constitutes the most evident examples of this inquiry, theatricality marked her work as a whole. Her early sentimental poems, as Beatriz Sarlo suggests, were verses to be performed, and their repetitive rhetoric and grand finales were perfect for an aspiring *poetisa*-declaimer (*Una modernidad periférica,* 79). Rachel Phillips has argued that much of Storni's poetic work exhibits a proclivity for scenarios of dramatic conflict, dialogue, and interior duplications through a poem within a poem (26, 40). Kirkpatrick proposes that the "staginess and theatricality" of the "landscape" of personal emotions in Storni's earlier poetry is unmasked in her later work by a conscious shift in the poetic speaker from observed to critical observer (*Dissonant Legacy,* 232). Comparable conflictive scenarios and dialogue, in a penchant for epistolary narratives and for a critical repositioning of narrative voice, permeate Storni's prose as well, as in the story of the tailored dress. Theatricality saturates not only Storni's public persona but also her writing and gives consistency to her intellectual project. She herself intimated that performance was a cognitive enterprise when she highlighted the integral role of its "sensorial activity" in her early formation (quoted in Nalé Roxlo, 39). Similar to their creator, the female protagonists in Storni's major plays and several male characters are portrayed as self-conscious performers, and characters in her prose sketches display a proclivity for the metadramatic as well. Along with the theatrical quality of some of Storni's poetic speakers, these portrayals display her keen scrutiny of the force of cultural scripts, the rehearsal of which she cast as a rich source of knowledge and a site for social change.

FROM FASHION TO BOOKS:
ELASTIC REHEARSALS OF CULTURAL MEMORY

In her journalism, Storni displayed the essentialist view of gender typical of a time when even the most active Argentine feminists lobbied for women to be "as good as men but not the same as men" (Lavrin, 5). But her sharp eye for the impact of cultural scripts on social identities appeared in her earliest creative work. The first two stanzas of "Del teatro" from *La inquietud del rosal* (1916) focus on a young actress whose theatrical presence masks a tubercular hunger and a "life without aroma"

(*Obra poética completa,* 70). The ambiguous portrayal of this figure as both consumptive character in a romantic play and as the actress playing the part poses the inseparability of scripts from their enactment. A more explicit blurring of actors with their roles unfolded years later in Storni's skillful farce *Cimbelina en 1900 y pico* (Cymbeline in about 1900; 1931). This work's characters are actors who execute two performances: on one side of the stage they play their parts as traditional figures in Shakespeare's Cymbeline, while on the other side they recast their Shakespearean roles in a modern farce set in Buenos Aires. Crossing the stage from Shakespeare to farce, the actor-characters change clothes in a neutral in-between space, a strategy that underscores the volatility of identity and the role of fashion in its constitution. But as they address the audience to discuss the play, they are always clothed as Shakespeare's creations or as the personages in the farce, never—as one would expect from the performance-free middle space—simply as actors, sans scripts or costumes, inhabitants of a putative real world. As in the poem, then, identities emerge through their enactment of historical contexts they embody.

Throughout her work, Storni accentuated the cultural constitution of social roles, an inquiry for which fashion and books provided central motifs in several genres.[7] Shaped by the idiom of her time, for "culture" in the ethnographic sense Storni generally used the term "education." While she argued in "La complejidad femenina" that the source of women's complex singularity was organic, educational, and economic, she devoted minimal attention to biology, some to economics, and a great deal to education or culture (*Nosotras,* 146).[8] Through this analysis, Storni debunked reciprocal gender typecasting and exposed prevailing images of women as myths perpetuated through the bodies and books that enact and transmit them. In this context, Storni's prose fiction and journalism reveal a love-hate relationship to fashion. While she often dismissed it as a trivial pursuit, she devoted exhaustive attention to fashion's power. In keeping with her theatrical training, fashion for Storni encompassed the makeup, body language, and tone of voice that constitute an individual's interaction with the social world. Drawing on Pierre Bourdieu and Marcel Mauss, Jennifer Craik argues that codes of dress and bodily demeanor constitute "technical devices which articulate the relationship between a particular body and its lived milieu, the space occupied by bodies and constituted by bodily actions," adding that clothes "construct a personal *habitus*" (4). Thus fashion for cultural theorists is both a "tool of self-management" and a "technique of acculturation" into a concrete social world (46, 10). Moreover, just as Judith Butler poses a tension between the unavoidable "citationality" of gendered social practices and their "unanticipated" new meanings in individual performances (23, 28), so do fashion theorists argue that, in the personal habitus created by clothing and demeanor, there is a dynamic relationship between the "prestigious imitation" of "structured and disciplined codes of conduct" and the "licence and freedom" of "untrained impulses" in the "way the body is worn" (Craik 56, 5).

Storni's fashion inquisition focused precisely on this fault line between the power of fashion codes to generate "prestigious imitations" through the "wearing" of bodies and the individuation of those norms through more novel enactments. As a progressive, Storni addressed this dynamic between discipline and freedom in fashion's practical presentation of class, gender, and historical context. Kirkpatrick observes that she used dress to signal class change ("Journalism," 120). In the story of the tailored dress opening this chapter, for example, the transformation of an affluent *porteña*'s garment into the attire of a working mother incarnates the women's contrasting class experiences.[9] Drawing on the shifting economic fortunes of her immigrant family and on her struggles as a self-supporting single parent, Storni was keenly attuned to class inequities. But while she highlighted class hierarchies enacted through dress, Storni asserted that the models of the masculine and feminine executed through fashion were far from timeless, and she suggested that modern men's attire had become less apt to signal class distinctions than women's (*Nosotras,* 77). If fashion norms had hampered the working class,[10] Storni argued that in the modern era they were even more rigid for women.

This is not to say that Storni saw masculinity as any less normative than the feminine. A comic scene in *Cimbelina en 1900 y pico,* for example, presents youthful male characters performing their masculinity through self-conscious bodybuilding. But Storni dedicated far more attention to limitations that cultural scripts imposed on women and highlighted the painstaking "techniques of femininity," to use Craik's term, that forged women's presentation to the world. Thus in Storni's satirical prose sketches, young women's hyperbolic mimicry of fashion standards renders the boundaries indistinguishable between a woman and the cultural norm she enacts.[11] Above all, Storni censured women's reiteration of social rules to the detriment of their own agency. The ironic "Diario de una niña inútil," for example, traces a young's woman's failure to produce an original diary as she recounts her pursuit of a husband through the ten commandments of the Secret Association of Useless Girls in Defense of Their Interests. Her diary degenerates into a litany of rehearsing these injunctions about clothing, bodily attitude, and comportment, and the protagonist observes with dismay her metamorphosis into a "decalogue in action" (*Nosotras,* 135). Storni stressed the incalculable scope of these techniques for gender acculturation and their bodily inscription through the comic sketch "La irreprochable." This exhaustive inventory sums up the 45,000 scripted movements (220 per social outing) required to catch a man, from discrete nose powderings to periodic bosom "affirmations" (*Nosotras,* 135).

Their disciplining power notwithstanding, the bodily norms parodied in these accounts also grounded Storni's pursuit of change. For her, the enactment of cultural memory through repetition constituted a fundamental human activity, as in an infant's first perception of its surroundings in "El hombre." In this poetic portrait of the human life cycle, the infant studies the "muscle play" of the anonymous face before him, which he in turn "copies by smiling" (*Obra poética completa,* 373). Storni locates this cycle of imitation in a body that does not always choose its models, as in the poem "Cara copiada" (Copied face) that characterizes a child's resemblance to his father as an act of bodily memory through mimicry. Thus the father's face, hidden behind the child's fine skin, organizes the gestures that we see (*Obra poética completa,* 270). "Autoretrato barroco" (Baroque self-portrait) poses a comparable image of bodily cultural memory that inexorably carves human presentations of self. Here an ancient Greek mask "cuts through" the face that the speaker wears (*Obra poética completa,* 397). Together these poems pose a dynamic between the power of cultural memory to enforce imitation and the energizing facility of the human agent who reenacts it.

Storni's analysis of gender renders this tension in bold terms. Exemplifying such autonomous impulses against the force of inheritance, women who mimic gender stereotypes to their advantage make numerous appearances in her work. Their self-aware maneuvers recall the resistant "tactics of the weak" that Josefina Ludmer highlights in Sor Juana Inés de la Cruz's subversive response to the ecclesiastical ban on her intellectual pursuits. Storni gave mixed reviews to this ploy, but she was ultimately intrigued by its creative possibilities. Thus the beautiful, manipulative Zarcillo, one of two women protagonists in Storni's first staged play, *El amo del mundo* (The master of the world; 1927), incarnates this fashion-conscious manipulation. Zarcillo, with her "imagination, calculation . . . and cunning," dresses in high fashion and fakes weakness to "control those who are stronger" (*Obras escogidas: Teatro,* 11). Although Zarcillo stands by, and wins, her man, the playwright judges her more harshly than Márgara, her more intellectual and artless counterpart who ends up alone but on higher moral ground. But even as she censured women for the play of "infinite veils" with which their education had "enveloped the feminine soul" (*Nosotras,* 146), Storni argued that as long as women lacked economic or political autonomy, their capacity for dissimulation remained their "defensive cloak," in the words of one dramatic protagonist (*Obras escogidas: Teatro,* 191). In fact, Storni proposed that marginality was the source of women's "feminine complexity," "idiosyncrasy," or "elasticity," defined as a capacity for creative resourcefulness and performative range that she attributed to all marginalized groups. In any power situation, she added, those submitted to the will of others develop a highly sharpened imagination that evens the playing field (*Nosotras,* 148).

Even as she lamented the social hierarchies that had shaped women's "complexity," then, Storni highlighted the capacity for change embodied in this performative elasticity, through the unanticipated move in the embrace of a stereotype or the recasting of timeworn roles in self-fashioning. Arguing that most human beings "borrowed" their lives through imitation ("Derechos civiles femeninos," 877), she placed a high premium on the personality that might "differentiate and separate" from the scripts it enacted through the unexpected gesture or word (*Nosotras,* 111). The paired stories "Niñas" portray two young girls who, through ultrafeminine clothes and corporeality, employ refined techniques of gendered self-management but also manifest a "delicious" originality through subtle realignments: the first through unfeminine retorts of disgust toward the pigeons she demurely feeds in the park and the other by transforming herself from a sweet young thing into a bold tightrope artist through the ingenious manipulation of her umbrella ("Niñas," 57–59). Other Storni characters realize more explicit androgynous recastings of cultural scripts, such as the predatory women in the poem "Divertidas estancias a Don Juan" (Entertaining stanzas to Don Juan). Here the poetic speaker urges the legendary but diminished womanizer to remain asleep underground. Not only are the updated women of these humorous verses impervious to his seductive powers and drawn to other readings (the "thin Doña Elvira" and the "chaste Doña Inés," who now read the erotic poetry of Delmira Agustini and Stendahl in French), some have even stolen his seductive thunder to "assume his manner" and "rehearse his power" (*Obra poética completa,* 291–292).

Early in her career, Storni cast a jaundiced eye on such androgyny, as in the ambivalent portrayal of a woman who combines her more "masculine" feminism with her feminine wiles (*Nosotras,* 32–33). This hesitation manifests anxiety about shifting gender roles that typified public discourse in Buenos Aires in the 1920s, an atmosphere exacerbated by the 1926 Civil Code reforms that increased civil rights for women, particularly in domestic matters. Piecemeal as they may seem in retrospect, such advances generated sensationalist cautionary tales in *Caras y caretas* about "amazons," cross-dressing males, or obscure tribes supposedly ruled by women.[12] But increasingly over the years, Storni cast gender hybridity as a powerful locus of change in the ostensible reiteration of inherited scripts. The lead female characters in her plays all display an androgynous turn. In *Cimbelina en 1900 y pico,* which recasts Shakespeare's play into a contemporary farce, Storni draws on a genre that traditionally enacted anxieties about relationships between the sexes (as in the nineteenth-century bedroom farce) to generate hybrid substitutions. In the play's modern segment, characters hyperbolize their gendered techniques of "self management," to recall Craik's term, through modern activities and fashion artifacts. Thus the male lead, Héctor (counterpart to Shakespeare's Postumo), and his friends assemble their masculinity in an exercise workout in which they engage in sexual locker-room banter. On the other hand, the identity of María Elena, the play's female protagonist and New Woman counterpart to Shakespeare's Imogene, mutates in the Gillete razor she gives her husband as an icon of fidelity. As María Elena's signature prop, whose gender value shifts with its users, the razor announces her incipient androgyny, and María Elena's dominant role in the play reinforces this identity. It is she who leads the others out of the Shakespearean roles into the modern-day farce and addresses the audience about the social change the play represents.

The play's farcical tone may have made such gender bending more palatable to its contemporary audience. But in an article on changing norms enacted through fashion, Storni imagined an androgynous future woman who would neutralize stereotypes by combining the "athlete's force, the delicacy of a butterfly, the clarity of water, the understanding of a philosopher, and the grace of a nymph" (*Nosotras,* 81). Only such a woman, Storni argued in a piece on women's "relative incapacities," could outgrow the frivolity, false authority, and dissipation produced by their marginality, discard outdated roles, and assume responsibility for the "new air moving through the world" (*Nosotras,* 88). *Cimbelina en 1900 y pico* dramatizes these concepts through the onstage presence of a giant leather book, with Shakespeare's title on its cover and from which the play's characters emerge in the opening scene, introduce themselves, and assume theatrical poses. A palpable artifact of cultural memory, the book remains on the stage throughout the transformation from Shakespeare to farce, and when the modern characters conclude their performance, they cross the stage to reenter it. However, the book's shrunken door now poses too small a fit, as they have literally outgrown their historical roles. In this scene only María Elena, the work's modern protagonist, remains attired exclusively in contemporary attire, while the others resume fragments of Shakespearean dress. Thus the play locates its historical consciousness in its contemporary independent woman as she articulates a new relationship with her world.

In Storni's three principal plays, books—multitudinous or larger than life—give visual testimony to the presence of cultural memory in intellectual life and simultaneously generate cognitive practices for overturning its power. But the fact that the imposing Shakespearean volume remains onstage throughout *Cimbelina en 1900 y pico* signals that, for Storni, new social roles may not simply be fashioned out of whole cloth. Rather cultural memory is both burden and resource, and the roles engendered by Shakespeare's script can change only as the modern actors rehearse them. Rehearsal for Storni constitutes not only a form of creating something new through imitation but also a lifelong process of learning by doing. Thus both *Cimbelina en 1900 y pico* and its companion farce *Polixena y la cocinerita* are structured as rehearsals that embody contemporary performances of timeworn texts (Shakespeare's *Cymbeline* and Euripides's *Hecuba*). As in a dramatic rehearsal, the character-actors also halt and restart their enactments, comment on their progress, and alter the script they rehearse.

As an omnipresent, accessible resource, cultural memory, for Storni, provoked the irreverence toward literary tradition enacted in the two farces and portrayed as well in her sonnet "Versos a la memoria" from *Ocre*. While acknowledging the forceful impact on her writing of the "populous library" of inherited cultural memory, which is also the "thread itself of creation," here the poetic speaker asserts autonomy from memory's full authority through the androgynous irreverence signaled in the Diana myth rehearsed in the poem's closing lines. Here the speaker identifies simultaneously with the "muscular male youth" in pursuit and the "muscular maiden" who eludes them (*Obra poética completa*, 286–287). At the same time, rehearsing cultural scripts constitutes for Storni an arduous cognitive method. Thus the speaker of the poem "El ensayo" recounts her lifelong rehearsal of an "unlearned drama," a process of multiple posture changes and of "falling down and getting up" (*Obra poética completa*, 236–237). Beyond the weight of mortality motivating the speaker (a burden not coincidentally inscribed by dramatic tradition in the lone actor-character contemplating life options onstage), this poem's images of apprehensive, alternating postures embody the rehearsal's epistemological mode.

Drawing on Artaud and Brecht, contemporary performance theory, akin to Storni's poem, locates the cognitive force of rehearsal in its "jerky

and disjointed, often incoherent" moves with "high information potential" (Schechner, 182) or in the "stumbling, erratic shorthand through
which facts are lost, collided with, found again" (Harold Pinter quoted
in Blau, *To All Appearances,* 43). Moreover, as in the seditious inversions
performed by actor-characters in Storni's farces toward their classical for-
bearers, this view of rehearsal as an embodied "center for . . . research"
(Schechner, 210) privileges the choices weighed by rehearsing actors over
the definitive performance that might be truer to an original script. Such
rehearsed betrayals provide, as Richard Schechner argues, a way of "trying
out what may never be shown" (209). In this vein, the androgynous New
Woman director, María Helena, of *Cimbelina en 1900 y pico* upends the
Shakespearean libretto not only to try out a different role but also to reflect
with fellow actors and audience on social and intellectual change.

The resolute presence of books in Storni's dramatic scenarios underscores that the crucial object of inquiry in her staged rehearsals was not
merely gendered scripts but also the impact of intellectual life on women
and, in turn, the roles modern women might assume as literary figures.
Her recurring juxtaposition of fashion and writing, moreover, blurs distinctions not only between script and performance but also between body
and language, intellectual life and mass culture, masculine and feminine.
If fashion for Storni acculturates the body to gender through tools of self-
management in a historically specific world, books, as inscribers of cultural
memory, offer comparably pliable cultural tools depending on how they
are read and by whom. As with the transformation of the bourgeois dress
into a working woman's garment, the trajectory from fashion to books in
Storni's writing foregrounds the challenging and intricate self-fashioning
of the New Woman intellectual from the paucity of hand-me-down scripts
at her disposal, specifically the popular role of *poetisa.* Notwithstanding
her ambivalence toward the talent for dissimulation she ascribed to unlib-
erated women, moreover, Storni ultimately suggested that their performative agility constituted a cognitive resource that could serve them well for
this daunting task.

(UN)MASKING INTIMACY:
THE PATH FROM *POETISA* TO INTELLECTUAL

As early as 1921, in a piece on women as novelists, Storni perceived radical
dissonance between the social role of the writer who is a woman—*la escri-
tora*—and that of the woman who actually inhabits the writer (*Nosotras,*
162). Storni's early poetry and public appearances as a declaimer of her

own verse provided an entrée to public literary culture. But her early essays and the overt ironies of the poems themselves, in which the voice of the feminist critic breaks through the sentimentality, manifest Storni's uneasiness from the start with the *poetisa* role and her skepticism toward its claims to expressive intimacy. While doubting the intellectual substance of the poetry for which she won recognition, Storni displayed conflict and uncertainty as to what a truly intellectual woman might be like and pondered what sources from their own experience women might be forced to deny in considering models of intellectual authority elaborated by men. In her own life, Storni changed from a woman designated a *poetisa* to one recognized by several male writers as a peer and a fellow poet. At the same time, in analyzing women's participation in literary life, she gradually imagined a more nuanced intellectual role for women, not only in its incipient androgyny but also in its crossing of prevailing boundaries between the mass culture she embraced as a performing *poetisa* and the intellectual work with which she identified as a serious writer.

Storni often criticized her own work, in particular those early poems that reiterated gender norms in their focus on love, and she occasionally even relinquished any claims to their status as "literature."[13] Cultural expectations for a *poetisa* in Storni's day were that she would write "intimist" verse about matters of the heart, that her poetry would be emotive but self-abnegating, devoid of excessive passion, and expressive of "feminine" qualities of gentleness, softness, purity, beauty, fragility, and moral superiority.[14] Even as Storni's early sentimental poetry and declamation style mimicked these norms, her acerbic wit, incensed chastisement of men, and resistance to self-abnegation defied them. Although she adopted the formal elements and motifs of latter-day Spanish American *modernismo* in her early poetry, these, too, offered an uneasy fit. Even before Storni's verse underscored the inadequacies of *modernista* models by moving beyond them, a 1916 short story challenged the ethical suitability of the *modernista* aesthetic for a woman poet. Well versed in the arts and endowed with a presumably refined artistic sensibility, this story's cold-as-ice female protagonist, Amalia, embodies both the *modernista* aesthetic and its pristine ideal of feminine beauty. The story portrays Amelia's objectification of a female friend whose "divine beauty" she contemplates in order to "reproduce it" ("La fina crueldad," 1365–1366). Amalia's repulsion by the realization that her friend would be even more artistically perfect were she dead signals not only her rejection of *modernismo* but also the ethical turmoil it generates in women who embrace it.

In part, Storni's ambivalence about the *poetisa* mode manifested the artistic biases of the time. A *poetisa,* for those in the cultural loop, was something less than a full-fledged poet. Roberto Giusti's high praise for Storni's metamorphosis from the former into the latter testifies to this hierarchy. From the "vague promise" of her early work, he noted, the "cordial little teacher" had gone beyond the "sub-literature" that constituted women's writing and become an "honest comrade" in their gatherings and an "authentic poet" (97–98). Storni's own critique of *poetisa* practices synthesized gender with genre. In a less-than-enthusiastic essay on "Las poetisas americanas" (1919), Storni contrasted proliferating women's verse (like the tropical vegetation of Latin America) to the dedication and mental discipline of prose and drama (*Nosotras,* 52). The prevailing social milieu, she argued, provided women with "light-weight culture" and reinforced mental laziness in those with the available free time to write (*Nosotras,* 52).

For Storni, then, *poetisa* aesthetics embodied this "light-weight culture" lacking the requisite intellectual rigor for original thought or art. She displayed keen awareness of the cultural hierarchies that assigned lighter fare to women when, after dutifully declaiming a poem for the Anaconda literary group, she suggested that her good friend and co-member Horacio Quiroga "declaim" one of his short stories, "complete with gestures" (Nalé Roxlo, 99). Storni's critique of *poetisa* aesthetics, moreover, addressed its limitations for women seeking to draw on their own experience. As early as 1916, in the heyday of her own *poetisa* phase, she suggested that the intimacy ascribed to women's poetry was itself a literary mask and cultural convention akin to a *poetisa*'s declamatory performance. The narrator of an epistolary tale, for example, laments that writing an intimate letter to a loved one requires an interior quest for the "stock phrases" that can produce something beautiful but "low on sincerity" ("Algunas líneas," 1308). Years later, in "Autodemolición" (Self-demolition), a parodic self-portrait that Storni published during a 1930 trip to Madrid, she mocked fashionable techniques of women's self-presentation in a tongue-in-cheek inventory of her own outer "wrapper"—her physical traits and dress style—and then summed up her more intimate self as 70 percent sugar, a condition she ascribed to her history as a *poetisa* (319). If the *poetisa*'s outward presentation was nothing but fashion and gesture, the "intimate" interiority it enveloped was itself a saccharine mask. Similarly, in a preface to an anthology of her work in preparation at the time of her death, Storni described her early poems as "romantic honeys" (*Antología poética,* 9–10). But in the same lines she praised the antipatriarchal critical position she had forged through *poetisa* aesthetics.

At the same time that Storni highlighted the expressive limitations of the *poetisa* role, she scrutinized obstacles to women's full intellectual development. In surveys of women's work in Buenos Aires, she lamented the low number of women professionally identified with academic pursuits or the arts. Whatever women's deficiencies as thinkers, Storni argued, they derived from inadequate education and conventions that castigated those who displayed their intelligence by withholding the rewards of romantic love and marriage.[15] She also suggested that the epoch's characterization of women as moral models further proscribed women's potential for thought. In the sketch "Tijereteo," a fictional *tertulia* of women artists and intellectuals, the dialogue inventories their frustrations in finding an intellectual home in the confectionery where they meet. The painters, musicians, and writers lament the marginalizing of any woman who tries to live by her ideas. One woman observes that their designated role as guardians of bourgeois morality, coupled with their preservation of the "discrete lie" of feminine wiles, had impeded their pursuit of the intellectual anarchy essential for true artistic creation (*Nosotras*, 171–176). In a related piece on women's enmity to women, Storni argued that a lack of philosophical training impeded their capacity to analyze their situation collectively and forge an androgynous "Masonry" of women (*Nosotras*, 163, 166), an image that calls to mind the habitat for fraternity shaping vanguard literary activity.

Storni contended that women lacked talent for prose and drama because of meager life experience produced by proscriptions of their assigned roles as moral arbiters. Paradoxically, Storni's own life experience and that of other women constituted the rich substance of her own prose and theatre. Her assessment of women's incapacity for abstraction, moreover, rested largely on an essentialist conception of analysis as a dry and by definition male activity and of intuition as the more subjective purview of women.[16] But Storni simultaneously rejected this binary opposition. More faithful to her own analytical style in writing about women, she explored a conception of philosophical thought and intellectual inquiry based on the activity of life that, she proposed, might well render women the true philosophers (*Nosotras*, 130). Most important, Storni's search for models of the new intellectual woman through her drama manifests a drive to synthesize her own propensity for analysis with her life experience as a performing *poetisa*. Thus Storni sought to recuperate for women's intellectual activity the performative resourcefulness she believed they had acquired in manipulating cultural norms that policed them.

The play *El amo del mundo* articulates the failed quest for such a synthesis between a woman's intellect and the performative dexterity she has won through hard experience. The original title Storni chose for her play—*Dos mujeres* (Two women)—manifests this duality, but the director persuaded her to alter it in response to lead actors' demands, which shifted the focus onto the play's principal male character: the handsome, educated, forty-something bachelor Claudio. Márgara and Zarcillo offer contrasting examples of gender interaction with Claudio, a man they both desire and who, in turn, wants both of them. Lovely, proud, strong, and soberly attired, the older Márgara forges her insightful vision of the world "from the exercise of reading and the observation of life from superior points of view"; she is, the stage directions explain, the "woman who escapes her environment and overcomes it" (*Obras escogidas: Teatro*, 11). The younger, beautiful, and frail Zarcillo is, as noted, fashionable, stagy, fun-loving, and brimming with manipulative guile, and she channels her wit toward the search for the social position and material security embodied in a husband like Claudio. While Márgara and Zarcillo incarnate two versions of the New Woman, their common ground includes their singular intelligence, voracious reading, and unconventional sexual pasts that, if revealed, would summarily disqualify them as Claudio's intended.

The abundant books and magazines that fill Márgara's home, where the action unfolds, underscore the relationship to reading and cultural scripts in the play's contrast of the two women.[17] For Zarcillo, who masks her intellect, reading, like dressing in style, constitutes a form of modern consumption, as it did for the trendy Beba of *Caras y caretas* described in this book's introduction. As an activity that she feels compelled to mask except with women's magazines, reading provides Zarcillo with scripts through which to decipher the world and men quixotically. Noting that she successively compares him to Solomon, an Oscar Wilde character, and a futurist creation, Claudio affirms that reading harms a woman's "fertile imagination" (*Obras escogidas: Teatro*, 32). By contrast, reading for Márgara, whom Zarcillo admires, constitutes a site for analytical thought and the source of her unabashed honesty with men, whom she regards as equals. For Claudio, drawn to and repelled by Márgara, her intellect deforms her into a "hybrid" that lacks both the boldness of a man and the modesty and flirtatiousness of a woman that, he argues, represent her best weapons (*Obras escogidas: Teatro*, 75). As Márgara discloses the identity of her illegitimate son to Claudio, her honesty poses a rejection of these wiles that might have won him. If only, Claudio laments, she had been willing to deceive him through theatre like a real woman.

Storni's indecision about the viable course for an intellectual woman stands out in the fact that, although Márgara refuses to deceive Claudio with artful wiles, she oversees a cover-up of Zarcillo's sexual indiscretions so that the younger woman and Claudio may launch an honorable marriage. While as an intellectual woman Márgara blasts double sexual standards, then, in keeping with the higher morality assigned to women by Argentine society and by feminist movements of the time, she paradoxically engineers the preservation of family and bourgeois morality. But this was precisely the role that, Storni had argued, prevented women from realizing their writing potential. Márgara's characterization in *El amo del mundo* as a nascent writer, her complex relationship with a man with whom she shares an intellectual rapport (analogous to Storni's with Quiroga), and her status as a single mother all make an autobiographical reading of the play tempting.[18] Moreover, Márgara's insistent refusal of sugar in her tea, a preference she attributes to her own masculinity, recalls Storni's own critique of the sugar and romantic honey she ascribed to her *poetisa* identity. But the play also underscores Márgara's incapacity for fun in contrast to the lively and entertaining Zarcillo, and this distinction discourages too literal an autobiographical take on Márgara. In contrast to Zarcillo's theatricality and love for the grand entrance, a quality noted by contemporaries in Storni herself, Márgara despises performing, in particular dance, a disinclination most certainly not shared with her creator. In light of its failed reconciliation between Márgara's hybrid, predominantly "masculine" intellect and Zarcillo's "feminine" performative dexterity, the play suggests that a site for synthesis is Márgara's analytical mode as a writer. When Claudio explains that he lacks the vanity required to write for an audience, Márgara counters that writing for her, by contrast, constitutes a mode for "thinking out loud" (*Obras escogidas: Teatro,* 65). This image recalls Storni's conception of the inventive rehearsal of cultural scripts as a path to change, an idea that she developed more fully in her experimental farces.

In fact *El amo del mundo,* which opened in March 1927 in the Cervantes theatre in Buenos Aires, fell short of both critical and artistic success. The former derived from the play's feminism: Storni was accused of man-bashing by an audience that had failed to grasp that the work, divested of the title she had intended, had relatively little to say about men and focused instead on the life choices available to women. Just as Márgara failed to find her place as a woman intellectual, Storni, too, had yet to find the dramatic idiom capable of imagining one. But Zarcillo's elastic theatricality harbored the seeds for the dramatic form that Storni found in the two "pyrotechnical" experiments, *Cimbelina en 1900 y pico* and *Polixena y la cocinerita*. These plays' farcical mode and satirical content provide a way of "thinking out loud." Both plays recast inherited scripts, Shakespeare and Euripides, respectively, into a critique of gender norms. But *Polixena y la cocinerita* poses a way to incorporate the cognitive dexterity acquired by women as performers into a model of intellectual activity congruent with their own social experience.

Aptly dedicated to Berta Singerman, *Polixena y la cocinerita* also constitutes Storni's most artistically effective meditation on the critical potential of the *poetisa*. The play explores the cultural activity of a self-styled Buenos Aires *poetisa* in Storni's own time, particularly declamation. Here a kitchen maid, accompanied by her sidekick, the *mucama* or household servant, counters the tedium of her job and the unwanted advances of her employer's son through the irreverent recitation of a scene from Euripides's *Hecuba*: Polyxena's voluntary, sacrificial death at Achilles tomb. The antimimetic reflection of this scenario materializes in extravagantly stylized characters and props and in the *cocinerita*'s mercurial identity. A fugitive from a middle-class family, the declaiming cook has held numerous jobs from the limited repertoire available to single women: caretaker, nurse, laborer, and office worker. Frequently checking her hair and makeup, the *cocinerita* hyperbolizes the performative elasticity of Storni's female characters. She proclaims that she will overcome her tough situation in the guise of Hecuba's heroic daughter, Polyxena, and, similar to the ideal *poetisa,* she "mixes her own drama with the one she relates" (*Obras escogidas: Teatro,* 260). Thus her onstage activity alternates between imaginative replays of conflictive encounters with her seducer and, while she cooks, her flamboyant recitations of Euripides's verse, subject to considerable poetic license. The cook's passionate oration of these hybrid lines culminates in her suicide when she stabs herself, not with the oversized cucumber she wields in her farcical mode but with the real-life kitchen knife that it masks. The play's epilogue expands on the cook's commentary to Euripides that he would be amazed to see a twentieth-century *cocinerita* reciting, and changing, his work. The epilogue includes dialogue between Euripides and a giant fish, a character that, as Phillips has suggested, recalls the comedies of Aristophanes, who portrayed Euripides as a misogynist (Phillips, 73). Reporting on his time travels to the modern world, the fish tells Euripides that *poetisas* are declaiming his verse in distant Argentina, a revelation that causes the horrified playwright to hurl himself into the fish's mouth.

This tragicomic farce places the role of *poetisa* on center stage and showcases the force of women's experience with performance for their own intellectual style. Moreover, the cook's self-portrayal as a "repeater of songs" (*Obras escogidas: Teatro,* 239), her declaimer's props of a lectern and book, and her diminutive label, *cocinerita,* which echoes the comparably diminishing "*poetisa,*" structure the play's inquiry into and celebration of the *poetisa* role. Ultimately the piece affirms the creative power of the *poetisa* identity, its epistemological affiliation with women's experience, its generative strength for the unexpected insight, and its foundational potential for intellectual alliances among women. Thus the cook calls on the *mucama* to join in the boisterous and powerful song of water boiling in pots, silver hitting the sink, the mortar and pestle grinding spices, the grater slicing bread and cheese. At the same time, the *cocinerita*'s desperate struggles with her seducer give her song an acerbic edge that counters the "romantic honeys" implicit in the *poetisa* mode. The work challenges expectations of confessional intimacy conventionally ascribed to women poets through the cook's unsettling culinary imagery and the mercurial emotional gamut she runs while shifting from one level of her metadrama to another: a single woman seeking a viable job, a decrier of social inequities, a well-read domestic employee, and the martyred Polyxena in Euripides's play. Thus as she recites her own version of Polyxena's sacrifice, the kitchen maid reenacts, reflects upon, and reinterprets her own experience, an epistemological process that fuels the irreverent recasting of Euripides and her suicidal act.

The work situates the cognitive force of these metatheatrical moves in the specificity of women's experiences. Thus the *cocinerita*'s proclamation that she "untangles Einstein" while timing the rice (*Obras escogidas: Teatro,* 244) affirms the intellectual power of her own feverish pursuits, recalls Sor Juana's linkage of frying eggs with learning physics, and anticipates comparable ties between cooking and knowledge forged by late-twentieth-century Latin American women writers. The play's juxtaposition of food and books as the objects of the *cocinerita*'s consumption and the tools of her performative trade further upends the derogatory equation of the New Woman with mass culture that circulated in literary circles and middlebrow magazines' cautionary tales of the New Woman as consumer. The piece also hints at the kind of intellectual "Masonry" that, as noted, Storni argued could counter the enmity of women toward one another. Thus the play highlights camaraderie between the *cocinerita* and the *mucama* and invokes Sappho as the predecessor of the twentieth-century Buenos Aires *poetisa.* Above all, these validations of women's intellectual dexterity garnered from lived knowledge counter Storni's earlier assertion that women had failed to write good novels or drama because of experiential poverty. Indeed the play's most striking feature is the generative force of the kitchen poet's feverish declamations and their radical new ways of imagining the world. Calling on the *mucama* to join her, she executes a form of verbal incantation—a performative "thinking out loud"—that sets objects around her into motion in a vertiginous accumulation of unexpected images, an estrangement of ordinary things. In their unexpected opulence and eschewal of affective intimacy, these images generated by the *cocinerita*'s incantations parallel what Kirkpatrick has called the "stunning and unsettling vistas" of Storni's vanguard poetry of the 1930s (*Dissonant Legacy*, 239). The *cocinerita*'s imagery also translates to the verbal realm the hard-won performative elasticity that, Storni had argued, accrued from women's artful manipulation of their constrictive social roles. Even as Storni openly rejected the sugared lyricism she had embraced in forging her own public role in literary culture, the cook's indomitable oral energy—her power to set words and objects into motion—salvages the creative and epistemological force of that role for an intelligent woman in pursuit of an elusive intellectual home.

Alfonsina Storni's own intellectual home was marked by its definitive itinerancy. Akin to the circuitous path of the mercurial *cocinerita*, her public identity continued to unfold in multiple venues, even as she gained a significant measure of status in literary circles that eventually included the prestigious Sociedad Argentina de Escritores. At the moment of her untimely death in 1938, Storni was more highly sought after than ever, not only as a popular declaimer of her latest poems but also as a knowledgeable lecturer and interpreter of Argentina, someone we would today call a public intellectual. In 1936 she was called upon to lecture at anniversary celebrations for the founding of Buenos Aires, and her observations on the city, its poetic history, and the character of its inhabitants appeared in a nationalist volume honoring the city on its birthday.[19] In this imposing tome, Storni once again kept company with *Nosotros* editor Giusti and with such rising luminaries of Argentine cultural life as Manuel Ugarte, Leopoldo Marechal, and Borges. During the same period, she lectured on Latin American women poets by invitation of the Ministerio de Instrucción Pública in Montevideo, prepared the first anthology of her own work for publication (posthumous, as it turned out), personally performed the *cocinerita*'s tale for the Sociedad de Arte y Cultura Popular organized by María V. Müller, also at the University of Montevideo, and continued publishing chronicles and poetry in the Buenos Aires daily *La nación*. Her strikingly innovative verse of these years included estranging views of Buenos Aires, fragmented and deformed representations of the poetic speaker, dispiriting portrayals of an urban underclass, and continuing inquiries into the redemptive promise of art, which, as the democratic poetic speaker in "Los coros" had affirmed, held no control over who produced it or how (*Obra poética completa,* 280).

This activity highlights the rich eclecticism of Storni's art of living as a writer in Buenos Aires. Paradoxically her eulogists by and large disregarded this complexity. Instead they shored up "romantic honeys" of her *poetisa* image, stripped of the irony, wit, critical edge, and intellectual depth with which Storni had transformed the role. Thus Ugarte memorialized her as a "soul of light," a woman possessing the "ingenuous and free sincerity of nature and children." (quoted in Delgado 235). Over the years, these public portrayals of Storni, along with the popular torch song "Alfonsina vestida de mar" (Alfonsina dressed by the sea) transmuted a suicidal liberation from terminal cancer into the escape of a victimized woman, à la *poetisa,* from the pain of love lost. Never fully relinquishing the role, Storni herself fueled this image in the enigmatic final lines of "Voy a dormir" (I am going to sleep), the farewell poem she submitted to *La nación* and that calls upon the reader to tell an unidentified "him" if he calls that she has "gone out" (*Obra poética completa,* 440). This was certainly not the first time that Storni, in the spirit of the artful Zarcillo, had self-consciously enacted a particular version of her public persona. But from the mid-1920s on, the poetic speakers of Storni's verse more often exhibited a critical perspective on their milieu, an unrelenting struggle with inherited social roles, and a mounting alertness to the sheer power of words. Just as the *cocinerita* decried the inhumanity surrounding her, so did some of Storni's poems portray a meaningless bourgeois life that called the artist's own activity into question.[20] Akin to the *cocinerita*'s lush verbal gala as a response to desperate straits, Storni's final poems, in *Mundo de siete pozos* and *Mascarilla y trébol,* counter increasingly dystopic images of the modern world and the speaker who views it with laudatory affirmations of the eccentric lyricism that brings those images into focus. Thus "La palabra" (The word) celebrates the "highest pleasure" of resisting the "dark genius that disintegrates us" (*Obra poética completa,* 290–291), and "Un lápiz" (A pencil) exalts the speaker's writing as the "hidden bomb" in her purse that will outlive her sudden death (*Obra poética completa,* 290–291). The linguistic liberation executed in the imagery of her late poetry marks a triumph of sorts in Storni's struggle to refashion available social personae and expressive forms into a comfortable fit. Interestingly, "Naturaleza mía" (My nature), the closing poem of Storni's 1925 collection *Ocre* that foreshadowed the radical shift of *Mundo de siete pozos* nine years later, highlights the uneasy habitus of social persona and culturally scripted attire established in the "Historia sintética de un traje tailleur." That sketch documented the re-making of hand-me-downs in keeping with the needs and experience of the wearer. But "Naturaleza mía" depicts a "diminished, ataxic, and robbed" being, the product of self-flagellation and forced fittings into "hair shirts" too restrictive to accommodate its paradoxically "voracious . . . incon-stant" nature (*Obra poética completa,* 303). Torturous as these forced fits may have been, Storni never discarded the hand-me-downs altogether but rather disassembled them and remodeled whatever might be salvaged into a groundbreaking public presence and singular forms of artistic expression.

chapter 2

WALKING BACKWARDS

Victoria Ocampo's Scenes of Intrusion

Victoria Ocampo's first play, *La laguna de los nenúfares* (1926) enacts the journey to maturity of its protagonist, Copo de Nieve, portrayed initially as a "snowflake that doesn't melt" (14). Shipwrecked, the orphan Copo de Nieve is raised in an idyllic forest by an overprotective Magician and two tutors, Optimio the dog and Atrabilis the cat. But Copo de Nieve prefers play with animals to formal lessons and, in a search for self-definition, imitates his companions' singularities. He walks on all fours with the hare, strives to grow a camel's hump, and walks backwards with the crab. In a strikingly comparable anecdote, Ocampo's autobiography describes a sheltered, privileged childhood in Buenos Aires and in the family home in Villa Ocampo, surrounded by doting parents and aunts. As did Copo de Nieve, Ocampo sought escape from governesses through play, and she recalls an adolescent inclination to mimic. She recounts impersonating the first young man to provoke her infatuation. In a perfect imitation of his style, she began walking with her head bent over, and when her mother remarked that they needed to attach her to a brace, the young Victoria imagined herself as Cleménce of the Countess of Ségur's *Comédies et Proverbes,* wearing a contraption to hold up her head (*Autobiografía,* 1:175).

The parallels between these tales illuminate key elements in Ocampo's assumption of a public persona and the formation of her unique genre of literary and cultural commentary, the *testimonio.* Both stories highlight performance as a site of learning, and the second tale links the performing body to readings, an analogy that, Sylvia Molloy argues, marks Ocampo's autobiography.[1] The two stories underscore Ocampo's fascination with theatre, as both youths enact the gestures of another. In both accounts, parents and teachers discourage the mimicry, just as Ocampo's parents forbade the theatrical career she desired. But these warnings only generate more performances. Most important, the imitation in both cases yields a jarring image: a young boy walking like a crab and an adolescent girl posing like a hunchbacked youth. Beyond the audacity of the two performers, this disjuncture points to the interventionist quality of Ocampo's dialogue with writers and books and her deliberate intellectual strategy to write against the grain and in the gaps. The best books, she argued, were those whose disorder obliged one to "read them backwards" ("El hombre que murió," 7–8), an image that mirrors Copo de Nieve's crablike gait.

Victoria Ocampo (1890–1979) enjoys a position in Latin American literary history unique for a woman of her time. She was a founder and director and the driving force for the journal *Sur,* which appeared from 1931 until 1971 and provided a rich intellectual forum throughout Latin America.[2] This literary midwifery, along with Ocampo's multiple volumes of *testimonios,* two plays, and six-volume autobiography, resulted in her appointment in 1977 as the first woman in Argentina's Academia de Letras. One could argue that Ocampo's achievements were compensatory for an unfulfilled dramatic career.[3] But her experience with performance was key to her literary activism and the emergence of the *testimonio.* These essays, the format for which she began crafting at the same time as her first play, are marked by abrupt narrative shifts in the conversations they stage between Ocampo and particular writers, books, or ideas. The *testimonios* also posit an intrusive narrating persona, a convener of the conversation who interrupts and redirects it at will. This aesthetic posture and style derives from Ocampo's early theatrical training and emergent feminism.

Although some see a contradiction between Ocampo's imposing public persona and more modest writing voice, the performative elements and motifs in her work illuminate a marked consistency between her public activity as a literary impresario and her evolving conception of her own writing.[4] In the *testimonios,* she staged a disorderly, fruitful dialogue among the voices populating the cultural universe of her richly diverse readings. Moreover, in keeping with the high awareness of an audience derived from her theatrical training, Ocampo fancied the conversations in which she joined as public events. Because she initially wrote in French, the language of her upper-class, tutorial education, and frequently interacted with noted international figures, it is tempting to portray Ocampo as aloof from the Buenos Aires cultural scene of the 1920s, the years when she began publishing there.[5] Yet her interventionist mode of intellectual activity in the 1920s and 1930s manifests her affinities not only with European modernism but also with Argentina's cultural avant-gardes, her formal affiliation with which emerged with the founding of *Sur* in 1931. This mode also highlights Ocampo's willful confrontation with the gender tensions of Buenos Aires literary culture.

BAUHAUS ON THE RÍO PLATA:
A WOMAN OF THE VANGUARDS

In light of Ocampo's achievements, a striking feature of her early career is the repeated refusal of the term "writer" to describe what she did. Molloy contrasts this paradoxical self-effacement to Ocampo's authoritative personal presence (*At Face Value,* 71). But the negation of the moniker is actually consistent with her sustained characterization of her cultural role as a work in progress, in response to her upper-class parents' prohibitions against "the public manifestation" of her "thoughts and sentiments" (*Autobiografía,* 3:104) and in a milieu that offered no inviting intellectual home to an intelligent, ambitious woman. Her denial of the label "writer" may signal less a lack of confidence in her own expressive ability than a determination in the absence of suitable models to intervene in the cultural dialogue she accessed through voracious reading. Ocampo described her writing as an irresistible personal drive and, like Márgara in Storni's *El amo del mundo,* a mode of "thinking out loud"(*Domingos,* 71). Ocampo also characterized her writing as an unending "search for a form of expression" and a struggle to write "more or less well . . . or poorly . . . but as a woman" (*Testimonios,* 1:12). But Ocampo's writings of the 1920s and early 1930s also exhibit an unwavering resolve to engage in a public conversation with leading male intellectuals, and a few women, of her time. Responses to her contributions to that conversation predictably focused on her public presence rather than her ideas. Thus one critic described the appearance of her early writing as a "mental" act of indecent exposure analogous to the bodily kind (Angel de Estrada quoted in Ocampo, *Autobiografía,* 3:106). Ocampo assumed an interventionist stance in response to such elisions of her work's actual content: If the conversation was to proceed oblivious to her input, well, then, she would just interrupt it. Although most of her interlocutors of these years were European and male, moreover, her assertive *testimonio* mode and self-representation bear the marks of the literary vanguards and of the gender debates circulating in Buenos Aires.

In contrast to Storni, whose entrée to literary culture as an actress and declaiming *poetisa* derived partly from the need to work, Ocampo accessed the literary world through privilege. Born to a family of the *criollo* oligarchy, she was educated by English and French governesses and through two extended Parisian sojourns designed to broaden her knowledge of the humanities and arts.[6] After abandoning a promising dramatic career out of sensitivity to convention-bound parents, beginning in the 1920s Ocampo threw herself into a self-aware art of living as a writer and intellectual. During this decade, through correspondence and face-to-face encounters, she embarked on formative dialogues with Ortega y Gasset, Rabbinath Tagore, Ernest Ansermet, Count Hermann Keyserling, María de Maetzu, and Waldo Frank. With the founding of *Sur* in 1931 and its publishing house in 1933, Ocampo's circle of interlocutors widened to include major Argentine, Latin American, European, and North American literary figures. Although she had been writing privately for years, Ocampo's public debut as a writer coincided with this active pursuit of intellectual exchange. Her essay "Babel," an inaugural example of the *testimonio* genre, appeared in 1920 in *La Nación,* followed in 1921 by her reflection on Dante, *De Francesca a Beatrice,* published in 1924 in book form by the Revista de Occidente Series (directed by Ortega y Gasset) and *La laguna de los nenúfares,* published in 1926 in *Revista de occidente* itself. Ocampo published her first collection of *testimonios* in 1935, including essays written over previous years. Ocampo's intellectual work in the 1920s and 1930s included lecturing for the literary society Amigos del Arte and organizing public events in the city or small *tertulias* in her home around visiting artists, intellectuals, and performers.

In his study of *Sur,* John King characterizes the site of these *tertulias* in Ocampo's home as a "salon chapel" that stands in contrast to Buenos Aires literary café life. Beginning with the *Nosotros* generation and continuing with the lively vanguard groups of the 1920s, this literary culture had, in King's words, been "open to all" (14). However, "all" generally meant all men and the few women who might accompany them. We should recall that male contemporaries regarded Storni's full-fledged participation in *Nosotros* as groundbreaking. While King posits a private-public opposition between Ocampo's style of literary life and that of the Boedo and Florida vanguardists, the latter had their own early "salon-chapel" in the private gatherings at the home of Norah Lange's mother. Although Ocampo was slightly older than the men of the 1920s Buenos Aires vanguards, her 1931 merger through *Sur* with Martinfierristas from the Florida group (Borges, Oliverio Girondo, Eduardo Mallea, and Eduardo González Lanuza, among others) brought to the fore longstanding intellectual affinities. While Ocampo herself downplayed her limited contacts in the 1920s with Borges and his contemporaries (*Autobiografía,* 6:52), a fundamental link was her close friend Ricardo Güiraldes, the revered mentor of vanguard writers and their collaborator on the little magazine *Proa*.[7]

Within the gender restrictions of her class, unless she had been personally tied to a Martín Fierro group member (as was Norah Lange to Girondo), it would have been unthinkable for Ocampo to join these young men in their urban wanderings in bars or cafés or confrontational artistic events. But Ocampo, who began publishing at the same time they did, shares striking qualities with their distinctive art of living as writers: an ambivalent relationship to the rapidly changing city, a fascination with the radically new in international culture, and a simultaneous nostalgia for the vanishing *criollista* world embodied in her own family and which Güiraldes transmuted into nationalist myth with *Don Segundo Sombra* (1926). Like the vanguardists, Ocampo nurtured a preference for artistic experiment, as she worked to introduce Buenos Aires to Stravinsky, Jacques Copeau, André Gide, Ansermet, Virginia Woolf, Le Corbusier, and Sergey Eisenstein. Her writing investigates the role of the writer with the consequent autobiographical affinity for the first person that marked vanguard literary culture but that in Ocampo was sometimes criticized as a peculiarly "feminine" quality in her writing.[8] Even as she favored the essay, Ocampo's *testimonios* share with vanguard modes irreverence toward genre boundaries (incorporating lyrical, dramatic, and narrative elements), a fundamental orality, and a self-aware posturing toward readers.[9]

Assaults on public expectations and urban wanderings constituted requisite gestures for the art of living as a vanguard writer in Buenos Aires. Ocampo (unlike Lange) was not on hand for *Prisma* (1921–1922), the broadside on city walls, or for the boisterous "issues" of *Revista oral*.[10] The main venue for her official public appearances was the more staid Amigos del Arte. But for her gender and class, Ocampo's public activity was as confrontational as a vanguard manifesto or performance. Although discreet about her private life, in the 1920s she flaunted her mobility as a New Woman, a flanêuse on wheels, cruising the city in her convertible, hair cropped and arms bare. In a chronicle titled "The Pleasure of Vagabonding," Roberto Arlt summed up his generation's urban nomadism, as he documented wandering through Buenos Aires with a critical eye, an activity he equated with his writing (*Obras completas,* 2:446). If Ocampo's meandering was merely automotive, it provided grist for her work.[11] Ocampo, too, linked these wanderings to her writing, but she also highlighted the reception this activity provoked when executed by a woman, as pedestrian shouts were "not exactly indulgent" and resembled readers' responses to her writing (*Autobiografía,* 3:105).

Beyond publishing that writing, Ocampo executed an aesthetic assault on her surroundings. While the vanguardists generally launched their performance events through words and an occasional prop,[12] Ocampo implemented her encounters theatrically, through transmutations of the domestic into the public. Thus while the Martín Fierro group assailed convention through daring metaphors, broadsides, and happenings, Ocampo contested traditional Buenos Aires architecture by building two Bauhaus-style homes, the first in Mar de Plata, and the second, inspired directly by Le Corbusier, in Palermo. An installation art of their time and a performative challenge to the norms of neighborhood styles, these architectural interventions effected dramatic intrusions on the city's landscape and, she reported, scandalized neighbors. Ocampo's choices of confrontational media—a trendy car steered by a woman, an aggressively experimental dwelling—manifested her economic privilege. But they also expanded her locus of control into the urban domain, endowing her with a sharp public profile and paving the way for her merger with vanguardists in *Sur*. These urban disruptions also underscore her inventive negotiation of available choices for women of her class.

A familiar story, Ocampo's feminism grew from personal experience: family-imposed prohibitions; condescension from male mentors (even from those who admired her intelligence); patronizing reactions to her early writing. But if Storni's feminism was rooted in class-consciousness gleaned from economic struggle, Ocampo's was fundamentally literary, generated by thwarted efforts to participate in a public dialogue through writing. As did Storni, Ocampo eventually made an enduring place for herself in a predominantly male cultural world, although she directed less attention over time to the overall situation of women. But in the 1920s and 1930s, Ocampo's interactions with women were fundamental for her feminism and her self-conception as a cultural activist. These include an adolescent correspondence with the older Delfina Bunge de Gálvez (wife of Argentine novelist Manuel Gálvez);[13] a dialogue with the Spanish intellectual feminist Maetzu, whom she met in 1926; and a decisive association with Virginia Woolf, whose works she began reading in the 1920s and whom she met in 1934. Woolf encouraged Ocampo to write more about herself, and in 1935, Ocampo prefaced the first volume of her collected *testimonios* with a "Letter to Virginia Woolf" that invoked the English writer as her mentor.[14] In a 1929 trip to Paris, moreover, Ocampo forged contacts with midwives of Anglo-European modernism, including Adrienne Monnier, owner of the Left Bank bookstore La Maison de Amis des Livres, and Sylvia Beach, manager of the equally renowned

Shakespeare and Company bookstore.[15] In the 1930s Ocampo helped found the Unión Argentina de Mujeres. She delivered eloquent speeches on women's rights during this brief period of feminist political activism, stimulated in part by Argentine reverberations of the rise of European fascism and by countless legislative attempts to reverse gains women had made in the 1926 Civil Code.

Ocampo detailed her positions on women's rights in "La mujer y su expresión" (Woman and her expression; 1935) and "La mujer, sus derechos y responsabilidades" (Woman, her rights and responsibilities; 1936). To some degree her views coincided with feminist political discourse that posed special civic roles for women through the social motherhood model.[16] Thus she invoked the image of Marie Curie boiling baby bottles while working in the lab alongside her husband to argue that women should not replace men but rather should "occupy" their own "place" (*Testimonios,* 2:164) and added that Hispanic women could liberate themselves by raising less sexist sons. But two singularities of Ocampo's feminism countered the social motherhood ideal and helped fashion her writing mode. Ocampo, like Storni, gradually challenged the essentialist conception of gender implicit in social motherhood. At the same time, she elaborated a more confrontational model of the intellectual woman as the disruptor of a public conversation that cast her as its passive listener.

Astonishing experiences with stereotyping stimulated Ocampo's anti-essentialist view of gender divisions, as when Ortega y Gasset baptized her the Gioconda of the Pampa or Keyserling called her the primordial woman or, smarting under her rejection of his advances, portrayed South American women as spiders who ensnare men in their webs (quoted in Meyer, *Victoria Ocampo,* 80). More positively, Ortega used his epilogue to the 1924 edition of Ocampo's *De Francesca a Beatrice* to character-ize its author as "an exemplary apparition of femininity" in Western cul-ture and to observe that the proper role of "woman" in history lay not in her deeds but in her "immobile and serene presence" (Epilogue, 136, 161). In a 1931 response, Ocampo politely told Ortega he had missed her central points on love, ethics, and art in Dante, which she then explained (*Testimonios,* 1:187–224). But objecting to his characterization of Anna de Noailles poetry as "beautiful, voluptuous, and warm" and, as with Penelope, woven from her "previously unraveled work," Ocampo later took Ortega to task for condescension toward women's talents; although he had stopped short of Otto Weininger's assertion that women lacked souls, Ortega, Ocampo argued, saw "woman as a gender, not an indi-vidual" (*Testimonios,* 1:27–28).

A key stimulus to Ocampo's challenge to gender norms was Woolf's *Orlando.* Her enthusiasm lay precisely in the characteristics of a life over time, irrespective of the character's gender metamorphoses. For Ocampo, the most significant facet of Orlando's gender knowledge lay in the fact that she realizes she has been transformed into a woman only when she notices she is wearing a dress. As an outward technique of gender performance, this clothing revealed for Ocampo (and Orlando) that women were naturally neither "obedient, nor chaste, nor perfumed, nor covered with adornments" and that they assumed these qualities only by submitting themselves to the *"most bothersome discipline"* (*Testimonios,* 2:30; my emphasis). Drawn to the fluidity of Orlando's gender performance and ultimate androgyny, Ocampo's negotiation of the "most bothersome discipline" of gender paved the way for her distinctive self-conception as a writing woman, a position she articulated polemically in "La mujer y su expresión."

Ocampo first delivered this piece as a transatlantic radio address that she cast as a conversation by repeatedly invoking her audience and inviting them to speak up (*Testimonios,* 2:173). By contrast, she offered the anecdote of an overheard conversation, in which a man (at her end of the exchange) repeatedly admonished his evidently silent wife (at the other end) not to interrupt him. Appalled by this scenario, Ocampo called on her female audience to speak up and interrupt not only her but also the "monologues of men" toward women they have silenced with a "Don't interrupt me!" or the "monologues in dialogue" that, she argued, characterized men's own exchanges. A true conversation could be achieved only through the free movement from interruption to interruption (*Testimonios,* 2:182). This call to arms underscores Ocampo's ideal of collaboration between women and men through dialogue (*Testimonios,* 2:182). More important, however, is her conception of writing as a performative interruption, an image played out in not only the interventionist writing persona that Ocampo first developed in the 1920s but also in the structure of her *testimonios* as a stylistic intrusion into a conversation *in motion.* This writing mode drew as well on Ocampo's years of immersion in theatre and the powerful impact of this apprenticeship on her worldview.

THE *MISE EN SCÈNE* OF THE *TESTIMONIO*

In her self-avowed search for a distinguishing style, Ocampo read the world—its books, their authors, and their contexts—as if it were theatre, through scenarios that the speaker who constructs them simultaneously scrutinizes and intrudes upon, inserting her voice and persona into their gaps. Her inquiry in the *testimonios* combines the tactics of the actor assuming a role with those of an experienced spectator attuned to the interplay of spatial, bodily, and verbal cues and to the sites of convergence between stage and audience. This mode of interpretive activity highlights populous essayistic scenarios marked by dialogic mobility and thematic porosity. It also stages a dynamic authorial voice that refuses a fixed location and instead takes up temporary residence in the interruptions of the conversations it rejoins. These features in Ocampo's writing transmute her theatrical background and performance training into her public role as a cultural activist, her writing style, and her intellectual self-portraiture.

The story of Ocampo the performer weaves through her autobiography. True to her roots, Ocampo was educated to provide entertainment for others that would please the senses and reinforce gendered conventions of decorum appropriate to her class. She was trained to perform classical music and lyric dramatic art destined for select, usually private, audiences. As a child she organized family performances, including dramatic dialogues in the style of children's stories by the Comtesse de Ségur. Following the model of her French governess, Ocampo apprenticed in declamation with lines from Racine's *Phèdre,* took private diction lessons from the French actress Marguerite Moreno, and learned the repertoire of French theatre. Under Moreno's tutelage, she gave exclusive dramatic readings, and she recited from Victor Hugo's *Stella* at her own social debut. Foreshadowing Ortega's portrait of her as "immobile and serene," she also performed in a society benefit *tableau vivant* of Musset's *Le Nuit de Mai,* a romantic dialogue between a poet (played by Moreno) and his muse (Ocampo), complete with white tunic. But as she matured, Ocampo voiced impatience with the performative exercises allowed to women of her class and their attendant social protocols. Rankled when a suitor described her as "a woman who declaims" (*Autobiografía,* 2:88), she denigrated "the fictitious life" that she led as an invention "of the silliness of men" (*Autobiografía,* 2:111).

In fact Ocampo's absorption with theatre drew her far from the *tableau vivant* toward the open-ended dynamics of a changing international dramatic scene. Initially, theatre as Ocampo portrayed it in her autobiography constituted a path of resistance to societal controls and a way to imagine personal transformations embodied in an actor's work. The very class status that foiled her goals gave Ocampo an enviable dramatic education:[17] readings of Hugo, Racine, Moliere, Shakespeare, de Musset, Wilde, and Sarah Bernhardt's memoirs; private lessons with Moreno; and firsthand contact in Buenos Aires and Paris with the dramatic creations of Edmond Rostand and the renowned actor Constant Coquelin, as well as with performances of Wagner's operas. During the 1910s and 1920s, moreover, Ocampo witnessed sea changes in the European dramatic and musical world that shaped her perception of performance as a site reflection. She was drawn to the work of French actor and director Jacques Copeau (cofounder of *La Nouvelle revue française*), who beginning in 1913 took up the antirealist revolution in French theatre at his Théâtre du Vieux-Colombier. Ocampo eventually witnessed radical Shakespearean productions in Paris under Copeau's direction. In the 1910s she also saw the avant-garde performances of Sergey Diaghilev's *Ballets Russes* and the debut of Stravinsky's *Rites of Spring.* In the early 1920s she became friends with the *Ballets Russes* director, Ansermet, who also introduced her to Stravinsky. With Ansermet, she supported the nascent Argentine national symphony and tried to bring modern music to Buenos Aires.

Although Ocampo reluctantly abandoned plans to become a professional actor, these innovative developments shaped her debut before a large Buenos Aires audience in groundbreaking roles that were a far cry from the silent muse of the *tableau vivant.* The first, in 1925, was the part of dramatic narrator for Arthur Honegger's oratorio, *Le Roi David,* a performance conducted by Ansermet and a role created by Copeau to be filled by a man. In 1936 she executed a recitation of Stravinsky's *Persephone* (based on Gide's poem) at the Teatro Colón in Buenos Aires and later in Rio de Janeiro and Florence. Even after turning to the essay as her expressive form and to the role of cultural activist through *Sur,* Ocampo continued to declaim in Buenos Aires, and she was a lifelong theatre spectator, particularly for rehearsals where she might offer discerning advice.[18] These experiences manifested a view of dramatic processes as a form of reflection, the kind of inquiry embodied in Copeau's turn from realist-romantic drama to what he termed "pure" theatre, that is, synthesizing scenarios of "movement, gesture, and attitudes" and of "facial expressions, voices, and silences" (quoted in Brown, 376).

Copeau's account of innovative theatre, a model Ocampo admired, could well describe her *La laguna de los nenúfares* (The white water lily lagoon), noted in this chapter's opening anecdote and a key work in her writing apprenticeship. Noteworthy features in this rarely read or performed piece include the lyrical simplicity of its visual cues (particularly for light and dark), its economic uses of theatrical space, and its sensitivity to intonation and gesture. The play also showcases its author's keen ear for lively dialogue. Ocampo recast the piece from an Estonian fairy tale, and others have described it as a children's fable and a version of the life of the Buddha.[19] Most important, this play, written when Ocampo was vacillating between theatre and prose, is the staged *Bildungsroman* of a young man's acquisition of wisdom through his teachers and his outward voyage from an overprotected childhood to a reality populated by love, war, suffering, death, and hope. With the autonomy thus acquired, he returns to the forest and reconciles with his possessive magician father. Ocampo wrote this play around 1922, just as she was defying family by abandoning her estranged husband's home and taking up residence on her own for the first time. This was also when she began publishing in *La nación*. The play's thematic focus later permeates her *testimonios:* problems of knowledge and creativity and ethical issues of human relationships—love and possessiveness, good and evil. Key for Ocampo's emergent prose style are the work's pliable notion of character, its interactive conception of dialogue as a succession of interruptions, and its portrayal of the protagonist's search for identity as a cognitive process that is simultaneously corporeal and verbal. Copo de Nieve's apprenticeship among the animals is particularly instructive. Like an actor trying out roles, he mimics, as I have noted, an essential bodily feature of his models. At the same time that he tries on these gestures, Copo de Nieve's cognitive odyssey unfolds in his ongoing conversations with his tutors, the dog and cat. As they converse, these mentors lead the protagonist from scenario to scenario, brief plays within the play that enact the life lessons they teach. While the sententious Atrabilis favors conclusive definitions, the more flexible Optimio counters with open-ended observations.[20] Of key significance is the fact that stage directions require that Optimio deliver his rejoinders to Atrabilis's retorts by interrupting. Thus Copo de Nieve's dramatized journey unfolds through the chain of lively interruptions that liberate the protagonist from isolation.

The intersection of bodily irreverence and open-ended dialogue that shapes Copo de Nieve's journey to knowledge highlights the malleability that Ocampo identified in theatre's making and unmaking of options, a flexibility that marked her emerging *testimonio* style. *Hamlet,* she affirmed, could never be transposed to the screen because the film medium would fail to embody a character's indecision. In the staged Hamlet, she argued, each "thought, each feeling for him blooms in *gesture, an action that alleviates and leaves us to meditate on a thousand possibilities and impossibilities*" (*Testimonios,* 1:70; my emphasis). Together with *La laguna de los nenúfares,* these lines underscore Ocampo's fascination with live performance as the rehearsal-like process assumed by Copo de Nieve in walking backwards like the crab and analogous to the epistemological rehearsals showcased in Storni's farces. As in Copo de Nieve's cognitive apprenticeship, Ocampo's *testimonios* of the period unfold as peripatetic conversations between the narrating authorial figure and readers and with the characters, books, or ideas that populate her scenarios. The *testimonios* also draw on the porous model of character and dialogue first enacted in this play.

While Ocampo often protested that she lacked talent for creating fictional characters, during the 1920s and 1930s, she fashioned memorable portraits of figures she had encountered in life or through readings: Tagore, Mussolini, de Noailles, Woolf and her Orlando, Paul Valery, and Dante characters, among others. She described a penchant for weaving interpretive "spiderwebs" around the physical appearance of people she did not know (*Autobiografía*, 2:39), and she saw faces as "entities to be deciphered" (*Autobiografía*, 2:39). Ocampo constructed her *testimonio* characters theatrically, through links between their personae and distinguishing gestures, the space they inhabit, or surrounding objects. Thus she embodied characters in a particular *mise en scène:* Emily Brönte in the windswept heath of Haworth, de Noailles in the sumptuous ornamentation of her boudoir. But what most fascinated Ocampo in her characters were their defining "tics" or "manias," as she called them ("Sobre dos poetas," 11–12). These performative inflections of singularity, like Copo de Nieve's crablike walk, constituted for her the "small acts" of daily life that "make or unmake a character" (*Testimonios,* 1:73).

Ocampo's absorption in this performative process not only manifests the cognitive role of the corporeal in her writing, a feature already well noted by critics.[21] Ocampo often described breakthroughs in learning as bodily events, as she compared first reading Dante to being tossed by a wave (*De Francesca a Beatrice,* 35). Yet Ocampo showcased anatomical gaps above all, that is, the defamiliarizing body awareness that marks an actor's assumption of a role. Thus she described a forced distancing at puberty from a gendered body that had betrayed her (*Autobiografía*, 1:147–148) or the estranging impact of studying anatomy (*Autobiografía*, 1:151–152). Bakhtin once postulated that the knowledge of self from a perspective outside the self required attentiveness of corporeal disunity (*Art and Answerability,* 42–43); likewise, Ocampo proposed that a willful disruption of bodily norms was fundamental for a self-aware identity.[22] As in the scenarios of Copo de Nieve's odd gait or young Victoria mimicking a hunchback, performative reflection, in Ocampo's view, interrupted the "embodying of norms," to borrow Judith Butler's term (22).

Through the mimetic, then, her characters rehearse a simultaneous identification with and differentiation from others. For Ocampo, the very tics through which character was performed constituted the "viable and tangible extremity of . . . [their] ideas" (*Testimonios,* 1:73). Thus she affirmed that people, like actors on a stage, harbored a variety of potential personae, but through their daily small acts chose among options (*Testimonios,* 1:73).[23] These reflections, whose outward manifestations were repeated physical gestures, she argued, activated the malleable process of moving, as do Jekyll and Hyde, from one expression of selfhood to another. Above all, they constituted the foundation for communicating individual experience. Thus people defined themselves precisely in their "gestures, their labors, their works" and search for "expression" (*Testimonios,* 1:375).

Ocampo also scrutinized the bodies and faces populating her *testimonios* for their fissures open to conversation. Characters did not fully enter these scenarios until they began to speak. In fact "to enter the scene" (*entrar en escena*), a phrase Ocampo employed often, equaled starting to talk.[24] Ocampo's opus is shot through with longings for interlocutors that began with early readings and theatre performances; lacking the opportunity to converse about what she had seen, she chose books whose resonance provided for dialogue, like "a recital hall with perfect acoustics" (*Autobiografía,* 2:60).[25] In Ocampo's expressive system, conversation and debate provide a differentiating locus for self-understanding. Thus, in *La laguna de los nenúfares,* Optimio tells the argumentative Atrabilis: "Learning to know you, I learned how to know myself" (11). Verbal interaction, moreover, offered liberation from bodily limitations imposed by the gender norms inscribed in the *tableaux vivants* of Ocampo's youth or the muselike immobility that Ortega ascribed to artistic women. Her autobiography links her gendered coming of age to the constriction of bodily freedom, a tie nowhere more poignant than when she described posing for the portrait painter Dagnan Bouvert. Ocampo reported escaping the immobility of these sessions through incessant conversation with the painter. Significantly, their conversation addressed Ocampo's readings of Dante, destined to be the focus of her first extensive prose work, *De Francesca a Beatrice,* which enacts a similar tale of bodily liberation through dialogue. This guided tour of a selection from Dante moves from the possessiveness inscribed in bodily connections, as personified in Paolo and Francesca, toward the more dialogic "intelligence of love" ascribed to the arts and to Dante's idealized connection with Beatrice. Thus in order to see and hear Beatrice, Dante must first "pass beyond the wall of [the] flesh" (80).

The dialogue of writing for Ocampo, then, comprised a persistent striving to "pass beyond" walls of embodied gender norms that limited her access to intellectual conversation. Interruptive images of "getting in the gaps" pepper her scrutiny of people, books, and language in the *testimonios*. In all cases, she preferred those whose porosity and performative tics invited interruption and, by extension, collaboration. Mussolini's countenance, she observed as a counterexample, was, like his pronouncements about women, impenetrable, offering a "terrible resistance" to her discerning gaze (*Domingos,* 12). Similarly, some books were so "concluded" as to discourage readers from "inserting themselves," while other volumes invited readers to slide through the "interstices" of their disorder ("El hombre que murió," 7–8). In a similar vein, translation for the multilingual Ocampo consisted of one language "interrupting" another, as when Ramón Gómez de la Serna "calmly quarter[ed] French to insert Spanish into it" ("Ramón Gómez," 207). In the context of Argentine literary culture, the dialogue Ocampo sought, then, required interleaving one's words into those of another. As an intellectual woman seeking conversation, she sometimes complained that the language of her chosen interlocutors, like Il Duce's impenetrable countenance, discouraged response. Yet by the time that she called on other women to interrupt her 1935 transatlantic speech and the monologues of men, Ocampo's own art of writing in the gaps was long established. In fact, her first published article, "Babel," begins in the midst of a conversation it interrupts. Following a quote from Pascal, the essay opens with a resounding "No! This is not totally convincing" (*Testimonios,* 1:45).

Ultimately, however, Ocampo was more collaborative than contentious, and her *testimonios* construe interruption less as an assault on the words of the men with whom she wanted to talk than as a dialogic intervention with the authors she read and their readers. Calculated intrusions structure many of her essays, as the dialogue between authorial speaker and reader maps an intricate, itinerant maneuvering of well-chosen insertions, parenthetical asides, anticipatory reactions to reader comments, and narrative digressions. The speaker's engagement with a particular figure or book catalyzes this winding discursive course, as prior readings, remembered conversations, or letters find their way onto the scene. Ocampo's 1935 "Al margen de André Gide" provides a fit example. While reading his work, she begins with a quote from Gide, who in turn is quoting Nietzsche, to argue that the latter leaves the former with a sense of nothing left to say. While initially affirming a similar response to Gide's text, Ocampo then contradicts Gide's assertion—"I am far from believing that there is nothing left to say" (*Domingos,* 51)—and launches a running conversation with Gide interrupted by digressions to Proust, to her own previous writings, and to Dante, among others. Through this multivocal intervention, Ocampo lays out her ideas about the ethical exigencies of her own writing, the activities of readers, and the problem of cultural hierarchies. As in many *testimonios,* the digressive course provoked by her self-interruptions weaves numerous voices into the staged dialogue with Gide. Similarly, in her guided tour of Dante, *De Francesca a Beatrice,* her interruption of Dante and Virgil's exchange incorporates interventions from other commentators and her own related readings. The overall effect is a rich, populous conversation of starts and stops, detours and returns. As do many *testimonios, De Francesca a Beatrice* builds a visual scenario for this conversation. Just as Dante and Virgil review what unfolds before them, so does Ocampo, speaking to her reader, watch and disrupt the conversation between Dante and Virgil.

THE ACTOR APPEARS:
OCAMPO'S INTELLECTUAL AS TOUR GUIDE

If the *testimonio* creates a scenario for the rehearsal of ideas, exactly where is Ocampo in that performance? Neither her earliest readers nor recent critics doubt her persistent presence on the scene. Ortega celebrated her palpable presence in *De Francesca a Beatrice,* noting that his "gaze" sometimes moved from Dante's characters to her gestures, as the poet himself had done with Beatrice (Epilogue, 133). But Ocampo fiercely resisted this muse role, from her dismissal of the *tableaux vivants* to her insurgency against portrait posing to angry rejoinders from the pedestal of inspirational grande dame on which Keyserling placed her. She in fact fashioned a far more itinerant persona for herself in the *testimonios.* She conceived this labile role as something *more*—not less—than a writer. In denying herself the title, Ocampo underscored that her quest for a role in literary culture "as a woman" was marked by the absence of a "climate propitious for its flowering" (*Testimonios,* 1:17). Manifesting her class and intellectual orientation, the resistance to the name also reveals Ocampo's ambivalence toward the emergent role of professional writer in tandem with journalistic media culture. At home neither in the latter nor among the vanguard fraternities that shared her ambivalence, and in the spirit of the resounding "No!" that opened her first published piece, Ocampo instead imagined herself as an informed, invasive guide through a spectacle of ideas. She first rehearsed this identity in the Dante essay and later unpacked it in the *testimonio* "Domingos en Hyde Park" (Sundays in Hyde Park).

De Francesca a Beatrice evokes the same sense of movement through time and space inscribed in the original, as the essay takes the reader on a circuitous tour through the work it glosses. The speaker guides the reader through a journey that, in turn, frames Virgil's direction of Dante from purgatory to heaven. In a virtual scene within a scene, Ocampo's speaker and projected reader watch and listen to Virgil and Dante as they observe and gloss *Divine Comedy* characters.[26] Early in the journey, Ocampo as speaker spells out her role. There is nothing more annoying, she notes, than the kind of guides, "veritable bodies in purgatory," who "haunt" museums, ready to "pounce on" and "hound" unfortunate tourists. Notwithstanding the exasperation they produce in the people they lead with their "inexorable common places," she adds, one must recognize their ultimate "usefulness" as those who know things. As she strives to be "useful" to readers, she will go "chatting along the path" of the Dante tour, hoping her limited "means of expression" will not exasperate (25–26). In this concurrently assertive and apologetic assumption of the guide role, Ocampo "bodies forth" her writing persona, to borrow Joseph Roach's term, and assumes a conversational tone. Here the guide and the reader-spectator, mirroring Virgil and Dante, examine a scene populated by a "herd of souls" (literary figures, their books or ideas), while the guide provides running commentary. Although ostending a mask of humility, she lays claim to cognitive power that authorizes her intervention as a cultural actor in this intellectual scenario. This portrayal of readers as "tourists" and the critical essay as a *Baedeker,*[27] moreover, recasts Ocampo's Virgil-Dante dialogic model into the discourse and motifs of modernity, images that along with the transatlantic, the propeller, and the skyscraper, peppered vanguard discourse. Notwithstanding her 1930s epistolary affirmation to Woolf that she had yet to find her style, in this gloss of Dante, Ocampo already by 1921 had created a blueprint for her essay form and a conception of her interventionist cultural role.

The title essay of Ocampo's 1935 collection *Domingos en Hyde Park* coincided with the consolidation of her role in *Sur* and details the performative nature of her assumed role as intellectual escort. Here she describes the engaging "portable tribunals" that populated London's Hyde Park on Sundays, religious or political preachers of diverse casts holding forth before distinct audiences. This revivalist display, she argued, offered a spectacle for tourists. Ocampo was drawn especially to the spontaneous dialogues between preachers and the impromptu pedestrian audiences they attracted. She cast herself in this scenario as a "foreigner" and, much like guide in the Dante piece, as "hovering around these fishermen for souls" (*Domingos, 96*). The piece then compares the tour of Hyde Park's revivalist scenarios with *God Is My Adventure* by Rom Landau, a survey of countercultural alternative thinkers such as Keyserling and Rudolf Steiner. Ocampo highlights the performativity implicit in the display of singular ideas and constitutes the essay as an excursion through belief systems. This scenario casts the reader as a curious tourist scrutinizing the spectacle of ideas and aided by friendly interruptions from the well-informed conductor, Ocampo, who privileges the relativity of ideas and the reader's right to interpretation. The open-air essayistic arena analogous to Sundays in Hyde Park underscores that Ocampo imagined her activity in the *testimonios* as a definitively public intervention in intellectual debates.

In assuming the role of a dialoguing guide who leads readers on an excursion, Ocampo laid claim to a powerful stance in the marketplace of ideas that paradoxically garnered authority from its very mobility and ambiguity. Although she situated herself ostensibly outside the scenarios evoked by the books or writers that she addressed—"On the Margins of Gide," "On the Margins of Ruskin,"[28] or chatting from the margins of Dante—her self-assigned location was anything but marginal. The literal margin of a book, in fact, offers the site of a reader's authority and intervention: the runway for proofreading, copyediting, and the gloss.[29] As she accompanied her *testimonio* readers through literary spectacles, then, Ocampo rarely stayed to one side. Instead she interrupted the reader's perspective by positioning her writing voice in the gaps *between* her reader and the scenarios she constructed. We can recall that for Ocampo to speak was to enter the scene. Having been denied a career as an actor, Ocampo, as noted, frequently observed dramatic rehearsals and sent suggestions to the director. But her role as critical tour guide in the *testimonios* parallels that of a director, stopping the rehearsal in progress to offer up her views. In her writing Ocampo as a cultural actor adopted an interstitial position within the scenarios she conjured up, simultaneously in and out of the scene, falling back only to launch her next interruption.

Although Dante provided a literary model for this position, one cannot overemphasize its debt to Ocampo's experience as a woman and to public debates about women's roles in early-twentieth-century Argentina. On one level, her dialogue of interruptions harks back to her education with private tutors. We can recall the roles of Optimio, the upbeat dog, and Atrabilis, the sententious cat in *La laguna de los nenúfares*. As they lead Copo de Nieve past panoramas that depict old age, illness, war, and finally death, the play assumes a Dantesque structure in which the teaching guide and student comment on framed scenarios unfolding before them. Thus the guide role's pedagogic function speaks to Ocampo's experience as the student of private teachers who opened the world through books. But this persona's tutelary air also manifests the acceptable roles assigned to modern women by Argentine feminist debates, particularly injunctions that, in the spirit of social motherhood, they be useful. In affirming her role as pesky tour guide in the Dante essay, Ocampo justified the intrusion above all on the grounds of its usefulness. We should recall, too, that Ocampo's piece on modern women's rights and responsibilities underscored their potential contributions to the social order through intelligent mothering and collaboration with men. In considering the pedagogic cultural role she imagined for herself as a virtual docent, it bears repeating that Ocampo's *institutrices* were her first mentors and that teaching was one of the few arenas in which women's public presence was deemed respectable, certainly far more than in the forum of writing.[30] Ocampo, by contrast, actually imagined less conventional roles for herself in the public scene, first as an actor and then as an intellectual joining an exchange of ideas. But the notion of contributing something useful envelops her rebellious writing persona in a cloak of respectability and also manifests the humanistic, ethical concerns that imbued Ocampo's writing. Thus Ocampo describes the guide Virgil's "usefulness" to Dante; in a purgatory scene, Virgil erases from Dante's face the soot and tears of Hell, a "sweet gesture, full of human tenderness" (36). This focus on suffering and altruism points to the ambitious focus throughout Ocampo's work on the big questions: the search for truth through variegated belief systems, the ethics of human relationships, human inequalities, and unanswered questions of final causes.

While validating her authority as a person with something to say about these issues, Ocampo's artistic self-portrait as guide highlights her projection of an interactive relationship, from interruption to interruption, with readers. The oft-noted conversational tone of the *testimonios* casts the on-again-off-again rhythm of Ocampo's appearances in her own writing as the collaborative entrances and exits of someone who invites interventions from readers. Ocampo's informal tone and authorization of the reader she goads to talk back call to mind Woolf's conception of the "common reader" that Ocampo admired and that has produced critical comparisons between the two.[31] But the conversations she set in motion through the *testimonio* were "common" only in their distance from pedantry and more academic writing. By no means did Ocampo imagine that she was interacting with the kind of broad, eclectic audience addressed by Storni in her popular columns for Buenos Aires periodicals. Rather Ocampo's writing projects a reader who, if not as conversant with Western arts and culture as was their guide, would confirm their value. Although she took a stand against social and economic injustice based on what she termed "artificial inequalities," she dismissed the "mediocrity" of mass culture, for example popular theatre in Buenos Aires, whose growing audience mixed all social classes: "The rich have just as much bad taste as the poor and are in just as great a need of education," she wrote, adding that she found it "impossible to commune which such masses" (*Domingos, 63*).[32] In this vein, Ocampo's concept of literary culture was in many ways consistent with that of her intellectual mentors like Ortega, her aestheticism with that of international modernists like Woolf or of the Martín Fierro vanguardists who joined her in *Sur*.

In comparison to Storni's work, Ocampo's writing of the 1920s and 1930s intimates less discernment that these cultural categories themselves might be gendered or marked by hierarchies other than what she saw as legitimate intellectual ones. Storni, as I have traced, shifted from lamenting women's lack of talent for abstract thought to questioning the definition of "philosophical" and proposing what we might today call a standpoint epistemology whereby women, like the declaiming kitchen maid–*poetisa* of her farce, could "untangle Einstein" from the specificity of their own experience. Where Storni embraced the *poetisa* role and its mass culture affiliations to critique the cultural and gender hierarchies marking it, Ocampo distanced herself from mass culture to the extent possible.[33]

But just as Storni transformed the socially acceptable role of *poetisa* into something else, Ocampo, too, enveloped the feminism implicit in her cultural activism with the aura of respectability accruing to women who became teachers rather than the actor that she wanted to be. At the same time, just as Storni flirted with androgynous notions of women's intellect, Ocampo also imagined a nongendered identity. Thus even as she affirmed the desire to write "as a woman," the great appeal she saw in Woolf's Orlando, we should recall, derived from the character's freedom from the "bothersome discipline" of gender. Moreover, although Ocampo's alter ego character, Copo de Nieve, is grammatically male, his amorphous, not-quite-human personality as a snowflake that does not melt suspends the character's gender identity in midair. This appeal to androgyny marks Ocampo's assumed role as an intellectual tour guide whose persona is inflected more by its interruptive style than by any discernible gender markings.

Storni once observed that no matter how much she imagined herself as their equals and forgot she was a woman when she conversed with men, it was clear that the men themselves never forgot it, which led her at times to imagine an alternative intellectual "Masonry" of women (*Nosotras,* 166). The mythologizing of Ocampo as a reaction to her intelligence and imposing presence documents that the men with whom Ocampo conversed never forgot she was a woman either. She, by contrast, imagined herself as an authoritative cultural actor whose gender might somehow be set aside. In Ocampo's case, a widening circle of contacts with artistic and intellectual women like Moreno, Maetzu, and Woolf undoubtedly reinforced her feminism and self-confidence in this role. But in contrast to Storni's journalism, Ocampo's writing addressed women explicitly only on a few exceptional occasions. Instead her imagined intellectual community was one populated primarily by men and into which, as she conceived it, women would gradually insert themselves as authorized collaborators. If the hindsight of twenty-first-century feminism and cultural criticism brings into focus Ocampo's blind spots of gender and class, it does not by that token authorize us to chastise her drive to participate as an equal in what she regarded as the intellectual banquet of her time. Amy Kaminsky eloquently exposes the double standard that has taken Ocampo to task for eschewing an interest in the autochthonous in favor of the attraction to international cultural innovation that she shares with almost all of Argentina's major male writers of the past two centuries. A woman who refuses the gendered charge of passing on customs and traditions, Kaminsky argues, "who is drawn to intellection, reason, artifice, is breaking the gender code that ostensibly maintains the societal balance of innovation and tradition" (127). Likewise, castigating Ocampo in the name of feminism for intervening in conversations undertaken primarily by men and for fashioning her intellectual home in their midst could lead to the disquieting, untenable conclusion that this was somehow not her place.

chapter 3
NO PLACE LIKE HOME
Norah Lange's Art of Anatomy

In the radically transformed landscape of Buenos Aires in the 1920s, the urban nomads of the literary avant-garde enacted a nostalgic quest for fraternity and familiar terrain. "Llaneza" (Plainness), a well-known Borges poem from his first collection, *Fervor de Buenos Aires* (1923), inscribes this yearning for participation in the analogy between a welcoming place and the literary kinship of an oft-read book. Here, with the "docility" of a turning page, the speaker's perspective glides from outside a garden gate to a house within filled with well-remembered objects and "glances," a place that, along with its inhabitants, knows him equally well (*Obras completas*, 1:42). For the initiated readers invoked by Borges's work, those versed in its "customs" and "dialect of allusions" (*Obras completas*, 1:42), the poem's dedication to Haydée Lange and the opening image of a garden gate might also have brought a specific place to mind: an aging home on Calle Tronador in the Belgrano suburb of Buenos Aires. Endowed with a high iron fence that enclosed an intimate interior garden, this abode housed Berta Erfjord de Lange, the widowed mother of a son and five daughters, including Haydée, named in the Borges poem. In keeping with the poem's analogy between a visit to this locale and communing with a good book, this house also enjoys a legendary status in Argentine literary history as the site of the renowned *tertulias* of the young vanguard writers who launched the experimental broadside *Prisma* (1921–1922) and little magazine *Proa* (1922–1923 and 1924–1926) and who in 1924 coalesced around the more enduring *Martín Fierro* (1924–1927).[1]

This house was also the residence of Norah Lange (Haydée's younger sister) and the location of her privileged adolescent initiation into Buenos Aires literary culture. Beginning in 1922, on Saturday and Sunday evenings, Argentine writers of older and younger generations enacted the public ritual of the artistic *tertulia* in the domestic privacy of Lange's home. Over time, Norah Lange (1906–1972) authored three poetry collections, six prose works, and a compilation of ribald, parodic *discursos* that she had delivered to the Martín Fierro literary fraternity in which she enjoyed the status of the group's sole woman writer.[2] Lange's home came to be known as the terrain of the group's collective origins and, as intimated in the Borges poem, a refuge from dislocation and loss of community in a city besieged by demographic change. At the same time, the group's male writers assigned to Lange, who declaimed poetry at their *tertulias,* the role of modern muse to inspire their artistic experiments. As a writer in the making herself, Lange paradoxically came to embody both the lost home sought by Buenos Aires vanguard writers in response to the upheavals of modernization and the modern, innovative aesthetic they sought in their writing.

In fact, Lange's connection with the literary vanguards was stronger and more enduring than that of any women writer in Latin America during these years. She is one of only two women among the sixty-seven poets anthologized in the *Índice de la nueva poesía americana* (1926) edited by Alberto Hidalgo, Vicente Huidobro, and Borges and widely regarded as a foundational collection for the movements.[3] Born in Buenos Aires to immigrants (a Norwegian father and Irish-Norwegian mother), she spent most of her childhood in Mendoza with her four sisters and a brother before returning to Buenos Aires in adolescence. In Mendoza, Lange received a tutorial education, and when the family's situation worsened after her father's death, she eventually attended Normal School in Buenos Aires. But the literary salon that her mother began hosting when Lange was in her mid-teens consolidated her emerging role as a writer and performer. Lange began writing at age fourteen and came of age in the heart of the Buenos Aires vanguards, a public phenomenon that invaded her private, domestic, and predominantly sororal world. Drawing on her multilingual background, Lange began working as a translator for General Motors in 1929. But the shape of her life was profoundly literary, and throughout her life, her activity revolved around her art of living as a writer.[4]

In the heart of the Buenos Aires literary fraternity that cast her as its muse and modern performing woman, Lange simultaneously embraced those roles and upended them in the service of her memorable artistic persona and idiosyncratic, "anatomical" narrative style. Some have found a disjunction between Lange's exhibitionist public role among the men of her literary circle and the ostensible intimacy of her more domestic poetic and novelistic worlds populated largely by women.[5] But the connections between Lange's public art of living as a writer and her poetic and narrative projects are compelling, not only in a continuity of eccentric authorial persona and startling critical perspective that inform them all but also in the anatomical style of her performative art of living among the Martín Fierro fraternity and her idiosyncratic writing.[6] Just as literary culture and domestic space overlapped in Lange's early apprenticeship in the predominately male Buenos Aires vanguards, so do her poetry and prose of the 1920s and 1930s manifest an artful negotiation of seemingly disparate universes. A striking fascination with community, the kind of home and "human grouping" evoked by the Borges poem, characterizes Lange's self-aware positioning in relationship to both worlds. At the same time, the distinctive art of anatomy that marked both her outlandish public performances as a mutinous muse and her inimitable prose style ultimately rendered such belonging elusive. Thus Lange's writing reveals a deft maneuvering between disparate worlds—the lively fraternity of the literary avant-gardes and a vanishing community of familial women—by a writer who portrays herself as an interloper in both.[7] As a result her work challenges the inscription of modernity's lost home in a female figure.[8] These maneuvers play out as well in Lange's interloping style, a verbal dissection and fragmentation that ostends the bizarre.

FROM ETHNOGRAPHER TO ANATOMIST: ULTRAÍSMO'S RECALCITRANT MUSE

In her art of living as a writer, Lange willfully confronted the muse role: rehearsing it in the early poems of La calle de la tarde (1925) and El rumbo de la rosa (1930); inverting it in her first prose work, Voz de la vida (1927); subjecting it to probing critical scrutiny in her novel 45 días y 30 marineros (1933); and radically metamorphosing it into the exhibitionist verbal displays of the 1930s eventually published as Estimados cóngeres (Esteemed congeries). Ultimately this intricate transmutation of Lange's assigned role as a performing New Woman unfolded into the workouts of a personal art of anatomy that coalesced in her fully realized narrative works, beginning with the autobiographical Cuadernos de infancia (1937). Lange's collaboration in the 1920s little magazines Prisma and Proa and her early poetry coincided with her initial immersion in the Martín Fierro wing of the Buenos Aires avant-gardes. Moreover, her lifelong relationship with one of the group's leading poets, Oliverio Girondo, began in 1926 and consolidated her enduring association with the circle.[9] Critics and biographers coincide in their consecration of her status in the vanguard fraternity: "the muse of ultraísmo" (Miguel, 103); the "angel and siren" of the ultraístas (Sofovich, 139); the "companion" and "mascot" of the vanguard writers (Muschietti, 91); their *salonnière* and *damisela* (Masiello, *Between Civilization and Barbarism*, 154); and "the muse and inspiration of the vanguard Martín Fierro group, a thin, redheaded walkyrie" (Domínguez, 44).[10]

These recent designations echo widespread representations of Lange during her early years as a writer. Commenting on her poetry in 1930, for example, the anthologist Néstor Ibarra observed that *"ultraísmo* needed a woman" (72), and Macedonio Fernández, mentor to the Martín Fierro fraternity, praised Lange's "submissive majesty" and "willful artistic spirit" (quoted in Nóbile, 15).[11] A reviewer of her work, Valentín Pedro, portrayed her as the embodiment of the new art itself: "Her soul casts off all of the traditional veils and her feet free themselves of all chains to dance—sing—magnificently free" (quoted in Lange, *45 días y 30 marineros*, 4). In the first section of Girondo's 1932 lyrical prose work *Espantapájaros (al alcance de todos)*, a comparable dynamic, mobile female figure that inspires the radical verse of male writers appears as a woman in perpetual flight (n.pag.). But it was Lange's good friend and admirer Borges who first established a metonymic connection between her presence and *ultraísmo* aesthetics.[12] In a preface to her poetry collection *La calle de la tarde* (1925), Borges linked her to the geographic locale of her home and the *tertulias* from which the group had emerged: "The days and nights of Nora[13] Lange are pooled and shining in a country house that I will not delimit with deceptive topographic precision" (Prologue, 5).[14] He then endowed her with the liberating traits of *ultraísta* verse— "Light and proud and fervent, like a flag fulfilled in the wind" (Prologue, 5)—and highlighted the role of her poetry "moving like throbs" as the inspiration for what he designated "our fraternity," to which, implicitly, she did not belong (Prologue, 6). Finally, he summoned her as the muse for his own artistic originality, equated in a typical vanguard mode with primal origins. Thus his laudatory words would resemble the "cedar bonfires that . . . announced the new moon to mankind" (Prologue, 8).[15]

In Borges's metaphoric maneuvers, the freedom that the woman he admires has inspired contrasts with her own passivity. Thus the pages of the magazine *Proa*, in which Lange had participated, transformed her "immobile grace" into a "shifting and varied" reflection (Prologue, 6). Lange's early poetic speakers enact this role much as Borges represented it, not in their passivity but rather in their constitution as images reflected in the eyes of a masculine viewer. Thus one speaker sees her own childlike visage in the "windows" of her interlocutor's eyes (*La calle de la tarde*, 27). In another poem from this inaugural collection, the speaker depicts herself as the inspiring muse of the "seer" that her verse addresses, a role she recognizes "along the little path of his glances" (*La calle de la tarde,* 14). While this interplay of seeing persists in much of Lange's poetry, in the later collection *El rumbo de la rosa* (1930) the imagery expands to incorporate voices, a shift that forecasts her move to narrative. Here one poem challenges the foundation of masculine creativity on feminine beauty. Here the speaker self-reflectively addresses herself as "you" and underscores her lack of "grace," fast walking, and "ugly face" (71). Beginning with the lyric prose of *Voz de la vida* (Voice of life) and confirmed with the more conventional narration of *45 días y 30 marineros* (45 days and 30 sailors; 1933), Lange's shift from poetry to prose coincided with her more critical stance toward the traditional muse role and a decision to highlight its performative power. But even as she upended the role inscribed in her verse, the interplay of seeing and being seen implicit in the muselike performing woman remained fundamental in her writing.

In comparison to Storni and Ocampo, Lange was the least openly feminist writer of the three. Her work contains no overt commentary on the real-world situation of women, and the subject does not surface in the few interviews she gave. Similarly, although scattered scenes in her narrative memoir, *Cuadernos de infancia,* manifest empathetic cognizance of an underclass, the social world represented in Lange's work is limited by the constraints of her own experience in a once-prosperous upper-middle-class family that fell on hard times. But although the world circumscribed in her fiction and literary activity was relatively small, she scrutinized it with a clinical eye. Like Storni and Ocampo, Lange turned that eye on gender relations, particularly within the literary culture that constituted her experience as a poet, and while the fraternity that provided her an intellectual home ostensibly welcomed her, like Storni and Ocampo she labored to find her place. Thus with her first narrative experiment, *Voz de la vida,* Lange embarked on a more explicit inquiry into the gendered role of muses in artistic production. This novella also marks the debut of the unconventional, modern woman in Lange's writing.

An epistolary narrative of lyric prose,[16] *Voz de la vida* presents the story of Mila, who writes yearning letters to her absent lover, Sergio. When she learns that Sergio is married, Mila seeks a cure in marriage to another man, but when she learns that Sergio still wants her, she abandons her husband for her lover. As Francine Masiello has noted, the work plays with melodramatic conventions of the popular romantic *novela semanal* (weekly novel) published in Buenos Aires mass-circulation weeklies (*Between Civilization and Barbarism,* 155). At the same time, the contrived plot is less important than image, tone, and situation in this sparse work of poetic prose. Reviewers of the time praised the piece's presentation of "the voice of a woman" (quoted in Nóbile, 78) on the one hand and on the other censured the "masculine turns of phrase" employed by protagonist Mila when speaking of love (Doll, 36).[17] While this reproach clearly manifests a negative reaction toward the affirmation of female eroticism in Lange's work, the critic correctly perceived a violation of the literary order. Inverting the conventions that had assigned her the identity of muse to vanguard writers, Lange's narrator in *Voz de la vida* imagines an absent and desirable masculine muse as the source for feminine creativity. In this sense, the novella manifests a kinship with the vanguards' portraits of the artist, for example Jaime Torres Bodet's *Margarita de niebla* (1928) or Martín Adán's *La casa de carton* (1928), and Girondo's *Espantapájaros (al alcance de todos)* (1932), in which a masculine intellectual speaker forges his narrative identity through feminine imagery that inspires him.

In *Voz de la vida,* the narrating protagonist evokes Sergio as her source of lyrical inspiration—"My verse required your name to be strong" (38)—and it is precisely the absence and inaccessibility of this male muse that stimulate the woman's writing: "I read, I write, and I think, and thus I finalize one more day, absent for you, pained for you" (36). Mila's invocation of Sergio as muse, moreover, is self-aware and voluntary: "I pass the hours . . . writing you, thinking you" (25). Just as Borges linked Lange metonymically to a specific creative terrain, a country house on the afternoon street of her poetry collection, so does Mila inscribe Sergio in the city streets that he travels. Thus she moves to the city center, the better to experience his presence and conjure him up in her writing, and, like André Breton in pursuit of his Nadja in Paris, she wanders the Buenos Aires streets in search of his memory. The text's greater emphasis on the male muse's voice than on his body, however, provides a more striking inversion of muse conventions: Mila pursues the enigma of the man's word, not his image. The focus on desire notwithstanding, this reversal offers a gentle critique of the visual eroticism enveloping modern renditions of the feminine muse. More importantly it signals the narrating protagonist's search for a dialogue with her muse, Sergio, portrayed not only as the object of her desire but also as a source of knowledge: "Teacher of the intense word" (10). In contrast to the paradoxically immobile and distant image of the muse Norah as invoked by Borges, Mila seeks a collaborative exchange with Sergio, not unlike the dialogue of interruptions with her male mentors imagined by Ocampo: "Your voice, along with mine, sounding any theme, any art" (Lange, *Voz de la vida,* 44).

The work reinforces this concept of dialogue with its crossings between intimate and public spaces, between the small room where Mila writes and the streets she wanders in pursuit of Sergio's memory, which provides the inspiration for her work. If we read this narrative as a kind of poetics, an interpretation encouraged by the muse theme and the focus on writing, these spatial elisions between the domestic and the urban also signal a move outward in Lange's own maneuvers from the *tertulias* on Calle Tronador to her public activity as a writer in the heart of a literary fraternity of men.[18] In this context, both the protagonist's unconventionality in matters of the heart and her mobility in increasingly public settings stand out. Significantly, by 1927 when *Voz de la vida* appeared, Lange was not only working as a translator outside her home, she had also participated in the more public activities of the Martinfierristas, including the Revista Oral at the Royal Keller café and other daytime gatherings of young Buenos Aires writers.[19] In 1928, at age 22, Lange traveled alone to Oslo on a cargo ship populated entirely by men, and by 1930, after her return to Buenos Aires, she had established dual residence between her mother's home and Girondo's.

A lengthy contemporary critique of *Voz de la vida* by Ramón Doll, castigating Lange for the modernity of both the content and style of her work, provides an example par excellence of what Susan Suleiman calls the "double margin" of aesthetics and gender facing the women of the avant-gardes. On the one hand the critic took Lange to task for "vulgar" erotic abandon of her protagonist, who would provide a negative model of morality for young women, and on the other he criticized the "cold abstractness" and "mathematical theorems" marking the work's vanguard economy of style, including the character Mila's "unsexed" and "male" language (35–36). But ignoring antimimetic vanguard premises and literally equating author with protagonist, Doll argued that Mila's experience as a woman was neither grammatical nor rhetorical but rather physiological and that Lange should therefore have eschewed *ultraísmo* or vanguard strategies as her protagonist's language and should have drawn instead on the "passionate virginal trembling" found in the (in fact antifeminist) poetry of Anna de Noailles (36). Undaunted by this admonition to adhere to traditional gender norms through her characters and conceptions of the literary on the one hand and of women's literature on the other, in her second novel, *45 días y 30 marineros,* Lange created an even more outrageous female protagonist. Published in 1933, this work undertakes a more direct inquiry into the role of a modern muse and highlights the creative power and cognitive potential of her reincarnation as the New Woman.

This work narrates the adventures of Ingrid, the lone woman on a cargo ship that crosses the Atlantic from Buenos Aires to Oslo. Although narrated in the third person, by privileging the protagonist's perspective the work focuses on how this woman maneuvers between the dangers represented by the thirty sailors who would seduce her and by the temptations of her own erotic desires. Both Lange and her recent critics mention this novel's questionable literary merit; narrated in conventional prose, the work does not yet offer the stylistic interloping—the estranging focalizations on the uncanny—of her later work. Still it constitutes a key moment in her development of an authorial persona; through its interplay of characters seeing and being seen it also points to her future signature style. Because Lange herself traveled under similar circumstances to her father's homeland in 1928, critics of her time and biographer Miguel have read the work as a transparent source of information about Lange's own trip. However, the fact of the novel's publication in 1933 provides a less literal but more telling link between Lange's art of living as a woman writer in Buenos Aires and the situation represented in *45 días y 30 marineros*. When we consider that by 1933 Lange had long been the central female figure in the *tertulias* and banquets of the Martín Fierro literary fraternity, the novel's narration of a lone woman's intricate survival tactics among a large group of men stands out. Moreover, the characterization of this woman as a dynamic performer for the male circle evokes the centrality of performance in Lange's own development of a public artistic persona among the Martín Fierro cohort. Two related events reinforce such a reading. For the official presentation of the book when it was published, an event recorded in a photograph, the male writers in Lange's group dressed up as sailors, with Girondo as the captain and Lange, in the center of the photo, dressed as a mermaid.[20] In 1936, to celebrate the baptism of Girondo's recently acquired brig, the *Martín Fierro,* in one of her ribald *discursos,* Lange extended the maritime metaphor to characterize the group, naming her audience of literary men the "crew, cabin boys, and shipwrecked," Girondo as the admiral, and herself as the godmother of the launching (*Estimados cóngeres,* 26–29).

Published in the very years when Lange had begun to perform her outrageous *discursos* among the Martín Fierro group, then, the novel *45 días y 30 marineros* rehearses a woman's discovery of the cognitive power of her assigned role as a performer among men. The protagonist not only embraces this role, she also celebrates it, clearly enjoys it, and manipulates it into a position of observational power. From the opening scene, the protagonist Ingrid who, like Lange for the *ultraístas,* "looks like a walkyrie" (26), recognizes her status as an image for the men who surround her: "As she climbed aboard, a multitude of celestial glances chased her legs" (5). In her first encounter with the thirty sailors, Ingrid assumes her designated part as a performer; invaded by the "conviction of her cordial role" she "lets herself be carried along by the voices of the men" and "totally located in her destiny as a woman" (13). At this moment, she climbs up on the berth and begins dancing a jazz rhythm, provoking an exchange of stories and toasts among the men who surround her. This scene and others like it, in which Ingrid dances a tango or delivers a talk, call to mind the image of Lange herself performing in the 1930s before the Martinfierristas. The novel simultaneously celebrates these displays and chronicles Ingrid's manipulations of the role. Aware of being incessantly observed and like Mila with her muse Sergio in *Voz de la vida,* Ingrid inverts the dynamics of watching. As she evolves into a meticulous observer, Ingrid subjects the masculine façades to her objectifying eye: the captain "no longer so odd to her retina" who presents the "standard contours" of a middle-aged Norwegian man and the others who neither provoke "profound, inquisitive reflections on masculine beauty" nor offer any "enduring, memorable exterior" (10–11).

Such observations constitute a learning process for the protagonist, whose own role as a performing woman gradually evolves into that of an ethnographic participant-observer, fascinated by this strange masculine culture. In this encounter, Ingrid initially performs a role comparable to Lange's own displays at the Martín Fierro fraternity banquets or to the ceremonial displays of an anthropologist in the field aiming to put her informants at ease. Thus she "launches an *abundance of words*" to make her nervous dinner companions "as comfortable as when they tell loud stories on the dark decks" (100; my emphasis). In the resulting relaxed atmosphere and while she dances, Ingrid scrutinizes what the men are doing. Her estranging perception imbues their activity with the air of an odd ritual in which they "dance to the rhythm of a music of their own composition" and their silhouettes, "distorted, take on a fantastic aspect in the night illuminated by searchlights" that scatter "their contours in a slow confusion." They "appear stealthily, as if driven by a strange force" (102–103). Lange's selection of an ocean voyage as the framework for a novel is congruous with her propensity, noted by critics, to construct worlds outside of temporal and spatial norms, settings that provide the opportunity, they argue, for her to rehearse alternative stories of the self or the nation.[21] But such settings, particularly in *45 días y 30 marineros,* can also reinforce a work's constitution as an ethnographic situation that, in this case, upends normalcy both for the masculine culture under invasion and for its woman interloper as well.

This deciphering of a masculine world constitutes the foundation for Ingrid's emergent definition of her function within it. Instantly mindful, as I have noted, of her status as a projection of male desire, she also recognizes from the start that everybody except her carries out a daily assigned task on this voyage. With the noteworthy exception of a male intellectual with whom she converses intermittently, Ingrid is the only actual passenger on this cargo ship. The novel's organization of its fictional space reinforces this singular circumstance, as the protagonist's mapping of a viable role unfolds with increasing fluidity between the intimate ambiance of her cabin and the more public spaces on the ship and in the ports in which it anchors. Initially Ingrid reads and writes only in her cabin, while performing her dances and speeches in the more open spaces. But the narrative gradually obscures these divisions. On the one hand, the periodic entrance of various men into her cabin unleashes scenes of failed seduction that the protagonist melodramatically deconstructs as part of her scrutiny of the masculine world and gender relations. At the same time, Ingrid gradually intercalates her own more intellectual and private activity into her emerging public role. Thus she begins reading on deck, in part as a defense against advances from men and also as the point of departure for a dialogue with them, particularly with the intellectual who shares her readings.

Drawing on her superior linguistic knowledge in the multilingual world of the ship and the ports where it docks, Ingrid also assumes the public identity of an informal language teacher and translator, activities that are clearly linked to her ethnographic position as participant observer (and to Lange's real-world work). In developing this singular role, Ingrid maneuvers between a variegated world of masculine tasks and her own position as a lone woman lacking a clear job in this masculine culture. Significantly, the role Ingrid creates for herself in this world that she visits emerges precisely from her assigned identity as image and muse, the experiential source as well of her analytical sharpness as an observer and her skills as a cultural translator. In addition, the novel sugarcoats with the flavor of respectability her risqué position as a lone performing woman among men. Thus Ingrid's assumed role as language teacher and translator, like that of Ocampo as a helpful tour guide, conforms to the social motherhood agenda of Buenos Aires feminism that posited a requisite utility for modern women in the changing social order.

The ethnographic identity of Lange's protagonist Ingrid in *45 días y 30 marineros* as a perspicacious participant-observer, who now and again seizes center stage with an arresting performance before the men whose world she has invaded, bears striking parallels with Lange's own performative strategies in her celebratory *discursos* among the Buenos Aires writers in the 1930s and early 1940s. From the days of her participation as an adolescent in the *tertulias* of Calle Tronador, Lange had performed for audiences of literary men, be it declaiming poetry, dancing the tango, or playing the piano or even the Argentine concertina or *bandoneón*. By the early 1930s, however, she had recast this respectable role for an upper-middle-class young woman into the startling, oddball *discursos* she delivered while standing on a case of wine at Martín Fierro events. According to Lange, she preferred this position because of the commanding visual advantage it provided, a privileged spot from which to inspect her audience and "dominate the multitude" (quoted in Nóbile, 20). This activity, as Sylvia Molloy aptly points out, echoes the linguistically playful adolescent displays that, according to Lange's autobiographical *Cuadernos de infancia,* she performed for neighbors from the roof of her house (*At Face Value,* 135). On one level, the parodic character of the *discursos* at literary banquets clearly constitutes a hyperbolic critique of the performance roles assigned to middle- and upper-class women. Thus in one of her *discursos* Lange openly assailed the performative fare undertaken by bourgeois women: "lectures, recitals, piano duets . . . and other lamentable effervescences" (*Estimados cóngeres,* 46). But her confessed zeal for "dominating the multitude" also signals a studied redirection of her designated identity as a muse toward a viable position in the public literary culture to which she had access as well as toward the consummation of a personal literary style.

At first glance, the exaggerated and exuberant proliferation of words in Lange's *discursos* of the 1930s and 1940s seems radically contrary to the economical and polished style of her most successful prose works: the autobiographical *Cuadernos de infancia* and the novels *Antes que mueran* (1944), *Personas en la sala* (1950), and *Los dos retratos* (1956). However, the principal stylistic strategies of these discursive "anatomies" (as she called them) of celebrated individuals, combined with the incisive imagery of her earlier poetry, provide the foundation for the fragmented style and the estranging perspicacity that mark Lange's language and uncommon strategies of characterization in her narrative work.[22] The *discursos* are "anatomical" both literally and figuratively. With their irreverent and skeptical dissection of the intellectual and cultural activity of Lange's contemporaries, these high-spirited addresses possess a satirical air and signature traits of the classical literary anatomy: the stylized portrayal of characters; a focus on mental attitudes and orientations; the exuberant and encyclopedic accumulation of details with which to assault the object of the anatomy with their own jargon; the ostentatious erudition of the satirist; and a digressive inclination in the exposition.[23]

Like the anatomist, in her *discursos* Lange casts the clinical eye of the performative synecdoche to ostend a select physical detail—the navel, the epidermis—or a psychological one—idleness, a lust for exotic food or drink—as the point of departure for a more profound character inquest. In one of her addresses, Lange described this anatomical process, linking it explicitly to literary practice: "Etymologically, anatomy implies the deferred enthusiasm to separate [the part from the whole, I would add], by means of an instrument . . . the diverse parts that comprise a waking being, with the ambiguous urge to pry into their sometimes disordered distribution" (*Estimados cóngeres,* 39). "Literature or dissection," she continued, "can construct that instrument that will separate, with pointed vehemence, the most uneven segment of the writer or poet" (39). A characterization of Girondo in one of Lange's *discursos* exemplifies the procedure: "After lingering, devotedly, on his circulatory system, on his perfect foot that he tends to exhibit during fluvial excursions or on nights populated by literary imprecisions on his little, Mediterranean finger that does not tolerate repeated touching . . . I quivered with sudden feminine intuition: Oliverio Girondo, electro-dynamic" (*Estimados cóngeres,* 67). Lange's irreverent anatomies cast a comparably penetrating eye on numerous writers, painters, or sculptors and their work.[24] In their presentation of the dissector's ostension of select parts, they correspond to the focalizing style of her best narratives.

THE ANATOMIST AS INTERLOPER IN ELUSIVE COMMUNITIES

Lange's *discursos* constitute a creative achievement within the public sphere of her acquired art of living as a woman writer in early-twentieth-century Buenos Aires. Although she delivered them with an improvisational flair, she researched and designed them carefully in advance, just as she did with her novels.[25] Notably, the *discursos* coincide in time with her first important success as a writer of prose fiction, the autobiographical *Cuadernos de infancia* (Childhood notebooks), which received a first-place municipal prize of Buenos Aires. Lange organized the narrative as a memoir and imbued it with the air of childhood notebooks.[26] The work encompasses remembered scenarios from the narrator's childhood, roughly from ages five to fourteen. Told through the voice of an adult and the perspective of a child, this structure typifies the dual perspective of autobiographical fiction, particularly the novel of formation or *Bildungsroman*. The narrative opens with the move of the narrator at age five along with her parents and siblings from Buenos Aires to provincial Mendoza, where her father will work. It concludes with scenes of economic readjustment and change after the father's death and the family's consequent return to Buenos Aires. Within this frame, the narrative encloses scenes of domestic life, enacted primarily by the children and their mother, and recollections of people and quotidian situations filtered through the narrator's childlike perceptions.

Although *Cuadernos de infancia* offers no traditional plot, the narrator's gradual awakening to her place in the world, combined with her eccentric, "anatomical" style for perceiving and describing it, provide developmental continuity to the account as a narrative of formation or, more specifically, as an account of the artist's style in the making.[27] Evoking the conventions of this genre are the odd role models for the narrator's development: a female circus gymnast who can balance men from her teeth and a cook who tells anatomically detailed stories of the scissors left inside her during a surgical intervention. Also typical of a novel of formation is the location of the narrator's apprenticeship in a spatial and temporal break from the normal routine, the family's years in Mendoza, and the placement of the narrator's self-conscious dislocation in the "awakening" from childhood to adolescence that exemplifies the singularity of this genre in the hands of women writers.[28] The work's clipped, telegraphic style, startling visual synecdoches and distortions, and thematic attention to the materiality of language situate it unmistakably in the literary vanguards and draw on the anatomical *discursos*.

Because of its thinly disguised references to Lange's own childhood years in Mendoza and Buenos Aires on the one hand, and due to its anonymous narrator, unconventional structure, and studied narrative style on the other, critics read this work as both biography and fiction. While it is tempting to contrast the narrative's sparse style and domestic locale with Lange's irreverent verbosity in the public *discursos,* reading it as a portrait of the artist underscores the continuity of the hyperbolic public addresses and the fictional world of childhood and family in Lange's art of living as a writer and highlights her intricate transmutation of conventional roles in pursuit of an uncommon writing style and authorial persona. Lange's extravagant performances while poised on the wine case or while dressed as the Martín Fierro mermaid comprised a critical (though required, Judith Butler might say) mimicry of the New Woman muse role circulating in literary and mass culture in Buenos Aires. But in the metamorphosis from muse to satirical anatomist, Lange produced the unanticipated: the discriminating eye of an anatomical authorial style in her prose.[29] In its portrayal of a stylistic apprenticeship *Cuadernos de infancia* also offers concrete connections between Lange's public experience as a performing woman among artistic men and this discerning narrative eye cast on a fictionalized world of women. As with the *discursos,* on the surface this narrative manifests the "compulsory citationality" of prevalent thematic standards for women's writing. The single women protagonists of *Voz de la vida* and *45 días y 30 marineros* are unconventional not only in their unabashed eroticism but also in their high public visibility, on the streets of Buenos Aires and on a cargo ship and in its ports of call, respectively. By contrast, *Cuadernos de infancia* situates its women in the safe propriety of childhood, family, and a quotidian domestic world.[30] Nonetheless, the narrative's creative distortions of perspective and eccentric authorial persona transform that safe haven into the dwelling of the uncanny and the site for a critical disfigurement of domesticity.

As a narrative of formation, *Cuadernos de infancia* actually traces two different apprenticeships, one in gender rules and one in artistic style, that share a common corporeal source. On one level, the narrator deciphers gender codes through scenarios in which she or her sisters voluntarily rehearse key roles and situations they observe around them. Prototypical roles identified for modeling including the frail, fainting woman with the romantic allure of "perpetual convalescence" (81) or a woman who exudes maternity while nursing. The narrator also rehearses representative situations scripted through gender relations, including killing a chicken for an imagined husband's dinner, conveying condolences with feminine respectability, or executing a lingering goodbye. While in some cases these are the narrator's mental exercises, in others the sisters carefully craft an actual scenario, for example an imaginary baptism. In either case and as when an actor dissects a role in order to assume it, the narrator portrays these trials as exercises in the kinesthetic imagination, to borrow Joseph Roach's term (26), as knowledge acquisition through the body. Thus while rehearsing the frail woman, the narrator holds her breath to provoke fainting spells and recreates the "voluptuousness" (168) of a long goodbye as an intricate assemblage of ambiance, gesture, and language. As the future dutiful wife, she experiences the chicken-slaughtering as the encounter of two bodies: "I could see myself imprisoning its body between my knees, trying to sling its head backwards, but the neck stretched like a rubber band, and as it interrupted the tug, the head returned, with a dry little sound, to its habitual posture" (147). The ultimate consequences of these rehearsals are choices made and roles rejected, as when the narrator vows that if chicken-slaughtering is required, she will never marry or when she rejects the fainting female role as more perilous and less empowering than that of circus gymnast.

The narrator's apprenticeship in a singular way of perceiving and portraying her world parallels the corporeal orientation of her gender rehearsals. In a prose style distilled of verbosity, the dissector's gaze of Lange's anatomical *discursos* undergirds her distinctive mode of character construction based on a physical or psychological eccentricity. In evoking memorable characters, the narrators in *Cuadernos de infancia* and her subsequent fiction manifest an overwhelming preference for synecdoche, an apt stylistic tool for the verbal anatomist, and the performative ostension of the singular. Thus she showcases the part—"a dampened eye, the piece of a nose, an angle of the mouth" (27)—dissected from the whole, for example, in the progressive framing of her sister's head by petticoats: "her figure expanded until her little head became a blonde point atop an enormous hoop skirt" (28). Moreover, with a concentration on the corporeality of words (typical of the vanguards), the narrator creates a metonymy of body and language. Thus she reports cutting out words that fascinated her from printed material because of their physical stature— she especially liked capital letters—or material peculiarities, say, the "stiff downward strokes of the l's and the t's" (51). Inversely, the narrator's novel bodily experience, the "electrical contact" and "nervous sensation" of a finger healing from a knife wound, undergoes a metamorphosis into an odd new word: *Itilínkili* (72–73).

The most arresting feature of the anatomical style in *Cuadernos de infancia* is the narrator's physical projection of her own persona into the corporeal eccentricities of the characters she scrutinizes. Frequently cited passages from the work describe this anatomical insertion of a creator into her characters, or of an actor in an identified role, in a child's literal and concrete terms. Thus the narrator recounts her penchant from early childhood to "nail her eyes" into a visitor and to imagine their profile from within. It is as if, she explains, "I inserted myself into the person, physically, but only into the face" (35). She then describes an afternoon when she introduced herself into the face of a visitor to "form his factions" with her own body, a process that required the constructing of "many imaginary figures, many fallen arms, many tangled legs" (35). The special case of the engineer Bok provides a more detailed account of how the body mimics the profile: "I had to install myself head down, so that my hair would form his beard, my hands barely united in his back, my legs folded, forming an obtuse angle with the body" (36). The rehearsal strategy here described resembles what Lange in her *discursos* called visual "auscultation" (*Estimados cóngeres,* 21), a word that underscores the interplay of vision and hearing, image and word in Lange's anatomical cognitive mode. Key moments in *Cuadernos de infancia,* moreover, frame the narrator's development of a particular style as a self-conscious act conceptualized in adulthood but originating in a childhood talent for deforming the quotidian. The narrator explains that people and things offer her a "miniscule world" she can refashion with "favorite words and gestures" (155).

Two remarkable scenes of performance frame *Cuadernos de infancia* and seal the connection between the anatomies of Lange's public *discursos* and the anatomical style of cognitive inquiry in her memoir. In the narrative's opening selection that describes the family's move to Mendoza, the narrator and her family cross paths with a circus impresario and "the strongest woman in the world" (12). The five-year-old girl vacillates between perverse fascination and fear as she contemplates this massive performing woman who can reportedly lift multiple men with her teeth (12). But by the end of the account, when she is fourteen and back in Buenos Aires, the narrator generates outrageous feats of her own: polyglot rooftop performances executed with odd costumes and ribald gestures. After calling out several words in different languages, she recounts, she would beckon all of the neighbors by name, and as soon as people's heads began to appear over the walls, her "stentorian voice" and "gesticulation" would "bounce against the walls, against the windowpanes, against the zinc roofs" (277).

In both language and gesture, the narrator explains, these scenarios were alternately inquisitive, ironic, nonsensical, insulting, obscene, strident, and mannered. As the culmination of an artistic apprenticeship that began with the powerful circus gymnast, this scene seals the connection between the work's world of performance and the authorial persona. Whether or not Lange as an adolescent actually executed such feats is less important than the fact that she wrote this account precisely during her years of performing *discursos* as the New Woman muse for a literary fraternity. The arresting similarity between the rooftop performer of *Cuadernos de infancia,* not to mention her predecessor Ingrid in *45 días y 30 marineros,* and the verbal gymnast of Buenos Aires literary gatherings underscores the intimate tie between the estranging verbal maneuvers of Lange's anatomical prose style and her eccentric performances as a New Woman muse. Through her fictionalized memoir, Lange situates the origins of her performative power in the dislocations of early adolescence.[31] But one could easily tell the story the other way around: that Lange's hyperbolic embrace of the part of performing woman for a Buenos Aires literary fraternity provided an apprenticeship in the bodily inquiries of performance and in the penetrating power of "auscultation" necessary for the anatomical, eccentric, and ironic conceptions of character, style, and, above all, authorial persona that coalesce in her best prose work.

One particular similarity between the rendition of this persona in *Cuadernos de infancia* and in the *discursos* highlights a woman writer's interaction with the ostensibly disparate worlds that her work seeks to bridge. Both the speaker in Lange's ribald addresses and the narrator in *Cuadernos de infancia* insistently identify themselves with a specific, concrete community at the same time that they portray themselves as outsiders. In the published collections of the *discursos,* third-person-plural verb forms—*festejamos* (we partied), *celebramos* (we celebrated), *ofrecimos* (we offered) (*Estimados cóngeres,* 30, 39, 45)—pepper the explanatory notes with which Lange linked each address to the group occasion of its performance. In the same vein, the descriptive phrases of direct address that launch each performance underscore the communal relationship of the speaker to the audience: "fellows," "consecrated contemporaries," "temerarious colleagues," "hypersensitive and abstemious co-*tertulianos,*" "esteemed fellow diners," "contemporaneous and worthy attendees" (*Estimados cóngeres,* 39, 15, 49, 62, 81, 86). Although the pronoun *we* and nouns of direct address typify the vanguard manifesto's aura of collectivity, Lange employed them with extraordinary tenacity. Some *discursos* chronicle from the perspective of an initiate the group's origins in the *tertulias* of Calle Tronador, while others assemble countless insider allusions and coin a plethora of inside jokes and communal neologisms, a shared "dialect of allusions," to recall Borges's quest for artistic community in the poem "Llaneza." In her 1938 *discurso* dedicated to the Lange family as the protagonist of *Cuadernos de infancia,* Lange chronicled the overlapping of her birth family and her literary one. Here nostalgic but ironic recollections of key events in the Calle Tronador *tertulias* follow similarly comic evocations of her mother and siblings. Interestingly, although the *discursos* as "oral incursions" or "guttural tasks" (*Estimados cóngeres,* 97, 45) evoke the present tense of their delivery, several of these speeches recollect events of the group's past with an intensity that is somehow greater than the moments they celebrate.

A comparable celebratory nostalgia for a community somehow lost weaves through key scenes in *Cuadernos de infancia,* as in the evocations of comfort and camaraderie of family storytelling on Saturday nights or the scenarios of the solidarity in the making among women implicit in the sisters' inventive misadventures. But the verbal gymnast of the *discursos* and the autobiographical narrator of the prose work both cast themselves as interlopers in the communities they commemorate. In part this is a question of location. If Lange preferred to deliver her addresses from a box because of the powerful perspective this spot provided, her characterization of her talks as anatomies speaks to a literary tradition in which the anatomist's physical position and power of perception were always superior to those of the anatomized. Similarly, the narrator in *Cuadernos de infancia* explains that she liked to execute her verbal panegyrics from the rooftops because it allowed her to see inside the surrounding houses of her neighbors. Both situations point to Lange's confessed penchant for "spying" or to what Molloy, citing Felisberto Hernández, calls the "lust for looking," *la lujuria de ver* (*At Face Value*, 130).

Lange's authorial persona not only spies on the communities she anatomizes, however; she also invades them and lives in their midst. In *Cuadernos de infancia,* the narrator's description of her anatomical strategy of taking possession of others through bodily rehearsal evokes this interloping activity as well—"to glide into the profile of others" (36–37)—and points again to Lange's writing style. Be it as a spy or an interloper, Lange's performative self-portrayals map out a relationship to her imagined communities that is both intimately participatory and willfully estranged. But the answer to the question of which venue constitutes Lange's authentic home as a woman writer, the private familial world of childhood origins constructed in *Cuadernos de infancia* or the public literary commune of the Martín Fierro group, is neither one and both. In fact the memoir blurs ostensible differences between them. An ensemble of odd characters inhabits the vanguard club as Lange represents it, from "demons" and the "extra flat-nosed" to "thirsty invertebrates," "tumultuous addicts," "lily pads, sponges," and "lepidopterous nymphs" (*Estimados cóngeres,* 45, 53, 67, 72). But family and home in the memoir are equally bizarre, characterized by Molloy as a "community of voyeurs" without lineage or fixed location (*At Face Value*, 130), by Domínguez as the site of dissonance within the hegemony of genders norms, and by Masiello as an alternative family cut off from the state (*Between Civilization and Barbarism*, 147). If the performing Martinfierrista Lange cut an odd figure from her perch on the wine case, the perspicacious and clever narrator of the memoir also portrays herself as an assemblage of phobias, compulsivity, and a fascination with the uncanny.[32]

But for all of its eccentricities, from *Cuadernos de infancia* onward, a domestic world inhabited primarily by women endures in all of Lange's prose fiction. The general absence of pathos in Lange's tone and novelistic worldview notwithstanding, however, the communities of women in all of her work constitute scenarios of loss, reflections on worlds in the moment of their vanishing, with a family move, the death of a loved one, the sale of a house, the disconnection among family members. The general paucity of dialogue and erotic unions in most of Lange's prose reinforces the aura of disengagement. The estrangement of the narrator from the world she inhabits and writes about persists as well, and the suggestive title of the incomplete fragment of Lange's final novel—"La casa de vidrio" (The house of glass)—echoes the blurring of public and private spheres in all of her work as well as the privileged position of an interloper who has equal access to both.[33] If Lange's writing consistently underscores an estrangement of the artist from the domestic worlds she creates, why then, we must ask, does she insist on locating her creative origins in that world, particularly when she could just as easily, as I have suggested, have situated them in her experience as a creative performer in the literary fraternity of the Martinfierristas? Why did the Latin American woman writer who was the most welcome over time in a continuing fraternity of the literary vanguards construct an enduring portrait of the artist as interloper, irrespective of the world in which she found herself? Was she never quite at home?

A key to an answer lies in the narrator's inscription in *Cuadernos de infancia* of her childhood's end. The memoir concludes with two momentous events: the narrator's trip to the barber to exchange her long locks for an updated bob and her recognition of the consequent alteration in the old gardener's treatment of her. Suddenly more reserved before her more mature look, he withholds the playful finger poke with which he had customarily greeted her. She was immobilized, she reported, by a gradually sharpening "sense of emptiness." She then experienced the sensation, she explained, of moving away from everything she had been before and felt that the finger was pointing to something that would gradually confine her, something that, while offering her other emotions and risks, would separate her from all the little "incidents . . . fears . . . and manias" of her childhood and all of its "tenderness" as well (284).

With this conclusion, Lange's New Woman narrator situates the loss of her community of women precisely in the crossroads of modernity and gender. The crossover to the modern, the fashionable hair bob, and to the gendered sexuality of adolescence locates the culmination of her aesthetic apprenticeship in the requisite moment of loss embodied in a modern woman's journey from a world of women to a fraternal community of artistic innovators. This loss unfolds neither in one world nor the other but from the transition between them, from the negotiation of private and public implicit in Lange's self-assumed artistic persona as a performing interloper who inhabits worlds that individually are not quite her own but collectively constitute her life. Lange's self-portrayals preempt any temptations to read the vanishing domestic world as more authentic or the Martinfierrista fraternity as less real. In this sense, she upends Borges's nostalgic equation of Lange the muse with the "immobile grace" of a lost Buenos Aires embodied in the house on Calle Tronador. Rather Lange's artistic practice and self-portrait as an artist in *Cuadernos de infancia* showcase an unending process of choice. Just as the child alternately rehearses and rejects certain gender roles, so does the adult Lange embrace certain personae and transform others.

These masquerades, in particular the public displays among the Martinfierristas, were in fact no less real than the childhood scenarios. The contemporary U.S. actor and playwright Anna Deavere Smith tells an instructive tale about the visit of her two-and-a-half-year-old niece, Elizabeth, to a freshman acting class she was teaching. Drawing on Peter Brook's admonition that a child is the hardest role for an adult actor to portray, Smith asked her students to observe Elizabeth coloring and playing and take notes so that they might later mimic her behavior. As the child quietly played at the center of this intense, silent inspection, she slowly began engaging her audience, first by covering her eyes and trying to get them to play peek-a-boo and when that failed, to divert them from their concentrated watching behavior by suddenly roaring loudly and ferociously like a tiger. Later Smith explained to her class that in order to gain power over the moment in their scrutinizing presence, Elizabeth had chosen to roar at them not as herself, but as her favorite animal, a tiger: "Elizabeth had created a fiction. Her fiction was not a lie. It was a persona. It was a tool that gave her power . . . and allowed her to speak . . . in fact it allowed her to roar, and thus to rule the room, for a moment" (Smith, 146–147). Norah Lange's self-elected personae in the *Discursos* and in *Cuadernos de infancia*—the irreverent roars of a muse launched from wine cases and rooftops—constituted her fictions that were not lies. These strategies allowed *ultraísmo*'s "immobile" muse not only to rule the room for many a moment but, in a milieu that still regarded her presence as uncommon, to upend the imagery with which male writers absorbed her presence into their own aesthetics and to map the terrain of her inventive art of anatomy and uncommon identity as a writer.

In the closing lines of the autobiographical essay that prefaced the 1960 anthology of her writing, *Mis libros* (My books), Nellie Campobello (1900–1986)[1] described the adolescent frustration she experienced while seeking the "state of mind" of a writer: "I would throw myself on the floor and resting my elbows on the rug . . . I would . . . scrutinize the poses of my protagonist" (45). This portrait of the artist in a bodily quest for a writer's disposition echoes the inaugural appearance of the narrator in Campobello's first successful prose work, *Cartucho* (1931), the only novel of the Mexican Revolution of its generation written by a woman. Here, as a visiting soldier thanks her mother for mending his shirts, the narrator depicts herself as a child who interrupts the scene with a brief, comic retort from her hideout "under a table" (*Cartucho,* 929; DM, 6). Although these two authorial personae strike a brief, stationary pose, they are poised, like the dancing Campobello, to leap into action. The same year that *Cartucho* appeared, Campobello performed at the Mexican National Stadium as the lead dancer in the renowned *Ballet de masas 30-30* (Ballet of the masses). As her first large-scale choreography for the Escuela Nacional de Danza under the auspices of the Secretaría de Educación Pública, this official performance helped institutionalize revolutionary ideals and was reprised throughout the country over the next decade and a half. In contrast to Campobello's artistic self-portrait of a writer down on the floor, spectators and participants in the mass ballets recalled the arresting figure of Campobello in a spectacle including up to three thousand citizens. Dressed in red and waving the torch of the Revolution, Campobello would run from one end of the stadium to the other provoking the other dancers to grab their 30-30 rifles and set off for battle.[2] Campobello's impact on the Mexican dance world was profound and enduring, as she joined the postrevolutionary movement to nationalize Mexican artistic expression in a synthesis of aesthetic innovation with autochthonous forms and themes.[3] But for all her renown as an innovative choreographer, dancer, and teacher, Campobello imagined her writing, not her dancing, as the privileged location for her own creative independence. In fact, her preface for *Mis libros* portrays her art of living as a writer as a rejoinder to the creative and ideological compromises required for her successful dance career. At the same time, the shifting dynamic between the writer striking a pose and the dancer on the move accentuates the interaction of body and word—the movement of writing—in Campobello's creative practice and her malleable position as a woman writer.

Campobello emigrated from northern Mexico to the capital in 1923. She made her mid-1920s debut in the city's cultural life as a dancer, but she published her first book, the pseudonymous poetry collection *Yo, por Francisca* (I, by Francisca) in 1929. As the childhood scene from *Mis libros* suggests, Campobello conceived writing itself as a performative act, a self-conscious pursuit of a particular style and creative persona. Amidst the gender-charged polemics of Mexican postrevolutionary cultural na-tionalism, in her writing more than her dance, Campobello's work defied the polarized oppositions shaping the public conversation about art. Her conception of the literary was nationalist, politically engaged, and pep-pered with truth claims, an orientation she shared with the left wing of the Mexican avant-garde, the *estridentistas,* as well as with cultural national-ists favoring realist conventions to depict the Revolution in the manner of Mariano Azuela's *Los de abajo* (1916). Similarly, through her literary and choreographic portrayals of the Revolution as the collective heroism of ordinary people, she embraced the populism of postrevolutionary cul-tural missions. Yet, in the spirit of the more aestheticist Contemporáneos group, Campobello's writing also executed an unremitting "will to style"[4] and exposed its own fictive status to tell a story not only of the author's childhood perceptions of the Revolution in northern Mexico but also of its creator's select status as a writer. In the revolutionary, autochthonous settings of her dance and fiction, Campobello reiterated the patriotic artis-tic "virility" espoused by cultural nationalists. But throughout her writing she mapped a more androgynous tale of a woman's search for a form of expression and an identity as a writer bent on interventions in the cultural dialogue of her day. This alternative story unfolds through the early poems of *Yo, por Francisca,* the lyrical prose of "8 poemas de mujer" (8 poems by a woman; 1930) and her best-known works, the narratives *Cartucho* and *Las manos de mamá* (My mother's hands; 1937). Collectively these writ-ings present a kinesthetic portrait of an artist and the willful assumption of variable poses. Even as Campobello imagined a primordial, indigenous world of origins rooted in her Villa Ocampo homeland far from Mexico City, the authorial persona portrayed in *Cartucho* and *Las manos de mamá* was quintessentially urban and modern, as removed from the Tarahumara roots to which she laid claim as was Antonin Artaud on his Mexican quest for the authenticity of the surreal.[5] The debates that shaped Mexico's diverse cultural scene traverse Campobello's artistic project, from the mass-media world of the imagined Eva Moderna to the vanguard innovations of *estridentista* and Contemporáneos aesthetics, and the postrevolutionary cultural missions initiated by José Vasconcelos and radicalized into overtly political art during the Lázaro Cárdenas presidency (1934–1940). Campobello was fully at home in none of these settings. Although she sought creative refuge in the sometimes nostalgic world of provincial origins in which she set her fiction, she also moved with assertive agility through Mexico City's cultural fray of the 1920s and 1930s. This sense of movement also imbues her writing, from her changing lyric or narrative voices or focalizers to the brief, telegraphic sentences of her prose.

THE NEW EVE, THE NEW MEXICO, AND SNAPSHOTS OF THE NEW NELLIE

When the twenty-three-year-old Campobello and her siblings relocated from Durango to Mexico City in 1923, she marked her arrival in a city undergoing a full-scale refashioning by assuming a new persona. Born María Francisca Luna in 1900 and nicknamed Xica and/or Nellie by family and friends, she took the last name from her sister Gloria's father, Ernest Campbell, and Hispanicized it to Campobello.[6] She also adjusted her birth date, a fiction she never relinquished. Their mother deceased, the siblings left behind hardship wrought by the Revolution in their hometown of Villa Ocampo and later in Chihuahua and Durango. With the support of Campbell's family, the sisters entered the capital's elite anglophone community. Here, through private schooling in the Colegio Inglés and its social world, Campobello pursued theatrical inclinations already evident in her adolescent dramatic posing and her exposure to theatre as a ticket taker for the Teatro Los Héroes in Chihuahua. In her new milieu Campobello acquired the performance training typical of an upper- or middle-class woman's education into respectability, through declamation, dance, song, and literature. Ana Pavlova's 1925 visit to Mexico City stimulated Campobello's decision, with her sister, to take up dancing. Their teachers included the well-known Stanislava Moll Potapovich, but her public debut with the popular Lettie Carroll dance group in 1927 proved decisive for Campobello's experience in Mexico City's changing dance scene of the 1920s. This apprenticeship with Miss Carroll's Girls, founded by the Texas-born Carroll, generated the dynamic interaction between innovation à la Isadora Duncan and a quest for *mexicanidad* that would characterize Campobello's long career. A performance tour of Florida and Havana in 1929 and early 1930 proved pivotal in her turn toward autochthonous forms. Back in Mexico, Campobello began teaching at the Escuela del Estudiante Indígena and soon joined the national music and dance section of the Departamento de Bellas Artes. She was a founding member of the Escuela Nacional de Danza in 1932, and she became its director in 1937, a post she held at least nominally until 1984.[7] Through this agency's incarnations, Campobello participated in a growing cultural bureaucracy, the legacy of the cultural missions initiated in the 1920s by Vasconcelos. The identity-building reclamation and dissemination of indigenous dance forms was an ambitious cultural venture analogous in imaginative scope to postrevolutionary muralism. Along with Gloria,[8] Campobello researched and taught regional dances and published *Ritmos indígenas de México* (1940). Historians situate Campobello's contribution to Mexican dance not only in her training of individuals who became key figures in Mexican modern dance in the 1940s and 1950s but also in her innovative choreographies and performances of the 1930s. The *ballets de masas* in particular epitomized the interdisciplinary quality of the new dance initiatives, in their synthesis of artistic innovation with nationalist ideology, of high art and popular culture, and in the collaboration of choreographers, dancers, musicians, theatre practitioners, and muralists in large-scale productions.

For all the collaboration that marked these projects and the ideological emphasis on collective art, however, Campobello stands out in contemporary accounts as remarkably individualized, a commanding presence and strong personality.[9] As with other powerful women, descriptions assumed a larger-than-life quality. Felipe Segura, a dancer who worked with the Campobello sisters in the late 1930s and 1940s, highlighted Nellie's strong personality: "she was *the* director of the National School of Dance, *the* director of the Mexico City Ballet, *the* writer, *the* chatterbox, the one who monopolized the attention of the public, the journalists, the officials" (Segura, 8; emphasis in original).[10] Campobello fostered her imposing image, characterized herself in personal interviews as an Amazon, and revealed that her cultivated fashion style included wearing "pants like the soldiers of Genghis Kahn" and "walking like a beast."[11] Such imagery of physical prowess weaves through Campobello's first work—the small poetry collection *Yo, por Francisca*—in which the speaker configures herself as powerful, free (barefoot), playful, engaged with the land, and endowed with a strong body.

Campobello's 1927 entrée to Mexico City cultural life through dance, particularly as one of Miss Carroll's Girls, set the stage for these early literary guises. This apprenticeship epitomized the tensions between dance as high art and as mass culture and between the modern New Woman and the local *soldadera* or revolutionary woman marking Campobello's creative choices. Most of Miss Carroll's Girls came from well-heeled society, and the group frequently performed at charity functions or in private salons. But their aura of respectability and class also allowed a measure of mobility within the city's growing dance culture. Under Miss Carroll's tutelage, "nice girls" could perform in settings otherwise deemed unsuitable.[12] In fact Miss Carroll's Girls performed at commercial theatres and select nightclubs, and the members' photos appeared in product advertisements geared toward modern women.[13] While ballet predominated, the group's eclectic choreographic lineup exposed the members to classical, folkloric, and contemporary dance forms, including the middlebrow style of the musical review. Most important for Campobello's growing visibility in the city's artistic world was the strong presence of Miss Carroll's group in the widely read *El universal ilustrado*. This weekly offered a prime forum for proliferating images of the New Woman and for airing anxieties about changing gender norms. Weaving through the magazine were manifestations of the New Woman as variable as the young Greta Garbo and Miss Carroll's Girls. In June 1927 a review explicitly characterized the group's dancers as modern Eves, set free from gender restrictions by gymnastic body work (Noriega Hope, 32–33).[14]

As a member of the Carroll Girls, Campobello reiterated mass culture's conception of the athletic New Woman at the same time that she rendered her first performance of Mexican *machismo*, a cultural standard tied to revolutionary ideals through gender-charged debates about politically correct art. She frequently assumed male roles, including a boxer and a Mexican *charro*. Such crossovers were not uncommon for performing women in a post-Bernhardt era, and we can recall that Alfonsina Storni and Victoria Ocampo also assumed male roles on stage. Transgendered performance raises actor and audience awareness of gender instability. Women performing men, moreover, reiterate the power invested in the guise, at least temporarily. But while it is culturally embodied through gesture, attire, and voice, that power may be more than corporeal. Sarah Bernhardt attributed her predilection for male roles to the intellectual complexity invested in them by their creators and the potential for unlocking larger fields of exploration (*Art of the Theatre*, 139). Similarly, Campobello's repeated crossover performances gave her the opportunity for reflecting on the gender norms they highlighted. On several occasions in Miss Carroll's group she enacted a culturally specific maleness: the *machismo* inscribed in the folkloric figure of the *charro* in command of his woman, or *china*. Accompanied by photos of Campobello and her sister posing as these figures, a 1930 performance review detailed the power play: "Nellie, aided by her origins in mountain life, her taste for adventure, her silhouette, is the admirable man who reins in, pursues, vanquishes the woman, dominating her with a final show of joy" (quoted in Segura, 13).

The photos of this scenario freeze this story into a pose. A dance composition choreographed around character (as with the *charro* or *china*) relies on a mobile sequence of poses for telling its story. Sylvia Molloy conceptualizes posing as a destabilizing activity that "offers (and plays at) new sexual identities" ("Politics of Posing," 147). One could argue that performance does the same thing, as when a man performs a woman and vice versa. But while performance highlights the process of reiteration and deviation from (gendered) cultural scripts through motion, the pose captures a single posture or attitude at the moment of its assumption, intensifying its potential for discomfiting recognition.[15] In examining the cultural politics and homoerotic tensions of posing among turn-of-the-century Latin American *modernistas*, Molloy underscores their enmeshment in "hypervirile constructions of nationhood" ("Politics of Posing," 147). In a comparable vein, players in Mexico's cultural politics of the 1920s and 1930s construed the artistic proliferation of postrevolutionary images of *mexicanidad* as "virile" while assigning the label "effeminate" (and by implication "unpatriotic") to more style-conscious art freer of obvious Mexican referents. In this context, Campobello's assumption of the *charro* pose in a choreographed tale of *machismo* in action ostensibly affirms a gendered conception of Mexican ethnicity dominant in the late 1920s and early 1930s. But even in a context that represents *machismo* as patriotic, a woman posing as a man who "joyously" vanquishes another woman produces unsettling effects not found in conventional icons of nationhood.

The culture wars over so-called *literatura viril* and *literatura afeminada* were more than a litmus test for the patriotism or aesthetic value of certain ways of writing. The fact that they often enclosed personal attacks on writers known to be homosexual highlights as well cultural anxieties about gender roles during decades undergoing material changes in their everyday construction amidst both feminist activity and the coming out of gay writers in Mexican cultural life.[16] These changes, including women's greater visibility in the workaday world and social settings, generated in middlebrow media like *El universal ilustrado* a mix of critical imagery in columns, photo essays, drawings, and cartoons: the emasculating feminist, the masculine woman, and the emasculated, if not explicitly effeminate, male. Although comparable images peppered the weekly's counterparts in other Latin American cities, in Mexico this iconography of gender trouble was especially intense and ensnared in cultural nationalism. Mass media displayed a simultaneous fascination toward flappers and the New Woman and anxiety over their negative consequences for Mexico.

Through her work with Miss Carroll's Girls, then, Campobello's inauguration to public artistic life catapulted her into the cultural dialogue through which competing ideologies of gender identity, Mexican ethnicity, and nationalism and artistic form and production converged. As the terms of this debate permeated Mexican literary culture with contending standards for modern writing, a woman writer faced a curious set of options, beyond the conventions of lyric sentimentalism traditionally available to her. Campobello's casting as a modern Eve in *El universal ilustrado,* a figure celebrated as well in the vanguard rhetoric of Mexico's *estridentistas,*[17] aligned her with an alluring rendition of cultural modernity. At the same time, and whatever contortionism in verbal art and writing persona these choices might entail, postrevolutionary cultural nationalism offered the option to "write like a man" (*literatura viril*) or, were she to pursue a more vanguard style, to "write like a man writing like a woman" (*literatura afeminada*). For a woman actively seeking the "state of mind" of a writer, as she called it, Campobello's inaugural dance work constituted an apprenticeship in multiple posing: as the gymnastic modern Eve, as a (cross-dressed) virile *charro* emblematic of postrevolutionary *mexicanidad,* and, beginning with the mass ballet *30-30,* as a populist, masculinized female surrogate for the Revolution itself. Campobello transmutes this conscious assumption of attitudes allowed by the posing of dance into her writing: in a preference for synecdoche, which as I have argued in the introduction constitutes literature's performative stylization of character, and through a serial rehearsal—a trying on and taking off—of authorial personae. The critical turns and claims for creative autonomy of these writerly poses enact an intricate advance toward and retreat from prevailing ideologies of gender, ethnicity, and nation reiterated in her dance.

A *WOMAN OF LETTERS:*
DANCES WITH BULLETS AND IRON SONGS

In the 1960 autobiographical account that prefaces *Mis libros,* Campobello characterized her inaugural writing activity of the late 1920s as a world apart from the headline notices she was receiving for her dance (14). Her audiences would be surprised to learn, she had imagined, that the young woman they admired for her dancer's body harbored pretensions of a "woman of letters" (15). Campobello linked her initiation to both dance and writing to the corporeal freedom she attributed to a rural childhood of horseback riding and play. Becoming a dancer as an adult, she explained, constituted reclaiming "ownership" of her own "moves" (*Mis libros,* 10). But the unfolding account of her dance career in the 1930s depicts a gradual dissolution of that creative independence into a sequence of patriotic obligations as she traveled the nation with the mass ballets and other choreographic spectacles. While embracing the populism that construed these command performances for "the people," her chronicle highlights the control by a growing cultural bureaucracy, "the men who had the law" (*Mis libros,* 31). The lengthy poem "Estadios" underscores Campobello's ambivalence about the absorption of her creative efforts by a vast institutionalizing project. The dancer-speaker celebrates in heroic tones her travels from one regional stadium to another, but she concludes in the frozen pose into which the nation has transformed her: a "statue in silence" (*Tres poemas,* 39). In contrast to this story of creative mobility arrested in a patriotic pose, the preface to *Mis libros* offers the world of writing as a scenario in which Campobello could craft the "truths" about the Revolution that, she argued, needed to be told. Images of secrecy and detachment infiltrate the space of writing in her autobiographical account: the private crafting of *Yo, por Francisca* parallels spectacles with Miss Carroll's Girls, behind the public performances of the Havana sojourn lies the gestation of *Cartucho,* and writing *Las manos de mamá* in Morelia during a tour provides refuge from alienating patriotic *fiestas.* While the social world of Mexico City and her dance career constituted the "entry hall" of her life, she argued in an interview contemporaneous with *Mis libros,* the secluded upper story of her home and the adjacent roof provided the space for her "most intimate" writing and access to a "country beyond" (Carballo, 414). But at the same time that Campobello imagined writing as a private performance executed elsewhere, a concurrent determination to intervene in contemporary debates through original representations of Mexican reality that she billed as the "truth" drove her project as a writer.

Campobello fashioned this biography of her writing in *Mis libros* when her publishing career was actually nearing its end.[18] "Estadios" appeared in *Tres poemas* in 1957 and *Mis libros* in 1960. But this tension between writing as private enactment in a place removed and writing as engagement with the world had already permeated her work in the late

1920s. Molloy has cogently argued that a willful "relocation" to a *different* place" characterizes Latin American women's self-conception as writers during these years (Introduction, 107; emphasis in original). But a conception of writing as an activity that is simultaneously autonomous and immersed in life typifies vanguard portraits of the artist, for example the first-person fictions of Mexico's Contemporáneos writers.[19] Notwithstanding an apparent kinship with the more politically engaged *estridentistas* and dedicated chroniclers of the Revolution such as Martín Luis Guzmán, Campobello shared with Contemporáneos writers her search for the persona of an author and a distinctive style, the quest for "technique" and "discipline" that she highlighted in *Mis libros* (15).

Campobello published her first writing as a journalist, with columns on exceptional events and people in the widely read periodicals *El universal gráfico* and *Revista de revistas*. As with her dance, then, she came to writing through a bourgeoning mass culture. But the drive to a more independent art of living as a writer paralleled Campobello's immersion in the middlebrow. In describing her search for the "state of mind" of a writer, she took distance not only from the "sweet verses dedicated to butterflies, mountains, and friends" that upper- and middle-class young women were encouraged to write but also from the "vulgar attitude of serial literature," the common ambiance of commercial theatre, and the mass entertainments—bullfights, cockfights—that she regarded with disdain (*Mis libros,* 17–18). Instead, and much like the early artistic projects of her vanguard contemporaries Alejo Carpentier, Miguel Angel Asturias, Mário de Andrade, and, in Mexico, Xavier Icaza, Campobello's writing is marked by a cultivated autochthony as an antidote to modernity's mass culture, combined with an aestheticist attention to style and a self-aware authorial stance.

These vanguard affiliations notwithstanding, as a participant in literary culture Campobello presents a solitary figure. A familiar group coalesced around her dance projects: performers and functionaries of the National School of Dance and a range of other artists, including the muralist José Clemente Orozco and later the writer Guzmán. But as a writer Campobello never enjoyed even the temporary intellectual home experienced by her compatriot Antonieta Rivas Mercado in the Contemporáneos fold, Alfonsina Storni with Anaconda, Norah Lange with the Martinfierristas, Victoria Ocampo with *Sur,* Magda Portal and María Wiesse with the *Amauta* circle, Mariblanca Sabas Alomá with Cuba's Minoristas, or Patrícia Galvão with Brazil's Antropófagos. In Mexico the lines between writers of diverse orientations were not nearly so sharp as the polemics of artistic correctness suggest. While it has been argued that Guzmán's influence dominated Campobello's later work,[20] her writing evidences her eclectic literary affiliations. At the same time that the *estridentista* Germán List Arzubide helped publish *Cartucho* in 1931 and composed its preface, in the early 1930s Campobello collaborated with Contemporáneos writers Xavier Villaurrutia and Jorge Cuesta in the avant-garde Teatro Orientación, successor to the group's inaugural venture of the late 1920s, Teatro Ulises.[21] Moreover, although she always insisted that her writing bore no specific influences, her 1929–1930 visit to Havana brought Campobello into contact with major currents of international modernism: the poetry of Vladimir Mayakovsky and Lorca, Afro-Cuban art and the Africanist primitivism of the avant-gardes, and the Harlem Renaissance through Langston Hughes.[22] Hughes later translated samples of Campobello's poetry for Dudley Fitts's landmark *Anthology of Contemporary Latin-American Poetry* (1942), where she cohabited with the continent's major vanguard poets. In Cuba, José Antonio Fernández de Castro, a founding member of the vanguard Grupo Minorista (1923 to 1928–1929) and a promoter of innovation in Havana, hosted Campobello, encouraged her writing, and published it in the *Revista de la Habana*.[23] In 1936, moreover, she advised surrealism's most radical practitioner, Artaud, on his journey to the Tarahumara Indians in Chihuahua.

Building on Campobello's modern Eve dance performances, these crucial vanguard encounters play out in the experimentalism of her writing and her self-portrayal as a modern woman. In *Mis libros,* she accurately noted the residual romanticism of her early poetry in *Yo, por Francisca,* evidenced particularly in the woman-nature metonymy. But these poems already intimate Campobello's creative kinship with the vanguards in their short verses, sparse descriptors, and irregular versification. "Collar" reinforces the increasingly "elongated" silhouette of an absent figure who will never return with the typographic display of a vertical column of single words or brief phrases (*Mis libros,* 261).[24] The collection's lyric speaker displays a dynamism that evokes the modern Eve of Campobello's public persona for Miss Carroll's Girls, an androgynous, gymnastic mobility typified in "Juego" (Play), in which a clamorous, youthful collectivity "pound[s] . . . sidewalks" and "smash[es] pots" (*Mis libros,* 252).[25] The poems locate this power in the female speaker's rural origins and ties to nature, such as the "clarity" of a mountain's "dark corner" in "Yo" (*Mis libros,* 251).[26]

This contraposition of the modern world with a primal authenticity with which the speaker identifies typifies the vanguards' myth of origins, to use Rosalind Krauss's concept, as well as its specific location in the feminine, as noted by Rita Felski.[27] The collection also displays a paradoxically expansive and imploding poetic ego, a characteristic of much vanguard poetry and manifestos, most flamboyantly executed in Vicente Huidobro's *Altazor.* Thus the speaker in "Mi pobre grandeza" (My poor greatness) on the one hand celebrates a mind and body "inebriated" by greatness and hands capable of pulverizing trees and on the other apologizes for this audacity (*Mis libros,* 262–263). This apology also manifests an uneasy undercurrent in the collection: the speaker's ambivalent (dis)location in a predominantly male ambiance. The speaker of "Juego" joyously shares her prowess with an androgynous group of boys and girls. By contrast, "Tenacidad" portrays a lyric voice whose song is ignored or rejected by the male figures it persists in following.[28] As Campobello's inaugural literary affirmation, then, *Yo, por Francisca* offers a range of authorial guises and an incipient experimental mode. The collection also represents the first step in Campobello's strategic distancing from the media culture in which she had made her creative debut. The poems situate the creativity of their speaker not in the problematic Mexican modernity that generates her, but in an imagined primordial world that she equates in all her writing with the northern Mexico of her childhood. The title's paradoxical assumption of a pseudonym that is, in fact, the author's given name—the Francisca of her baptism—offers an antidote to the "Nellie Campobello" of her rising public persona and signals the increasing complexity of her identity as a New Woman and modern writer.

These moves anticipate Campobello's "8 poemas de mujer" (1930), also signed "Francisca." With an afterword by Fernández de Castro, this compendium of eight lyrical prose fragments appeared in the *Revista de la Habana* shortly after her return to Mexico in 1930. The autobiographical sequence explores Campobello's ambivalent artistic affiliations more openly. The eight segments tell the story of the narrator's emergence as a writer, highlight key creative choices, rehearse a series of authorial poses, and herald the genesis of *Cartucho* (1931) by presenting two of this work's anecdotes as the final two of the "8 poemas de mujer." The loosely knit narrative sequence also documents a self-styled modern woman's search for a disposition for writing, a concrete subject matter, and an appropriate style. The first two sections, "En mi Azotea en la Habana" (On my roof in Havana) and "Tarjetas Postales de la Habana" (Postcards from Havana) situate her in Cuba, while "La Llegada" (The arrival), "En las calles de Mexico" (On the streets of Mexico), and "Mi Cuarto" (My room) narrate the return home and the creative awakening generated by the Cuban sojourn. Section 6 showcases a well-known caricaturist as an artistic mentor for the narrator's emerging style, while the final two sections put the creative choices into action in two segments from *Cartucho,* which was published soon afterward. Stylistically, the pieces execute vanguard innovations, rehearsals of narrative structures that would culminate in Campobello's best work: short narrations beginning in *media res* with few coordinates of time and place, rapid accumulations of telegraphic images and short sentences or phrases, and an investment of creative power in the narrator's kinship with motifs of modernity and occasional cubist imagery. Framing the six initial sections is the authorial voice of a modern woman who, just as numerous male vanguardists discovered the New World during an eye-opening sojourn to the old, reaffirms her *mexicanidad* through a Cuban pilgrimage and return.

Her "8 poemas de mujer" represents the Cuba experience as a life-changing event in which the narrator's exposure to the impact of mass culture on women, the cross-cultural conflicts of gender expectations, and the celebration of black culture in art all shape her assumption of a cultivated *mexicanidad* and an androgynous identity. A series of author poses weaves through the compendium, an acknowledgement that a particular stance or "state of mind" as a writer, to recall Campobello's words, alters the perspective and version of an experience through writing. The composition's opening segment renders the narrator in a self-contemplating pose on the roof of her Havana dwelling, a site that anticipates Campobello's portrayal years later of her home's high point as the location of her writing and access to a "country beyond" (Carballo, 414). Here a futuristic metonymy of the narrator's body and the building blocks of modernization augment this earth-woman's strength: "Iron bars, streetcar rails, tubes, pieces of sun, squares of moon engrave themselves in my eyes and expand in my soul. Sometimes the rails sparkle like two great daggers in a heart, my eyes follow them to the end of the street and then they resemble two steel curtains on the land of my body" (133). As the passage continues, the figure takes shape as a dancer, the scene her rehearsal of a pose: "My body half hanging on the roof, my hands reddened by the pressure give me the appearance of a dancer conquering the sun, the backs of the houses in front give me the new rhythm for the steel dance that hammers in my brain" (133).

The more whimsical "Postcards from Havana" that follow open out the speaker into five alternative stances toward the same cross-cultural encounter: "As a Tourist," "As a Mexican," "As a Woman," "As an Artist," and "As a Friend." These five poses invest the narrator with the dispositions framing her experience. Collectively they highlight her intricate negotiation of the contending cultural expectations that traverse her identity as a Mexican woman writer. The first three postcards underscore the gender trouble marking tourist encounters and challenge the prowess of the performing woman on the roof. With a feminist appeal to modernity—"We're in 1930, Sirs"—the narrator resists the salacious *piropos* of taxi drivers and "dirty old men" and highlights with irony their characterization of her as a *mexicanita* (134). The postcards consider as well the estranging ostentation of difference generated by the cross-cultural eye that transforms a Mexican woman on the streets of Havana into "a little idol" (134). While "as a woman" the narrator problematizes the gender tensions in such cross-cultural recasting, "as an artist" she considers the creative potential of highlighting difference. Thus Africanist art exhibits provoke her ruminations on the international popularity of art by blacks and the representation of blacks in art. Evincing a preference for an autochthonous art that displays "six steel girders raised by two strong brown hands," the narrator responds to Afro-Cuban art with the pose of a self-aware Mexican, evoking, "with lowered eyes," the sound of the *jarabe tapatío* (Mexican hat dance), the lace flowers of her *tehuana* attire, and the rhythm of her *guaraches* (134–135). While the otherness of Afro-Cuban art stimulates the choices of local Mexican motifs that will culminate with *Cartucho,* the narrator's expression of solidarity with the Cuban laborers in "As a Friend" presages that work's populism.

The subsequent three segments consolidate the creative choices ascribed to the Cuban awakening. Set in the paradigmatic locale of cultural transitions, the customs checkpoint, "The Arrival" blurs the speaker's dual identity as a dancer-writer, as she defends her Mexican Victrola as a tool of her trade analogous to her typewriter. "On the Streets of Mexico" portrays, through a tourist's eye, the narrator's rediscovery of Mexicanness in Veracruz, while challenging the proliferating mass culture that would obscure it. Rejecting Parisian hairdos and modern fashions that compromise the "beauty of Mexican braids," the narrator embraces a poetics "embroidered" with the flowers of Xochimilco and of Indian hands laboring over water jugs and woven mats (136–137). The return to Mexico City intensifies the critique of homogenizing mass culture, as the speaker contemplates her room with new eyes. Her fashionable Japanese furniture, bric-a-brac, and doll collection negate her new art of "fresh streetcar rails and horizontal drawings" (137). Recasting herself as a woman reborn in Cuba who dislikes dolls, the narrator likens her roomful of them to a dance hall bazaar, separating herself from traditional conceptions of femininity and from her middlebrow performances as one of Miss Carroll's Girls. As she rejects the "sugared" substance of her dolls and traditional women's writing and the infantilizing moniker *mexicanita* acquired in Havana, she claims the more androgynous authorial pose forecast in her opening appearance on the Havana roof: "I am . . . a doll . . . who was born . . . across the sea . . . above a rail . . . a doll of steel . . . who cannot eat honey" (137; ellipses in original).[29]

"Massaguer as Seen by a Mexican Woman on a July Afternoon" frames these choices in a verbal caricature of a caricaturist, the renowned Cuban cartoonist Conrado Massaguer. Here the speaker selects what will become Campobello's signature characterization technique—the stylization of a single trait—from the very mass-culture bazaar she eschewed as a "woman of letters" (*Mis libros*, 15). Campobello had already exhibited a penchant for framing the strange in her journalism. The irony of her choice was apparently deliberate. Thus in the spirit of the artist she admired, the speaker in the epigraph to this segment of "8 poemas de mujer" assumes the position of the caricaturist behind the caricature, simultaneously secretive, revelatory, and critical: "playing hide and seek, with a paper smile" (138). Not only does this image anticipate the interplay between the (visible) child perspective and the (invisible) adult narrator of *Cartucho,* it also calls to mind the narrator's opening stance in that work as I described earlier: bunkered down under a table, poised to launch critical barbs. Appropriately, the two *Cartucho* episodes that conclude the "8 poemas de mujer" share key features. Both "Zafiro y su Hermano" and "Cuatro soldados sin 30-30" rely on synecdoche, the verbal caricaturist's performative exaggeration of a crucial trait or gesture: the "shoes like two houses being dragged clumsily" while worn by Zafiro and his brother, and the "trousers of a dead man" worn by the soldier with no rifle (138–139). Both pieces also include the hide-and-seek interplay of child and adult perspectives, as an encounter with death transforms the child's irreverent laugh into the critical dismay of the adult "doll" who can no longer sing with honey.

First published in 1931, *Cartucho: Relatos de la lucha en el norte de México* constitutes, along with *Las manos de mamá,* one of Campobello's major literary achievements. Told retrospectively in the first person, the short work presents a child's-eye view of characters and events in the northern Mexico phase of the Revolution as they traverse the narrator's world, directly or by word of mouth. With the double voicing of autobiographical narration, the account filters the child's perspective through the words of the adult, who expands on what the child saw or thought. Incorporated into the child's perceptions are the intercalated narratives that augment the narrator's tale with the words of family (above all her mother), neighbors, and soldiers. The first section of this tripartite work—"Men of the North"—includes seven short sketches of soldiers the narrator has encountered in person or by reputation. The twenty-one segments in Part 2—"The Executed"—focus on killings witnessed by the narrator, her mother, or others, and Part 3, "Under Fire," presents six reported accounts of action in the line of fire. An expanded edition of *Cartucho,* published in 1940 and anthologized by the author as definitive, augments the incorporated stories and collective sources, including a selection of *corridos,* but respects the original's narrative structure, content, and most important, narrative voice. *Cartucho's* collage-like disposition of scenes eschews plot conventions of time and space, and the segments easily stand on their own. This absence of hierarchical relationships in characters or events shapes the work's representation of the Revolution as a continuum and a collective experience in which none are heroes unless all are heroes. At the same time, the narration privileges the revolutionary role of northern Mexico and of Pancho Villa in particular. A defining feature of *Cartucho,* alternately praised and condemned in its time, is the uncommon juxtaposition of graphic images of violent death with the matter-of-fact fascination of the child witness.[30] The work's avant-garde style, akin to "8 poemas de mujer," underlies this effect: bold, cumulative imagery enhanced by the predominance of nouns and verbs, generally brief, matter-of-fact declarative sentences, and temporal references unmoored from clarifying contexts. The predominance of synecdoche in characterization juxtaposes the singular and the ordinary with a periodic inclination toward the grotesque. Together these stylistic features propel Campobello's prose. The account of Colonel Bufanda being killed in the middle of the street—"'That expanding bullet was well spent,' said the men who passed by"—typifies this style: "The pouch of his jacket, the left pouch, shredded like a rose, said my eyes, taking their bearings from the voice of the cannon" (937; DM, 26).

Equally striking is the work's paradoxical construction of a strong authorial persona through the narrator's circuitous self-portrayal. Critics have aptly highlighted the intricate relationship of *Cartucho's* narrator to its intercalated stories, a connection germane to its "collective" and "testimonial" quality.[31] But the novella also engenders a well-defined creative persona with a self-aware disposition toward the world she narrates and who assumes alternating stances of engagement and distance. Although the narrator seldom describes herself, her definitive presence in the opening scene—emitting a retort from under a table—underscores her centrality to the work, a feature reinforced with the reiterated first person in almost every episode. Gradual changes in the narrator's childlike perspective, from inquisitive observation to awareness of injustice, suffering, and the finality of death, provide the novel's sustaining thread and consolidate her as the work's central figure. In contrast to novels of the Revolution that catapult characters into the eye of the storm, in *Cartucho* the Revolution seeks out the child, and its protagonists, its fallout, and the stories it spawns overtake her world. Just as Campobello the dancer stood out as the star in the populist *ballets de masas,* so does *Cartucho*'s adult writer-narrator subject her tale and its incorporated voices to her willful artistic interventions. Notwithstanding the edition changes, this writerly presence remains consistent in both versions, and in fact, in the later edition it grows in corporeal substance and artistic authority.[32] The speaking adult and the observing child merge in the qualities they share as artists and in their shifts from a stealthy presence to outbursts of interpretive authority.

Recalling the multiple orientations assumed by the narrating observer of Havana in "8 poemas de mujer," the ironic guise of the child in *Cartucho* constitutes a deliberate, ironic pose assumed by an aspiring woman writer, a choice framed in the Havana experience by the introduction to the first edition. Here Campobello underscores the diminutives *muñeca* and *muchachita* (little doll and little girl) repeatedly assigned to her in Havana, even by Fernández de Castro, who encouraged her to write *Cartucho.* But as in Norah Lange's *Cuadernos de infancia,* this is no ordinary child. Much like the "doll" who no longer sings with honey in the "8 poemas de mujer," Campobello divests the observing child in *Cartucho* of the diminutive sweetness ascribed by cultural scripts to children and, in literary culture, to writing women.[33] Instead the pose of the child playing under the table harbors the critical potential of the unseen observer. Because of the cultural ascription of innocence, moreover, the mask of childhood itself allows the narrator autonomy and mobility unavailable without it, particularly for a woman. Thus *Cartucho* reinforces the opening portrayal of the child narrator as omnipresent and opinionated but barely perceived, listening to stories and observing events without being noticed (944). Just as the child suddenly reveals herself in the opening scene with a wise remark, so do the startling images of killing filtered through her eyes jolt readers with her presence throughout the work. Similarly, the adult narrator intrudes on the reader's experience of the account with periodic judgments repeatedly introduced by an intrusive *Yo creo,* "I think."

In *Cartucho*, the child is mother to the woman, who in this case happens to be a writer.[34] Just as Campobello's "8 poemas de mujer" situates the narrator's artistic awakening in her trip to Havana, so does *Cartucho* document the narrator's apprenticeship in human suffering, gender trouble, and the emerging power of her art. Framing their accounts of revolutionary characters or events, numerous segments of *Cartucho* tell a simple, pointed story of a change in the child's perceptions, an awakening to what lies beyond her initial wonderment at death. "Zafiro y Zequiel," for example, opens with the child squirting water through a large syringe at two Indian men who pass her house daily, laughing at their huge shoes. Shaken after they are shot, the narrator notes that the shoes are now only "hunks of black leather that could tell me nothing about my friends," and she breaks the syringe (934; DM, 19). Among such eye-openers, the shock of gender limitations experienced by a narrator self-portrayed as a *marimacha* (tomboy) who could fight with boys is crucial (937; DM, 27). Thus the child and her siblings watch anti-Villa soldiers tear up their house while the general abuses their mother at gunpoint; a subsequent encounter with the same officer provokes the now-adolescent narrator to imagine herself as a man with his own pistol who fires at the general (941). This episode links the child's quest for vengeance to the work's provocative title, *Cartucho* or (gun) cartridge, and a subsequent segment expands the title's metaphor by linking bullets with the *corridos* (collective ballads) that right history's wrongs, a liquidation of "debts" with bullets and songs (965).

Such metaphoric ties, performed through the rapid-fire, telegraphic sentences and narrative fragments of Campobello's signature prose style, cast the narrator's creativity as the product of revolutionary horrors and rude gender awakenings and intertwine the war's bullet power—as performed by Campobello in the *Ballet de masas 30-30*—to her own writing style. Thus, the General Rueda episode also offers the adult narrator's first textual self-revelation at the site of writing the memoir, *Cartucho*. The episode reverberates not only "two years later" when the family has moved to Chihuahua and the narrator sees Rueda, but also "one day, here in Mexico City" when the adult narrator reads a news report of his court martial and execution (940–941; DM, 33). Assuming the pose of the child avenging her mother's harassment, the Mexico City narrator launches "a child's smile" toward the executing soldiers who carry her "pistol with a hundred shots" in their hands (941; DM, 34). This androgynous move reclaims the power of those shots for her writing. These textual exposures of the adult narrator also locate the work's composition in a time and place that is simultaneously removed from the experience it recounts and linked to it through the child's metamorphosis into the adult writer. References to the narrator's imperfect memory highlight the fragility of this tie, but the creativity of her unfolding story reinforces it. Just as *Cartucho* portrays the child observer as an agile *marimacha,* so does the adult who forgets the precise wording of stories once heard still enjoy, like a dancer, an expansive kinesthetic memory that renders the Revolution through a choreography of bodily gestures, visual details, tones of voice, and sounds. As an artist in the making, moreover, the child displays a keen alertness to the individual styles of the storytellers crossing her path, as she admires one man's capacity to speak "synthetically" (929; DM, 6). Paralleling the child's ear for style, the adult underscores her work as a crafter of tales that, while collective in origin, are hers for the retelling. She highlights this creative control through references to the moment and place of her composition. Thus she imagines General Urbina receiving bad news: "Urbina, . . . his veins enlarged" and "opening his rolling eyes wide *would* emit a general's snort at that news" (948; my emphasis).[35] The narrator highlights her own inventive activity, implicit in the scene's conditional verb: "This is just innocent guesswork, thought up today" (948; DM, 48). This passage is from *Cartucho*'s second edition, but in both editions, the narrator employs the phrases "I think" or "I know that" to frame comparable scenes of her own imagining as supplements to reported stories.[36]

These scenarios showcase the speaker's self-aware fictionalizing as she transmits not what necessarily happened but what she affirms certainly might have happened. While the incorporation of more stories from multiple sources in the second edition reinforces the work's collective air, the later edition also augments the adult narrator's affirmations of control over the stories' telling. Thus she recasts the death of a soldier with a reputation for timidity: "I think he was very pleased to die . . . He embraced the bullets and held on to them" (956; DM, 66). In a strategic episode close to the conclusion, the narrator candidly identifies such imaginings as a writer's craft, first by framing the story of a character's death with an attributive "they say that" and then by augmenting the account with the generative "I think": "I think Pablo Mares stopped spraying bullets from his rifle . . . His blue eyes didn't close. His rosy face died little by little. His broad shoulders lay at peace" (961; DM, 76). Continuing, the narrator underscores her own intervention in the tale: "He never dreamed I'd write this rhythm-less verse to him" (961; DM, 76).

The sharpened presence of an already strong author's persona in the second edition of *Cartucho* enacts a resolute authority over how its stories will be told and anticipates Campobello's account in *Mis libros* that she had entrusted the publication of the work's first edition to List Arzubide only because he had promised it would appear *"exactly as it was written"* (17; my emphasis).[37] An epigraphic dedication to her mother that opens *Cartucho*'s second edition casts these tales as "true stories" in contrast to Mexico's "fabricated legends" of the Revolution, a claim reiterated in *Mis libros* that characterizes the tales as "historical truth" (17). But more than shoring up the truth status of her stories, the narrator's frequent use of "I think" for her own accounts in *Cartucho* paradoxically invests authority in her own versions while underscoring their status as fictions. The claim staked here, then, is for the authority to tell the stories as she chooses, the ultimate power of a writer. This conception of writing as the site of interpretive authority, strengthened in *Cartucho*'s second version, coincides in time with the onset of Campobello's disillusionment with the dance world. The work's location of the writer's activity in Mexico City, moreover, signals the narrator's distance from the rural setting posited as the source of her authority. Produced in the intervening years of *Cartucho*'s first two editions, *Las manos de mamá,* written in 1934 and published in 1937, both exacerbates and mourns the separation.

Set in the same childhood world and revolutionary era as *Cartucho,* this retrospective portrayal of the narrator's mother includes sixteen segments and an epistolary conclusion—"A Letter for You"—that addresses the deceased mother. The episodic structure, absence of a plot line, and autobiographical air resemble *Cartucho.* But *Las manos de mamá* possesses greater structural complexity and a more studied style, and here telegraphic phrases alternate with more lyrical prose. Shifts in the first-person voice from "her" to "you" for evoking the mother give *Las manos de mamá* a more pronounced experimental air. Even so, the novella enjoyed a smoother critical reception than *Cartucho,* probably because its mythification of the maternal, reduced violence, and lyricism appeared to conform to unwritten rules for women's writing.[38] But the work actually challenges such gendered divisions of literary labor and, as some have explored, recasts patriarchal conventions long embodied in the *Bildungsroman* to offer new ways of conceiving a national Mexican subject.[39] In comparison to *Cartucho,* and in Campobello's ongoing search for the "state of mind" of a writer, the narrator of *Las manos de mamá* is a more sharply drawn modern woman, mentored by a dancing mother. The work also intensifies the speaker's distance from the increasingly mythical northern Mexican life of her origins and underscores her dislocation within the modern cultural world she actually inhabits.

Las manos de mamá constructs an experience of loss, articulated by the narrator in an arduous return through memory to a distant childhood land where she gropes for orientation in time and place: "I am crawling on the ground, my hands are red, my face red, and the sun and my street—everything red like children's landscapes" (971; IM, 97). This self-portrait of the artist on all fours reiterates the narrator's opening pose in *Cartucho* and anticipates Campobello's description of her adolescent quest for the pose of a writer in *Mis libros* (45). Presaging the narrator's urban adulthood, *Las manos de mamá* counters her journey back in time with the story's relentless movement forward from the mother's youth to her daughter's childhood, adolescence, and young adulthood and the moment of the mother's death. Repeated family relocations accompany this trajectory, from the small-town life of Villa Ocampo, to the more urban Chihuahua and Durango, beset by fragmentary modernization.

Over the course of this odyssey, the narrator loses not only her mother but also a bond to origins forged through the mother-land link in a dancing figure whose gesturing assumed "the precise outline of the mountains" (973; IM, 101). A lyric epigraph in the language of the Tarahumara and occasional indigenous references reinforce the narrator's Spenglerian location of her creative apprenticeship in a non-Western, primal world. This opposition between (mother) nature and urban culture typifies the avant-garde's guiding fiction that, as Krauss aptly argues, equates creativity with origins: "originality becomes an organicist metaphor referring not so much to formal invention as to sources of life" (157). As Lena Hammergren observes, moreover, in the body culture that shaped modern dance in the early twentieth century, a strong tie to nature provided a common framing device (57). In this vein, and reiterating the autochthonous pose of "8 poemas de mujer," the narrator in *Las manos de mamá* portrays herself and her siblings as a preliterate "tribe" with "red hands" tied to the earth and ignorant of city life, "not even from books" (975–976; IM, 103, 105). The work contrasts this primitivist ambiance with encroaching change that marks the family's moves to a world "where the tram rails were nailed to the ground . . . shining with long reflections like daggers and making a grimace that was a cruel smile if we looked down on it from the roof" (975; IM, 104). As the narrative progresses so do these urban intrusions, in accounts of a "bitter city" that "shrinks the spirit" and "crushes . . . brain power" (986; IM, 123). Thus the power of the narrator's rural childhood derives above all from all that it allowed her to ignore in the chaotic urban world: fast-walking people, windowless homes, the "fetid atmosphere" of soirees inhabited by people with "pallid flesh" resembling "fish bellies" or "fetuses pickled in alcohol" (976: IM, 105).

In her dystopic rendition of the urban, the most striking feature is the narrator's intimate familiarity with a world she rejects in meticulous detail, a milieu that, as Elena Poniatowska has observed, Campobello herself knew and traveled well (160). The novella's penultimate segment—"When We Came to a Capital City"—leaves no doubt that this setting, and not the rural North, constitutes the narrator's quotidian experience. Thus the work's idealization of the Chihuahuan plains and inhabitants—"simple . . . free . . . strong, and agile like the mountain deer" (986; IM, 123)—reiterates what Rita Felski has termed modernity's "nostalgia paradigm." Moreover, in linking the narrator's mother to the indigenous, the work exemplifies what Felski identifies as the nostalgia paradigm's location of lost presence in the feminine (54–60). From a contemporary perspective, Campobello's portrayal of the Tarahumara resonates with racism: "ancient Indians, peaceful, sensitive, artistic, exponents of noble life, resigned by nature albeit without the civilization of the white man" (986; IM, 123).[40] She indeed partook in prejudices of her time. But in an analysis of literary modernism's "prehistoric woman" as a refuge from dislocation, Felski argues for a critical rather than conservative nostalgia whereby "yearning for the past may engender active attempts to construct an alternative future" (59).

Considered in this light, *Las manos de mamá* renders a nostalgic conception of the narrator's past as a critique of a specific situation—the dislocation of a modern woman—and imagines an alternative persona to those available to a Mexican woman in the 1930s. Thus the narrator transforms her mother into her artistic forbear, a retrospective projection of the creative persona she envisions for herself. Portrayed as both a dancer and a storyteller who encourages her children in "rhyming [their] steps" (988),[41] the mother provides a model for integrating verbal art with the body's performative power, a way to "own" one's "moves," as Campobello put it in *Mis libros* (10). Although here the mother reiterates cultural values assigned to women—physical beauty, caretaking, self-abnegation—she is also strikingly unconventional. In contrast to the frozen dance pose of Campobello's patriotic poetic speaker in "Estadios," *Las manos de mamá* casts both mother and narrating daughter as youthful women in perpetual motion. The narrator "run[s] with the wind" and calls to her mother: "dance for me, sing, give me your voice" (974). This mother-daughter duo reiterates the dynamism of the modern Eve in Campobello's early poems and public performances with Miss Carroll's Girls. At the same time, the narrator distances the mother's primal world, idealized as "ignorant of money" (986; IM, 123), from the commercial culture that rendered New Women as "little dolls."

As a chain-smoking, independent woman who moves in and out of the revolutionary fray, the mother reinforces the androgyny in all of Campobello's self-portrayals, as the narrator refuses to compare her to virgins or angels and likens her only to herself (983). The mother's sewing machine, with its "iron song," analogous to the "voices of the cannon," underscores this androgyny and a fruitful negotiation of modernity and, as with the metonymy of rapid-fire bullets and writing in *Cartucho,* points again to Campobello's own telegraphic prose. Countering the voracious machine-woman of international modernism, however, here a metonymy of woman-machine invests the mother with a productive power that contrasts with the lethal cannon.[42] Most important, the narrator draws her own art from this productive interaction: "*She* singing to the rhythm of the machine; the machine, a steely little girl in her hands, allowing itself to be led by her and her singing" (983; IM, 117; emphasis in original). This apprenticeship epitomizes the mother's approach to the education of her *marimacha* daughter, to whom, in the narrator's account, she offers the home schooling of "strong feet" and "agile legs" in lieu of schoolbooks and First Communion (987). Lacking the frivolities that Campobello ascribed to her anglicized training in Mexico City, here the narrator's no-nonsense education unfolds in the company of strong women, including an aunt who teaches her to read. But the critical element in the narrator's artistic apprenticeship is the mother's insistence on telling her children the kinds of stories she chooses: neither fairy tales nor ghost stories but the "real events" of the Revolution (974). Thus *Las manos de mamá* invests the narrator's artistic forebear with the same interpetive authority claimed by the adult speaker in *Cartucho* and by Campobello herself when she insisted that its first edition appear "exactly as it was written" (*Mis libros,* 17).

Nellie Campobello's unusual literary style and the unconventional poses assumed in her work attest to the fact that she did indeed tell some of her stories as she chose. But the critique of urban modernization unleashed in *Las manos de mamá* and the preface to *Mis libros* suggests that she did not succeed in telling all of the stories she had planned. In the early 1940s, she and her sister published a detailed study of indigenous dance forms, *Ritmos indígenas de Mexico* (1941), and a quasidocumentary tribute to Pancho Villa, *Apuntes sobre la vida militar de Francisco*

Villa (1940). But she never published several works in progress that could well have thrown more light on the story of a Mexican woman writer that weaves through her poetry and fiction of the 1920s and 1930s. These unfinished projects include a biography of Isidora Duncan, a collection of sketches of accomplished Mexican women, and, most intriguing, an epistolary narrative of her own experiences in Mexico City. In their absence, the preface to *Mis libros* and an interview she granted Emmanuel Carballo in the 1960s flesh out her story to inform us that the same woman who enjoyed a thriving performance career in the heart of Mexico's postrevolutionary artistic nation-building also characterized modern Mexico City life as a "simulation" (Carballo, 412) and argued that artistic innovation often served only to mask a fundamentally stagnant society (*Mis libros,* 22). Most important, Campobello repeatedly highlighted the negative impact of the forces of modernization on women, setting as favorite targets the superficial education and life choices available to middle-class women and the "modern custom" of showering them with ostensible privilege and praise, whose price was conformity to societal norms (*Mis libros,* 33). Writing constituted a particulary formidable challenge, she argued, as she described her own intricate negotiations with networks of male writers in order to publish her own work. What lingers from the totality of Campobello's self-portraits is that this woman who labored as a dancer in the heart of the city's official artistic world and enjoyed enthusiastic support of such notables as José Clemente Orozco and Martín Luis Guzmán never wavered in portraying her writing, protectively, as a covert activity rendered in an imagined "land beyond" of her own making. These images, along with that of the clever child narrator hiding under a table in the opening scene of *Cartucho,* may well construct a commentary on Campobello's experience as a woman writer in postrevolutionary Mexico City more eloquent than whatever her unfinished work might have offered.

chapter 5

"DRESSING AND UNDRESSING THE MIND"

Antonieta Rivas Mercado's Unfinished Performance

In the final weeks of her short life and from a self-imposed exile in Bordeaux, France, Antonieta Rivas Mercado (1900–1931) wrote four chapters of the novel *El que huía* (The fugitive). Here the Mexican novelist Esteban Malo decides to end his voluntary Parisian exile and react "in real life" to the problems facing his country in the early 1930s (*Obras completas,* 466). In her Bordeaux diary, Rivas Mercado described the chronicle of the José Vasconcelos presidential campaign that she was also writing as a comparable confrontation, a chance to "settle up with Mexico like a man" (*Obras completas,* 443). Rivas Mercado contemporaries knew her as an intelligent, learned woman with a commanding public presence. Her artistic and political activism and her writing, like Malo's anticipated Mexican return, constituted a rigorous encounter with the most important cultural debates of her day. But soon after she created this novelistic alter ego, she carried out a real-life reaction of her own: her suicide in the Parisian Cathedral of Notre Dame. Beyond the complex sources for such a deed, Rivas Mercado's final, tragic performance cut short her productive pursuit of the larger questions that shaped her life and work: What was the proper role of artists and writers in postrevolutionary Mexico? What viable roles did postrevolutionary intellectual life offer Mexican women? In a milieu that ascribed "virility" to cultural activism, how could an artist or writer "settle up with Mexico" as a woman rather than as a man?

Rivas Mercado's complete works, most of which appeared posthumously, testify to her intricate negotiation of the conflicts surrounding these questions. On one level, her multifaceted cultural activism laid bare the pulls typical of Latin American vanguard activity between self-reflective aestheticism and more immediate engagement with the world. As in the career of Nellie Campobello, the intense and often acrimonious postrevolutionary cultural politics of *mexicanidad* reinforced this tension. Rivas Mercado's short-lived economic independence, unconventional public profile, and radical ambivalence toward U.S. models of the New Woman further complicated her position, as did her enthusiasm for international artistic experiments in an environment dominated by nationalistic cultural correctness. Still, she pursued an active role in the artistic and political debates of Mexico City in the 1920s and sought a viable art of living as a Mexican writer that might somehow integrate her nationalist commitments, her penchant for artistic innovation, and her complicated options as a woman. The 1981 publication of her complete works generated critical studies that highlight the unresolved conflicts marking her life and work.

While not denying these conflicts, I want to argue here that her enduring engagement with performance constitutes a pivotal element for her public identity as a cultural activist and her speculative inquiry through writing. In searching for an intellectual and ideological position from which to intervene in the cultural debates of the day, Rivas Mercado rehearsed multiple public roles: cultural benefactor, *salonniere,* dance hall owner, theatrical artist-of-all-trades (actor, playwright, set designer), political chronicler, feminist commentator, creative writer, and unconventional New Woman. As a writer she navigated the conflicting positions that constituted the turbulent cultural field of Mexico City in the late 1920s: gendered debates about the role of writers and artists in postrevolutionary cultural missions, the appropriate artistic style and form for a Mexican writer ("virile" and realist or "effeminate" and experimental), and the viable public and personal roles for modern women. Through mobile conceptions of character and subjectivity, as a writer Rivas Mercado acted out the "collision of readings," to borrow Charles Lyons's term for the rehearsal of character in drama, that is, the ideologies in conflict that traversed her cultural world.[1] As with Campobello, her resolutions of these collisions often defied the polemics from which they emerged, leading to positions that were simultaneously "virile" and "effeminate," Mexicanist and internationalist, artistically innovative and politically engaged. Over time, Rivas Mercado became one of the most mythified of Latin America's women writers of this century, myths that intertwine the tragedies of her personal life with hyperbolic assessments of her actual achievements.[2] Moreover, in her hagiographic portrait of the renowned cultural figure José Vasconcelos, whose ill-fated election campaign she supported and chronicled, she collaborated in myth-making herself. But in her cultural activity and creative writing, Rivas Mercado more often than not challenged the received truths of gender, politics, and art circulating in the cultural world she inhabited.

THE MASKS OF CHARACTER IN LIFE AND ART

Rivas Mercado's renown derives primarily from two roles she played in Mexican cultural life between 1927 and 1931. She provided organizational and artistic stimulus, financial backing, and, according to one contemporary observer, the "soul" (Novo, 21) for the group of intellectuals who in 1928 launched the innovative Teatro de Ulises and later became known as the Contemporáneos, the name of the journal they published from 1928 to 1931.[3] She also supported the publication of novels by Contemporáneos writers, including Gilberto Owen's *Novela como nube* (1928) and Xavier Villaurrutia's *Dama de corazones* (1928),[4] and she helped finance and organize the Orquesta Sinfónica Mexicana under the directorship of composer Carlos Chávez. She also donated a large portion of her inheritance and energy to Vasconcelos's failed 1929 electoral campaign, and she was the meticulous chronicler of that undertaking. Luis Mario Schneider's edition of her writing, *Obras completas de Antonieta Rivas Mercado* (1981), a chapter in Jean Franco's critical study *Plotting Women* (1989), and Fabienne Bradu's biography, *Antonieta* (1991), generated overdue attention to Rivas Mercado's own work,[5] contributions recognized as well in the exhibition hall of the Mexican Museum of Modern Art and the theatre critics award that bear her name.[6] Even so, the dramatic details of her personal life rather than the substance of her intellectual career have shaped numerous creative interpretations of her life, in film, theatre, narrative, poetry, and paintings.[7] But Rivas Mercado's promising, truncated intellectual project provides a compelling counterpart to this tumultuous personal odyssey.

The daughter of a renowned architect for the prerevolutionary regime of Porfirio Díaz, Rivas Mercado grew up surrounded by her country's cultural elite. Drawing on a rich tutorial education and two extended Parisian sojourns, she was well versed in classic and modern European literature, Hispanic literatures, symbolist poets and French modernists (Gide, Valery, Verlaine, Baudelaire, Gourmont, Superville, Radiguet), contemporary Spanish writers (Juan Ramón Jimenez, Lorca, Ramón Gómez de la Serna, Ortega y Gasset), the politically engaged (Romain Roland, Waldo Frank, Trotsky), and the philosophical (Dostoyevsky and Nietzsche). She expressed considerable literary ambition, imagining not long before she died that she would become the first modern Spanish American woman playwright (*Obras completas,* 440), and her letters and Bordeaux diary propose an astonishing array of possible projects. The hybrid collection of her actual writings is more limited. In addition to the chronicle *La campaña de Vasconcelos* (The Vasconcelos campaign), it includes two plays (one incomplete), four stories, two essays, and a review of a feminist work, four chapters and a detailed outline for *El que huía,* a collection of eighty-seven letters to Manuel Rodríguez Lozano, and the Bordeaux diary. Rivas Mercado also translated André Gide's *School for Wives,* as well as several of the European plays staged by the Teatro de Ulises. This relatively small compendium of writings provides a revealing document of an intelligent woman's frustrated search for a viable role as a cultural activist and of the impact of her experiences with performance on her ways of understanding the cultural conflicts around her.

As a woman of class privilege, Rivas Mercado, like Victoria Ocampo, was broadly trained in multiple modalities of performance: poetry recitation, song, and classical dance, including ballet. She was particularly drawn to the theatre and to the most innovative trends, as she bridged the gap with ease between high art and popular culture. In Paris at an early age she was fascinated by the Guignol Theatre and Sarah Bernhardt's singular acting style (Bradu, 35). With Rodríguez Lozano she founded the Mexico City dance salon El Pirata, where the urban elite, out of place in the burgeoning middlebrow dance clubs, could embrace the contemporary crazes: the *danzón,* the tango, the fox-trot, and the shimmy.[8] The jazz of New York cabarets enthralled her as well. Her biographer proposes that during her second Parisian sojourn she most likely witnessed the dramatic experiments unfolding at Charles Dullin's Théâtre de l'Atelier, in which Antonin Artaud participated (Bradu, 74–75).[9] The Teatro de Ulises embraced a comparable workshop mode as members shared the preparatory work to their performances and established a close informal exchange with their audiences.[10] Beyond collaborating in every detail of the *mise-en-scène,* Rivas Mercado performed—with considerable success, according to reviews—in plays by Claude Roger Marx, Jean Cocteau (in the role of Orpheus), and Eugene O'Neill.[11] In 1929 she took charge of the set details for a staged version of Mariano Azuela's novel of the Revolution, *Los de abajo.*[12] During her 1929–1930 stay in New York, she met and became fast friends with Lorca, whose plays she wanted to translate into English (*Obras completas,* 403). With Lorca's help, she initiated negotiations with the New York Theatre Guild to stage nine Mexican and Latin American plays,[13] including an English translation of the dramatic adaptation of *Los de abajo.*[14] These activities nourished the two plays she authored. In her own ample performance activity and in her letters and diary, Rivas Mercado displayed a strong preference for experimental, antimimetic theatre, evidenced in her positive reactions to surrealistic Theatre Guild performances (*Obras completas,* 397)[15] and to the inventive plays that Lorca was then writing and to which she had access through small group readings and drafts.[16]

On one level, this propensity for theatrical self-consciousness marked the presentation and reception of Rivas Mercado's public persona. Numerous contemporary descriptions highlight a studied modern style, and male observations in particular evoke her presence as a self-aware performance. Vasconcelos's verbal portrait, for example, endows her with a certain modern agility and self-consciousness: "Dark, well made and *elastic,* exemplary of the fine native race, her power, on the other hand, lay in her spirit. With large, understanding eyes and appealing conversation, a certain *skeptical irony* seduced one, aggravated by the urge for frivolity that infected her turbulent post-war generation" (Vasconcelos, 718; my emphasis). Others focused on details of gesture and voice: "Black hair, combed back, coldly intelligent eyes, elegant, *she disguised her tall and slender figure* with the latest fashion extravagances of the mad 1920s. She wasn't beautiful, but impressive . . . *and even more when she spoke*" (Skirius, 97; my emphasis). Beginning in her youth, Rivas Mercado parodied Bernhardt (Bradu, 35). But in contrast to the pondered drama of a Bernhardt era, the reviews of Rivas Mercado's stage presence reveal more subtle attention to nuances of gesture and voice. The similarities between descriptions of her in ordinary life and onstage suggest the deliberate creation not only of dramatic characters but also of a public persona. A review of Rivas Mercado the actor for the Teatro de Ulises, for example, praised her style as both carefully executed and modestly subtle: "Antonieta speaks in a voice so simple that it just reaches the back of the room without filling it with useless resonance. Her hands . . . (does Antonieta have hands?) . . . move only when indispensable, in those moments when they need to move . . . The force of Antonieta's expression is in . . . the genuine gesture, in the expression of her eyes, of her lips, of her eyebrows that contract and expand like arcs" (El Joven Telémaco, 55). A similar portrait of the offstage Rivas Mercado by her Ulises colleague Xavier Villaurrutia highlighted her quotidian self-consciousness of gesture and word: "She has found a way of moving her hands when she speaks that matches her inflexible softness perfectly" (608).

Evidence abounds that Rivas Mercado greatly enjoyed the onstage opportunities of everyday life and that she relished the central position for an audience's attention. In Mexico City life of the 1920s, middle- and upper-class women played semipublic roles with a strong performative air, for example during "receiving days" when they entertained guests with food, conversation, song, or poetry recitation (Collado, 111). In a similar vein, Rivas Mercado gathered an audience around herself as hostess for the soirees of the Teatro de Ulises or when she executed grand entrances and danced the tango at El Pirata (Bradu, 127–128).[17] The young followers of the Vasconcelos electoral campaign also noted her habit of summoning them around her and her propensity for creating a circle in which she would occupy the center: "She was a most noble lady," one recalled, "whose sanctuary we would enter surrounded by the most religious discretion" (Magdaleno, 46). During her New York stay, she participated in the *tertulias* of the Hispanic artists and intellectuals living in the city and with them frequented the movies, the theatre, and cabarets. Writing to Rodríguez Lozano about these encounters, she noted that her own arrival had generated this circle, in which she had "automatically" become the center (*Obras completas,* 405). But Rivas Mercado often displayed a comparable capacity for serving as her own audience. Bradu observes that as a child she loved to dance in front of the mirror (37), and in a letter to Rodríguez Lozano about dances in a New York cabaret, her own performative abandon—"plastic," laughing, and a "complete fool" (*Obras completas,* 389)—provides the central focus of the tale. Her letters and diary highlight a pondered inclination toward imagining herself as others might see her. She also stressed the essential importance of this self-scrutiny through the eyes of another for constructing her own sense of self, for example as she wrote to Rodríguez Lozano that his gaze had "cleansed" her, invested her life with "a new sense of dignity," and "permeated" her life with meaning (*Obras completas,* 354).

This ostensible reliance on a male audience for validation hardly appeals to contemporary feminism. But it reveals Rivas Mercado's finely tuned understanding of the subtle shifts in gesture, attitude, voice, and the implicit relationship to an audience that shape individual identities. These understandings are consistent with a Bakhtinian view of subjectivity as a dialogue not only of words but also of perspectives, a drama always "*containing more than one actor*" (Holquist, 18; emphasis in original). In Michael Holquist's exegesis of Bakhtin, subjectivity is "the tale of how I get myself from the other . . . I see myself as I conceive others might see it. In order to forge a self, I must do so from the *outside*. In other words, *I author myself*" (Holquist, 28).[18] In Rivas Mercado's case, this process of self-creation is marked by a capacity for transformation, as one reviewer observed: "In interpreting Orpheus, Antonieta Rivas displayed herself in a different aspect from the previous ones and was able to be nimble, tenuous, almost impalpable: between a shadow and a spirit" (El Joven Telémaco, 65). Another review underscored her onstage talent for blurring boundaries between performance and life: "she lived her role so intensely that she succeeded several times in erasing the idea of the fiction and making it as if we were witnessing a real . . . scene" (Dalevuelta, 67).

This fluidity between staged scene and life constituted a self-aware rehearsal of the conflicting positions and perspectives that traverse the formation of a character, lived or theatrical. Rivas Mercado's palpable experience with performance also manifests itself in her writing through a process of authorization that she described in a letter: "In dissolving myself, I make myself, the incomprehensible process of creation" (*Obras completas,* 383). This process assumed a dialogic form through the "intimate conversation" of her letters to Rodríguez Lozano, a phrase she used to characterize a similar exchange in her incomplete novel, *El que huía.* Here the exiled protagonist Esteban Malo exchanges letters with his friend Salvador Dorantes in Mexico. This epistolary liaison resembles the literary conversation between Rivas Mercado and Rodríguez Lozano in what she called a "nurturing" exchange of novels, biographies, travel accounts, monographs, and poems (*Obras completas,* 294). In both cases the dialogue provides "integration . . . centralization, concentration" and "synthesis" (*Obras completas,* 360). This interactive conception of self-authoring also emerges in the dialogue of perspectives or ideas initiated in Rivas Mercado's writing through a series of fictitious subjectivities or lifelike positions that unfold through a performative process. This transition from Rivas Mercado's real-life performances to her writing underscores the interaction of body and language in her intellectual inquiry. Thus her two dramatic works constitute a testing ground for shifting ideological positions embodied in variable characters.

The one-act *Episodio electoral* examines the military manipulation of public opinion through the disposition of a political prisoner. The more extensive, though incomplete, *Un drama* represents the interrogation, torture, and trial of José de León Toral, assassin of the ex-president and presidential candidate Álvaro Obregón in 1928. These pieces possess a realist air, but their technical and scenic economy evokes the modern, self-reflective theatre that Rivas Mercado admired. *Episodio electoral* attributes a defining body language or voice style to each character: a prisoner with the nervous tic of picking bits of straw from his body, a general who obsessively caresses his pistol, an engineer whose voice shifts from incisive to opaque in an ironic manipulation of audience perception. This sharp awareness of the spectator underscores Rivas Mercado's sensitivity to position and perspective.

A similar understanding emerges in *Un drama,* which offers a more intricate notion of identity and individual autonomy. Rivas Mercado was fascinated by the real-life Toral and by his alleged collaborator, the nun Madre Conchita. A Catholic zealot, Toral had shot Obregón in the aftermath of the Cristeros rebellions against the anticlericalism of postrevolutionary governments. In her campaign chronicle, *La campaña de Vasconcelos,* Rivas Mercado painted Toral as a mystic believer of "rare moral stature" (*Obras completas,* 39) whose depth of commitment appealed to her activist inclinations. The play's more ambiguous portrayal, by contrast, links shifting identity positions to their performance.[19] On one level, the piece represents Toral and Madre Conchita as Antigone-like figures that, grounded in a higher law, hold to the belief that they are right. Onstage body imagery underscores Toral's martyr status, as stage directions call for him to stand before the altar with his profile toward the audience and his head down and periodically to bring his hands together (in prayer, one might surmise) (*Obras completas,* 214). But the work undermines this notion of unified character and rehearses alternate versions of Toral through other characters who enact competing disciplinary discourses: religion, criminal law, medicine, social work, and Mexican postrevolutionary politics. In this fashion, the play stages an interpretive struggle, a "collision of readings" to recall Lyons's term, less over events themselves (Toral's authorship of the fatal act remains unquestioned) than about how to characterize the responsible individuals. Thus Toral is variably cast as a "martyr," a "religious fanatic," a "penal character," a "victim" of his bad background, a "pacific" man, and a "defender of freedoms" (*Obras completas,* 199–247). Initial stage directions, which require that the audience not see Toral's face throughout the first act, intimate that he is in fact a blank slate whose character is to be shaped by his audience (*Obras completas,* 201–202). Most importantly, during the interrogations, stage directions characterize Toral through his resistant silence, a portrayal that constructs on the one hand the committed believer that Rivas Mercado described in the Vasconcelos chronicle but on the other the man whose identity will only emerge dialogically through interaction with his audience, as he begins to move and speak. Stage directions marking this moment provide an image strikingly similar in its focus on understatement of voice and gesture to the descriptions I have cited of Rivas Mercado's own studied demeanor, suggesting that this character, too, is self-contemplative and self-authored through an "intimate conversation" of perspectives. Thus, as Toral starts to testify, he is to remain calm and serious and to speak in modulated voice "without exaltation," much like a "dispassionate spectator" (*Obras completas,* 237).

Rivas Mercado's prose fiction offers a comparable performative inter-play of perspectives and shifting identities. On the surface, even her most politically committed writing, the Vasconcelos chronicle, deploys the dramatic metaphor, for example in references to the "farce" of democratic elections, Mexico's "tragicomedy," the "pantomime" of its military in-terveners, the "ornamented operetta figurines" embodied in its *caudillos,* or the Mexican public as "actor and spectator" of the aborted electoral process (*Obras completas,* 37, 36, 38, 41, 70). More profound is the sensitivity to the performative connections between identity, voice, and perspective that characterizes Rivas Mercado's short stories and unfin-ished novel. Even the more intimate letters and diary rehearse a range of personae. Notwithstanding Villaurrutia's complaint that her demeanor was always the same—Rivas Mercado "has only one tone of voice and one tone of the spirit" (608)—the speaking voices in her prose parallel the shifting characterizations of Toral in *Un drama.* Moreover, as a writer she deliberately assumed distinct voices for diverse projects, a choice that bespeaks the agency of the chooser.[20] As she explained in her diary, she would write two different texts on postrevolutionary Mexico: one the campaign chronicle, the other a novel. For the former, which she described as an arduous patriotic duty, she would assume the voice of an "intelli-gent and pained observer" and seek a unified account of events which, in and of themselves, she confessed, moved her little (*Obras completas,* 443). The novel, by contrast, would open up multiple perspectives and through manifold character positions would allow free rein to her prefer-ence for acting out over telling. She noted that she was far more interested in creating events than in narrating them (*Obras completas,* 443).[21] Thus the reader of her prose experiences a kind of "taking on and putting off ideas," to recall Herbert Blau's phrase for a performance (*To All Appear-ances,* 41), a masquerade of quick changes in narrating voice and perspec-tive in which the authorial persona divides herself not so much between body and soul (as many have suggested about Rivas Mercado's own life)[22] as among subjectivities that embody the conflicting views she entertained in search of an intellectual anchor. Nowhere is this process more evident than in Rivas Mercado's writings about women.

RIVAS MERCADO'S MEXICAN WOMAN: A "COLLISION OF READINGS"

Rivas Mercado's radical ambivalence about women's roles materializes in the contradictions between the relative autonomy and nonchalance toward convention with which she lived and the irresolute feminism weaving through her writing. Two works that she selected for translation exemplify this deep division. André Gide's *School for Wives* (1929), which she translated into Spanish with Villaurrutia, presents the epistolary, first-person account of an upper-class woman's metamorphosis from the self-effacing adulator of her new husband to a critically thinking, mature woman who, in rejecting him, challenges romantic love and marriage and exposes women's subordination of themselves. Otto Weininger's *Sex and Character* (1903), on the other hand, a work that she wanted to translate, offers pseudoscientific study of "characterology" that, while extolling the qualities of emancipated, literary women poses the essential moral and intellectual inferiority of most women, along with homosexuals and Jews. The indecisiveness about women's nature and place embodied in the unlikely combo of Weininger and Gide manifests the contentious conversation about gender circulating in Rivas Mercado's postrevolutionary cultural world. The Mexican feminist movement of the period found less common ground among its participants than contemporaneous feminism in Argentina, Cuba, or Brazil. The postrevolutionary governments consistently subordinated women's issues to nationalist concerns, and feminism itself focused more on "the Mexican woman" than women in general (Miller, 76). This nationalist subtext permeated the alternately adulatory and critical images of the New Woman in mass-circulation periodicals. The cover art for a June 1927 issue of the widely read *El universal ilustrado,* for example, projected the message that women adopting new ways might betray their *mexicanidad:* here a young Mexican woman (with male companion) sporting the cropped hair and short skirt of the New Woman buys flowers from a forlorn-looking Indian mother and her barefoot child.

The mixed messages about modern models of women's behavior in Rivas Mercado's work rest in part on such nationalist concerns. Her essays on women, "La mujer mexicana" (The Mexican woman) and "Ideales de mujeres: Maternidad vs. igualdad de derechos" (Women's ideals: Motherhood versus equal rights), reveal strong admiration for modern women of the United States, whose liberation she overestimated.[23] But she took distance from them on the terrain of cultural identity. She condemned U.S. intervention in Mexican political life. A strong dose of anti-American *arielismo,* with its position on the spiritual superiority of Hispanic cultures, permeates her writing, and her utopian discourse of ethnicity in some way resembles Vasconcelos's "cosmic race." She observed, for example, that in contrast to Anglo-Saxons, Latin women (and she included the French in this category) descended from a long tradition of moral values different from those of the United States or England (*Obras completas,* 324), and she attributed these values in part to a Christian heritage.[24] Rivas Mercado actually had limited contact with Mexico's political feminists, although she praised their support of Vasconcelos. But although she argued that Anglo-American feminism could not take root in Latin America, in the essays on women she espoused quintessential feminist views. Much like her successor Rosario Castellanos, she invoked Sor Juana Inés de la Cruz as her mentor and alluded to critical studies she was writing on Sor Juana and La Malinche. The piece on Mexican women affirmed that their behavior rested on a "strange concept of feminine virtue" based on "'not doing'" (*Obras completas,* 319). Similarly, she launched a polemical critique of women's self-subjugation in relationship to men. Without a life of their own, she wrote, they depended on the men they followed "not as companions" but rather as "subject[s]" to their "will" and "whim." The result, she added, was that men neither esteemed nor respected women who took refuge in their ostensible "goodness" (*Obras completas,* 319). In the same essay, Rivas Mercado supported universal female education in Mexico comparable to that of the United States and lobbied for a feminine form of logic or analysis or, in its absence, the adaptive appropriation of male models (*Obras completas,* 313). Although her contact with working-class or indigent women was framed by her upper-class origins, her commentary was noticeably sensitive to experiential differences of Mexican women from diverse backgrounds, and she resisted the temptation implicit in her title "La mujer mexicana" to produce a unified account of "the Mexican woman."[25]

Along with these relatively progressive ideas, Rivas Mercado shared gender biases of her context. She proclaimed that the only interesting idea in *En torno a nosotras,* by the Spanish feminist Margarita Nelken, was the affirmation that women should showcase their difference from men (*Obras completas,* 313). This difference feminism rested on essentialist notions. Women's singularity, she argued, derived from their valuable "intuitions," drawn from their "intimate contact with vital forces" inaccessible to men (*Obras completas,* 320). She also reiterated the doctrine of social motherhood widely espoused by Latin American feminists: the ultimate value of more liberated, active Mexican women would derive from their dedication through marriage and motherhood to creating better men. But motherhood in Rivas Mercado's writing is also the site of a particularly intense interpretive struggle. While she declared that Mexican women should educate themselves to better support their husbands and sons, her own mothering was less conventional, as when she took her son on the Vasconcelos campaign trail. In letters to Rodríguez Lozano, she described a novel, suggestively titled *La que no quiso ser* (She who did not want to be), whose central character would be a "sensual and terrible mother" (*Obras completas*, 419). The Bordeaux diary includes a list of projects in progress on motherhood, a vertiginous enumeration of identities in conflict: the "animal" and possessive mother who "devours" her son, the "virgin," "lover," "transcendent," and "intellectual" mothers and the "Mother cat who eats her kittens" (*Obras completas*, 444–445; 461).

Rivas Mercado staged these maternal identities in conflict in her short stories protagonized by Mexican women. Because of her own stormy divorce and custody battle, they are often read as literal biographical sources.[26] Without denying the productive interaction of fiction and biography, however, the strategies of narrative voicing and perspective constitute three of these tales—"Equilibrio" (Equilibrium), "Páginas arrancadas" (Pages ripped out), and "Incompatibilidad" (Incompatibility)—as a fictionalized inquiry into women's conflictive roles. Their performativity lies not only in the theatrical qualities of the prose, including scene construction through stage direction-style phrases or dominance of scene and speech representation over summary, but also in the distinct style in which each is written. Stylization in narrative, as Bakhtin argued, constitutes the palpable manifestation of diverse speech representations and multiple voicing ("Discourse Typology in Prose"). Such style shifts discourage reading these stories as direct autobiographical accounts and underscore instead the varied experiential positions they perform. Rather than a unified account of feminine subjectivity, collectively they offer a speculative "collision of readings" embodied in the dramatic rehearsal of character.

"Equilibrio," for example, presents in a sparse, realist mode a traditional family's tale in which the father controls the mother and daughter, while the mother, without overtly disagreeing with her husband, gives the daughter license to go dancing with friends. As a consequence of this transgression, the daughter eventually runs off with a divorced man, a disastrous fate in the story's worldview. With stage direction-style phrases the story constructs highly visual scenes that reinforce the thematic focus on performance, in this case dance, as a potential source for women's liberation, albeit with a high price. On one level, this story constitutes a kind of morality play about the tragic consequences of marriages in which men and women neither communicate nor share authority over children. But although the tale unfolds in a conventional third-person narrative, through free indirect discourse the reader perceives primarily what the mother sees and hears. Evoking Rivas Mercado's own periodic release through dance, this perspective enacts a radical ambivalence toward the New Woman as a liberationist role model for Mexico. In forbidding her to dance, the father shelters his daughter from the modernity he portrays as the century's "contagion" (*Obras completas,* 257); in allowing her to dance, the mother undertakes an ostensibly liberating act for herself as well as her daughter but loses her daughter to an uncertain fate.

While this story presents the tale of a traditional mother with little autonomy in her marriage, "Páginas arrancadas," the composition most often treated as biography, lays out the first-person account of an emphatically modern woman. Through the intercalated narration of a diary that recounts events as they have just happened, the story depicts a failed marriage, quarrels and accusations of infidelity, and the narrator's lack of love for her husband. It includes a scene in which the husband burns the wife's books, a scenario that Bradu offers as a factual event in Rivas Mercado's biography and that Carlos Saura incorporated into his 1983 film *Antonieta.* But the narrative unfolds in a more studied, consistent style than the author's actual entries in her diary or personal letters to Rodríguez Lozano. These qualities, along with references in the story to the act of writing a diary, underscore Rivas Mercado's self-aware assumption of a specific authorial persona and narrative style to enact one version of a Mexican woman's experience.

"Incompatibilidad," Rivas Mercado's most theatrical story, also offers her most effective narrative enactment of this contested ground. This *mise-en-scène* of ambivalence constitutes a process of self-authoring in Bakhtinian terms in a dialogue of self-contemplation from three perspectives. The narration of the opening scene resembles the stage directions for an expressionist drama of shadows and murmurs as it describes "two women, two forms" who sit quietly in "semi-darkness" from which "women's voices" emerge (*Obras completas,* 265). A dialogue follows between giving voice and keeping silent, as one woman speaks of the failure of her marriage, her passions, and her yearnings for a suicidal escape, and the other, invoking religion, urges stifling such thoughts and attending to daily responsibilities. One voice suggests that the other is merely her echo. Just as a third woman awakens to discover that this conversation has been only a dream, a variation on the opening scene intimates that, through this Freudian dream-work, the speakers have enacted conflicting personae of the same woman: "the enlaced modulations of a single rhythm" (*Obras completas,* 268). The woman who awakens recalls having read a newspaper account of a divorce immediately before falling asleep. As she regains self-awareness, she recognizes her own red shoe and gray silk dress, garments that suggest a liberating evening of dance.

But the critical detail in this story surfaces during the dream dialogue when the woman voicing unspeakable thoughts is asked about her love life and the narrator personifies her response through an abrupt gender shift: "—Are you in love? / The answer was a *young male warrior armed* with all of his weapons. / —Not yet; I will love" (*Obras completas,* 206; my emphasis). In Spanish, the gender crossover emerges through grammatical inflection: "la respuesta fue *un joven guerrero*" (my emphasis). In the environment of this sentence, "una joven guerrera" (a young female warrior) would have worked equally well, but Rivas Mercado chose the masculine form. This gender cross-over is far from casual. The protagonists of the three stories I have just described are all Mexican women, and the tales focus on their vicissitudes as wives, mothers, or doomed lovers. As a group they struggle with the passivity—a "not doing"—that, as I have noted, Rivas Mercado ascribed to Mexican women (*Obras completas,* 319). In this context, the move toward the masculine inscribed in a woman's protest in "Incompatibilidad" is key to Rivas Mercado's critical account of women's roles in Mexico. The only truly active woman in her fiction is Madre Conchita, the nun portrayed in *Un drama* as the "intellectual co-author" of Toral's assassination of a corrupt president. Rivas Mercado also portrays her as an imposingly masculine woman, tall and large, with short, manly hair (*Obras completas,* 213). Significantly, this autonomous woman appears in a work focused not on women's roles but on the integration of ideas and action. This question—how to combine a life of intellectual reflection with critical engagement in the world— constitutes the central concern in Rivas Mercado's writing from 1929 to 1931. The gender tensions manifested in "Incompatibilidad" permeate this inquiry as well.

A "SPY OF GOOD WILL": THE ART OF A CULTURAL ACTIVIST

The problem of intellectual activism provides the central theme of Rivas Mercado's unfinished novel, *El que huía.* While she regarded the Vasconcelos chronicle as an unfinished piece of patriotic business, she esteemed *El que huía* as her most important project. As in the short stories about women, the novel enacts a contentious dialogue of perspectives through multiple character masks. But in a transferal of both gender and culture, Rivas Mercado performed this debate in the guise of two Mexican men and two U.S. women, underscoring the tensions of gender, politics, and art that shaped her search for an intellectual position. In the nationalist climate of postrevolutionary Mexico in the 1920s, as I have observed, the Contemporáneos writers with whom Rivas Mercado made her cultural debut sustained attacks for an aestheticism labeled as "effeminate," their interest in international currents, and their resistance to facile signifiers of *mexicanidad*. Rivas Mercado shared these preferences, particularly during her peak engagement with the Contemporáneos group, as evidenced in her many modernist readings and her translations of Gide and European playwrights and affirmed her antipathy toward the art of local colorism that she referred to as literary *jicarismo*. Her propensity for masking, moreover, constituted an apt bond with the Contemporáneos writers, some of whom negotiated their coming-out as homosexuals—particularly in their writing—with leadership roles in the growing cultural bureaucracy.[27] At the same time, through the Vasconcelos campaign Rivas Mercado intervened in political life, and her efforts to disseminate Mexican drama and art in New York bespeak the nationalism marking her literary thinking. In the context of these ostensibly incompatible interests and commitments, she struggled on the one hand with how to communicate Mexican experience without an affected regionalism and on the other with how to reconcile literary inquiry with political activism. Rivas Mercado staged this debate through the multiple positions embodied in her novel characters. Comparable to the construction of Toral in *Un drama*, this process reveals the irreconcilable views that traverse Rivas Mercado's intellectual posture.

Combining the four chapters that she completed—"Sobremesa" (After-dinner conversation), situated in Paris, "Tren de barco" (Boat train), "El trasatlántico" (The transatlantic), and "Nueva York"—with the detailed narrative plan provided in her letters and the Bordeaux diary, we have a pretty clear idea of what the completed novel would have been like. In the first chapter, the novelist and intellectual Esteban Malo converses with a group of artists (a Russian, a Frenchman, and a Spaniard) about the problem of creating a viable Mexican and Latin American literature. This exchange reproduces the incandescent debates about "autochthonous" versus "universalist" (essentially European) art circulating in Mexico and the rest of Latin America at the time and responds specifically to observations on the subject by the Mexican intellectual Alfonso Reyes in the 1930 essay "Un paso de América," published in his journal *Monterrey*. Reyes had argued that recent Mexican literature, including works such as Azuela's *Los de abajo* and Martín Luis Guzmán's *El águila y la serpiente* that focused on Mexican reality and more modern, less locally specific writing by Contemporáneos writers, had successfully overcome the mediocre exoticism or "local color" plaguing early Mexican writing (Reyes, 275–276). Reacting to this essay, Rivas Mercado wrote in the Bordeaux diary that she wanted to transpose into the characters of her novel the debate that Reyes's "platitudes" about "local color" had generated in her (*Obras completas,* 448). While sharing Reyes's views on the insufficiency of literary localism, Rivas Mercado's diary reveals that she wanted *El que huía* to avoid both superficial autochthonism and the kind of modern experiments she had supported for the Contemporáneos writers and now viewed as insubstantial.

Rivas Mercado imagined a new kind of novel that would capture "what was most purely Mexican" (*Obras completas,* 421). Similarly, in order to come to terms with his country and write a more authentically Mexican novel than his first work, Malo in *El que huía* returns to Mexico via New York, reversing the itinerary of Rivas Mercado's own pilgrimage to France. On the ship-bound train, Malo reads a letter from Salvador Dorantes, an equally learned but more activist friend who is an orator for a Mexican election campaign. On the ship, Malo meets the seductive New Woman Joel Nolan, a dancing American blond, with whom he spends time in New York. A letter from her sister to Joel introduces the reader to her more intellectual twin, Frances Nolan, who is in Mexico completing a doctoral dissertation titled "The Relationship between Strong Peoples and Weak Nations." The novel plan suggests that in Mexico Malo will have a love liaison with Frances and, launching himself into political action, will suffer a violent end. For her part, Frances will chronicle Malo's death, as Rivas Mercado did with the Vasconcelos campaign, to share the episode's "truth" with the world. She will also, as Rivas Mercado did in the campaign's aftermath, lose her illusions and face her own country in a new way. But, as Rivas Mercado was ultimately less able to do, her fictive character Frances will face the future with hard strength, like a "mountain on the move" (*Obras completas,* 421).

As in Rivas Mercado's other works, the novel draws its characters in performative terms through gendered inflections of voice and gesture. Thus the aesthete Esteban Malo possesses a "plastic" countenance, another character speaks with a pasty voice, and Malo's activist friend Dorantes writes with a "virile hand" (*Obras completas,* 280, 292). Joel Nolan, the "cold and perverse" New Woman, dances the tango and executes staged entrances that recall Rivas Mercado's at El Pirata. She lights her own cigarettes with "masculine" gestures and, recalling Rivas

Mercado's self-portrait in a New York cabaret, dances with abandon (*Obras completas,* 288, 297). Comparable to Rivas Mercado when she wrote *El que huía,* Malo, as the novel opens, is removed from the action in his own country, and the narrative portrays him as a spectator yearning to participate. Most important, Rivas Mercado characterizes him with the gendered rhetoric of her time: "Malo is never a determining agent, but rather essentially feminine; he receives impressions, he doesn't provoke them" (*Obras completas,* 466). Dorantes, by contrast, "active" and "virile," writes that reading the "precious trifles" of Gide and Cocteau recommended by his friend is merely an idle pastime in his career as political orator (*Obras completas,* 292). A similar opposition marks the two women: the "vague" and intellectual Frances and the sensual, aggressive, and masculine New Woman, Joel.

These characters are consistent with the modern "types" that Rivas Mercado affirmed in her diary she wanted to portray (*Obras completas,* 421). But the novel's staging of the debate between art and political engagement assumes more complexity than these oppositions suggest. In fact, the work and the plan for its completion exemplify a drive less to choose between the activism of body and words than to conceive writing and intellectual work, like performance, as acts. Thus, the activist Dorantes dedicates his literary talents to his political oratory, and the Bordeaux diary conveys that Frances Nolan will abandon her dissertation and dedicate her intellect to writing truths as she sees them. These characters embody Rivas Mercado's affirmation in her Bordeaux diary that the proper labor for a writer was not to reflect but to intervene (*Obras completas,* 449), a view that intensified with her reading of Trotsky's autobiography. But her short story "Un espía de buena voluntad" (A spy of goodwill) provides a more developed image of the committed aesthete who directs his genius to a social cause. In its stylistic simplicity and allegorical air, this tale has the quality of both a children's story and an artistic manifesto. The protagonist is Cornelio, a youthful poet with an androgynous air possessing many qualities we find in the self-portraits of Latin American vanguard writers: his playful spirit, his coming of age in the World War I era, his European training and internationalist orientation, his propensity, like Huidobro's Altazor, for flight, and his iconoclastic way with words. Cornelio, the narrator explains, "played with the weight of words, with the rhythm of verses" (*Obras completas,* 215). But much as the protagonists of a vanguard portrait of the artist, Cornelio descends to the world as an orator who professes "the truths of the spirit" (*Obras completas,* 252), a more developed version of the character Dorantes in Rivas Mercado's novel.

Cornelio and Dorantes both resemble the youthful, learned orators allied with the Vasconcelos campaign, in particular Germán del Campo. After his assassination, del Campo was transformed into a martyred symbol of the students who participated in the Vasconcelos campaign. Although Bradu argues that he was actually the least capable orator in his cohort (160), Rivas Mercado, in her campaign chronicle, invested him with an iconoclasm of ideas and language that resemble her fictional Cornelio. Del Campo, she wrote, "had the fresh and rosy skin of a little boy, eyes brilliant with illusion, golden locks, *rebellious toys* of the breeze . . . His familiar chatter evoked more than one of those *piercing mistakes that unsettle*" (*Obras completas,* 143; my emphasis).[28] Cornelio's greatest importance in Rivas Mercado's fictional world lies in the talent that allows him to bridge the gap between art and action. Thus the story portrays him simultaneously as a verbal performer whose power with words can move others to action and as a more speculative and detached observer, a spy who watches with goodwill and collects "whys" (*Obras completas,* 254). In this sense, Cornelio embodies the performing cultural activist, balanced between reflection and action, most akin to Rivas Mercado's ideal for how she could intervene through writing (*Obras completas,* 449). As she mapped out her own intellectual project in the Bordeaux diary, she imagined a comparable balance for her own two works and hoped to publish them simultaneously. Thus the campaign chronicle would direct her verbal talents to a political stand of "exaggerated sobriety" (*Obras completas,* 451).[29] The novel, by contrast, would give rein to her "doubts and disquiet" and in its conclusion leave open multiple perspectives in a speculative inquiry akin to Cornelio's penchant for collecting whys. Like Cornelio, moreover, Rivas Mercado conceived of her own writing as a performance, a taking on and putting off of ideas, to recall Blau's term. "The phrase," she observed, "*dresses or undresses the mind*" (*Obras completas,* 463; my emphasis).

Even as she sought harmony between them, Rivas Mercado's diary ruminations on the chronicle and the novel reveal an unresolved struggle between action and critique whose synthesis she was ultimately unable to perform as a Mexican woman. In the writings of her final months, the novel chapters and the Bordeaux diary, the unsettled conflicts of gender and art merged in a failure to imagine their resolution within either the feminine or masculine terms of the period's discourse of gender. The novel's Russian character, Plekanoff, conceptualizes artistic action metaphorically as a *machista* act of sexual dominance,[30] and the "virile" orator Dorantes offers a comparable "manly" model of artistic activism. But the novel devotes far more attention to its transgendered characters, those who, notwithstanding authorial intentions, appear to enact elements of Rivas Mercado's experience most closely. The more effeminate protagonist Malo, like Rivas Mercado and unlike Plekanoff or Dorantes, reveals deep conflicts about his public role and, like her, unburdens himself in the "intimate conversation" of his letters.[31] Joel Nolan, although portrayed as cold and perverse, embodies the performing New Woman whom Rivas Mercado sometimes imagined herself to be. With the androgynous spirit of the "spy of goodwill," Cornelio, the novel portrays these characters in gender-bending terms, as with Madre Conchita in *Un drama* and the woman on the verge of acting in "Incompatibilidad." Malo, through whose masculine eyes we perceive Joel Nolan as an object of seduction, is in other arenas "essentially feminine" (*Obras completas,* 466), and the modern woman Joel, with a masculine name, is both the object of Malo's seduction and, as I have noted, the agent of masculine gestures. Most important, Malo's reaction to Joel highlights the total absence of Mexican women in the novel's fictional world, as he observes that she represents a "complete affront" to his masculinity, and he resolves to seek out in Mexico a "reserved," "modest," and "dark-skinned woman," like a "closed jewelry case" (*Obras completas,* 309). This stereotype, moreover, reiterates Rivas Mercado's essayistic portraits of her women compatriots as submissive.

The characters that receive the greatest attention in the novel's fictional world, then, include an "effeminate" aesthete out of touch with Mexico and a masculine New Woman. Only the vague, intellectual Frances Nolan, whose story Rivas Mercado ironically never completed but who embodies the novel's eye to the future, offered another option. Although she is from the United States, the novel plan leads us to understand that through the learning process awaiting her, Frances would have become somewhat Mexicanized through radical changes in her national consciousness and more activist in her intellectual goals. In many ways, this yet-to-be-developed character incarnates the unfolding cultural role for an intellectual woman that Rivas Mercado was on the verge of imagining at the time of her death. But ultimately, her novel constructs a mercurial authorial persona, precariously poised between the Mexican and the international, the masculine and the feminine, engagement and reflection. In a politically charged cultural field that sought to align specific writing styles with concrete ideological positions, Rivas Mercado's variable prose style manifests comparable balancing acts, resistant to any set artistic categories of the time. Thus modern shifts in perspective generated by free indirect discourse mark the somewhat conventional realism of her novel, and in the short stories about women she cultivated the experimental and lyrical "prose of intensities" that characterized the writing of her colleagues in the Contemporáneos group.[32]

Taken together, Rivas Mercado's complete works, particularly her letters to Rodríguez Lozano, the Bordeaux diary, and the novel in progress, communicate the tumultuous struggle of a writer who sought simultaneously to transmit truths as she saw them and to "violate the truth" of her times through her writing (*Obras completas,* 440). Not long before her suicide, she identified the key quality of Esteban Malo, the novel protagonist—his "borrowed personality"—while noting that his "true" one, which is "unknown to him," will assert itself only when he returns to Mexico and "react[s] in real life" (*Obras completas,* 466). Rivas Mercado's strong public presence and ambitious cultural project notwithstanding, her final performance of a fundamentally private act, her suicide in the Notre Dame Cathedral, suggests that in her frustrated search for a viable art of living as a modern Mexican woman writer and cultural activist, her talent and intellectual power remained for her, as did Malo's character to him, essentially unknown. For more recent women writers, a convention-defying cultural performance like Rivas Mercado's might provide a compelling source of creative and life-sustaining power. But in her case and in her time, the balancing act of a "spy of goodwill" apparently proved too precarious to be survived. Although she crossed paths with numerous artistic and intellectual women, she sustained no evident enduring connection with any of them, links that may have offered an anchor. Her class position, moreover, evidently obscured from her line of vision the option, chosen by some of her female contemporaries, of making a living with her writing in order to maintain the economic autonomy that, having spent her inheritance, she was about to lose. As with her unfinished life work, Rivas Mercado's final performance remains open to contradictory interpretations as a final defeat or a final rebellious affirmation. In either case, her writing reveals the creativity of her performative maneuvers in forging a public identity as an intellectual woman and in fashioning a productive dialogue with the most important cultural debates of her moment.

ACTS OF LITERARY
PRIVILEGE IN HAVANA

chapter 6

Mariblanca Sabas Alomá and
Ofelia Rodríguez Acosta

In 1929 the young Cuban feminist Ofelia Rodríguez Acosta published a novel, *La vida manda* (Life commands), which soon became a two-edition best-seller. The story of the novel's ill-fated protagonist, Gertrudis, encompasses the experiences attributed to emancipated women by Cuban feminist debates in the 1920s. She works in an office, seeks economic independence, has open love affairs while unmarried, hand-picks a man to father her out-of-wedlock child, and reads to improve her mind. She also joins a *tertulia* of literary types and political activists, and in one of the novel's early scenes, on the street she encounters Enrique José Varona, a man she admires as an intellectual and "model of action" (43). An essayist, poet, philosopher, and literary critic, Varona (1849–1933) was a central cultural figure of late-nineteenth-century and early-twentieth-century Cuba. His achievements included modernizing the country's educational system during its early republican years.[1] In the 1920s he was also the revered mentor of Cuba's vanguard Grupo Minorista, some of whose members founded the influential avant-garde periodical *Revista de avance* (1927–1930). Varona's cameo appearance in *La vida manda* is apt. Young Cuban male writers of the 1920s consistently sent their work to Varona for his response and his seal of approval. Moreover, in November 1927, the *Revista de avance* offerings included the supportive article "Feminismo" by Varona. Other *Revista de avance* pieces with a feminist cast included a review of *La vida manda,* in which Francisco Ichaso (a founder and editor) noted the singular problems facing any woman wanting to be a writer. Other major outlets of Minorista activity, the monthly *Social* and the popular periodicals *Carteles* and *Bohemia,* devoted even more attention to feminist activity and the work of women writers.

These crossings between Cuban feminism and the country's literary avant-gardes of the 1920s are striking; nowhere in Latin America were they quite so strong. In part, this tie emerged from the heterogeneity of Cuban cultural life in the 1920s, when artists, intellectuals, and political activists of diverse stripes joined against the corrupt government of

Alfredo Zayas (1921–1925) and the brutal dictatorship of Gerardo Machado (1925–1933). While the bond between feminism and literary journalism in Latin America dated to the nineteenth century, in Cuba's ideologically diverse women's movement of the 1920s a conspicuous number of feminists undertook literary or journalistic work as their primary careers.[2] As feminist leaders and literary figures in Havana, Mariblanca Sabas Alomá (1901–1983) and Ofelia Rodríguez Acosta (1902–1975) exemplify these ties between feminism and the culture of Havana's literary modernity. Sabas Alomá was a founding member of the Grupo Minorista, successful journalist, author of vanguard manifestos and verse, and activist for feminism and anti-Machado campaigns. Although Rodríguez Acosta was neither an official Minorista member nor a signer of the group's manifestos, she participated in its cultural events, joined its members in literary experiments, and was the feminist correspondent for *Social,* essentially a Minorista organ. A widely read novelist and journalist in the 1920s and early 1930s, Rodríguez Acosta, like Sabas Alomá, lobbied for women and against Machado. The two writers reviewed one another's work and exchanged interviews and correspondence in their regular columns. Both participated in women's congresses and the leftist wing of Havana feminism, both enjoyed a strong public presence, and both subscribed to the ideal of intellectual activism—a synthesis of cultural innovation with radical political change—that permeated Cuba's literary scene.

For all their social commitment, in their art of living as writers Sabas Alomá and Rodríguez Acosta ultimately privileged the literary but also challenged emerging notions of literature as an exclusive cultural category. As Ana Cairo has demonstrated, the Minorista conception of intellectual culture was remarkably hybrid and inclusive, particularly in the early to mid-1920s. Francine Masiello highlights a comparable eclectic quality in the offerings of *Revista de avance,* which was founded in the group's later years by its more illustrious members, including Jorge Mañach, Alejo Carpentier, and Juan Marinello. But as Cairo demonstrates (166–168), the group's interweaving of politics and art unraveled in these years as the *Revista de avance* contingent, in particular Mañach, moved to solidify a more discrete conception of literature.[3] By contrast, as they imagined a special role for literature in feminist struggle, Sabas Alomá and Rodríguez Acosta, like Alfonsina Storni in Argentina and Nellie Campobello in Mexico, mined the boundaries between literature and mass culture. Sabas Alomá pursued a more democratic relationship between writers and ordinary readers than the increasing distance assumed by male Minoristas. For her part, Rodríguez Acosta juxtaposed in her fiction the ostensible banalities of a modern woman's tortuous love life with reflections on post-war modernization and modern literary culture. Both writers showcased the singular challenges of the woman writer as a central concern in their work. While publicly enacting the role of modern women, both attacked stereotypes of the performing New Woman and advanced more complex notions of the woman intellectual. At the same time, the two forged quite different portraits of the woman artist in their writing and enacted distinct interventions in the cultural scene. A born performer, Sabas Alomá crafted a bold journalistic self-portrayal, executed an aggressive populist campaign with readers, struggled to find her intellectual home within Havana's male vanguard community, and, in a gendered literary world, embraced stereotypes of the feminine that she also challenged. Rodríguez Acosta, by contrast, elaborated more oblique strategies of self-representation, cut a more intricate figure in her own writing, showed less interest in intellectual alliances, and launched a more thorough inquiry into gender norms and the shifting coalition between literary culture and feminism. The contrast between the hyperbolic reception both women enjoyed in their time and their relative obscurity in official histories of Cuban literary culture today underscores that even in a cultural milieu as ostensibly open to women's participation as was Havana's, the woman writer was still cast as anomalous, her career a singular event. The work of Sabas Alomá and Rodríguez Acosta illuminates the character of that singularity.

STAGING THE FEMININE:
MARIBLANCA DE CUBA'S WRITER AT WORK

Midway through Lesbia Soravilla's feminist novel *El dolor de vivir* (1932), the Cuban protagonist and advocate of free love, Ana María, talks with her Mexican writer friend, Marta. Their conversation ranges from avant-garde painting to feminism and motherhood. Encouraging her friend to put her ideas to paper, Marta sings the praises of a certain "Mariblanca" as an extraordinary woman. She also notes her great surprise on meeting her for the first time: Was that woman with a languid walk, elegant gestures, and smooth hands the same "Mariblanca of the civic fury, of the valiant outcries, of the political campaigns, who launche[d] her creed from 'Carteles' and [was] read and admired from one end of the sensual and lyrical Island to the other[?]" (155). This narrative incorporates the live personage Mariblanca Sabas Alomá into its fictional world. For her part, in a review of Soravilla's book for *Carteles*, Sabas Alomá reproduced the passage in its entirety ("Un libro; una mujer," 44). These intertextual moves highlight crucial features of Sabas Alomá's career, including her proverbial popularity and powerful interaction with readers. More important, it displays the peculiar reception that marked a woman's cultural activism whereby unexpected good looks and femininity offered reassuring antidotes to a woman's feminism and, above all, to the threats to the status quo harbored by her success as a writer. Sabas Alomá's verbatim reproduction of the passage in *Carteles* also signals the hyperbolic self-portraiture in her journalism. In her column, published regularly from 1927 to 1933, she took on a panoply of feminist issues: suffrage, free love, double standards, juvenile justice, and the rights of striking women, battered wives, and children born outside of marriage. She also reviewed a range of literature and artistic activity and attacked the Machado dictatorship, press censorship, the death penalty, and the rising tide of European fascism. But the central, recurring subject in Sabas Alomá's writing was herself. On one level this exhibitionist self-representation mimicked prevailing mythifications of women writers as somehow larger than life and reiterated discursive tension between being "feminine" and acting in public. But through this recurrent self-portraiture, Sabas Alomá also scrutinized images of the New Woman, meditated on women writers' situation, imagined the intellectual community that might embrace them, and, while assigning literature a special role in cultural activism, challenged elite conceptions of the literary.

Soravilla's novelistic account in *El dolor de vivir* was not far off. In the late 1920s and early 1930s, Sabas Alomá was in fact one of the best-known cultural figures on the island. Jorge Mañach, a Grupo Minorista regular and founder of the *Revista de avance,* baptized her "Mariblanca de Cuba."[4] Through the continental circulation of *Carteles* as well as a network of vanguard magazines and more broadly based Americanist periodicals like the *Repertorio americano,* she also enjoyed name recognition in other Latin American countries and Florida. Born and educated in Santiago de Cuba, Sabas Alomá relocated to Havana in 1923.[5] While establishing herself as a journalist, she held government jobs for the postal service and the census bureau in Santiago and Havana. She first gained public attention through frequent contributions to Santiago periodicals and with the anticlerical tract *La rémora* (The remora; 1921). Here she charged Catholic education and religious confession with a nefarious impact on women and was promptly excommunicated. In Havana she attended women's congresses and emerged as a feminist leader. She lobbied vociferously against Machado, and even after his fall, her enduring radicalism brought her a brief prison term in 1936.[6] She settled on a journalism career in 1927, writing regularly for *Bohemia* (1927–1930), *Carteles*

(1928–1933), *El país excelsior* (1938–1940), *Avance* (1940–1946), and *El mundo* (1961–1968), among others.

An enduring commitment to cultural and especially literary radicalism marked Sabas Alomá's turn toward feminism and politics. She had in fact made her public debut as an artistic performer, declaiming her own poems and receiving two gold medals at the Santiago Juegos Florales (literary contest festivals) in 1923 for such conventional fare as "Canto al carnaval" and "Soneto patriótico." During the 1920s her poetry became more avant-garde, and she studied art and literature intermittently at Columbia University, at the University of Puerto Rico (with Pedro Salinas), and in Mexico. Her poems appeared widely in literary magazines including *Social* and in two landmark anthologies: María Monvel's *Poetisas de América* (1929) and *La poesía cubana en 1936*, edited by Juan Ramón Jiménez. In 1930, Sabas Alomá published *Feminismo*, a collection of her newspaper columns, and its subtitle, "Social Issues—Literary Criticism," highlighted the literary in her cultural politics. Most important was her visible role in the Grupo Minorista. Sabas Alomá was one of only two women among the thirty-two signers of the group's 1927 culminating manifesto or "Declaración" that advocated political, intellectual, and artistic change.[7] She participated actively in the group's earlier incarnations, including ventures supporting the university reform movement and against the Zayas government. From their inception in 1924, she was a regular at the Grupo Minorista's "sabbatical luncheons," convened in the law office of Emilio Roig de Leuchsenring, the literary editor of *Social* and chronicler of the group.[8] Sabas Alomá's name and photograph appeared habitually in accounts of Minorista activities in *Social,* which also published her poetry. Along with Nicolás Guillén and Juan Marinello, among others, she was also the subject of one of *Social's* full-page "Positivos," a series of biographical sketches on Minorista members or writers whom the group supported.[9]

Beyond her active role in a predominantly male intellectual assemblage, Sabas Alomá produced the only vanguard manifesto in Latin America openly authored by a woman.[10] In 1928 her polemical "Vanguardismo" appeared in Havana's *Atuei* and in Latin America's widely read *Repertorio americano.* The same year, in the literary supplement to Havana's *Diario de la marina,* she published the satirical performance piece "Primer congreso de poetas de vanguardia" (First congress of vanguard poets), subtitled "Prose Poem with Five Edges and One Final Revolution" and dedicated to the city of Havana, the "Geneva of America." This piece stages a fictive gathering of vanguard delegates from Cuba, Latin America, and Europe, a ribald celebration of iconoclastic artistic activity that brings together Sabas Alomá and her Minorista cohorts with the likes of Ramón Gómez de la Serna, Miguel de Unamuno, Vladimir Mayakovsky, Vicente Huidobro; Ecuador's Hugo Mayo; Mexico's Manuel Maples Arce, Germán List Arzubide, and Salvador Novo; Guatemala's Miguel Angel Asturias; and Peruvians Magda Portal and Alberto Hidalgo, among others. Here Sabas Alomá offered a particularly entertaining version of a performance genre employed by other Latin American vanguardists to constitute an intellectual community and artistic stance.[11] Her characters engage in the requisite vanguard posturing against the usual targets: traditional verse, bourgeois intellectualism, punctuation, and canonical poets of a previous generation such as Leopoldo Lugones and José Santos Chocano. But adhering to an avant-garde that would entwine artistic and political change, which is also the view of her "Vanguardismo" manifesto, the piece concludes with an acerbic note on the illusion of an exclusively artistic vanguard promoting real "prodigious revolutionary accomplishments" (321).

Through this performance manifesto Sabas Alomá claimed membership in a large vanguard club, a network linking the Grupo Minorista with politically inclined artists throughout Latin America.[12] The piece also casts other women into that community, including Magda Portal, Blanca Luz Brum (Uruguay), María Monvel (Chile), and Argentina's Berta Singerman. Most striking is Sabas Alomá's self-assigned role in this imaginary congress: while Carpentier speaks on Cocteau and Apollinaire, Huidobro quips that "property is a trick," and her Minorista cohort Mañach lectures, she herself, "the cultivated and distinguished Eastern poetess," performs by reciting her poems ("Primer congreso," 324).[13] This self-portrait as a captivating performer surrounded by a vanguard community intertwines Sabas Alomá's engagement with literary innovations and the creation of her public persona as a writing woman. Literary historiography often chooses poetry, the microcosm of verbal experiment, as the paradigmatic vanguard genre. But as a critical cultural activity that challenged multiple norms and institutions, avant-garde practice used whatever expressive outlets were available. In the context of an undersized book industry, as Cairo points out, Cuba's Grupo Minorista actually made its primary impact through periodicals. Whereas these journals published a variety of work and although a few accomplished Cuban poets such as Mariano Brull and Guillén debuted during the vanguard period, according to Cairo, the essay and the article constitute the enduring legacy of the Grupo Minorista. Thus Sabas Alomá's engagement with the Havana vanguards provided the rhetorical strategies for her journalism and self-portrayal as a writer. This portrait, combined with her columns' singular style, fashioned her intervention in a cultural conversation about the nature of intellectual activity and the status of the literary author.

Singular stylistic features, an exploration of the author-reader pact, and the aggressive staging of an authorial presence mark Sabas Alomá's inquisitorial journalism.[14] During the 1920s and early 1930s she published prototypical vanguard verse. But the vanguards' signature typographic gestures, particularly hyperbolic capitalization, peppered her journalistic columns. Along with the orthographical pyrotechnics, assertive pronouncements, conversational asides in parentheses, ironic twists, and an unrelenting first-person speaking voice give her columns the oral immediacy and illusion of presence typical of a manifesto. Although her columns could be verbose, she often employed a vanguard accumulation of telegraphic phrases for staging a scene, as in describing a sugar exporting center: "continuous movement, millions of dollars, millions of mosquitoes, drunken sailors, boats, boats, boats" ("Ah! . . . si fuera así!," 16). Her hybrid pieces conformed neither to the ostentatious oratory that typified nineteenth-century journalistic prose in Latin America nor to the ostensibly more objective, empirical style that was increasingly dominant after the turn of the century.[15] By turns reflective, polemical, objective, intimate, and oratorical, Sabas Alomá's journalism interwove genres and fragments—interviews, anecdotes, lectures, letters, quotations from readings, and confessions—to craft a dialogue with readers. She often incorporated reader letters, congratulatory or condemning, into a virtual conversation or confrontation. The radical engagement with an audience was the quality she most praised in experimental art, such as radical innovations by Jean Cocteau.[16]

Sabas Alomá's vanguard experience provided the foundation, above all, for the larger-than-life self-portraiture that propelled her inquiry into the concept of authorship and the challenges facing writing women. This bold, assertive "I" made its first grand entrance in the anticlerical, feminist tract *La rémora,* published when she was nineteen, a "diatribe in eight chapters," as the poet and critic Regino Boti baptized it in the prologue (*La rémora,* 10–11). The book's final chapter, "Yo" (I), authorizes the tract's first-person voice. Declaring that the "Supreme I" constitutes the "superior part of all beings," here Sabas Alomá as identified speaker lays out her motives for writing—to "enlighten" the "fanatic" element and stimulate a feminist movement against the Church—and grounds her authority in her experience and "detained study" (51–55). This inaugural self-portrayal as a careful reader reached fruition in her journalism. But her vanguard poetry also augmented this "Supreme I." The *ars poetica* "Poema en si bemol" (Poem in B flat; 1928) intertwines the religious iconoclasm of *La rémora* with artistic and feminist rebellion. Here the speaker draws power from her religious irreverence, decorating the label of the Christ child's jacket—as a twentieth-century groom—with "the perfumed white lily" of her "sweet smile" (34). She reinforces this impertinence with childhood memories of a powerful performing woman who, as a mentor, played with circus lions and tamed the child's beasts (34). The poem interlaces the speaker's religious, feminist, Marxist, and artistic revolt in a fitting invocation of Saint Cecilia, the patron saint of musicians, known not only for her resistant chastity in marriage but also for her superhuman strength in the face of death. Here the speaker challenges the traditional image of a chaste Saint Cecilia with her own outbursts of feminine desire: "YES, I WANT" (34). Nonetheless, this strong woman inspires her own song. The dedication to Magda Portal, Peruvian vanguard poet and Aprista political leader, reinforces the poem's convocation of a tradition of strong, artistic women, as does the closing image that celebrates with irony the "enormous disillusionment" provoked by morning newspapers that did not announce a "poetess's suicide" (34). This celebration of a tragic end that does not happen, the thwarted demise of the woman poet who (like Saint Cecilia) refuses to disappear, counters traditional imagery of the poet's sacrifice and, closer to home, the practice of obscuring a woman's art by sensationalizing her dramatic life or death.[17]

The patently Marxist "Poema de la mujer aviadora que quiere atravesar el Atlántico" (Poem of the woman flyer who wants to cross the Atlantic; 1928) urges the modern woman it apostrophizes to dedicate her high-flying impulses to social causes (218). Appearing just as Amelia Earhart was preparing for her first solo transatlantic flight, the poem's image of the woman flyer evokes the New Woman's modernity and athleticism. It also reiterates the expansive self-immolating impulses of the vanguards' discursive construction of the artist and the movement's concomitant portrayal of poets who descend from celestial tours into the contingent world. Thus the poem urges the modern woman to exercise her wings in the name of the poor, to spread the "new word" of her activist song from high over the Atlantic, and to use her aerodynamic talent to nail an anti-imperialist cry for justice to the top of the Eiffel Tower (218).

In recasting the larger-than-life poet as a woman, then, Sabas Alomá drew on the vanguards' rhetorical gestures. In constructing an exaggerated personal image throughout her writing, she also mimicked the widespread propensity to magnify the woman writer, embodied, for example, in Mañach's moniker "Mariblanca de Cuba" or in Boti's preface to *La rémora*. This exaggerated tribute equated her prose with a menacing nature-woman: "Miss Sabas Alomá's prose is bruising, red, turbulent, disorderly . . . It flows like an Amazon; and it overflows with the unruly clamor of a waterfall and a blizzard. At times it seems like an intermittent thunderbolt that advances and retreats; others like the resounding and flaming crack of a whip" (*La rémora*, 10–11). Such damning flattery undermines the phenomenon of a self-possessed woman writer by conjuring up what Rita Felski has called modernity's "prehistoric woman," a primal antidote to the fragmentation of modern life that constitutes the very milieu of such developments as women's writing. Boti's overblown portrait of Sabas Alomá's prose also typifies the practice, highlighted by Joanna Russ, of neutralizing women's writing by showcasing its ostensible anomalies (Russ, 76–86).

In fact Sabas Alomá's overstated persona in her *Bohemia* and *Carteles* pieces articulate her critique of emerging literary norms in Cuba, particularly the growing eschewal of an author's textual presence. Even as her vanguard poetry exalted the speaker's critical power, it usually respected the vanguards' aversion to a psychological "I." But the speaking Mariblanca of her journalism fiercely resisted such conventions and seized any opportunity to talk about herself. Over time, in fact, the faithful reader of her columns could piece together a short biography of their author, an account that incorporated conversations with brothers and sisters, memories of the family home in Santiago, accounts of the family's well-heeled origins, evocations of the tastes and smells of childhood, a summary of her prejournalistic work experience, and a detail or two of her private life. The strategy laced her descriptions of others with snapshots of herself. Thus she set the scene for an interview with Berta Martínez Márquez, a founder and director of the Lyceum women's cultural center, with details of its nineteenth-century lamps that generated a Proustian interlude: "When, while I was very little, they would take apart the [lamp] . . . (a family jewel that had belonged to my grandparents), I was happy if the old servant woman would allow me to discover marvelous rainbows through the lamp's 'tears'" ("Lyceum," 26). In keeping with the family's colonial roots invoked in this selection and with Mañach's epithet (Mariblanca de Cuba), she also claimed a privileged relationship to the Cuban nation: her father's ties, as "an authentic Bayamés," to Cuban independence, a maternal link to José Martí, and, during a Mexico sojourn, reaffirmation of her status as a "daughter of Cuba."[18] Although she often depicted her Havana haunts—her route to work, her *Carteles* office, and the Lyceum—and paid tribute to the city as the logical destination for a woman in search of culture, she also identified herself as a *guajira,* the Cuban peasant frequently invoked as a literary icon of Cuban identity.[19]

The autobiographical intertext of Sabas Alomá's journalistic corpus also seeks an image of normalcy as a counterpoint to the exceptionality by definition of the woman writer producing it. Thus she portrayed herself as part of a supportive extended family and a Cuban among Cubans. These images also constitute an antidotal undercurrent to Sabas Alomá's frequent citation of her own unusual traits: "irreverent" and "misbehaved," "informal, undisciplined, voluble" but also a "firm and tireless journalist."[20] Above all, she described herself indefatigably as a voracious reader (with accounts of favorite books), a thinker, and, modesty aside, a "woman of talent" ("Los siete puñales," 64). "I analyze, I investigate, I think," she recounted, in explaining her support of a battered wife convicted of killing her abuser ("El terrible caso," 18). Reacting to a reader's suggestion that she employ a pseudonym, she proclaimed, "I am a woman of ideas and ideals, who says what she thinks out loud" ("La moral," 43). Countering the same reader's judgment that she was a good writer but a poor thinker, she offered the self-portrait of a "young woman who studies, who analyzes, who 'sees far,' who dreams naively of a social organization unlike the one that currently exists, and who is, therefore, noble, equitable, amply generous, human" and who, on the contrary, "writes poorly and thinks well" ("La moral," 48).

Sabas Alomá's self-portraiture executed a complex dance of advance and retreat between convention and exceptionality. She forcefully rebutted readers who criticized her outspoken positions and self-assured style and, to the many who praised her work, emitted protests of modesty with self-critical asides about her own vanity. She celebrated her own popularity with reports of reader letters from throughout the Americas (including a few marriage proposals), of sighting her image in Mexico City, Tampa, and Miami newspapers, and of enthusiastic receptions in those cities. At the same time, she claimed mystification at this popularity, attributed it to her privileged access through *Carteles,* and argued that there were many Cuban women writers with greater talent but less exposure.

Most important, a relentless claim to femininity permeated Sabas Alomá's campaign to normalize her public presence as a woman writer. Small photographic images accompany many of her columns, a practice rarer among her male peers,[21] and she highlighted her physical attributes in gender-charged terms. In setting the stage for an interview with a teacher, for example, she wished she could photograph the surrounding scene with her eyes and recorded her own gesture: "and the refined arm of a woman sketches out a moving semi-circle" ("Ana Abril," 26). She also recounted pleasure whenever a reader who met her would express surprise that she was pretty. In her most unabashed and extensive journalistic act of self-portrayal—"Un pie sentimental para un retrato" (A sentimental footnote to a portrait)—Sabas Alomá included a formal photograph of herself in a quintessential pose of feminine serenity: a well-made-up face, modestly low-cut attire, a contemplative Mona Lisa countenance, and her head resting delicately on her upraised, well-manicured hand. She explained that this photograph, which occupied more than a third of the full-page piece, constituted a response to numerous reader requests. But she glossed the image with copious verbal self-descriptors: "smiling and melancholy, with her recondite sweetness" and imbued with a "vague sadness," qualities that she contrasted to the "gossip," "perfidy," and "envy" that her journalistic success and feminism had generated (28). She interlaced these gendered qualities with images of resistance to attack: "stronger and stronger, taller, more secure, more understanding, more serene, more *composed*" (28; my emphasis).

This calculated composition of a feminine but powerful woman writer rearticulates, in unanticipated ways (to restate Judith Butler's terms), a discursive field in which "feminine" and "woman writer" are contradictory. The degree to which this was so in Havana, a city witnessing extensive feminist activism, becomes apparent in the fact that, as in Soravilla's novel, men and women alike represented the real Sabas Alomá as a surprisingly, emphatically feminine intellectual. Setting the stage for an interview, the Lyceum's president, Berta de Martínez Márquez, noted her remarkable discovery that Mariblanca had nice eyes and beautiful white hands ("Mariblanca," 42). More striking is the tribute to Sabas Alomá by J. Font Saldaña for Puerto Rico's influential journal *Indice*. He extolled by turns her "robust and precise prose," her "solid culture," and her "sage experience" and marveled that she was a beautiful woman who had chosen all this instead of the "vanity table" and a husband (291). As a "rebellious and ferocious woman" who possessed "all of the appetizing physical enchantments" and a mouth "so feminine, when it unfolds convulsively in an ironic smile," Font observed, Sabas Alomá had made "many an upright man, many a learned man, and many fathers of the nation lose their balance" (291). In hyperbolizing her own femininity, then, Sabas Alomá reproduced the reigning view that these qualities were discontinuous with intellectualism. Inversely, she trumped the compelling "denial of agency," to use Russ's term, whereby if a woman succeeds as a writer, she must be less than a complete woman.

The commanding threat of this denial of agency explains Sabas Alomá's propensity to exaggerate the femininity of other women writers as well. Ofelia Rodríguez Acosta, she argued in a review of *La vida manda,* was "very young, very beautiful and very feminine . . . in spite of the image of 'tiresome' that people generally have of women intellectuals" ("Ofelia Rodriguez Acosta," 20). The fear that a woman writer would be denied recognition through aspersions cast on her femininity accounts in part for Sabas Alomá's troublesome homophobia. Noting her campaign against what she called the decadent life of *garzonismo* (bachelor womanhood), Nina Menéndez argues convincingly that the femininity Sabas Alomá ascribed to the protagonist of Rodríguez Acosta's novel constitutes a denial of the work's inclusion of a lesbian character as an alternative to heterosexuality ("*Garzonas y feministas,*" 178). As Menéndez notes in a series on women's *garzonismo* and men's *pepillismo,* Sabas Alomá characterized lesbianism as an aberration.[22] But the reaction to *garzonas* in Havana in the 1920s reiterated the specific portrait of bachelor womanhood disseminated by the popular French novel *La garçonne* (1922) by Victor Margueritte, translated as *La garzona* (1922) in Spanish and *The Bachelor Girl* (1923) in English. In this work, which Sabas Alomá had read, the protagonist's temporary lesbianism coincides with her immersion in the trendy life of the performing New Woman, a scenario of cabaret nightlife, theatre, jazz, cropped hair, short skirts, and easy liaisons.

Sabas Alomá's ambivalence toward women's role in such a world testifies to the appearance of Havana's signature twentieth-century performance culture and nightlife. The 1920s and 1930s were key decades in the emergence of Cuban music and dance genres, theatre, radio culture, and, to a lesser extent, film. Reflecting the geographic proximity and cultural influence of the United States, *Carteles* and *Bohemia* propagated the new mass culture's display of women even more than counterparts throughout Latin America. For example, photographic campaigns and stories celebrated nudity, particularly female. In her critical portrayal of Cuba's *garzonas,* Sabas Alomá, in the spirit of Margueritte's novel, bought into the link Rodríguez Acosta's novel forged between a trendy social modernity and lesbianism or bisexuality. This reaction coincides with her efforts to distance political feminism from what she described as the upper-class "pleasure dolls" inhabiting a world of charity balls, cocktail hours, and mahjong or from the women of varied class backgrounds populating Havana's night world of jazz bands, shimmy-dancing, seminudity, and open sexuality. In her critical vision of this ambiance, Sabas Alomá was not simply being prudish; she in fact published a column defending nudity and her magazine's attention to the topic.[23] Rather the frivolous image of modern womanhood fostered by Havana performance culture, Sabas Alomá argued, detracted from feminism's serious purpose. She imagined a more politically radical New Woman dedicated to revolutionary change: "women who call ourselves *modern* for something more than the simple fact of wearing short hair, smoking a cigarette . . . , driving our automobiles at one hundred miles an hour, or breaking world records in swimming" ("Como queremos," 44). Drawing on Alexandra Kollontai's writings, Sabas Alomá argued that while women should have access to the freedoms of modern performance culture, the true New Woman would educate herself and maintain her "intelligence and her spirit in constant revolution" ("Palabras a la mujer dominicana," 28).

Beyond whatever prejudices she harbored about the range of sexual behavior, then, Sabas Alomá's adherence to images of femininity for women writers and her resistance to the label "masculine" ascribed in her day to liberated women manifested a well-grounded fear that the intent of such attributions was to denigrate women's writing, to deny its serious purpose, and, ultimately, to silence it. Thus in "Palabras que asustan" (Frightening words), Sabas Alomá protested the stereotyping of feminists as a way to dismiss the impact of their writing, a process that demonized "the woman who has stopped being a woman" as somebody "lacking in beauty and grace, with a baritone voice, enraged disposition" and "the shadow of an incipient mustache" (*Feminismo*, 47). Paradoxical though it may seem, then, exaggerating her own femininity was to insist on the seriousness of her writing, to resist neutralization by false categorization, in Russ's terms. Her blind spot toward homosexuality notwithstanding, Sabas Alomá actually rejected gender essentialism and argued that masculinity and femininity were categories undergoing radical revision. She affirmed that gender traits were "extrinsic" rather than "intrinsic" (*Feminismo*, 68–72) and argued that statements such as "what Cuba needs are more men like Mariblanca" exposed a crisis in norms of masculinity as well as femininity ("Feminidad," 44–45). Again drawing on Kollontai, she proposed that a changing society was producing not only "new women" but also "new men" who undermined the equation of masculinity with machismo (*Feminismo*, 81).

These moves toward a constructionist view of gender bring us back to Sabas Alomá's "Un pie sentimental para un retrato" that accompanied her large photographic representation in *Carteles*. As she homed in on her status as *"a woman who writes,"* her italics underscored the term's insinuations of aberrancy and oxymoronic charge. She rearticulated this contradictoriness in her self-characterization as an uneven mix of euphoria, optimism, gravity, balance, disquiet, anguish, skepticism, and faith, as "dynamic," "combative," and "demolishing" on the one hand and "placid," "contemplative," and "timid" on the other. The quotation marks with which she framed the litany of her possible identities—"a 'woman writer,' a 'feminist,' a 'poetess,' an 'intellectual'"—underscore their substance as social roles that, assumed or imposed, generated mixed reactions. What, then, was this new entity, she pondered, this woman who writes: "A temperament? A character? A person? A personality?" ("Un pie sentimental," 28). Sabas Alomá in fact confirmed that the "personalism" of her writing was an assumed stance that excluded her "modest private life" ("De mi humilde soberbia," 28).

The strong autobiographical presence in Sabas Alomá's journalism, then, embodies a conscious choice in the cultural politics of a feminist and a location of the woman writer's dilemma at the center of her work. This militant first-personism also enacted a particular conception of literature and intellectual activity within the cultural debates of the Grupo Minorista. She advanced a democratic view of the author-reader pact and a reader-engaged vision of authorial voice. Although her journalism far exceeded her poetry, in a cultural field in which boundaries between the literary and the nonliterary were under debate, Sabas Alomá repeatedly characterized herself as part of Havana's "little artistic and literary miniworld" ("Algo más que recitar," 44)[24] and of an emerging cadre of Latin American and Spanish peninsular women writers, including Juana de Ibarbourou, Blanca Luz Brum, Gabriela Mistral, Teresa de la Parra, Alfonsina Storni, Magda Portal, Concha Espina, and Carmen de Burgos ("A las mujeres mexicanas," 30). She praised high-quality artistic work, with Berta Singerman's recitations, Parra's novels, and Mistral's poetry among her favorites. She privileged reading literature as a form of mental calisthenics that could enhance the intellects and discipline of women. In praising the Lyceum, the arts center founded by Havana women, she lobbied for women's "emancipation through culture" as an antidote to the mental atrophy produced by mahjong and jazz. Through literature and the arts, she proposed, the "well-educated woman" could replace the "pedantic" woman or "babbler" ("A la emancipación," 16, 67). She often described her youthful move from Santiago to Havana as a quest for culture and alluded to Cuba's "cultural mediocrity" and "poor literary environment" ("Maledicencia tradicional," 32, and "Regino Pedroso," 40).

But Sabas Alomá categorically opposed institutionalizing literature as an esoteric activity. A writer, she argued, should never become an elite practitioner distanced from readers. She displayed the requisite literary competence to make valorizing judgments about literary works. While praising the content and ideological focus of many writers, for example, she also peppered her reviews of literary work with gentle criticism, noting "technical poverty" or "literary merits" inferior to a work's overall "sensitivity" ("Literatura femenina," 28). She was not above establishing hierarchies, as she noted that she regarded Parra and Mistral as more accomplished creative writers in the early 1930s than, say, Rodríguez Acosta. But although she dedicated a small portion of her article collection, *Feminismo,* to literary criticism, she insisted that she was neither a literary critic nor a *letrada* (learned woman) and declared that she was less interested in style and form than in a work's power to provoke debate. She in fact often highlighted the ostensible absence of literature in works she reviewed. She praised Carlos Montenegro's short stories for their "naturalness" or avoidance of "all style . . . and literariness" (*Feminismo,* 214) and Mistral's poetry for its power "without literature" ("Nuestra Gabriela," 18).

This gentle disparagement of the literary notwithstanding, Sabas Alomá characterized hers as a "literary career" and herself as a professional writer ("Ida Mola," 40). But her portrayal of her art of living as a writer highlighted neither creative inspiration nor style and instead characterized her writing, and reading, as rigorous cultural work with a higher purpose. This view of the literary at the service of social change (albeit indirectly) was consistent with the conception of literature widely promoted by the left wing of Latin America's avant-gardes, not only by Havana's Grupo Minorista, but by José Carlos Mariátegui's *Amauta* circle in Peru, by Mexico's Estridentistas, and by a continental network of writers joined by their allegiance to the Americanist goals of Peruvian *aprismo.* A repeated image in Sabas Alomá's columns reinforces this notion of writing as cultural work: herself bent over her typewriter and laboring (a word she employed often) into the night. She underscored this work image with allusions to the difficulties of putting ideas into adequate words. Above all she portrayed her work as writer and reader as an eminently practical activity engaged with the world and readers. A 1931 column for *Carteles,* "¡Me parece muy bien!," provides an excellent portrait of the author engaged in this art of living as a writer. This piece on modern marriage opens with a present-tense scenario in which she rushes to turn in her column at deadline and then narrates retrospectively the activities coalescing in this piece. The next scene presents Sabas Alomá conversing with her favorite bookseller at the Cervantes bookstore about readings on the column topic. While settling on Ben Lindsley's widely read *Companionate Marriage,* she makes ironic asides about traditional women's columns on fashion and offers this book discussion as an alternative response to readers' questions. In explaining the bookstore trip, she describes a conversation overheard on the streetcar between two women about a scandalous news story in which a socially prominent woman withdrew her divorce petition after her husband was charged with a highly publicized murder. Recognizing Mariblanca, the two women, fans of her column, ask what she thinks, a question, she explains, that provoked her bookstore quest and produced the column. Illustrating her emerging view of literary culture's role in the world, this scenario stages Sabas Alomá in the act of solving a practical problem through reflective reading and in direct response to a continuing conversation with her own readers.

This piece also depicts a writer at work—on the streetcar, in the bookstore, at her typewriter—and underscores the presence of the author's activity in her writing. Thus Sabas Alomá countered emerging conventions of literary journalism as practiced by the Grupo Minorista writers, particularly as they moved in the *Revista de avance,* to solidify the boundary between literary culture and the middlebrow. As Masiello argues, at the center of the journal's aesthetic discussions lay "a new vision of the role of the author, both as a leader of political activity and as a guide to alternative esthetics," as the editors worked to secure "a place for the modern intellectual as an arbiter of art and social life" ("Rethinking Neocolonial Esthetics," 8–9, 28). But in the broader Grupo Minorista trajectory, as Ana Cairo convincingly demonstrates, the *Revista de avance* years, 1927–1930, particularly in Mañach's work, also consolidated divisions between the literary and the "extra-literary" (137–144).[25] The magazine's editors and Mañach in particular accentuated the divide between the literary essay and more engaged journalism. On longstanding fluid boundaries between fiction and journalism in Spanish America, Aníbal González observes that as a "mouthpiece of modernization," journalism taught the literary writer "about the nature of writing as a process and as a product" and helped to "demystify writing and the notion of literature itself" (14). In the context of Grupo Minorista debates about the status of literature, Sabas Alomá tapped into this tradition, keeping fluid the divide with the literary and demystifying herself as author. But much like Spanish American *modernistas* and early vanguardists, she simultaneously cultivated a strong authorial presence.

Sabas Alomá undertook a virtual dialogue with Mañach on these matters in two 1931 columns, "Un muchacho de hoy," published September 6,
and "Letras a Mañach," published October 4, in response to intervening
commentary by Mañach in his column for the Havana daily *El país*.[26] In
the first, she recounted a visit to her office by a fourteen-year-old boy from
Matanzas, a reader of her columns who enumerated the literary journalists he liked (Sabas Alomá, Roig de Leuchsenring, and Marinello, among
others) and those he did not. Mañach stood out among the latter, credited with great talent and culture but also a superior air toward readers.
While Sabas Alomá reported having encouraged the young man to give
Mañach's writing another try, her comments provoked a debate with Mañach on literary language, a writer's presence in their work, and relationships with readers. In a second column she thanked Mañach for having included her in the "closed chapels" of literary writers, but she underscored
their contrasting conceptions of literary journalism. He had advised her
to use her vast, high culture toward more polished and adept writing and
to separate her "literary personality" from her social activism and will to
please readers. She responded that establishing a "shoulder-to-shoulder"
contact with readers was precisely her goal. To this end, she added, she
sought language accessible to any literate person, used the first person,
and addressed readers with the informal "tú." To his admonition that no
writer was important enough to talk about themselves, she defended self-
portraiture as a calculated strategy for connecting with readers, as a good
teacher would do with students. She argued that authors could talk about
themselves directly or indirectly, intimating that the distance and complex
language cultivated by Mañach itself constituted a strategic literary persona. Finally Sabas Alomá noted that they had each revealed something of
themselves in this exchange, surely more interesting to readers than had
they simply shared ideas ("Letras a Mañach," 16).[27]

Keeping the boundaries blurred between literature and mass communication was not simply an aesthetic or philosophical position for Sabas
Alomá as it was for many vanguard writers. Rather it provided a way into
a literary world that overdetermined the acceptable outlets for women's
writing and the models for the public persona of an intellectual woman.
Although she persistently claimed the literary scene as her cultural world,
over time Sabas Alomá gradually wrote less poetry, and her writing grew
even more politically engaged. She published award-winning journalism
after the 1959 Revolution, but she gradually disappeared from the literary
scene. Her contemporary Rodríguez Acosta offers an instructive contrast.
As a woman who interacted with the main literary groups in Havana but

who, unlike Sabas Alomá, never claimed them as her intellectual home, Rodríguez Acosta forged a more enduring literary career.

WOMEN ON THE VERGE OF A BREAKTHROUGH: RODRÍGUEZ ACOSTA'S PRACTICAL(LY) NEW WOMAN

If Mariblanca Sabas Alomá's public persona dominated every page of her work, Ofelia Rodríguez Acosta's authorial identity was subtler, her feminist critique of Havana's cultural modernity more intricate and radical. In contrast to Sabas Alomá, she was circumspect in deploying the first person. Instead she deflected the autobiographical toward a fictive investigation of women's peculiar position in Havana's literary culture, a tumultuous and contradictory world that, as she saw it, objectified them while simultaneously offering them a place for relative autonomy. Rodríguez Acosta, too, criticized the frivolity of mass culture's performing New Woman, but she was more intrigued than her contemporary by the figure's inventive potential. Although she periodically gave public lectures, she cast herself in her work as an active spectator more than a performer. But she rehearsed diverse positions through the characters in her fiction, and she conceptualized both feminism and literary work as sources of knowledge through practice. Although she was less flamboyant in her presentation of self than Sabas Alomá and less polemical in her journalism, she also was an anti-Machado political activist and a socialist somewhat influenced by Marxist thought who supported progressive causes and was arrested in 1931 with other feminists for helping to organize demonstrations against the government's murder of the university student Rafael Trejo.[28] Rodríguez Acosta also challenged gender standards more profoundly than did Sabas Alomá, not only through androgynous literary characters but also by unmasking in her essays the gender biases that permeated the cultural conversation about art.

As the author of short stories, seven novels, and a play, Rodríguez Acosta was a more productive literary figure than Sabas Alomá. This productivity was documented in the Grupo Minorista–backed reviews *Social* and *Revista de avance,* the latter of which praised her 1929 best-seller novel, *La vida manda,* and in the more academic *Revista de la Habana,* which dedicated a critical study to her fiction. Born in Pinar del Río to an intellectual family, Rodríguez Acosta was educated at the Instituto de la Habana in the mid-1920s, served as a librarian for the Club Femenino de Cuba, and was a member briefly of the Unión Laborista de Mujeres.[29] In the 1920s and early 1930s she lectured on feminism and politics for women's organizations and other gatherings, and from 1929 to 1932 she wrote a regular column on feminism and other political issues for the Havana weekly *Bohemia*. Among her longer critical essays, *La tragedia social de la mujer* (Women's social tragedy) rebutted Russian philosopher Anton Nemilov's *Biological Tragedy of Women* (1929). She published critical and fictional pieces in *Social* and, in the *Revista de la Habana,* the feminist essays "El carácter y la personalidad en la mujer" (Women's character and personality) and "La intelectual feminista y la feminista no intelectual" (The feminist intellectual and the nonintellectual feminist). But Rodríguez Acosta's fiction writing predated her journalism and political activism and outlived both by far. She began writing as an adolescent.[30] Her contemporaries dismissed her first novel, *El triunfo de la débil presa* (1926), as melodramatic thesis narrative. But the controversial feminist novel *La vida manda* put her on the literary map. Following this critical and commercial success, Rodríguez Acosta published five more novels between 1931 and 1953, including the autobiographical *Sonata interrumpida* (Interrupted sonnet). This 1943 work focused heavily on its protagonist's experiences in Havana political and cultural life in the intense 1920s and 1930s.[31] Beginning in 1933 she traveled widely in Europe and then settled in Mexico City, where she spent most of the 1940s and 1950s. She returned to Cuba after the Revolution and died in Havana in 1975.

Rodríguez Acosta was the most productive Cuban woman fiction writer of her time, though her novels vary widely in themes and philosophical orientation. Their penchant for thesis statements and uneven quality, elements that also typified much fiction by Cuban male writers of her generation, manifest her enduring, not altogether successful search for an integrated style. Her most engaging novels, *La vida manda* and *Sonata interrumpida,* enact the complex relationship of a woman writer and feminist to Havana's projects of cultural modernity. Rodríguez Acosta was never a card-carrying member of the Grupo Minorista, but she participated in one of their fiction experiments, and her writing bears the mark of the vanguards' artistic and cultural polemics. A less-known Minorista venture was the collective novel *Fantoches* (1926), a prose fiction work composed from narratives published by each of twelve Minorista authors in successive issues of *Social*.[32] *Social* editors launched a similar experiment in 1927—*Once soluciones a un triángulo amoroso* (Eleven solutions to a love triangle)—and Rodríguez Acosta, as did Minoristas Jesús López, Enrique Serpa and accomplished novelist Carlos Loveira, each authored an entry.[33] Moreover, in the story "Agonía" she traced the stylistic odyssey of a vanguard artist who fails in his quest to encompass all. The story alludes to vanguard experiments in its imagery ("The artist's thought is a bomb and a woman's womb"), in its echoes of Huidobro's *creacionismo* ("The uncreated would be his creation"), and its meditation on style: "Long ago, many characters, many adjectives. Volumes. Today, lines. Words served up in bottomless thimbles . . . Tomorrow? A sun. It is unknown" (39).[34] *La vida manda* includes some comparable telegraphic passages in descriptions of everyday modern Havana, and reviewers encouraged the author to cultivate this incipient vanguard style. But as the quoted passage suggests, Rodríguez Acosta regarded this clipped style as a passing fad and remained unconvinced of its expressive potential for women writers. She observed in an interview that "writing in vanguardism without talking nonsense is like balancing on a loose rope" (quoted in Martínez Márquez, "Ofelia Rodríguez Acosta," 60).

Her reservations about vanguard stylistic conventions notwithstanding, in her anti-institutional view of culture, activist conception of literary work, self-reflective novels, and portrayal of the epoch as unparalleled, Rodríguez Acosta was as avant-garde as Havana's most radical innovators. Reiterated throughout her work is that profound sense of temporal crisis ascribed by Matei Calinescu to international modernist culture (5), an image of "all that is solid melt(ing) into air" that Marshall Berman, quoting from Marx, underlines as the defining quality of modernity (Berman, 20–21). She made repeated journalistic references to her "uncommon century" and "transcendental period" as the most interesting the world had ever seen.[35] Similar hyperbolism situates the characters of *La vida manda* in "the century of aviation, the century of the ambition to reach Mars, the century of woman, the century of surprises and disenchantment, in which man remains, without parallel, the greatest experiment and the greatest ailment of the earth" (*La vida manda*, 192). This self-conscious modernity weaves through Rodríguez Acosta's essays in a sometimes futuristic utopianism: birth control on demand, voluntary paternity, eugenics, a liberalized family, the leveling of racial, social, and sexual differences, and the disappearance of "patriotism of hymns and flags" ("Concepto del patriotismo," 17).[36] But the gap between modernity's promise and its inequities constitutes a central theme in her fiction, particularly as these contradictions affect modern Cuban women.

These inconsistencies also underlie Rodríguez Acosta's activist model of cultural work, framed in resistance to the Machado dictatorship that mobilized her generation and as an attack on institutionalized culture that echoed anti-academic rhetoric of vanguard manifestos in a campaign against the "grammarians of life" ("La lepra social," 11). "De-mummify

yourselves," she admonished the icons of "human knowledge, the historical legacy, the official Culture" ("Por los fueros," 21). This activist view
of intellectual work permeated her conception of a "practical feminism"
of lived experience contrasted to a "salon feminism" of elitist debates or
even political lobbying. The true "practical feminists," Rodríguez Acosta
argued, might be ignorant of feminist doctrine but instead performed it in
their lives; the laborer, salesperson, teacher, professional woman, or artist
were all feminists though they might reject the label ("Feminismo teórico,"
9). The practical feminists embodied problems affecting women not in isolation but as one element in an assortment of pressing social issues, including the rights of workers, the freedom to dissent, and the abolition of the
death penalty. Thus would feminism be fully integrated with the practice
of an engaged life. Beyond the vote and women's social and economic independence, feminism's genuine triumph, she argued, would come only
with a practical change in women's "mental structures" and "concepts of
life" and their continuing "intervention" in the culture of the world ("La
intelectual feminista," 76).

The idea of feminism as practice coincides with Rodríguez Acosta's
conception of novel-writing as work in the "trenches" ("La lepra social,"
11). This she contrasted with the disengaged writing of intellectuals who
avoided sullying themselves with the messiness of life. *La vida manda*,
in fact, synthesizes the ideal of "practical feminism," epitomized in its
unconventional protagonist, Gertrudis, with the author's concept of novel-
writing as a rehearsal of character "attitudes" or "poses," as she called
them, and a testing out of multiple writing styles. She insisted that her
fictional characters, in particular the unconventional Gertrudis, were not
literally autobiographical. Rather she proposed in a 1930 essay, "Sobre la
manera de producir del novelista" (On the novelist's mode of producing),
that a novelist must undertake a rigorous "preparatory cultural labor"
through self-analysis and by assuming the know-how of others. The novelist, she wrote, "*incorporates* himself in the experiencing of others, characterizing himself, insinuating himself until he humanizes himself altogether
in the multiple and distinct lives that surround him" (255–256; my emphasis). Similarly, she argued, stylistic polishing encompassed observing
and studying the novel itself in all of its "poses" (255–256). Consistent
with this performative concept of fiction-writing, Rodríguez Acosta's short
stories constituted first-person rehearsals for what she subsequently recast
as third-person character experiences in her novels. For example, the short
narrative "Doscientos años atrás" enacts a first-person, meditative trip
to the Convent of Santa Teresa, a journey identical to one subsequently

undertaken by the character Ezequiel in the novel *Dolientes*. The revealing difference between the two accounts is that while the reader experiences the novel version through the perceptions of an anachronistic, heroic young man in love, the story concludes with the distancing words of a modern intellectual woman as she leaves the convent and rejoins the contemporary street: "clattering, honking horns, shouts, cars— . . . reintegrated to [her] very modern" personality ("Doscientos años atrás," 58).[37]

Rodríguez Acosta's popular *La vida manda* assumes a comparable distance from its unconventional, emancipated protagonist Gertrudis, though readers rushed to identify the character with the author. Gertrudis actually embodies the "practical feminist" the author theorized in her essays, a character situated neither in a feminist salon nor a writer's study but in the thick of a challenging life. She acts out the new morality in a world unprepared for her choices. The image of "balancing on a loose rope," to echo Rodríguez Acosta's phrase, is apt both for Gertrudis's struggle to integrate feminist ideals with her life's realities and for the writer's quest for an uneasy synthesis of melodrama and modern self-reflection as a way to express this clash. Situated in Havana in the 1920s, the plot traces Gertrudis's rocky path. An orphaned, independent young woman who lives with her godfather, she earns her living as an office worker and leads a sexually liberated life. After abandoning her fiancé, Antonio, to whom she is engaged out of propriety but whom she neither loves nor desires, she takes up with the more intellectual and sexually interesting Damián. Although Damián turns out to be married, Gertrudis continues the affair, believing he will soon leave his wife, but terminates the liaison when she learns otherwise. In search of a new focus, she opts for single motherhood. For the child's father she selects Antonio, since married and now divorced, because he will provide good genes for the baby while staying out of her life. She is fired when she appears pregnant at work, and the child dies at birth. Gertrudis's final autonomous gesture, an attempted suicide, fails when she blinds herself instead.

As a "practical feminist," Gertrudis acts out Rodríguez Acosta's modern ideals of economic emancipation, sexual freedom, even eugenics, always with tragic results. The ups and downs of minor characters, Gertrudis's aunt, uncle, and cousins, and the protagonist's arguments with her godfather showcase additional social issues debated by the author and her generation: women's suffrage, class inequities, domestic violence, sexual abuse, drug addiction, and prostitution. But a radical dissonance envelops the work's style and protagonist. Both the novel and its contemporary critics identified Gertrudis as a "transitional" character, with one foot in the past and one in the future and thoroughly miserable in the present.[38] The character's vertiginous flips from a lovesick woman prone to emotional meltdowns to a cool-headed observer of the Havana cultural scene and her own situation reinforces this portrayal of a woman whose own life doesn't quite fit her. Similarly, the style careens from melodrama and a high-blown rhetoric of suffering to a leaner, more modern prose for the routine of Gertrudis's life and for moments of greater pause and reflection for both narrator and character. Gertrudis's orphaned state embodies her dislocation as a New Woman lacking models in a new Cuba. Her godfather, a veteran of the independence wars, empathizes with her drive to live freely and offers support when she falls. But he trivializes her intellect. The public celebration of May 20 commemorating the founding of the Cuban republic, moreover, backgrounds Gertrudis's eye-opening discovery: Damián happily watches the parade and flag-waving with his wife and children. Harboring minimal patriotic pretensions, Gertrudis imagines herself "lost, isolated within that enormous, noisy mob" and "on the margin" of the domestic and national family alike (164, 169).

In fact Gertrudis's only viable Havana home is literary, although even in this intellectual milieu her role is problematic. Three times the novel interrupts the histrionic account of the protagonist's life with extended *tertulia* scenes, eccentric soirees of artists, intellectuals, and political activists, set in the basement apartment of the character Guzmán. These gatherings offer an enlightening time-out from whatever sentimental upheaval Gertrudis has just experienced. But this "social underground" (77) is far from utopian. Focusing from Gertrudis's perspective, in fact, the narrator describes this setting as "an impossible ambience," a "hostile and repugnant milieu" with a "confused abundance of weak wills, skilled intellects, poisoned hearts" (76–77). Still, the narrator intimates, in the *tertulias* new information circulates, and talk about art and cultural issues offers the necessary "fertilizer" to enrich the stifling banality of Gertrudis's everyday life (77). Here she abandons the melodramatic discourse of romance to reflect more philosophically on human interaction, women's situation, and ideas. These well-placed scenes are critical for the work's inquiry into the tenuous relationship between the modern woman and literary culture, in which the former emerges as a burning topic in the latter, its subject in more ways than one. Thus the *tertulias* provide a place where those women privileged to enter can feast on the banquet of cultural activism. At the same time, these sessions witness intense metafictional discussions about the art and commerce of novel-writing and the proper subject matter for modern fiction. In fact *tertulia* participants debate the viability of Gertrudis herself, both as a modern Cuban woman and as a credible character.

Although Rodríguez Acosta once proposed in an interview that Gertrudis was not sufficiently "intellectual" to face her own problems (quoted in Martínez Márquez, "Ofelia Rodríguez Acosta," 9), the work portrays her as a woman with intellectual aspirations and a privileged relationship to literary culture. Just as she embodies the "practical feminism" that Rodríguez Acosta espoused in her essays, so does the novel constitute her as a "practical intellectual" whose interaction with the literary milieu emerges through her singular work. Described as a woman of "masculine ambition" (44), Gertrudis does secretarial work in a government office. But her coworker Fonseca, a novelist of slight commercial success, provides her an entrée to intellectual life. Through his contacts, she moonlights typing for university professors and students, learns from their notes, and becomes editor of their prose: "Motivated by her acute intellectual curiosity, she began to acquire a serious enthusiasm to study by analyzing, to understand by observation and deduction. She would argue with that sympathetic and varied clientele, who increased her knowledge, transmitting their professors' explanations and lending her books" (23). Quickly gaining editorial and entrepreneurial talent, Gertrudis, like the New Woman of international modernism, becomes the literary midwife to a cadre of novelists who bring her their work, which she edits, places with printers and bookstores, and launches and advertises.[39] The autonomy gained makes her less dependent on the office job and, like a modern, male writer, she walks the city for reflection and new ideas. She also tries her own hand at writing, a venture her godfather dismisses as the accumulation of "literary scraps" that substitute for "original ideas" (26). Although possessed by a "generative creative fever" (41), however, Gertrudis prefers living over writing, an activist conception of intellectual life reinforced by her encounter on a Havana street with Jose Enrique Varona that I described earlier. In the spirit of the vanguard Minoristas, Gertrudis marvels at Varona's "example of action," as a man who knows how to "wield ideas and exhibit life at work, in the newspaper, in the street . . . in his own house" (43). Similarly, Gertrudis struggles to live her ideas through activism that encompasses both her literary midwifery and her radical life choices.

Her lover Damián's paradoxical reaction to Gertrudis points to the historical dissonance between these choices and her intellectualism, as the novel showcases the male literary world's radical ambivalence toward modern literate women. The narration posits that Gertrudis's intellect actually provokes Damián's interest, as he witnesses her repartee with Fonseca. But once coupled he transmutes her into an aesthete's silent muse, "ample, and harmonious" poetry, "like an ode" (114). He would rather know little about her, he explains, so as better to imagine her "alone, isolated . . . disconnected from time and life itself" (52). But Gertrudis's androgynous persona undermines such imaginings, as her *tertulia* cohorts struggle to square her intellectual qualities they regard as masculine with what the novelist Fonseca calls the *noñerías* or infantile banalities of her sentimental life. Pondering these ostensible contradictions, the *tertulia* characters discuss Gertrudis in her presence as if she, the New Woman subject of their salon, were not really there. They speculate in her presence how she can be so modern, so "manly, dynamic, precise, like an hourglass" (80), so "full of masculine traits, all of her potency concentrated in her will" and at the same time enact such a sentimental concept of life (82, 142–143). The discourse of the novel's *tertulias* equates modernity with masculinity, particularly as performed by the New Woman, while melodrama and romance stand for outmoded femininity. Only Delia, the novel's lesbian character, sees no paradox in Gertrudis's synthesis of intellect and sentiment. Delia, in fact, lauds the "grand imagination" with which Gertrudis lives—she "works, struggles, is poor," she "knows how to think," and she "practices the freedom to love" (142). For Delia, Gertrudis is a true "woman of the times" (143).

Nina Menéndez has argued that along with the *tertulias,* Delia's lesbianism offers a utopian alternative for a dislocated New Woman like Gertrudis. Delia is unquestionably the work's sole contented woman character and the only person talking *to* Gertrudis as well as about her. Yet the novel conspicuously situates its autobiographical impulse neither in Delia nor Gertrudis but rather in the contentious, heterogeneous intellectual world in which they meet, an "ambiance" that Gertrudis, "restless" and "as susceptible as a sponge," finds essential for airing her modern turmoil (189). While Gertrudis performs Rodríguez Acosta's concepts of practical feminism through her melodramatic life, the third (and longest) *tertulia* scene offers the only setting in which the narrating voice itself assumes a palpable, separate identity by speaking repeatedly in the (collective) first person. Here the narrator goes on at some length about the wages of post–World War I modernity as experienced in early-twentieth-century Havana and energetically debated in the very *tertulia* that directs so much attention to the *noñerías* of a young woman's life. Enumerating the trends that keep the city and the *tertulia* in perpetual activity—politics, vanguard polemics, scientific developments, sports—the narrator highlights feminism as "the only appealing thing left to us on the tray of History, by the thousand-times damned European War of 1914, in its postscript of economic landslides, moral confusion, and artistic reversals of fortune" (190–191).

The narrator's abrupt outing as the "we" of this passage, repeated in the pages that follow, startles the reader, as the authorial persona drops the impersonal mask and catapults herself into the novel's vivid scenes of Havana's literary culture, the scenarios for Gertrudis's self-reflection and heated debates about her New Woman status. The narrator's identification with the protagonist, then, emerges only in their mutual *tertulia* ties, a common world they inhabit. This identification underscores the novel's insistent location of Gertrudis's drama in the heart of the intellectual world. Moreover, this third and final *tertulia* scene, with its heated commentary on art and intellectual life, also witnesses some of Gertrudis's most histrionic moments as she drinks to forget her heartbreak, dances for an audience, winds up in bed with her novelist friend Fonseca, and awakens with little memory of the night before. The very incompatibility of the protagonist's melodrama with the intellectual debates surrounding her becomes one of the novel's central concerns. Fonseca does not know quite how to handle the messiness of her life, material, he emphasizes, that would never do for one of his own abstract novels. He, in fact, undervalues the middlebrow society women who constitute a significant portion of his own readership and regards the popularity that their interest signals as proof of its artistic failure. Moreover, he argues, Gertrudis's highs and lows constitute unrepresentative material for a modern novel. But Gertrudis's lesbian friend, Delia, counters with a view more consistent with *La vida manda* itself as she argues that the very disarray of Gertrudis's life embodies modern Havana and is therefore precisely what a modern Cuban novelist should address. The best-seller status of *La vida manda* provides an apt counterpoint to the work's fictional discussion about whether women's problems constituted suitable novelistic fare. The novel's internal debate about the relationship of writers to audiences and the appropriate subject matter for literature, moreover, resembles the heated discussion between Sabas Alomá and Mañach on similar topics.

The central role of the *tertulias* in the novel exemplifies Rodríguez Acosta's position that immersion in public literary culture could be fundamental for women's intellectual growth, social mobility, and agency, a judgment shared by Sabas Alomá. At the same time, Gertrudis's emotional seesaws and their negative outcome underscore Rodríguez Acosta's ambivalence toward the performance role assumed by women in cultural life. Gertrudis's night of conspicuous display at the *tertulia,* when she dances provocatively for an audience that desires her, triggers her melt-down that culminates in the novel's catastrophic end. Rodríguez Acosta implies, then, that a seductive public performance generates this particu-lar New Woman's dissolution. At the same time the narrator intimates that this performative coming-out harbors the incipient independence of a woman on the verge of a breakthrough. As Gertrudis dances, the narrator observes, her joyous laughter "like music that may have been sleeping un-sung in her throat might suddenly have burst into the playing of an entire orchestra" (193).

A comparable ambivalence toward performing women weaves through all of Rodríguez Acosta's writing. In journalistic columns com-parable to Sabas Alomá's campaigns, she assailed the "false feminism" embodied in the prostitution of "free" women's physical beauty on the Hollywood screen, criticized weddings as performative rituals that put women's bodies on display, and censured the frivolity of "salon feminism" as a "doubtful aristocracy" of women who had never undertaken serious study or the hard work in the "trenches" typical of a practical feminist.[40] Menéndez aptly points out that *La vida manda* usually avoids subjecting Gertrudis to the bodily scrutiny of readers and other characters. At the same time, Menéndez argues, when the narration observes that Gertru-dis's life is "narrow and tight, like a dress that is too short" (*La vida manda,* 24), Rodríguez Acosta was opposing both "consumerism that produces a fashion subject" and "biological arguments to justify the sub-ordination of women" (Menéndez, "No Woman Is an Island," 102). But as in Gertrudis's brief dance scenario, Rodríguez Acosta focused in other forums precisely on the potential power of a performing woman on dis-play. The short quasifictional sketch "Mujeres de cabaret," for example, showcases through the eyes of a discriminating observer women of varied personae brought together in the smoke-filled, sensuous ambiance of a nightclub: the "dancer woman," the "woman who waits," the "woman who resists," the "barometer woman," and the "curious woman," the narrator herself, who watches in voyeuristic pursuit of "a new sensation" and with high expectations about "all that happens" and "above all, all that does not happen" (45, 90).

This focus on what does not happen but could, like the outburst of song harbored by Gertrudis's laughter as she dances in *La vida manda,* highlights the "as if" or "subjunctive" condition of performance, its open-ness to possibility and liberationist promise.[41] While she denigrated the exploitation of women's sensuality for consumerist ends or for social roles grounded in their own subjection, Rodríguez Acosta celebrated bodily power as a characteristic of modern women worthy of emulation. The fusion of physical agility with intellectual or social work, in fact, epitomized Rodríguez Acosta's ideal of the "practical feminist." She gave top billing to Amelia Earhart as an effective New Woman ("La propia ruta," 13) and pointed to the musical and dramatic achievements of women on stage, above all Isadora Duncan, as harbingers of their emergence as social actors ("El gobierno," 13). She also argued that before they could change their thinking, women needed to perform. They should assume public "attitudes," take open stands on issues, and cultivate a public persona, for example, by taking the stage to give a lecture, recital, or concert ("El carácter," 313). In short, she implied, women must engage in an art of living through self-conscious public performances that defy traditional gender or class behavior. Thus she proposed that feminists substitute "personal respect for slavery, courage for useless self-denial" and "intelligent tolerance for tearful pardons" and that the upper- or middle-class feminist failing to identify with the woman laborer was defending only her "reclining sofa and her car" ("El carácter," 314–315).

While she was less the performer than Sabas Alomá, through lectures and columns Rodríguez Acosta took the stage and cultivated the "attitudes" and public persona of a practical feminist as she defined it. In contrast to Sabas Alomá's public enactment of an explicit, "feminine" presence, however, she worked against gender binaries. She affirmed that men and women should juxtapose in their behavior qualities typically ascribed to one or the other, and, by example, she infused her own writing with androgynous turns such as "virile tenderness" and "soft vigor" ("La raza humana," 17). The banalities of Gertrudis's love woes in *La vida manda* may have been typical for working- and middle-class Cuban women in the 1920s, but her role as literary midwife, her intellectual coming-out in Havana literary culture, and her characterization as a woman with few explicitly "feminine" attributes were decidedly not. Rodríguez Acosta's subsequent fiction continued to challenge gendered scripts, for example, in *Dolientes* (1931) through a liaison between a sentimental melodramatic man and a cerebral no-nonsense woman or in *En la noche del mundo* (1940), through the matter-of-fact portrayal of a gay male pair. This fictional assumption of multiple gender and class positions constituted for Rodríguez Acosta the practical work of a novelist, a virtual life in the "trenches" comparable to the lived activity of the "practical feminist."

Significantly, Rodríguez Acosta's *Sonata interrumpida* (1943), her most autobiographical work and from a literary standpoint probably her best, posits this practical art of living as the best path for a woman who becomes not a literary midwife like Gertrudis but a successful writer in her own right. Fernanda, the protagonist, repeatedly assumes public "attitudes" in Havana cultural and political life in the 1920s and 1930s. The *tertulias* of male artistic culture provide only one among several venues for her intellectual coming-out. Fernanda, although heterosexual, is even more androgynous than Gertrudis and, not coincidentally, better adjusted and integrated. But unlike Gertrudis, and in keeping with Rodríguez Acosta's ambivalence about women's performative role in public culture, Fernanda does not perform as an artist before an audience. In fact the work's performing woman, an accomplished pianist, is one of its more manipulative but ultimately powerless women characters. Fernanda, by contrast, comparable to Rodríguez Acosta, is an outspoken actor in politics but performs in the more dramatic sense only through writing.

Although both Mariblanca Sabas Alomá and Ofelia Rodríguez Acosta had long and productive careers, the 1920s and 1930s witnessed their greatest public presence in cultural life. As the divide between political activism and literary work sharpened in post-Machado Cuba, they moved in opposite directions, with Sabas Alomá dedicating herself more exclusively to political journalism and activism and Rodríguez Acosta devoting most of her energy to literary writing. Both grew less visible, although Sabas Alomá carried her activism into the postrevolutionary period and Rodríguez Acosta wrote several more novels. Not only did neither achieve the prominence of their Minorista cohorts, until recently they virtually vanished from literary institutional memory. It would be simplistic to attribute exclusively to gender obstacles or gendered norms of literary quality the fact that Rodríguez Acosta in particular never achieved the status of her better-known male contemporaries. Unlike her accomplished female contemporary the poet Dulce María Loynaz, who kept her clear distance from public cultural life in the 1920s, Rodríguez Acosta never became as good a writer as, say, Carpentier or Guillén. But neither, of course, did most of the male Minoristas who populate Cuba's literary histories. Moreover, *Sonata interrumpida,* certainly Rodríguez Acosta's best-written novel, never received the contemporary attention of *La vida manda,* with its more titillating content.[42] As the most prominent feminists in Havana's modern literary culture of the time, however, Sabas Alomá and Rodríguez Acosta enacted through their intellectual careers the tensions and complications of a cultural world that subsequently forgot them, and their writing offers a rich and intricate record of what it was like to be a woman writer in Havana in the 1920s. As feminists they promoted a key role for literature and literary culture in the intellectual formation and liberation of women even as they scrutinized women's subjection in the literary world. At the same time, they were as fully immersed in Havana's intense public conversation about intellectual activism, artistic standards, and the wages of modernization and modernity as any Minorista or *Revista de avance* writer. Their work, in sum, illuminates the profound ways in which gender shaped that conversation and the intricate strategies they crafted in order to join in.

chapter 7

AD-LIBS BY THE WOMEN OF *AMAUTA*

Magda Portal and María Wiesse

In a 1929 review of Magda Portal's essay on vanguard poetry, a contributor to José Carlos Mariátegui's renowned Lima magazine *Amauta* (1926–1930) said little about the work itself but waxed ecstatic about its author.[1] Calling her his "belligerent comrade" and "the purest feminine revolutionary ferment" of her time, the reviewer consecrated Portal as Peru's New Woman, a combative muse who could motivate the journal's radical cultural and political mission. She was, he proclaimed, "the woman who goes to the barricades with her unrest at her waist and a cartridge belt with incendiary metaphors . . . the agile woman of the steering wheel and the press, of the locomotive and the electoral outcry" (Delafuente, 102).

This image of Magda the muse as a grand inspiration for Peru's "new men," as Mariátegui called them, recalls other renditions of women writers as bold embodiments of a national imaginary or artistic program: Ortega y Gasset's Gioconda of the Pampa for Victoria Ocampo, Jorge Mañach's Mariblanca de Cuba for Sabas Alomá, or Borges's "proud" and "fervent" Norah Lange, a muse for the Argentine vanguards (Borges, Prologue, 5). Whatever feminist aura emanates from Delafuente's exaggerated portrait of Portal is misleading, not only in its relationship to her complex self-representation as an activist and writer but also as a gauge of *Amauta*'s cultural politics. In fact, if the careers of Mariblanca Sabas Alomá and Ofelia Rodríguez Acosta embody the exceptional ties between Cuba's artistic vanguards and the country's strong feminist movements, those of Magda Portal (1903–1989) and María Wiesse (1893–1964) exemplify by contrast the vast divide between the vanguards and Peru's incipient feminism. As Francesca Miller and Elsa Chaney have demonstrated, the slow start of Peruvian feminism provides a counterexample to the relative progress in women's civil rights during the same period in the Southern Cone and the Caribbean. According to Miller, the absence of a strong Peruvian middle class and the persistence of parochial Catholic schools as the foundation of women's education explain in part the late arrival of a broad-based feminist movement in Peru, as secular schoolteachers stimulated feminist critique elsewhere in Latin America (Miller, 79). The leaders of Lima's muted early feminism were upper-class and their politics considerably more conservative than those of Portal, Wiesse, or the cultural worlds that they inhabited.[2] In comparison to what one finds in Buenos Aires, Havana, São Paulo, or Mexico City, the images of women and gender standards circulating in Lima's popular publications *Mundial* and *Variedades* were generally more traditional, and descriptions of the New Woman were more often framed as models of how Peruvian women ought not to behave.

As a center of progressive thought within this milieu, Mariátegui's circle and *Amauta,* the dominant wing of the Peruvian vanguards, imagined a Marxist-inspired new Peru as a response to the Leguía regime, which despite its reformist cast still catered to oligarchic structures. But the *Amauta* group and other Peruvian vanguard circles highlighted class and indigenous ethnicity.[3] Given its internationalism, *Amauta* contributed less than one would expect to serious gender debates. In keeping with its eclectic cultural politics, the journal did designate its "women of the struggle," such as Rosa Luxembourg or the Uruguayan poet Blanca Luz Brum, and it published prose and verse by Spanish American women writers: Juana de Ibarbourou, Amanda Labarca Hulbertson, Nydia Lamarque, Gabriela Mistral, and Alfonsina Storni. In a cultural setting with no comparable opportunities, *Amauta* offered a provisional intellectual home for a few Lima women. Along with Portal and Wiesse, Dora Mayer de Zulen and Ángela Ramos assumed noteworthy roles among the diverse group of writers and artists that coalesced around Mariátegui and the magazine. It is not surprising that a Lima journal with a strong literary orientation should attract intellectual women. Already in the nineteenth century the literary circle constituted a center for feminist activity in Peru, for example in the cultural endeavors of Clorinda Matto de Turner, Mercedes Cabello de Carbonera, and Argentina's Juana Manuela Gorriti.[4] Despite the biases marking his youthful writings on gender, moreover, Mariátegui's views on women grew more progressive during the 1920s, coinciding with his Marxist conversion and his marriage to Ana Chiappe. Still, views of the New Woman weaving through the journal, Mariátegui's writing, and the overall ambiance of the Lima vanguards generated new stereotypes of the feminine or cast women in iconographic associations with larger cultural projects that revealed little about the experience of women writers themselves.

In this context the interpretations of the intellectual woman enacted by Magda Portal and María Wiesse illuminate the complex dynamic between writing and experience, between the affirmative art of self-portrayal and the power of dominant cultural scripts. A leading activist for the Alianza Popular Revolucionaria Americana (APRA), Portal edited two literary journals and wrote poetry, short stories, essays, and position papers on vanguard aesthetics. Wiesse, the film and music critic for *Amauta,* made her start as a women's columnist for *Mundial* and *Variedades* and authored plays, short stories, novellas, poetry, and biographical, artistic, and literary essays. Although their immersion in the major cultural scenarios of their day was impressive, both Portal and Wiesse portrayed a woman's search for creative autonomy as arduous. Both women embraced the Peruvian vanguards' leftist politics and defining focus on class and ethnicity but also posed the subject of women as a central in their work. So thorough was their rejection of the conservative ideology of Peru's upper-class feminists, however, that in the 1920s and 1930s both Portal and Wiesse avoided identification with official feminism per se.

More than any other women in this study Portal and Wiesse exemplify the power of contending cultural scripts to provoke unwitting imitation from those who might dispute them. Absent the level of irony that we find in Alfonsina Storni, Norah Lange, Patrícia Galvão, or even Mariblanca Sabas Alomá, Portal's early self-portraits at first glance offer uncritical correspondences between what male cultural observers in Lima wrote *about* her and what she sometimes wrote about herself. For her part, Wiesse ostensibly embraced conventional women's fare in her journalism and reiterated much of Mariátegui's and *Amauta's* cultural politics. But the multifaceted activity of both women in early-twentieth-century Lima reveals resourceful improvisations on reigning gender scripts, and their work testifies to their radical ambivalence not only toward traditional roles but also to the ostensibly liberated New Woman. Ethnicity and class issues marked the charged cultural debate about a new Peru, and the cultural politics of *indigenismo* permeated *Amauta* and other literary circles. But through considered, inventive responses to their meager choices as intellectual women, Portal and Wiesse established that the debate was, in fact, also about gender. Although their own engagements with performance and with literary culture were quite distinct, both Portal and Wiesse undertook forceful critiques of modern performance culture in its impact on women.

MAGDA PORTAL:
THE "IMPOSSIBLE BALANCE" OF A SOLO PERFORMANCE

In 1965, under the title *Constancia del ser* (Constancy of being), Magda Portal published the most comprehensive collection of her poetry.[5] She framed the poems with articles by two critics who had praised her work. The first, Mariátegui's response to Portal's writing of the 1920s, was originally published in his renowned essay "El proceso de la literatura" (Literature on trial) as part of the landmark *7 ensayos de interpretación de la realidad peruana* (1928; translated as *Seven Interpretive Essays on Peruvian Reality,* 1971). The other piece, by Ricardo Latcham, first appeared in the newspaper *La Nación* in Santiago, Chile, in response to the publication of Portal's collection *Costa sur* in 1944. The differences between the two pieces are arresting. In his reconstruction of a national literary history, Mariátegui, who had encouraged Portal to publish her poetry, consecrated her as Peru's first *poetisa*. He argued that while "asexual" women writers of previous generations had produced a neutered art, contemporary women like Portal had created a truly "feminine" poetry possessed of "fresh roots," "candid flowers," and, above all, greater *"elán vital"* and "biological force" than their nihilistic, skeptical male counterparts (*Obras completas,* 2:323).[6] Writing sixteen years later, Latcham affirmed that as a writer Portal differed sharply from "what with a little sarcasm and another little bit of tolerance" he and his contemporaries had commonly dismissed as a *poetisa* (217). Latcham praised Portal for producing poetry "completely divorced from . . . torrential feminine lyricism in America" (219).

Beyond whatever changes Portal's poetry may actually have undergone from 1928 to 1944, these two judgments document a volatile cultural dialogue about gender and art and exemplify yet again the mixed signals provoked by women's writing. In short, one critic congratulated Portal for writing "like a woman," while the other lauded her for electing not to. More important, that she herself selected these articles as bookends for a comprehensive assemblage of her work highlights Portal's own uncertain identifications as a woman writer. This indecision undercuts one meaning of the work's title while accentuating the other. In one sense *constancia,* or constancy, to designate a collection spanning forty years suggests an enduring self-conception linking the poems over time. This image coincides as well with Mariátegui's assertion in 1928 that Portal's writing offered a consistent self-portrayal, "a clear version of herself" divested of paradoxes, myth-making, idealization, or legerdemain (*Obras completas,* 2:324). By contrast, Portal's own creative writing of the 1920s and 1930s and her autobiographical novel *La trampa* (The trap; 1956) that revisits these years undermine the implied continuity of the anthology's title and of Mariátegui's reading of Portal.

Portal's art of living as an activist intellectual in the 1920s and 1930s in fact projects a frustrated search for a viable conception of self, particularly as a creative writer. More pertinent to this enterprise is the alternate meaning of *constancia* as evidence or proof, a connotation reinforced in Portal's prefatory note to the collection in which she explains that she lost much of her collected writing on a flight from Peru to Buenos Aires in 1951. The material in *Constancia del ser,* she noted, was gathered from work published widely in periodicals and could stand in for a much larger body of work written during twenty years of "precarious personal stability" and "unending struggle" (*Constancia del ser,* 7). The constancy in Portal's unfolding self-portrait as an artist, then, is its projection of instability, dissatisfaction, and turmoil. These tensions between politics and poetry, between Magda the activist muse for the men of *Amauta* and Magda the perilously located modern artist are particularly strong in the 1920s and 1930s and showcase her ambivalence toward feminism, models of the New Woman, and women's designated roles in public life. As a central participant in the Peruvian literary vanguard, Portal alternately embraced and subverted the gendered discourse that marked conceptions of cultural modernity in Peru. Above all, her self-represented experience of this period conveys the radical aloneness of an intellectual woman who was absorbed as no other in Peru's political and cultural life.

Portal's public inaugurations into literature and politics were simultaneous. She was born in the Lima seaside suburb of Barranco to a middle-class family that soon fell on hard times.[7] Following a childhood and adolescence of deprivation, Portal went to work once she had completed a basic education. In the early 1920s she sat in on literature and philosophy classes at the University of San Marcos, participated in student reform movements, taught classes for workers in the Universidades Populares Manuel González Prada, and began publishing her poems, short stories, and essays in *Mundial,* mostly under the pseudonym Tula Soavani. During these years she met her political mentor Víctor Raúl Haya de la Torre, who would soon found the APRA, and somewhat later, Mariátegui, with whom she forged both intellectual and political ties. As her biographer Daniel Reedy points out, 1923 was a banner year for Portal in both politics and art: she joined demonstrations against the Leguía regime and was awarded a prize in the Juegos Florales, a poetry contest at San Marcos. Beginning in 1926, Portal dedicated herself for more than two decades to national and continental Aprista activities and underwent intermittent political exile in Bolivia, Mexico, Cuba, and Chile. Between 1934 and 1936 she was incarcerated for almost two years in the Santo Tomás women's prison in Lima. In 1930 she cofounded PAP, the Peruvian branch of the APRA, and for years she directed the women's section of its executive committee. Disillusioned with the APRA on both political and gender grounds, she broke with it in 1950. During the 1920s and 1930s Portal also edited innovative literary magazines, published short stories, vanguard poetry, political essays, and position papers on the new art and played a central role in mapping the *Amauta* aesthetic that synthesized vanguard technical experimentation with social commitment.

These ties to major movements notwithstanding, the contradictions in Portal's identity singularized her experience as a woman writer. During these years her writing enacted unrelenting tensions between her political and literary selves as she cast a critical eye on the roles of muse, performer, and New Woman ascribed to her in public life. From early on Portal was a dedicated poetry declaimer and engaging speaker, roles that saturated her public persona and the reception she received. Male contemporaries and fellow political activists reportedly called her "The Doll" and later reflected on her "svelte figure," the "angelic" beauty of her red hair and blue eyes, and the deliberative tap dancing of her walk.[8] This imagery's corporeal dynamism anticipates Portal's incarnation as *Amauta*'s agile New Woman of the barricades. Accounts of Portal's legendary refusal to take the stage and receive her 1923 poetry award at San Marcos because of Leguía's unexpected presence in the audience transformed her de facto refusal to perform (and to accept the prize) into a performance unto itself that generated a standing ovation from the audience.[9] Portal's public performances often synthesized the political and the literary, for example in poetry recitations for the Fiesta de la Planta, a celebration for labor unions and workers studying in the Universidades Populares González Prada that included artistic soirees and theatrical and sporting events. (n.a., "La fiesta de la planta," 33–34). The characterization of her alter ego María de la Luz in the autobiographical novel *La trampa* underscores the value Portal placed on the power and artistry of performance and simultaneously sets her apart from other women. María de la Luz, the narrator emphasizes in a chapter aptly titled "Speeches," is the only woman among APRA party leaders fit to take the stage, and her performances are both artistic and political achievements. She possesses, the narrator notes, a "full" and "vibrant" voice that produces the "harmonious and solemn notes" of "musical tonality" and contrasts with the "strident voice" and "harangues" typical of women's speeches (104).

While this passage affirms Portal's embrace of the performing woman as an integral part of her persona, it also reveals her refused identification with other women and official feminism, an attitude that permeated her political writing of the 1920s and 1930s. The passage also reproduces derogatory stereotypes of activist women. Notwithstanding her roles as the APRA's spokesperson for women and lobbyist for the material improvement of women's lives and their equality within the party, Portal rejected mass-media versions of the New Woman on political grounds and affirmed the cultural inappropriateness of foreign models. She also replicated gender stereotypes from a heterosexist stance. Thus the polemical tract *Hacia la mujer nueva: El aprismo y la mujer* (Toward the New Woman: Aprismo and woman; 1933) describes the models that Aprismo was to avoid. These included the "asexual" and "ambiguous" "man-challenger," the liberated and "equivocal" *garçonne* trying to imitate men in an "absurd copy," and, above all, the "Yankee flapper, a species of feminine boy, sportswoman, agile, daring, with fear of nothing, but unsure of her own path" (51). Portal noted that through magazines and Hollywood films these imported models from "more advanced countries" attracted freedom-seeking Peruvian women drawn to a seemingly happier world (52). Images of the "asexual" flapper, she argued, served class interests inappropriate for Peru's women workers. But while she lobbied for Peruvian women's equality, throughout this polemical treatise references to women's "intuition" and "natural curiosity" reinforced gender essentialism and conveyed evident discomfort with androgyny. Portal's condescension toward the women on whose behalf she spoke, moreover, was conspicuous.

As befits the genre, Portal's pronouncements in political writings are categorical. In fact, the self-portrayal that emerges from these essays and in her most political poetry corresponds rather faithfully to the New Woman of the barricades described in the *Amauta* review, above all in the contentious tone of a voice that periodically projects its presence in capital letters. But this very feature gives Portal's political writing a monologic quality, in Bakhtinian terms, and defies readers seeking more nuanced self-representations. It is tempting for readers seeking to recast Portal as a late-twentieth-century feminist to interpret the rebellious voice of these polemics as the voluntary affirmation of the more autonomous thinker and open feminist that Portal became from the 1960s to the 1980s. But her political essays and tracts of the 1930s offer no unanticipated rearticulations (to paraphrase Judith Butler's term) of the negative view of upper- and middle-class civic-oriented feminism held by the Peruvian left of the 1920s and 1930s. As in other Latin American countries and as feminist historians demonstrate, the political left often viewed women as a conservative force that, if given access to the ballot, might thwart progressive goals. Thus Portal rejected the small group Feminismo Peruano Zoila Aurora Cáceres (founded in 1924) for sustaining an "excessively elastic concept of women's rights" that could lend itself to "praise a tyrant" ("Rol de la mujer revolucionaria," 332). As historian Francesca Miller aptly sums it up, during these years Portal the activist privileged class over gender, dismissed bourgeois feminism as frivolous, initially opposed women's suffrage, and expressed little faith in the capacity of Peruvian women for civic life (101–102). True, Portal attributed these limitations to the "corrupt environment in which the mentality of [Peruvian] women [had] been forged" ("Rol de la mujer revolucionaria," 332). But she argued that the Peruvian woman would be ready to participate in national life only under a new system that would give her "ample possibilities" to *"rehabilitate herself"* ("Rol de la mujer revolucionaria," 332; my emphasis). As the director of the feminine section of the APRA, Portal herself was charged with this "rehabilitation" of women for the imagined new society.[10]

Paradoxically, then, Portal in her political work assumed a pedagogic role toward other women that was compatible with the very goals of civic usefulness and social motherhood that characterized Latin America's feminist movements and that she ostensibly rejected. If one considers only her political writing, it is difficult to reconcile Portal's condescending tone toward other women with her own public role, assigned and self-styled, as the rebellious New Peruvian Woman. Her class-based critique of Peruvian feminism of the time leads one to expect, in fact, a more open reflection on feminism as a concept. Mariátegui, for one, saw feminism, its class origins notwithstanding, as fundamentally radical.[11] Although he labeled "dilettante feminism" a product of bourgeois liberalism, he argued that as a "pure idea" feminism was "essentially revolutionary" (*Obras completas,* 14:130). As embodiments of revolutionary feminism he pointed to the Russian activist Alexandra Kollontai and to Isadora Duncan, whose iconoclasm in art and life constituted a "permanent revolutionary impulse" (*Obras completas,* 6:201). Portal, too, admired Kollontai and drew on her work in imagining the new Aprista woman as a sexually liberated partner to the new man and a person disinclined toward the sentimentalism and romance associated with her gender.[12]

As an icon of revolutionary feminism, however, Mariátegui's choice of Isadora Duncan, a performing woman and genuine artist, is more apt when considering Portal's self-figuration over time. In her art rather than her politics Portal found terrain for more reflective considerations of gender and for illuminating her own precarious position in the cultural worlds she traveled. In poetry and fiction she crafted a more intricate image of the woman intellectual and a more compassionate perspective on women's experience. In recounting her political life, in fact, Portal linked literature and intellectual activity to intermittent loss and recovery. Thus she recalled that when Haya de la Torre urged her in the early 1920s to abandon poetry writing and study political economy, she dutifully tossed her unpublished collection *Anima absorta* into the river but felt "torn apart" by her action ("Yo soy Magda Portal," 214). Mariátegui, by contrast, who was more heterodox politically than Haya and saw cultural innovation as a foundation for social change, encouraged her to publish her work, a fact documented in Portal's presentation of *Constancia del ser* in homage to their friendship (9). As I have noted, her preface to this volume characterizes its contents as a recuperation of remnants lost. In the 1978 essay, "Yo soy Magda Portal," she insists that her "essential vocation [had] always been poetry" (231). Although both historians and literary critics have underscored the primacy of Portal's political activity,[13] the portrayal of her fictive alter ego, María de la Luz, as a performing artist underscores the high value Portal herself placed on the aesthetic.

Although Portal clearly reserved literature for cultivating a more autonomous voice, she hardly idealized it. But literary culture, in contrast to APRA politics, allowed her room for inquiry and the strategies to cast a critical eye on the culture itself. Thus some of her earliest writing, short stories, and sketches published in *Mundial* from 1920 to 1923 challenge the gendered discourse of art. While some of these stories, as Reedy points out, employ the imagery and conventions of Spanish American *modernismo* (*Magda Portal*, 40–48), as a group they actually expose the troublesome role of women in *modernista* aesthetics. To the extent that they document Portal's frustrated efforts to situate herself in relationship to *modernismo,* these stories exemplify what Sylvia Molloy has called (in another context) "the complexity of the woman's scene of writing" in the twentieth century's early decades (Introduction, 124). The rather plotless "Fantasía" (1922), for example, reiterates to the point of parody a style that Gwen Kirkpatrick has aptly termed *modernismo*'s "groaning" language from its "excess of sensory paraphernalia" (*Dissonant Legacy,* 7). In "Fantasía" a man and a woman located in an aristocratic setting and identified only by gendered pronouns speak in accelerating crescendos about their love of precious stones and Schubert's music. As they enumerate the jewels they desire, accumulated adjectives of preciosity and synesthesias enact a critical mimicry of *modernista* conventions. But the most interesting feature of this sketch is its elision of just *whose* fantasy, the man's or the woman's, this cornucopia of jewels and sensorial plentitude is supposed to be. The piece unfolds an enumerative list of questions and answers, but the reader is never certain who asks and who responds. A stylized drawing of a static female figure—scantily attired, adorned with orientalist bracelets and a jeweled mask and standing stiffly against the tree from which she emerges, mermaid-like—echoes prototypical renditions of women in the *modernista* aesthetic.[14] The artwork reinforces the piece's *modernista* air, but the obfuscation of its subjectivity highlights profound authorial discomfort with the very rhetorical moves that the sketch rehearses.

While "Fantasía" merely alludes to women's problematic relationship to *modernismo,* the more developed "Violetas" (1920), "Mujer" (1921), and "El fracaso" (1923) place it on center stage. Here women serve as models and muses for male creativity, and the three pieces challenge their consequent idealization. The first two stories demythologize the practice of converting women as aesthetic artifacts. "Violetas" offers the melodramatic tale of a consumptive seamstress of meager means who models for the bohemian painters who befriend her. Seeing her image on canvas, the young woman mistakes the "fantasy of the author" for love and dies heartbroken when she discovers that she is merely the model for an ideal (n.pag.). Through the volatile friendship between a bohemian painter and his favorite model, "Mujer" shifts the loss from the woman to the misguided male artist. The model, portrayed as a mix of "unconscious perversity" and "natural goodness," easily assumes the variety of poses necessary to inspire the artist who, the narrator observes, is still held captive by an "incapable *modernismo*" (n.pag.). The model's "plastic soul," the painter believes, can "interpret all of the human sensations" that could incarnate the perfect artwork he imagines (n.pag.). But the project fails when the model, an active New Woman, abandons a sitting to socialize with friends. Astounded that she could so easily postpone his great work, the artist destroys the canvas and weeps. The third story, "El fracaso," locates the inadequacy of the *modernismo* paradigm in a relationship between a male and female artist. Here an admiring composer in the audience is transfixed by the perfect performances of a classical dancer. He writes his magnum opus for her to perform and offers it to her anonymously in exchange for her agreement to meet him following her opening night performance. Their shared ideal of artistic perfection fails as a bond when the woman discovers that the man is black and his eyes are opened to her bigotry.

The shifting authorial identifications in these stories—from the young woman cast as a male artist's fantasy to the male painter grieving the dissolution of his aesthetic ideal into a flesh-and-blood woman to the disillusioned male and female artists—enact Portal's failure to craft her art of living as a writer within the *modernista* ethos. As early markers of her periodic reluctance to identify with other women, in "La mujer" and "El fracaso" the narrator sympathizes with the loss of the male artists when real women fail to validate their artistic ideals. On the other hand, as harbingers of Portal's own artistic liberation, this story trio traces the increasing agency of women characters who move resolutely away from the museum-like immobility of the César Moro drawing that accompanies "Fantasía." Portal's early fictional women evolve from the lovelorn, submissive painter's model in "Violetas" to the recalcitrant model in "Mujer" who casts off her poses as rapidly as she tries them on to the vibrant, all-too-human dancer in "El fracaso."

This gradual appearance of a dynamic persona in Portal's fiction coincided with her foundational role in the literary activities of Lima's avant-gardes, clearly a more comfortable milieu than *modernismo* but still lacking as a woman writer's ideal intellectual home. In October 1924 Portal, along with Federico and Reynaldo Bolaños (Reynaldo was better known as Serafín Delmar),[15] founded *Flechas,* Lima's first literary magazine with a vanguard air. The four-issue journal pledged to cast light on "all of the audacities of thought and art that may arise in Peru" (n.a., "Prólogo-manifiesto," 1). This artistic oath anticipated the opening charge of Mariátegui's *Amauta,* which did not appear until September 1926. Although it did not employ the word *vanguardia* or its derivatives, *Flechas* was avant-garde in its inaugural rhetoric and declared purpose. Subtitled the "organ of modern literary orientations and new intellectual values of Peru," the magazine debuted with a polemical manifesto that pitted the "spiritual renovation," "energy," and "committed ardor" of a "revisionist youth" against the "farces, literary senility, paper marionettes, conservative old age, and mental decay" of the existing literary environment ("Prólogo-manifiesto," 1). Much of the literary content of *Flechas* was actually the work of latter-day *posmodernistas* along with a handful of younger Peruvian writers who had yet to hit their stylistic stride.[16] But Portal and her colleagues deployed other tactics from the vanguard repertoire as they invoked a select audience of "pure and resolved spirits" charged with counteracting the "marble-like leveling" of Peru's intellectual elite (n.a., "En marcha," 1).

The role of *Flechas* in the formation of Portal's artistic persona was critical. Here she first established literary connections with other women, through pieces on Storni and Gabriela Mistral, and published her most experimental writing to that point, the lyric prose fragments of "El cuento de las estrellas." Most important was the emergence in *Flechas* of what would become Portal's signature authorial voice cloaked in rhetoric of vanguard dynamism. The magazine also marked the initiation of a network of Peruvian vanguard writers and activists that coalesced around several little magazines published in 1926, *Amauta*'s inaugural year.[17] The most flamboyant of these short-lived publications was Portal's own four-issue sheet, co-edited by Serafín Delmar, published from October 1926 to March 1927 and successively titled *Trampolín, Hangar* (or "extrampolín"), *rascacielos* (or "exhangar"), and *TIMONEL* (or "exrascacielos"). The sheets published work by Peruvian vanguard writers and such continental figures as Vicente Huidobro and Pablo Neruda.[18] With the exception of a few examples of "pure poetry," the writing in this review epitomized the Peruvian vanguards' synthesis of visual and syntactic experiments, *indigenista* and Americanist motifs, and social comment. A similar mix shaped Mariátegui's longer-lived *Amauta,* the signature journal of the Peruvian avant-garde whose original title was to be *Vanguardia.*

Portal's impact on *Amauta* and the magazine's role in her conception of a woman intellectual were strong, even though her association with the magazine was cut short in 1929 when she was deported from Peru. In *Amauta,* Portal published poetry, a short story, and the position paper on vanguard art "Andamios de vida" (1927). Here she defended radical artistic experiments, advocated their deployment to synthesize art and social action, and, in an implicit critique of Ortega y Gasset's widely read *Dehumanization of Art* (1925), affirmed that, conscious of a "double mission in aesthetics and in life," Peruvian and Latin American vanguardists were crafting a vitalist "HUMANIZATION OF ART" (12; upper case in original).[19] The central imagery in Portal's characterization of the new art is its "dynamism" and "action," words that, as materializations of her own voice, contrast with the stationary posing women she had subverted through her quasi-*modernista* fiction. Her subsequent piece on the new art, *El nuevo poema y su orientación hacia una estética económica* (1928), serialized in the continentally circulated magazine *Repertorio americano* and also published as a book, offered evaluative criteria for Latin American poetry.[20] As Melvin Arrington details, here Portal favored poets who interwove vanguard conventions with social engagement, for example Mexico's *estridentistas* and Cuba's Mariblanca Sabas Alomá, although Portal also valued less political poets such as Vicente Huidobro. In both essays, Portal reaffirmed that the iconoclasm and vitality of vanguard art constituted a foundation for social commitment.

While Portal's role in Peru's vanguards was foundational, however, the movement itself cast her differently. I have already cited the *Amauta* review that rendered her as the journal's New Woman of the barricades. Most striking was Mariátegui's discursive makeover of Portal through critical legerdemain and, no doubt, genuine admiration. In Mariátegui's writing, Portal, the author of one of *Amauta*'s important position papers on vanguard art, metamorphosed into a muse for Peru's "new men," her poetry into a gendered metaphor for Mariátegui's aesthetics. Ironically, then, the woman who had spearheaded Lima's literary vanguards in reaction to *modernismo*'s rendition of women as static embodiments of aesthetic creeds found herself recast as the gendered incarnation of the very artistic creed she herself helped launch in Peru. As I have observed, in his reconstruction of a national literary history, Mariátegui dedicated a significant section to Portal and consecrated her as the nation's first *poetisa*. More interestingly, his account of her writing portrays her and other women poets of her time as the quintessence of the anti-artifice aesthetic that, as I have argued elsewhere, characterized Mariátegui's artistic ideal.[21] Thus he argued that although the poetry of contemporary men manifested "nihilistic skepticism,"[22] the work of *poetisas* like Portal offered more "biological force" (*Obras completas*, 2:323). In contrast to the "mammal of luxury"—the bourgeois New Woman—Portal, he argued, avoided offering up her soul in the "full dress of finery," and her poetry, devoid of artifice, was "essentially lyrical and human" (*Obras completas*, 2:324). Thus did Mariátegui designate contemporary women writers not only as the rejuvenators of art but also, in Portal's case, as a synecdoche of the energy required to build a new Peru. At the same time Mariátegui's carefully articulated model of Peru's critically engaged organic intellectual was unambiguously male, and it was to these "new men" of Peru, not to their *poetisa* muses, that *Amauta* pledged in the "Presentación" of its inaugural issue to provide an intellectual home.

Although evidently grateful to Mariátegui for showcasing her work, Portal often worked against the grain of this gender-charged conversation, even as she sometimes embraced its terms in her lyric persona. Read in its context, her piece on vanguard aesthetics, "Andamios de vida," evidences a studied resistance to a metaphoric assignation between gender and art. Published in *Amauta* in January 1927, this position paper responded to a review by Miguel Urquieta from the journal's previous issue. Here Urquieta embedded his high praise for César Atahualpa Rodríguez's work, *La torre de las paradojas,* in a homophobic diatribe that contrasted the "rising tree" of the author's "virile art" with the "effeminate and pseudo-leftist puerility" of vanguard experiments. Attacking the lyric deployment of modernity motifs as an unnatural form of intellectual masturbation, he proclaimed that "the jazz-bandy extravagances" did to the brain what Onan did to sex ("César Atahualpa Rodríguez," 4). Portal's rejoinder to Urquieta, the artistic manifesto "Andamios de vida," chastised him as a bourgeois intellectual fearful of real revolution and took him to task for ascribing "inverted natures" to experimental artists (12). She defended the metaphors of modernity as the product of a postwar context and added that the new art had surely been born in an airplane cabin or on radio waves. Although she used a metaphor of (anti)conception to characterize *modernismo*'s idea of beauty as "sterile," she generally avoided such language and ameliorated the gendered potential of the sterility metaphor through repeated references to the creative power of a *human* art (12). Portal also emphasized the social power and energy of creativity, eschewing the word's associations with human reproduction.

But in the next installment of their debate, Urquieta, while heaping hollow praise on Portal as a public figure to be reckoned with, seized her conception metaphor with a vengeance to defend himself from the "hand of a woman" that, he complained, had attacked him. With more gay-bashing metaphors that compared new artists to dandies and sodomites, he responded to Portal's notion that *modernista* beauty was "sterile" with a full-blown metonymy of artistic creativity and the (hetero)sexual act in which a sterile woman could sabotage the most potent of (male) progenitors. The artist's internal beauty, he affirmed, "fecund" like "women of the countryside" could be impregnated at the lightest "exterior contact," adding that external beauty (of others) was equally fecund because it provoked the artist's creative instinct. Beauty, he continued, "excites and . . . receives . . . acts as semen and uterus," and he concluded: "If beauty were sterile, as Magda Portal affirms . . . if its ovaries had atrophied or been removed . . . it would be impossible to conceive anything, no matter how enormous the engendering power of the artist" ("Izquierdismo," 25–27). Urquieta's metaphoric contortions provide a stunning reminder of the discursive minefields intellectual women maneuvered simply to converse publicly about art. Portal curtly dismissed Urquieta's imagery, noting that even parasites have ovaries, and referred him back to her original article for illumination on her ideas ("Réplica de Magda Portal," 28).

In her creative writing Portal was less adept at sidestepping the gendered pitfalls of artistic debates. Still, her lyric self-portrait of this period and her fictional characterizations of women exhibit more nuanced perspectives on women's experience than her political writings of the same years. Far from Mariátegui's vitalist idealization of the feminine, for example, the lyric story "Círculos de violeta" provokes reader reaction to an infanticide perpetrated by a destitute woman to save her newborn daughter from life in an asylum, an "incubator of slaves and assassins" (1–2). Similarly the poem "Hijo" depicts the jarring education of a teenage girl when she is raped by her boss and gives birth to a daughter. These dystopic portrayals of motherhood manifest Portal's own challenges as a single mother and contrast with utopian imaginings in her political writing of educated wives and mothers building a new society with APRA men.

As the centerpiece of her creative production, however, Portal's poetry creates a woman speaker entangled in a web of irreconcilable cultural directives. Notwithstanding Mariátegui's claim of the essential "femininity" of Portal's work, her poetry actually shares concerns common to male contemporaries and poetic tradition. Thus most poems in *Una esperanza i el mar* (A hope and the sea; 1927), her most important work of this period, present a speaker who seeks, by turns, ties with humanity, an elusive clarity of thought, enduring love, power or serenity in the face of death, and liberation from the limits of being and the world. The collection's manifestation of experience attributable to a woman artist emerges less in these timeless themes than in the vacillations of the lyrical voice, sometimes within a single poem, and the intricate maneuvers of a speaker striving to incorporate conflicting roles.

Overall the collection generates the portrait of an artist struggling to square the exigencies of a prescribed, self-imposed social identity with a drive to communicate alternatives. As a composite of its varied manifestations, the collection's speaking persona takes up the larger causes celebrated in these pages but also seeks avenues for more idiosyncratic self-representations. Three poems with utopian projections of collective liberation—"Frente a la vida" (Facing life) and "Canto proletario" (Proletarian song) at the beginning and "Grito" (Scream) at the end—frame this collection. They invoke a human collectivity and link the speaker of the more inward-turning poems with a wider reality. In some poems the speaker lacks gender specificity, reaches out to "free men," and suppresses internal conflict. But "El mandato" (The command) communicates tension between the individual and the collective and provokes a shock of recognition in readers familiar with Portal's anecdote of having acquiesced to Haya de la Torre's admonition to abandon poetry for political economy. This composition manifests the compulsory quoting of social exigencies, to recast Butler's term, in a speaker struggling to perform a moral and political mandate while subjugating the very emotive impulses that could provide raw material for her lyrics. Thus the speaker in "El mandato" observes that she must stop dreaming and "tame . . . beasts" in order to be merely a "brain" and a "WILL" (*Una esperanza*, 43). Countering this vision of a speaker chained to the "wall of life," the poem "Quiero perderme de mi misma" (I want to lose myself) affirms the speaker's claim to "leap the circle" that "imprisons" her (*Una esperanza*, 35). "La tragedia común" (Shared tragedy) invokes the struggle between this impulse toward freedom of expression and the monologic force of the mandate, the "hard stone" of a "single idea" that "flattens" her brain and restrains her from taking flight with "agile wings" (*Una esperanza*, 48).

Although an apparently ungendered voice generates much of Portal's lyric, a more explicitly feminine speaker surfaces in several poems in *Una esperanza i el mar*. Here gender complicates pulls between cultural mandates and expressive singularity. Overall the self-portraits in Portal's verse waver between the earth woman as primal force, which Mariátegui recast as a source of artistic renewal and national energy, and a skeptical, critical woman-as-intellectual, akin to the modern cynicism that Mariátegui attributed to male poets but overlooked in her work. While in some poems one persona dominates the other, in many the two identities square off. The primal voice reigns in the opening poem, "Frente a la vida," a collective projection of liberation that juxtaposes a new humanity—"recently FREED MAN"—with a primordial self that has "no origin" other than the "Earth's bosom" (*Una esperanza*, 5). This imagery links originality with origins, a dominant motif of the historical avant-gardes. As the poem unfolds, it situates this myth in the feminine, as the speaker claims a gendered Old Testament foundation, her possession of the "red apple of Life" (*Una esperanza*, 7).

As Rita Felski has shown, this embodiment of a lost primal world in women permeates the discourse of international modernism, and I have already noted comparable appropriations of the motif, not only in Mariátegui's mythification of Portal but also in aspects of Nellie Campobello's self-figuration as an artist. Portal reiterates this metonymy in several poems, particularly through the speaker's identification with the sea, as in "Mar de Alegría" (Sea of Joy): "I am a Sea / *Genesis of Life*" (45; italics in original). But as in Campobello's work, this persona vies with a modern, intellectual, less "feminine" self, often in the same poem. The speaker in "Amistad" (Friendship), for example, juxtaposes her earth woman force with a modern potency of vision. Here a "savagely sister" speaker, likened to tropical winds, is also "cosmopolitan, and . . . bitterly antisocial" as she envelops cities from around the earth with the "ultra potent" Zeiss lenses of her eyes (*Una esperanza*, 17).

This poem's emphasis on a penetrating critical vision marking the speaker's interaction with the world recurs throughout the collection and aligns Portal's self-figuration with numerous artistic self-portraits by male writers in Latin America's avant-gardes. Although the poem's capitalized celebrations of "FRIENDSHIP" invoke a search for collective ties, it also highlights her solitude with comparable typographic hyperbolism: "I FEEL ALONE" (18). If Portal's poetry reproduces the primal woman as antidote to modernity's alienation, then, the "intercontinental" and misanthropic embodiment of that uprooted condition weighs in as well. In another poem, this contemporary woman speaker smokes her "spleen cigarette" and depicts a solitary self seeking "an *impossible balance*" on the "masts" of life (*Una esperanza*, 19–20; my emphasis). The collection associates this balancing act—between politics and poetry, between contradictory feminine identities, cited or self-fashioned—with intellectual work. Thus one poetic speaker, self-described in the "refined body" of a "civilized woman," invokes Oscar Wilde's admonition that "intellectual work" is bad for the looks, and she seeks beauty instead in a more primal, utopian self-portrait that imprisons life in an "iron cage" with a "small door of hope" (*Una esperanza*, 25). This poem negotiates the seeming disconnections between intellectual activity and femininity, between the "neurasthenia" of a civilized woman's intellect and the vitality embodied in the earth woman of other poems. Similarly, "Canto 1" (Song 1) juxtaposes the critical vision of the more intellectual persona with the energy of an elemental, typecast femininity. Thus life's "triumphant armies" march through the "arches" of the speaker's eyes, and her "red hair" unfurls like a flag in the sun (*Una esperanza*, 49).

The persistent image of a speaker seeking an "impossible balance" among competing cultural scenarios is reinforced by the penetrating dislocation and aloneness that permeate not only this collection, for all its collective imagery, but all of Portal's writing. Later she accentuated this portrait of a woman alone, immersed in politics and intellectual activism but lacking a political or intellectual home, in her autobiographical novel *La trampa*. Despite its artistic limitations (she wrote it in a hurry, Portal explained), this narrative reflects on her complex situation as a woman absorbed in a world of men. The novel focuses on two stories, both drawn from Portal's APRA experience. One is the tale of Charles Stool, a character the APRA sets up as a killer for the cause but abandons when others are freed. The other portrays Portal's alter ego, Marilú: her prison experiences, subjection to sexual harassment by male party members, and struggle with their denigrating views of women that she, too, has internal-ized. The novel depicts Marilú as a male-identified character who, initially uncertain what she thinks of other women, gradually questions her own views. Thus she reflects on her failed search for community in the APRA, even amidst the party's feminine hierarchy. Just as Portal acted as a leader among party women, so does Marilú instruct them to "prepare themselves for the struggle to conquer their rights" (90). "The truth is, Marilú really doesn't know the women," the narrator observes candidly, while the men, with whom she is more at ease, have been her comrades (91). But the novel also documents the protagonist's discovery of how little those comrades value her, as Marilú is "pushed aside, diminished." The narrator adds cynically that the party needs a woman to attract women, "so that it won't be said that women don't count, that they are only used to fill gaps and for inferior tasks, like selling raffle tickets, organizing charity functions, visiting prisoners" (102). The narrator's observations about how others perceive Marilú underscores the woman intellectual's isolation and blurs boundaries been author and fictional alter ego: "She has the prejudices of the intellectuals. The wives don't like her, because she looks down on them. The leaders don't like her because the presence of a woman among so many men is jolting. . . . She stands alone" (122).

Together with her biographical essay on the nineteenth-century figure Flora Tristán as the "foremother" of Peruvian feminism (1945),[23] this novelized reassessment of Portal's position in a male political and cul-tural world signaled a turning point in her thinking. It also forecast the more acute feminist consciousness that developed fully in the last three decades of her life and that marks her 1978 autobiographical essay "Yo soy Magda Portal." Nevertheless, the image of a solitary woman strug-gling to maintain an "impossible balance" that permeates her work in the 1920s and 1930s persists in Portal's more mature writing as an expression of her turbulent experience as a woman intellectual in Peru. From the van-tage point of age in "Yo soy Magda Portal," Portal recognized, even more than in *La trampa,* her tough apprenticeship as virtually a lone woman leader in the APRA and the challenges she had faced as a writing woman. Much as second-wave Euro-American feminism emerged from women's dissatisfaction with their lesser roles in the New Left of the 1960s, so were Portal's eyes fully opened to the gender prejudice she had endured (and unwittingly collaborated in) during the APRA years. But even as she rec-ognized and protested gender discrimination, Portal still resisted the idea that a separatist, collective feminism might be a necessary step for achiev-ing women's equality. In 1978 she joined the feminist group Acción para la Liberación de la Mujer Peruana but also underscored her enduring commitment to defend the rights of all, not only those of women ("Yo soy Magda Portal," 216). In the autobiographical essay she still projected the self-image of a lone crusader, for example when she downplayed the participation of women other than herself in the *Amauta* circle.[24] Although composed decades later, this deliberative exercise in self-reconstruction offers continuing testimony to the precarious balancing acts that shaped Portal's initiation into Peruvian cultural life in the 1920s and 1930s and her often solitary experience, even if self-imposed, as a woman intellectual in Peru.

NEITHER YANKEE NOR *HUACHAFITA:* MARÍA WIESSE'S INTELLECTUAL WOMAN

A concrete source of Portal's aloneness was many years of life on the move, to Bolivia, Cuba, Puerto Rico, and Mexico and later to Chile and Argentina. But as Sylvia Molloy and Francine Masiello have highlighted and as I have observed in this book's introduction, penetrating images of dislocation mark women's writing during the twentieth century's initial decades, even for those who rarely left home. The paradoxical juxtaposition of this quality with a career fully engaged in public cultural life constitutes one notable similarity between the work of Portal and María Wiesse. But although Wiesse, who was ten years older than Portal, remains far less known outside of Peru, she actually played a more enduring role in *Amauta* and was a far more prolific writer. Born to an intellectual family, Wiesse spent part of her childhood in Lausanne, Switzerland. In 1918 she published two plays, and in 1919 she founded and edited the Lima magazine *Familia*. In the early 1920s, under the pseudonym Myriam, she wrote for the popular weeklies *Mundial* and *Variedades*. Over the next four decades Wiesse published stories, novellas, poetry, plays, short biographies, children's literature, and essays on history and musicology. From the time of her journalistic debut, she participated actively in Lima *tertulias* around the publications in which she collaborated. With her husband, the well-known Peruvian painter José Sabogal, whom she married in 1922, she joined *Amauta*'s inner circle and gatherings in the mid-1920s. Possessed of broad literary, artistic, and musical knowledge, Wiesse authored much of *Amauta*'s music, film, and drama criticism.

To all appearances, Wiesse led a more conventional life than Portal, and her daily reality was certainly less precarious. On the surface, in fact, her life was the most commonplace of any woman in this study. Although she was not the only mother (Portal, Storni, Rivas Mercado, and Galvão were as well), she was the only one to raise her children in a conventional household, relatively free of economic hardship.[25] Although she sympathized with *Amauta*'s national and international politics, Wiesse displayed more interest in artistic culture than politics, in contrast to Portal. Although she published more in *Amauta* than any other woman, and one Peruvian literary history calls her "perhaps the most important woman writer of the first half of the century" (Arriola Grande, 422), Wiesse was less a public figure than Portal and is today all but forgotten outside of Peru.[26] As did Portal, Wiesse distanced herself from Lima's upper-class feminist movements and criticized images of the Anglo-European New Woman. Sentimentalism excessive by current norms dots her writing, and her literary work rarely achieves the promise of her evident knowledge and talent. But Wiesse's work of the 1920s and 1930s projects the resolute authorial persona of a self-aware woman intellectual.

As with her contemporaries in this study, the realm of performance marked Wiesse's entree to literary culture. She made her 1918 literary debut with two plays, *La hermana mayor* (The elder sister) and *El modistón* (The fashion designer). She wrote other plays on domestic topics in the 1920s, at least one of which, *El lazo,* was staged and reviewed in Lima.[27] During the 1920s Wiesse also published reviews and articles on theatre in *Variedades* and *Amauta*. But in contrast to Portal, Wiesse maintained a modest public profile and eschewed the theatricality of the New Woman in her own artistic identity. Instead, the studied, often subtle self-portraits weaving through her work highlight erudition, a passion for reading, and a penchant for critical observation and reflection. In contrast to the serious purpose ascribed to this authorial persona, Wiesse used theatricality as a sustained metaphor for what she dubbed the social farce of trendy tastes and social practices, whose effects, she argued, hindered women's intellectual development. This response to the performing New Woman as the embodiment of social contradictions and hypocrisy resembles the work of Ofelia Rodríguez Acosta in Cuba and Patrícia Galvão in Brazil. In a similar vein, Wiesse's writing of the 1920s, including her journalistic columns and the short novels *La huachafita: Ensayo de novela limeña* (1927) and *Rosario: Historia de una niña* (1929), explored the challenges facing women and highlighted the social factors thwarting women's intellectual development. But these concerns already marked her 1918 plays. The protagonist of *La hermana mayor,* Luisa, is well read, reflective, and independent, a thirty-something woman left to raise her younger sister after their parents die. Of course the learned Luisa fails to win her man, who, while enjoying her intelligent repartee, prefers her naive sister as a wife. *El modistón,* the *entremés* or interlude accompanying this play, targets the theatricality and duplicity of fashion as an obstacle to a sound matrimonial match.

The patronizing reception accorded Wiesse's early writing underscores the challenges she faced to serious consideration as a woman writer. In a *Mundial* article on her 1923 biographical piece on the Colombian liberator José María Córdova, for example, the reviewer adroitly reassigned Wiesse's authorial agency to the deceased protagonist of her account. While he praised her as an accomplished writer, Wiesse's reviewer recast her essay as the seduction of a star-struck woman by the masculine hero of her writing. Thus, Wiesse becomes the "spiritual, romantic lover" captivated by the "wild and amazonically virile" Córdova (Rebagliati, 10). In contrast to the "fire" of Córdova's "warlike ardor" and his "vigor," "bravado," and "intelligence," Wiesse's "passionate" writing, Rebagliati argued, was "fragrant with emotion," like a dragonfly scattering the "precious dust" of a "brilliant wildfire" (10–11). By contrast, a laudatory article on Wiesse's magazine *Familia,* written by her woman contemporary and sometime *Amauta* cohort Ángela Ramos, accentuated her enterprise as a writer and publisher, "distributing the work, correcting proofs, choosing the fonts for the letters, selecting prints to illustrate a poem or a story," to create an elegant magazine (Ramos, 2:13). But even Ramos was compelled to inflect her portrait of Wiesse the writer with her gender. Although Ramos showcased Wiesse's intellectual power as a "celebrated woman . . . cultured and extremely learned," she reassured the reader about the "exquisite femininity" of a journalist "equally well versed in the recipes of the boudoir and the disposition of the home . . . as the latest creations worn in Paris" (Ramos, 2:13).

Even as she embraced such culturally sanctioned roles and established herself as a professional writer in women's columns for *Mundial* and *Variedades,* Wiesse portrayed herself as an intellectual and cultural critic. Moreover, she negotiated her critique of Peruvian women's situation within the context of an ostensibly conventional life, as in the self-conscious debut of her authorial persona in the travelogue of her honeymoon trip from Callao to Cuba, Guatemala, and Mexico, with stops in Colón and the Panama Canal. Published as *Croquis de viaje* (Trip sketch; 1924) and illustrated with woodcuts by her husband, Sabogal, this account opens with the meditations of a first-person narrator-writer who seizes the "quietude" of shipboard life to engage in an "interior dialogue" (5). While she is surrounded by other passengers and accompanied by her husband, the narrator imagines herself in a world apart with "the most complete and delicious freedom, far from the foolish and the indiscreet, isolated from the human fauna, and accompanied by a piano, music, chosen books, and a favorite cat . . ." (5; ellipses in the original).

On one level this book is a conjugal venture. Sabogal's autochthonist woodcuts shape the reader's perception of some of Wiesse's points, and he appears in the text's "we" as the plural agent of their tours and interactions with hosts on the journey. But Wiesse's artistic persona, voice, and critical eye dominate the chronicle. Following the opening scenario of shipboard reclusion, the speaker portrays herself as an insatiable reader of classic and modern literature and displays knowledge of architecture, painting, and music. Her ostensible distance from "human fauna" notwithstanding, the narrator offers numerous critical interpretations of the people around her and displays cultural prejudices and hierarchies that likewise appear in her other writing of the time. Wiesse often focused on women. The couple travels on a British ship, and Wiesse reserves her most acerbic barbs for the "skinny" and "agile" English and American New Women who dance trendy jazz and foxtrots to the "brusque rhythms of the sour little music" emitted by a phonograph's "nasal voice" (9). At least the Latin American women read, she observes approvingly, but she laments their choices of pulp fiction writer Hugo Wast over Anatol France or Proust. Two key encounters provoke meditations on the fate of women. In search of Gabriela Mistral in Mixcoac, Mexico, Wiesse and Sabogal instead find an old Chilean woman who runs a boarding house and says she has little use for poetry. Wiesse notes that this woman's economic desperation has transformed her into a "harpy" comparable to a Hoffman story character or a *Macbeth* witch (52). When the old woman shows her a well-read copy of Jorge Isaacs's *María* and says she, too, read when she was young, Wiesse laments life's transformation of a young woman who reads into a despairing, somber caricature (52). In another village scenario seen from the train on the way from Veracruz to Mexico City, Wiesse spots a beautiful young woman with an intelligent look of "unrest" eagerly watching the arrival. She imagines the provincial woman's daily trip to the station "teeming for an instant with people and noise" (32) and foresees the loss of those stimulating interludes in her prescribed life: "when the girl with the restless gaze will have to stay home at the hour of the train; she'll have married the town druggist or notary, and she'll have some crying children who will give her a lot do . . ." (32; ellipses in the original).

In these anecdotes, Wiesse resists the temptation to mythologize the provincial *mestiza* or indigenous women who catch her traveler's eye or provide the subject matter of Sabogal's woodcuts. As she lauds their beauty, she also points out that their bodies are "deformed by successive pregnancies, work, and misery" (30). But a defining exception is the binary Wiesse constructs between the ostensible authenticity of Latin America's autochthonous people and a Europeanized modernity, as she praises the women of Merida, in paradoxically classical terms: "What are the Parisian *toilettes,* capital city fashions, or the *chic* of city dolls compared to the elegance of these women, who move and walk like the nymphs and goddesses of antiquity!" (27–28). Wiesse, as did many of her male Peruvian contemporaries, privileged the indigenous over the African, for example, in her troubling racist references to the "simian gestures and contortions," the "pungent discharge," and the "guttural, strange, almost savage" speech of Afro-Panamanians in Colón (11).[28] She also reproduced class prejudices in occasional disparaging comments about the petit bourgeois who came up short in her account, particularly when compared to the rural poor.

Most revealing of Wiesse's search for an acceptable self-portrait as a Peruvian woman intellectual is her binary opposition of indigenous Mexican women with the "manly" Yankee feminist, a model from which she, as did Portal, took great distance. In the Mexican National Museum, Wiesse targeted American tourists viewing the Aztec calendar, in particular the bald, spectacled professor who explains Mexican civilization to his students with a "doctoral tone" and "pontificates in a nasal and disagreeable English" (74). But Wiesse saved her most unflattering comments for the young American women hearing his lecture, criticizing them not only for "puerile" acceptance of his remarks but also for abandoning gender norms. Their abdication of "elegance and care in dressing" and their lack of "grace and femininity," she argued, undermined other women with intellectual aspirations (74). In contrast, Wiesse praised the "discrete muteness" of the Mexican peasants before the sculpture of the god Chac-Mool (74). The fact that Wiesse paid tribute to U.S. culture elsewhere, with high praise for Emerson, Longfellow, Poe, and Twain ("El alma americana," 11–12),[29] highlights her special aversion in the travel chronicle to Yankee *women.* It is their behavior, not the men's, that challenged her cultural conceptions of gender, as she, much like Mariblanca Sabas Alomá in Cuba, strove to be both "intellectual" and "feminine."

These scenarios in *Croquis de viaje* highlight the intricate interplay of cultural hierarchies of nation, ethnicity, race, class, and gender that marked Wiesse's pursuit of a viable role as a Peruvian woman intellectual. Setting aside for the moment her singular focus on women, the contraposition in this work of the authenticity of the autochthonous with a modern Anglo-European culture allied Wiesse with Sabogal and Mariátegui and shaped her own cultural project. Wiesse on the one hand directed her multifaceted writing throughout her career toward the recuperation and dissemination of Peruvian cultural information: autochthonous myths, traditional and contemporary social mores, and the lives of religious, artistic, or historical figures. In addition to her journalism on these topics, her books *Quipus: Relatos peruanos para niños* (1936); *La romántica vida de Mariano Melgar* (1939) and an anthology of his work she edited in the same year; *Antología de la poesía amorosa peruana* (1946); and *Vida del Perú y su pueblo* (1958) all contributed to this cultural agenda. In the spirit of *Amauta*'s cultural politics, this writing validated Peru in contrast to a long-standing fashionable fascination with France among Lima's cultural elite. At the same time, in her journalism and in *Amauta,* Wiesse disseminated information and critical reviews of international artistic currents. Her efforts complemented the aesthetics of a modernizing autochthony practiced by Sabogal and the politics of *Amauta,* including a simultaneously nationalist and internationalist agenda for Peru's "new men." But Wiesse's short stories, plays, novellas, and that part of her journalism specifically dedicated to women diverge from this dominant agenda to challenge modernity's mixed consequences for those it dislocated, particularly modern Peruvian women.

This critical perspective on modernization and modernity infiltrates all of Wiesse's writing, particularly in the 1920s and 1930s, even as she embraced the vanguard spirit. She characterized her century as "irreverent, artificial, complex, and bored" ("San Francisco de Asís," 3). But she shared Mariátegui's vision of material improvement through social change, and she flatly rejected dystopic portrayals of modernization, such as in Fritz Lang's 1927 film *Metropolis* ("Notas sobre algunos films," 99–100). Although critical of what she called the "disharmony" of some vanguard compositions, she praised the critical energy of the new art. The "spirit of the age," she observed, consisted not only of "asphalt and car tires" but also of "agile rhythm, spiritual dynamism, melancholy disguised as irony, acute and profound sensibility" ("900," 43–44). Thus she praised the creative power of modern film, especially the work of Charlie Chaplin and Sergey Eisenstein. But manifesting her class identifications, in her journalism about Lima and *Croquis de viaje* Wiesse censured visual manifestations of commercialism and worried that mass culture would either produce mediocrity or exaggerate the Peruvian version of supposed petit bourgeois bad taste: *huachafería.* Although she valorized the critical spirit of modern culture, then, she criticized its "frivolity," for example in the fascination with Hollywood stars and fashion novelties. This critique manifested an *arielista* prejudice toward many things Yankee but also her belief that new customs aggravated what she called the grand social comedy.

As an antidote to modern urban life, Wiesse at times idealized the provincial past, but like her contemporary Teresa de la Parra, she did so with dollops of skepticism. She described Querétaro, Mexico, for example, as the embodiment of "placid" provincialism that was gracious and poetic but also, particularly in its meager options for women, antiquated and narrow (*Croquis de viaje*, 79). Even as they inhabit nostalgic pasts, the protagonists of Wiesse's prose are uprooted by the social role changes generated by modernization. "El forastero" (The stranger), first published in 1928 in *Amauta* and later included as the opening story in *Nueve relatos*, locates this condition in the young protagonist who returns to the family *hacienda* following a long European stay. Replaced by his brothers who have modernized the estate and rejected local traditions and abandoned by the girlfriend of his youth now enthralled by everything new, the foreigner in his own home lacks a viable role in a changed nation. The story's ambiguous authorial perspective, through free indirect discourse, exemplifies a mix of critical perspective and nostalgia that typifies Wiesse's characters, displaced from a vanishing world or their social or artistic roles. Thus the play *La hermana mayor* (1918) and the rest of the collection *Nueve relatos* present displaced characters pursuing new identities: a storyteller disguised as a sailor whose invented past adventures serve as his creative source; an urban woman schoolteacher exiled to the provinces who assumes an adopted family identity; an aspiring romantic poet transformed into a tool salesman who finds his new muse in a rich widow; and a migrant Indian worker whose death from malaria the story attributes to his distance from home.

The link that Wiesse established between modernization and the uprooted brings to mind once again the moral extracted by Doris Sommer from the nostalgic evocation of colonized worlds in Teresa de la Parra's fiction: the "marches of progress might take note of where and on whom they step" ("Mirror, Mirror," 180). Similar to Parra, in a critical take on her own era Wiesse addressed, often with irony, modern culture's mixed consequences for women. Her writings on art and culture for *Variedades* and *Mundial* often addressed a general public. But under titles such as "La página femenina" (The feminine page) in *Mundial* and "Levedades" (Light fare) in *Variedades*, Wiesse engaged women readers exclusively. Notwithstanding the levity implicit in the headlines and drawings of feminine figures fashionably attired, she undermined women's-page conventions.

While addressing some item of attire, she scrutinized the relationships and values implicit in the cultural artifact. Thus in one piece Wiesse cited Oscar Wilde to reflect on the connection between the flirtation of the fan and deceit between men and women, while in another she highlighted the ignorance of an affluent Lima woman about the lives of the women who sewed her fashionable clothes.[30]

Just as Portal prepared other women for political activism, so did Wiesse instruct bourgeois women to avoid the traps of frivolity inherent in their designated gender roles, develop a social conscience, and examine their own situation. Thus she urged women to be tolerant toward women prisoners or street women; to resist "dispersing their faculties" in the "mindless frivolity" of modern social life; to take stock of women's sacrifices in varied economic straits; to avoid "draw[ing] and quarter[ing]" other women through gossip; to read women's writing; to cultivate camaraderie with men instead of flirtation; and to consider that ninety-five percent of marriages were based on "interest and convenience" instead of "reciprocal regard."[31] Wiesse's journalism clearly mimicked scripts of gender essentialism. As in Portal's political writings, Wiesse periodically referred to the fundamental "fragility" of women, their need for protection, their "natural" maternal instincts or propensity for gossip. Usually, however, Wiesse attributed her generalizations about women as much to their situation as to their nature. For example, she defended to contemporary feminists her position that Peruvian women should work outside the home only for economic reasons on the grounds that in Peru more than in Europe or the United States, men openly mistreated women in the workplace.[32]

Generally, however, Wiesse, whose activism was more literary than political, focused less on how to improve women's treatment than on their potential for self-apprehended autonomy and intellectual power. In the spirit of much feminist activism of her time, her two novellas of this period—*La huachafita: Ensayo de novela limeña* (The *huachafita*: Rehearsal for a Lima novel) and *Rosario: Historia de una niña* (Rosario: The story of a girl)—showcase the problematic formal and social education of modern Peruvian women. The first presents the cautionary satiric tale of the petit bourgeois Doralisa, portrayed to embody all that is *huachafo* in Lima of her day. This derogatory epithet was coined in the twentieth century's early decades as a label for the ostensible materialism and bad taste of a class seeking social ascendancy to accompany its material improvement. Through its very title, then, the work embodies the privileged class position implicit in citing this reigning cultural script. Although its satirical

passages detail the supposed bad taste of *huachafería,* the novel directs the
attention of its (implicitly feminine) readers to Doralisa's bad education
from her immersion in Hollywood films, piano training in tango, jazz, and
"operatic reductions," and readings of middlebrow serial fiction (5–9).
To lure her readers, Wiesse stylized the conventions of this literary form,
overlaid with a light didactic tone. Thus for the *huachafita* the Bovarist inclination to imagine her suitors as Hollywood stars leads to her moral and
economic demise at the hands of a wealthy young man lacking intellectual
sensibility. In an ironic touch, a vanguard poet courts the fallen *huachafita.*
Here Wiesse evoked rhetorical clichés of the vanguards in the poet's lyrical
declamation of love not only for her "kisses" but also for her "cadmium
hat" and her eyes like "headlights of cars" (23). This parody and the vapid
relationship between the poet and the *huachafita* challenge the ties between
vanguard aesthetics and the performing New Woman seen, for example,
in *Amauta*'s rendering of Magda the muse to inspire its cultural project.
La huachafita, moreover, underscores the insufficiency of modern performance culture in educating women for the challenges of modern life.

As the counterpart to the *huachafita*'s bad education, *Rosario: Historia de una niña* examines unforeseen consequences of an ideal education
enjoyed by a more privileged young woman. Educated in a Rousseau-like
ambiance where her intelligence and talent flourish, Rosario, in contrast
to the *huachafita,* enjoys a strong maternal bond that is fundamental
to her intellectual development.[33] Still, in encountering "the weight of
terrible daily life" (39), Rosario experiences a new challenge to her autonomy, and her rebellion toward rules and conventions mounts. In this
schematic *Bildungsroman* with marked autobiographical traces, Rosario
experiences adolescence and its implicit incorporation of men into her life
as an enormous loss of freedom.[34] The novel portrays the ensuing social
comedy as pernicious to women. Thus Rosario's parents postpone their
daughter's debut into the "complicated ritual of vanity, of flirtations, and
of the puerile and foolish lie" (32), encouraging her refuge in imagination
and books. A lover of the necessary solitude for these activities, Rosario
is disloyal to her requisite roles of gender and class. The novel depicts
her sister, by contrast, as more feminine and bourgeois because she masters the social niceties (57). The narrator prophesies that Rosario will
never be "a perfect homemaker," will "love solitude," and will live apart
even when surrounded by the world (57). With all the privileges of her
class and education, Rosario is destined to become an intellectual and,
the work suggests, to be as uncomfortable in the modern world as the
huachafita is unhappily immersed within it.

As forecast in the shipboard room of her own in *Croquis de viaje,* the work in which Wiesse's authorial persona debuted in 1924, the voluntary, affirmative dislocation embodied in Rosario permeates Wiesse's self-portrait as an intellectual in the 1920s and 1930s. In a journalistic essay on "feminine literature," she affirmed in 1920 that women could contribute to the "intellectual life of humanity" not by imitating men or "masculinizing" their style but by writing "as women" about their experience. In imagining a women's literature—"profound, subtle, tender, and charming"—Wiesse privileged an essentialist notion of women's writing and, as did Mariátegui, conceived it as a vitalist antidote—"warmth of [the] heart"—to the "library dust" and "polished chunk of marble" of erudite writers ("Algunos apuntes," n.pag.).[35] Her negative portrayal of the masculine Yankee woman embodied a comparable search for a model of the woman intellectual who might remain "feminine." But Wiesse's call to cultivate feminine difference paradoxically unfolded in the young intellectual in formation Rosario, whose "difference" in fact diverged sharply from the normative femininity of her conventional sister. "Infancia," a nostalgic piece in *Amauta* affirming the rich contribution of Wiesse's childhood years in Switzerland to her imagination and intellect, points to the autobiographical content of *Rosario: Historia de una niña.*[36] In another 1928 *Amauta* piece, Wiesse, like the young Rosario of her novella, showcased her own voluntary relocation as a source of creativity. In the light satirical sketches of eccentric Lima characters, the narrator portrays herself locked in a room of her own, contemplating the banalities that surround her ("Pequeñas prosas," 29).

The frustration inherent in Wiesse's search for a cultural space sufficient for a woman's intellect to thrive also surfaces in the vacillations of authorial tone and register that characterize her writing. From the moment of her journalistic debut she assumed a voice confident in its own erudition, the validity of its opinions, and its right to subvert, if subtly, the conventions of the women's page assigned to her. At the same time, a studied modesty marks Wiesse's work, in occasional apologies for a limited preparation to write about whatever she has taken on and in a penchant for characterizing individual works as provisional or incomplete: "rehearsal for a novel" for *La huachafita,* "fragments of an essay" for her reflections on women's literature; "facts" and "notes" for her biographical essay on Mariátegui. This vacillation between self-effacement and affirmation also marks Wiesse's biography of her husband, José Sabogal, composed shortly after his death in late 1956. Here she focused primarily on Sabogal, inserting herself into the account modestly and in expected roles as wife and mother. A caption for a family photograph, for example, identifies her without a name: "José Sabogal, his wife, and his children" (*José Sabogal*, 38). Other photos with her husband fail to identify her at all. On the other hand, the account portrays an intellectual and artistic collaboration that begins in their courtship and honeymoon and continues until Sabogal dies. Wiesse did not romanticize this partnership or eschew naming its challenges, noting that it was hard to be married to an artist who often demanded solitude (69). But although she portrayed him as her early mentor (he was significantly older), she depicted herself as a full participant in the intellectual circles they inhabited and the movements of their time. Her repeated use of the first-person plural, *nosotros,* reinforced her active presence in the cultural world they inhabited. This *nosotros* also embodies the work's conception of marriage as an intellectual partnership, an idea that attracted Wiesse from early in her career. The protagonist of her first work, *La hermana mayor,* as I have noted, enjoyed a close intellectual friendship with the man of her dreams but lost him to her sister in a traditional romantic liaison. A short story, "El hechizo," published in *Mundial* in 1921, offers a more sanguine outcome for a young woman committed to a life of the mind. Here her fiancé convinces her that conjugal love does not require a woman to sacrifice these pursuits and forecasts the story that Wiesse eventually crafted of her own collaborative marriage in the Sabogal biography.

Still, a lasting irresolution between self-effacement and assertion throughout Wiesse's writing career suggests that she, like Portal, never quite found her intellectual home as a woman writer in Lima, even as the cultural world of *Amauta*—to its credit—provided temporary quarters for these dissimilar women. In the face of powerful restrictions, both struggled mightily to map out an eminent zone of intellectual domain. For the more visible and activist Portal, the rhetorical and performative strategies of the vanguards, in contrast to the conventions of lyrical *modernismo,* offered an adaptable libretto through which to improvise her public persona, even as she replicated the scripts of New Woman muse or earth woman ascribed to her by *Amauta*'s new Peruvian men. But she conceived this performance as solitary and herself as a teacher rather than comrade among women, with whom she identified on the basis of gender only after decades of political disappointments. Although her own writing was always shot through with gender trouble, until after her break with the APRA, Portal placed class above gender and resisted inclinations to place women's experiences on center stage. Although she was as absorbed in the cultural scene as Portal was in politics, comparable notes of solitude inflect Wiesse's writing.

As a journalist, she, too, assumed a didactic stance toward other women. Although she was as class-sensitive as Portal, Wiesse wrote from a clearer position of class privilege and criticized the version of cultural modernity enacted by Lima's emergent petit bourgeoisie. Wiesse showcased the challenges posed by modernization to women and investigated the role of a woman intellectual more openly. She eschewed the performing woman model with which Portal negotiated her public identity, and she avoided the vanguards' more ostentatious gestures, drawing from them instead the artist's roving eye, which she cast by turns on gender tradition and fashionable trends. Both women simultaneously reproduced and challenged prevalent gender stereotypes in early-twentieth-century Lima. Although the men of *Amauta* did offer selected women a provisional cultural home, they were prone to incarnate literary women as artistic or political icons. But the marked differences in the intellectual trajectories of Portal and Wiesse highlight instead the thorny situation of flesh-and-blood women writers, including their common ground of disarticulation and the distinct modes in which they experienced that terrain through its written expression.

chapter 8

A REFUSAL TO PERFORM
Patrícia Galvão's *Spy on the Wall*

In a lecture on modern art for the March 1922 Semana de Arte Moderna at São Paulo's Municipal Theatre, a founding moment for the Brazilian vanguard movement *modernismo*,[1] Paulo Menotti del Picchia proclaimed that the new era demanded a new muse. "We want an active Eve," he declared, "beautiful, practical, useful in the house and on the street, dancing a tango and typing a counter current; cheering at a futurist soirée . . . Down with the tubercular and lyrical woman!" (291). The modern woman of this vanguard fantasy moves with extraordinary dexterity from private to public, a sanguine image that belies the considerable challenges faced by women of all classes in the rapidly changing São Paulo of the 1920s. But the city's artistic innovators eventually found their dynamic performing Eve, or so it appeared.

In 1928 Patrícia Rheder Galvão (1910–1962) joined the self-proclaimed radical wing of the movement, led by Oswald de Andrade and constituted in the "Manifesto Antropófago" and the *Revista de antropofagia* (1928–1929).[2] Galvão was the young protégé of Tarsila do Amaral (Oswald's mate at the time), the modernist painter who authored *Aba Poru* (Man who eats). The anthropophagists embraced this painting as an icon for a new Brazilian art of exportation that would consume and recycle colonizing European culture. The group adopted Galvão, a savvy, irreverent Normal School student, and transmuted her into the performing New Woman of *antropofagia*, the embodiment of its primitivist aesthetic. The poet Raul Bopp rechristened her "Pagu" and in the poem "Coco" for the Rio de Janeiro weekly *Para todos* celebrated her "come-and-go body . . . umbilical and slothful" (Bopp, in Campos, *Pagu vida-obra*, 39). Two drawings of Galvão by Emilio di Cavalcanti in the same magazine portrayed her as the juxtaposition between the primitive and the modern that characterized the *antropofagia* artistic ideal. One drawing depicts her as simple and voluptuous, playing the guitar and surrounded by cactus and huts, a scene, as David Jackson points out, that evokes Tarsila's painting (Afterword, 119). In the other drawing Galvão is the New Woman à la flapper, sporting exaggerated makeup, a short skirt, and a cigarette holder. A caption highlights antirationalism and originality: "Pagu abolished the grammar of life. . . . She has genius."[3]

True to her mission as a vanguard muse, in 1929 Galvão executed a startling display for a declamation festival in the same Municipal Theatre where Picchia had conjured up a vigorous modern Eve. Dressed in a white Goya-style Spanish dress, a large black and yellow cape, strips of palm leaves, and a Bahian silver belt buckle, Galvão strode to the front of the stage and recited her own erotic composition about a cat and Bopp's poem about her. Each time that she neared the refrain from Bopp's poem, she would run to the back of the stage, turn toward the audience, flash open the cape, and declaim "Eê, Pagu, Eê!" (in Campos, *Pagu vida-obra,* 271).[4] Newspaper accounts of this audience-flashing performance highlighted the "strange appearance," "impassivity," and "cold-blooded" quality of Galvão's recitation (Campos, "Roteiro," 321). These accounts suggest that Galvão unleashed a full-blown parody of the New Woman role she embraced. The audience's response—first nervous silence, then strong applause—accentuated the ambivalent charge of the show. Recent scholarship designates Galvão the "essential symbol of everything new [and] revolutionary" of her time (Besse, "Pagu," 103) and an "important intellectual" (Valente, 26). Galvão's three-decade journalistic, literary, and political career has generated a full-length film, two documentaries, and literary and historical scholarship; a feminist study group at Brazil's University of Campinas and its journal, *Cadernos Pagu,* bear her name.[5]

The path was arduous from Galvão's lyric striptease to writings that include two novels, poetry, a political tract, detective fiction, and a corpus of journalistic literary and dramatic criticism. But this display encapsulates the issues marking Galvão's intellectual project, as it challenged women's performing role in vanguard aesthetics and mass culture. "You want a performance?" Galvão seemed to ask of the literary culture that surrounded her, "*I'll* show you a performance!" The very excess of her self-ridiculing act set the practice of muse-ifying artistic women on its ear. Galvão's simultaneous embrace and burlesque of the role resembles Norah Lange's hyperbolic *discursos* for her Martín Fierro cohorts. But Galvão's critique was more expansive and politically charged. That she first executed this challenge on a stage highlights the centrality of performance in her work. Through metaphors of performance and theatrical strategies, Galvão dedicated her writing to a rigorous assessment of the impact on women of modern performance culture and its sexual dynamic. Her eccentric costume that evening forecast the centrality of fashion in

Galvão's feminist, class-based critique of São Paulo society, and her aggressive advance on the audience presaged the strong ties in Galvão's career between artistic and political activism. This one-of-a-kind show projected an authorial persona resistant to facile portrayals. Galvão was a dedicated progressive who was a thorn in the side of the Communist Party until they expelled her in 1937; a feminist who attacked feminist movements; a vanguardist who unmasked the radical pretensions of Brazil's vanguards; a theatre and film aficionado who denigrated bourgeois theatre and Hollywood film; and a profound believer in ideals who rejected idealist dogma. Flashing the audience from the municipal stage sent studied mixed signals about Galvão's singular portrayal of New Woman exhibitionism. If they were watching her, then she was casting an eagle eye on them. Whatever she revealed as she threw open her cape, closing it showcased what they could not see, a corporeal "sign of refusal" to adapt Doris Sommer's term for the resistance enacted by minority writers toward readers or audience (*Proceed with Caution,* 1–31). This pas de deux of public persona and private I/eye marked Galvão's intellectual activity throughout her career. Moreover, her gathering refusal to perform radicalizes the critique of performance culture undertaken by the women in this book and stages a new critical turn.

Galvão grew up in Braz, the fast-growing center of São Paulo's textile industry that would provide the setting for her "proletarian" vanguard novel *Parque industrial (Industrial Park;* 1933).[6] She attended the Braz Normal School and wrote articles for the *Braz jornal.* In 1928 she joined the artistic gatherings hosted by Oswald and Tarsila, and in 1929 she produced *O album de Pagu: Nacimento vida paixão e morte* (Pagu's album: Birth life passion and death), a self-portrait in drawings and lyric prose. She first engaged in street demonstrations in 1930, the same year that she and Oswald became a couple, but 1931 was the banner year in Galvão's emergent political activism. She joined the Communist Party, was jailed for the first time at a demonstration in support of dock workers, and joined a rally in homage to Sacco and Vanzetti. In March and April she and Oswald published the eight-issue news sheet *O homem do povo* (The man of the people), for which Galvão wrote the column "A mulher do povo" (The woman of the people), theatre and film commentary, and a cartoon strip. The next year she and Oswald moved to Rio de Janeiro, where Galvão worked in the factory sector, wrote for the *Diário de notícias,* and composed *Parque industrial.*

From 1933 to 1935 Galvão traveled as a journalist and joined international radical causes, spending time in Hollywood, China, Russia,

Germany, and France, where in 1934–1935 she worked as a translator, attended the Université Popular, wrote for *L'Avant-garde,* was active in the popular front, and was jailed several times. In 1935 she attended the International Congress of Writers in Defense of Culture and was later jailed and repatriated to Brazil to avoid deportation. A formalized break with Oswald marked her return to Brazil. Between 1935 and 1940, under the Getúlio Vargas regime, she spent four and half years in Brazilian prisons and was tortured. The Brazilian Communist Party not only expelled her in 1937 as a Trotskyite and "sexual degenerate" but also contributed a deposition to her prosecution by the fascist Estado Novo.[7] Released in 1940, she married the journalist Geraldo Ferraz, a former *Antropofagia* cohort. Between then and her death in 1962, Galvão published a large body of journalistic literary criticism,[8] a series of pulp fiction mystery stories for the magazine *Detetive* (published in 1998 under the title *Safra macabra* [Macabre harvest]),[9] the novel *A famosa revista* (The famous magazine; 1945) co-authored with Ferraz, and some poetry. She remained politically active and was the Brazilian socialist party's (unsuccessful) candidate for São Paulo state representative in 1950, the same year she published the political pamphlet *Verdade e liberdade* (Truth and liberty).

THEATRE AS *PESQUISA* IN GALVÃO'S INTELLECTUAL PROJECT

Although art and politics intertwined in Galvão's work, following her experience with Communist Party orthodoxy she lobbied for the autonomy of the aesthetic and disparaged openly nationalist art. But she repeatedly affirmed the power of even the most esoteric literature to make people see the world in new ways, and her experience with theatre and performance was pivotal for this view. Incarceration and torture clearly soured Galvão's taste for street-based political action, and her contentious relationship with the party cured her of any inclinations toward political orthodoxy. But Galvão's intellectual style was consistent over time, in her critical conception of cultural activism and her self-portrayal as a discerning, dissident presence in the artistic and political causes she joined. This constancy belies her multiple pseudonymous identities, for the most part voluntary, although two were imposed: the "Pagu" assigned by Bopp and the "Mara Lobo" she adopted when the party insisted she not release *Parque industrial* under her name. Galvão's array of pseudonyms, which also included Ariel, Brequinha, Cobra, G. Léa, Gim, Irman Paula, K. B. Luda, King Shelter, Léonie, Mme. Chiquinha Dell' Oso, Pat, Patsy, Peste, Pt, Solange Sohl, and

Zazá, highlights a theatrical penchant for disguise that marks her literary self-portraits and that resonates in the villain in one of her detective stories, known as "the man of a thousand faces" (*Safra macabra,* 121). But Galvão deployed masquerade for very specific ends as she mapped out her place as a woman intellectual in São Paulo's artistic worlds.

Not merely playful, Galvão's lifelong engagement with theatre and performance as an aficionado, student, critic, and practitioner, was central to the critical force of her writing and her evolving conception of art as simultaneously autonomous from dogma and engaged. Childhood and adolescent photos in carnival costumes and posing for a beauty contest document the performative orientation of her upbringing. Beyond the memorable Municipal Theatre event, Galvão declaimed poetry on numerous occasions, including on a 1930 trip to Buenos Aires. A caption for her photographic portrait in the society page of *Para todos* portrayed her as the very model of a proper performing woman: "she is a Normalist, she wears her makeup like a doll, she is a declaimer." [10] But propriety is not the word that comes to mind from eyewitness descriptions of Galvão's flamboyant appearance on São Paulo streets: an unruly coiffure, short skirts, odd clothing, and heavy make-up, described by one observer as "very stagy" (*Pagu vida-obra,* 272). Her aggressive retorts to suggestive remarks by law students ogling Normal School pupils anticipated her in-your-face confrontation of the Municipal Theatre audience.

Similar to Magda Portal's response to *Aprista* orthodoxy in Peru and Nellie Campobello's reaction to the cultural politics of the Mexican dance world, Galvão construed literature as a site of intellectual independence. But within the literary field she privileged theatre as a form of radical inquiry for practitioners and audience. She studied theatre at the São Paulo Dramatic and Musical Conservatory, contributed theatre reviews to the *Braz jornal* in the 1920s, and wrote theatre commentary for *O homem do povo* in 1931. Galvão oversaw this publication's exclusive artistic focus on theatre and film, usually under the column "Palco, Tela, e Picadeiro" (Stage, screen, and circus ring). This dedication to the performance arts paralleled the modernists' turn to theatre as their antibourgeois genre of choice.[11] As alternatives to bourgeois drama, in *O homem do povo* Galvão highlighted Brazil's popular dramatic forms and its most vanguard experiments. Thus the news sheet showcased the work of the famed circus clown Piolin, whom it named the honorary "stage director" of its theatre section. At the same time it highlighted confrontational, multisensory theatre in the work of *modernista* sculptor and activist Flávio de Carvalho, who soon created the radical Teatro de Experiência.[12]

Although political activism drove her travels in the 1930s, Galvão interviewed actors and film practitioners in Hollywood, attended diverse performance events in Asia and Europe, including Chinese pantomime and the Beijing opera and a performance of Stravinksy's *Rites of Spring* in Paris, and had close contact with Parisian surrealists. After she returned to Brazil, as critic and translator Galvão disseminated the work of such avant-garde European practitioners as Jarry, Ionesco, Beckett, Artaud, Brecht, and Lorca. In 1952, as an apprentice to Alfredo Mesquita at the Escola de Arte Dramática in São Paulo, an institution central in the emergence of modern Brazilian drama,[13] she executed the first Portuguese translation and Brazilian staging of Ionesco's *Bald Soprano*. She also translated and staged Fernando Arrabal's *Fando e Lis* in 1959 and Octavio Paz's *La hija de Rappaccini* in 1960. The aversion to explicitly social art that followed Galvão's disaffection from the Communist Party shaped her unfavorable criticism of the early work of Brazil's Augusto Boal, Oduvaldo Viana Filho, and Gianfrancesco Guarnieri. But consistent with her interest in popular traditions, she praised Ariano Suassuna's *Auto da compadecida* and Alfredo Dias Gomes's *O pagador de promessas*.

Galvão's favorable take on Brecht is not surprising given his radical aesthetic innovation and her own insights into the critical power of artistic form. As I have argued elsewhere, Brecht's self-reflexive *Verfremdungseffekt* is analogous to the Russian formalists' notion of *ostranenie* or "making it strange" or to Peter Bürger's concept of the "non-organic" vanguard work of art (*Latin American Vanguards,* 21–23). Galvão strove to make her public persona and literary texts deliberatively strange. She also promoted theatre as *the* vanguard, or estranging, genre par excellence because of its capacity to shake up audiences, encouraging them, as she did from the Municipal Theatre stage, to see in new ways. Two telling words appear often in Galvão's mature critical writing. One is *vanguarda* and its variants, repeatedly aligned with theatre, emphasizing the genre's structural capacity to promote the new.[14] The theatre, she wrote in 1957, had the power to illuminate unknown potential precisely because of its revelation of "new methods" and "new forms," and it possessed the "audacity" to demolish "all walls" and "confront a hostile public" (*Pagu vida-obra,* 223). Also reiterated in Galvão's criticism is the word *pesquisa*: inquiry, research, or investigation. After her falling-out with the party, Galvão defended literature's autonomy on the grounds that it promoted and projected inquiry in a politicized environment (*Pagu vida-obra,* 125). The power to promote *pesquisa,* she argued, was *the* defining trait of a vanguard writer and derived from the capacity to intensify and surprise (*Pagu vida-obra,* 240). Theatre in particular encapsulated both the vanguard spirit and the power of inquiry of the verbal arts.

For all her contributions to modern drama in Brazil, Galvão never published a play. She did compose several experimental one-acts while at the Escola de Arte Dramática, but their staging history is sketchy. Yet Galvão wrote exclusively about two topics in *O homem do povo*—theatre and film on one hand and the situation of women on the other—as she channeled her devotion to theatre toward larger critical objectives. Theatrical and performative motifs, strategies, and themes weave through Galvão's poetry, fiction, and journalism of the 1920s and 1930s, and these mechanisms underlie her class-based appraisal of Brazilian society and official feminism as well as her feminist account of Brazil's cultural and social worlds.

CHANGING THE SUBJECT:
O ALBUM DE PAGU AND "A MULHER DO POVO"

Similar to Magda Portal in Peru, Galvão disassociated herself from middle- and upper-class feminism. But the dominant focus of her writing in the 1920s and 1930s is the experience of women, as she examined their roles in modernist literary culture and their situation across classes in São Paulo society. Galvão's major work, *Parque industrial,* is a rich, multifaceted novel that invites numerous readings. That the novel's central focus on women is sometimes overlooked gives testimony to the fact that, as Susan Besse points out, "what it meant to be a 'feminist' was an issue of great contention in the late 1910s to 1930s in Brazil" (*Restructuring Patriarchy,* 164). Through her unconventional art of living and her artistic work, then, Galvão joined an intense public conversation about gender in Brazil and was largely critical about what she saw.

Although they were by no stretch feminists, some Brazilian modernist leaders implicitly contested gender norms. They ushered in a more powerful iconography of the feminine than romanticism's "tubercular and lyrical woman" (Picchia, 291) favoring, as I have noted, a modern, athletic Eve. Mário de Andrade's *Macunaíma* (1928), showcased in the *Revista de antropofagia* as the paradigmatic anthropophagous work, is populated by strong, if mythical, women. More ambitiously, Oswald's "Manifesto antropófago" presages the post-patriarchal, post-bourgeois Brazil—the "matriarchy of Pindorama"—as an antidote to the morality of "pater familias," "suspicious, Catholic husbands," and the pre-Freudian "enigma woman" (*Obras completas,* 6:13–19). But as Leslie

Bary has demonstrated, the document's equation of woman with nature, instinct, and the savage reproduces stereotypes it supposedly rejects (Bary, 14–15). Such (re)constructions of a nature-bound femininity typified, as Rita Felski has argued, the gendered discourse of international modernism. Oswald's manifesto also blends the nature woman with the trendy New Woman, invoked in the Golden Age of America and "todas as girls," all the girls (*Obras completas,* 6:14). While Oswald's novels of the period exalted sexual freedom, as Emanuelle Oliveira has shown in a discerning rereading of *Serafim Ponte Grande* (1933), Serafim's is a phallic liberation that celebrates male sexuality at the expense of the sexual and social roles assigned the countless women his protagonists seduce (Oliveira, 268). Even *A escada,* the 1934 novel that traces Oswald's own leftist conversion (and casts a fictionalized version of Galvão as the catalyst), reaffirms a masculinist identity as the protagonist struggles to divest himself of bourgeois notions of sex and romance. Thus the narrative reports the character's awakening to his own economic exploitation: "He felt virile. He felt manly" (*Obras completas,* 1:246).

Galvão was certainly not the only Brazilian woman writer of her day to focus on women, but hers was the only voice within the exclusive fold of the São Paulo-based early modernism to assert such a change of subject. Galvão's first self-representations reproduced gender imagery of the Brazilian modernists but executed unexpected improvisations. I am referring to her short collection of drawings and prose poems (or lyric prose), *O album de Pagu: Nacimento vida paixão e morte,* dated 1929, which remained unpublished during her lifetime but circulated among her *antropofagia* cohorts.[15] The work's twenty-eight prose poem-scenes are grouped into the four stages—birth, life, passion, and death—of the speaker-protagonist's experience.[16] Dedicated to Tarsila, *O album* reiterates the anthropophagous version of women but also presages the critique of literary modernism and of Brazil's uneven modernization that Galvão would instigate in later work. *O album*'s theatrical format, a synthesis of visual scenes captioned with first-person lyrical monologues, complements its portrayal of a dynamic performing woman. On the one hand, the character's nudity and simple appearance enact the descent into the city of São Paulo of the primitive woman of *antropofagia.* She is the daughter of the moon and the stars, and an enormous black bird delivers her amidst the tall urban buildings. Portrayed as "untamed" and "beastly" (IV, 49), she consumes "savage Manioc," lolls among the cattails, moss, and mud, is desired by Freud (V, 50), and has a special relationship with her "shameless" cat (XI, 51). The ingénue sketched in each scene incarnates incessant motion: she flies her kite, reaches to the sky on a swing, careens from a church bell, dances on the streetcar, and masquerades as a Hawaiian dancer.

As with Galvão's burlesque on the municipal stage, this characterization hyperbolizes the modernists' muse and casts her in espionage acts against her artistic creators as the character affirms autonomy from cultural scripts through the excess of her self-portrayal. In the opening scene, her flailing arms and legs overflow the reed basket in which the large bird transports her. Through repeated imagery of flight—in the bird's mouth, on the swing, swaying from the church bell—this muse come to life appropriates the vanguard dynamic between ascent and descent seen, for example, in Huidobro's *Altazor*. As described earlier, Mariblanca Sabas Alomá executed a comparable poetic recasting through an Amelia Earhart-styled lyric aviator who exercises her wings in a cry for justice. Although Galvão's *O album* also contains social commentary, her high-flying muse addresses a more immediate objective. Launched on her swing, she proclaims her desire to travel high with a "sensation of delicious superiority" so that she may "spy" on those who surround her (IX, 50). We have seen such a portrait of the artist as spy in Nellie Campobello's authorial child narrator in *Cartucho* who hides under a table or Antonieta Rivas Mercado's "spy of good will" who alternates between galvanizing others to act and detached observation. Galvão's spy is most similar to the persona crafted by Norah Lange who also inhabits the groups she spies on and "anatomizes." This similarity is not surprising, as both were immersed in male vanguard communities and cast as their muses. Galvão's fly-on-the-wall self-portrayal not only intimates a critical distance from her muse identity but also anticipates the more aggressive critical stance toward modernist literary culture she would take in *O homem do povo* and *Parque industrial.*

Other elements in *O album* presage the subversion. Galvão's hedonist nude is the most erotic rendition of the New Woman we have seen here. But flaunting this feature of the modern Eve defies the sexual objectification it implies. With the exception of the reader, nobody is watching this woman who watches—make that spies on—others. Moreover, *O album* projects a distinct self-pleasuring quality to the speaker's sexuality, much like her cat that plays with its own tail. This is by and large a solo performance, even in erotic scenarios. Some of the most important frames enact a refusal to be seen. In one scene she sits alone on a rectangular block with her back to the viewer, her arms in her lap, her head looking down. A large, rounded pitcher is by her side, and the caption refers to a warm "ampulla" with its "heady liquor" of "solitude" and "I" (XVII, 54). The word *ampulla* can denote a vessel for liquor, perfume, or drugs, a holy vessel, or vessel-shaped parts of female anatomy. The speaker appears alone even in a scene that portrays her, Eve-like, reaching for an apple from a tree.

O album's few male figures are sketchy and static, and the work actually nominates a female candidate for the speaker's passion. A sketch of the protagonist looking skyward bears the caption "I want . . . you" (IXV, 53),[17] a highlighted pronoun that in the context of the work's dedication—"for Tarsila"—poses this female mentor as its referent. A scene located between the depiction of the speaker's absorption with her own body and the one of her tasting the apple further links another woman to her sexuality. Here the protagonist appears as a mermaid or someone whose lower torso resembles the tail of her cat and describes the "madness of some almond eyes" (XVIII, 54). Almond-shaped eyes are the signature feature in Galvão's drawings of Tarsila, both in *O album*'s opening dedication and in a drawing of Tarsila signed "Pagu" that appeared in *Para todos* in March 1929 (*Pagu vida-obra*, 60).[18] In sum, the multiple referents for this New Woman's desire include her cat, herself, another woman, and, eventually, men.

Additional scenes in *O album* demythologize the work's earth woman and forecast the imminent shift in Galvão's writing toward the inequities of Brazil's modernization. While she may have swept into modern São Paulo from a primal land, the protagonist's apprenticeship is distinctly urban. Two scenes locate her on a streetcar, taking in languages, smells, and sights. Here she encounters a Portuguese woman "smeared with oil and rouge," a "melancholy" mulatto who rubs against her (XIII, 51),[19] and a man with a sore-infested tongue who spits blood and follows her home. The accompanying drawing presents the dancing protagonist framed on one side by flower chains and on the other by a serpent's head sporting a mouthful of teeth and a long tongue that grazes her leg. Subsequent scenes reinforce these tensions between festive and predatory faces of the erotic, as when two figures make love in the cemetery beside a tombstone inscribed "syphilis victim" (XXVI, 58). The final section, "Death," reinforces the work's mixed signals with irreconcilable images of the earth woman: toward the top a winged protagonist ascends to the sky while near the bottom she roasts over a fire surrounded by pitchforks.

If *O album* points to the contradictory status of musedom by juxtaposing a literary fantasy world with a dystopic São Paulo reality, in the eight "A Mulher do Povo" columns of *O homem do povo* and in *Parque industrial,* Galvão targeted the muse identity as one link in a damnable network of culture, class, and gender exploitation. Although they are markedly different in tone, style, and philosophical worldview, these are tandem projects: the first, a blueprint for issues treated in the fictional world of the second. While the polemical columns register Galvão's short-lived search for ideological absolutes, the novel presages a growing conviction that there are none. The appearance of O *homem do povo* in 1931 coincided with Galvão's entry into the Communist Party, a move that with the advent of the Estado Novo typified Brazilian modernism after 1930. As Randal Johnson observes, the Revolution of 1930 brought about "a new political reality in which indifference or political neutrality was no longer a viable alternative for writers and intellectuals" (210). Just as O *album* problematizes the construction of modernism's muses, so do Galvão's columns focus on women's situation in the very society that the news sheet lobbied to revolutionize.

Galvão's eight "A mulher do povo" columns offer a mordant critique of Brazilian bourgeois performance culture that, she argued, trained girls to be proper (or improper) New Women, to engage in public display, and, implicitly, to serve as the muse for some incipient poet. Here the discerning "spy" of O *album* metamorphoses into the bald-faced critic of the political tract. Although evident throughout Latin America, the modern performance culture that Galvão attacked was particularly pronounced in São Paulo and Rio de Janeiro. Here with growing industrialization and urbanization and the increase of middle-sector jobs, more middle- and upper-class women were out on the streets as workers and consumers. In Brazil's urban centers, simply *fazendo a avenida,* making the scene, even if chaperoned, on avenues or boulevards constituted an important activity for women (Hahner, 80). Galvão's account of this milieu recalls similar critiques by Alfonsina Storni, Ofelia Rodríguez Acosta, and María Wiesse. But Galvão located the behaviors she censured in bourgeois culture, although she added that working-class women might emulate them. Specific targets for censure were the excessive emphasis on clothes and makeup, the projection of Hollywood models of femininity, women's poetry declamation as an art of bodily ostentation, and the Catholic Church's tacit support of training young women for love. She directed scathing barbs at Normal School life, where, she argued, young women wasted their time talking about "an idiot tango," an "imbecile film," or young men with "syphilitic kisses" ("Normalinhas," 2).

In Galvão's view the family, the Church, the Normal School, and the artistic circle all conspired to train women for show. She launched a special assault on young women's declamation performances in parochial schools, where, she asserted, "made-up girls" would demonstrate to young Catholic men that they had "good legs, a symmetrical torso, and ok breasts" ("Liga de trompas," 2). As the continent's mother of all declaimers, Argentina's Berta Singerman received a distinctive roasting. Singerman, as noted, performed for huge audiences in Europe and the Americas (São Paulo in 1931), and male writers often described her as an awe-inspiring muse.[20] Galvão dismissed Singerman's work as the worst kind of "spoken opera" and "false modern art" ("As óperas," 1).

A strong current in Galvão's critique of performance culture is her assertion of its "unhealthy" sexuality. During the 1920s and 1930s, as Susan Besse documents, sex and marriage manuals and treatises on human sexuality circulated in Brazil, including writings of Brazilian legal and medical leaders and translations of Freud, Gregorio Marañón, Alexandra Kollontai, and Havelock Ellis, among others (*Restructuring Patriarchy*, 66, 221).[21] Galvão celebrated her sexuality in the late 1920s but subsequently evidenced critical ambivalence on the subject. Her focus on sex was certainly not unique. Frenzied sexual activity marks such classic novels of Brazilian modernism as Mário de Andrade's *Macunaíma* (1928) or Oswald's *Memórias sentimentais de João Miramar* (1924) and *Serafim Ponte Grande* (1933), and women writers explored sexual practices as well. The anarchist feminist Maria Lacerda Moura wrote essays on women's sexual freedom, and the literary feminist Ercília Nogueira Cobra explored women's sexuality in the essay *Virgindade anti-higiênica: Preconceitos e convenções hipócritas,* (Antihygienic virginity: Hypocritical preconceptions and conventions; 1924) and the novel *Virgindade inútil: Novela de uma revoltada* (Useless virginity: Novel of a revolted woman; 1927).[22] Other women novelists addressed women's sexual, moral, and marital issues.[23] As historian Margareth Rago argues, sexuality constitutes a central theme in Brazilian identity discourses of the time, in Paulo Prado's foundational *Retrato do Brasil: Ensaio sobre a tristeza brasileira* (Portrait of Brazil: Essay on the sadness of Brazil) from 1928 and Gilberto Freyre's 1936 classic, *Casa grande e senzala* (translated under the title *The Masters and the Slaves*). But Rago also emphasizes that attitudes toward the topic are complex and contradictory.[24]

Galvão's ambivalence on the topic of sexuality is striking, particularly the shift between representations of *O album* and the polemics of her "A mulher do povo" columns. This change encompasses not merely a maturing awareness of sexual politics and the gendered exploitation of girls and women that marked the emergent culture industry, as when she equated the history of film with the history of sex ("Freud e o cinema," 4). Suggesting that she had rethought her own performance of sexuality, in the news sheet she constructed a dichotomy between a theatrical sex of deception and a "natural" sex, free of artifice. Thus, among the stars of the "sexual cinema," she preferred European-born actresses such as Marlene Dietrich and Greta Garbo because, she claimed, they represented sexuality as a "biological simplicity" divested of false gestures, ornamental airs, or "artificial titillation" ("Cinema sexual," 1).

This conception of a nonperformative sexuality took Galvão down a slippery slope of denigrating what she termed sexual "deviations," including the "masochism" and "hysteria" of religious mystics or celibates ("O retiro sexual," 2). She attributed all "deviations" to bourgeois repression and forecast their disappearance in an era of "rationalized biological morality" ("O retiro sexual," 2). In the context of growing Freudian influence, the *antropofagia* call for the transformation of taboo into totem, and Galvão's recent political conversion, this view is not surprising. But her notion of sexuality without artifice unfolds in a peculiar brand of homophobia. She did not explicitly oppose gay sex. Rather, she implied, regardless of whom they slept with, boys should be boys and girls should be girls. Thus she criticized homosexual men not for desiring other men but for assuming the gestures, voices, or tastes of women. The Greeks, she affirmed, knew how to be homosexual and remain masculine ("Saibam ser maricons," 2).[25] Similarly, as did Sabas Alomá, Rivas Mercado, Portal, and Wiesse, Galvão assailed the "masculinized" American New Woman but in this case because of her ostensible artifice. She argued that America's movie-star model of the athletic woman was unnatural because of an exercise regimen directed at a specific ideal. By contrast the new Brazilian working woman—"very strong, very womanly"—would come by her physical health naturally and without a "glimmer of masculinity" ("Mulher mulher," 2). In forging this curious position, Galvão drew on her performance experience and theatrical knowledge to recognize the performativity of gender norms, say in men who supposedly "act like" women and women who supposedly "act like" men. But she stopped short of attributing these norms to culture. Instead she clung to essentialist axioms about "natural" ways for men and women to act, or in Galvão's terms, to behave *without* acting in the theatrical sense.

On many points Galvão's views align her with other dissenting feminists such as Moura, who criticized mainstream feminism. But Galvão rejected such potential allies. On the grounds that it ignored working-class women, she dismissed the suffrage campaign of the Federação Brasileira pelo Progresso Feminino (FBPF) under the leadership of Bertha Luz. Galvão's unconventional life in these years conflicted with the "social motherhood" goals that characterized Latin American feminism. Hahner and Besse document this orientation in Brazilian feminism, as in the simultaneous establishment in 1932 of (limited) women's suffrage and Mother's Day. As Besse details, Moura attacked official feminism in the name of women's sexual liberation and, as an anarchist, assailed the movement's ignorance of working-class women (Besse, *Restructuring Patriarchy,* 179–180). As did Galvão in *Parque industrial,* Moura included male intellectuals as well in her critique of bourgeois culture (63–64).[26] But Galvão censured Moura as part of the bourgeois problem, as a mere "reformist" and "poetisa" who did not understand worker women ("Maltus alem," 2).

That Galvão did not perceive a tie with other alternative feminists derives from her quest for identification with the working class. As did Portal in *La trampa,* Galvão periodically portrayed herself as a loner among women. But in "A mulher do povo" she idealized the potential for sisterhood among the proletariat. In the column on the Normal School based on her own experience, Galvão portrayed her classmates as a frivolous lot, while she, by contrast, was a more sincere rebel, already a revolutionary in the making ("Normalinhas," 2). A photograph placed alongside this column and titled "Revolutionary Joy" depicts two smiling, uniformed schoolgirls arm in arm, with the caption: "2 little girls of the people ready to fight for the proletarian cause."

NOT TO BE SEEN:
THE WAGES OF PERFORMANCE IN *PARQUE INDUSTRIAL*

Galvão acted out this fantasy of camaraderie among women most eloquently in *Parque industrial,* a novel that refines her inquiry into the issues she posed in *O homem do povo.* But where the columns frame her views as truths, the novel, written after an additional year of political experience, subjects these problems to a more discerning critical eye. *Parque industrial* is radical in its vanguard form and layered ideology critique: a socialist exposure of class inequities in São Paulo, a feminist critique of gender relations and Communist Party orthodoxy, and a leftist-feminist critique of artistic culture. Through a series of synoptic sketches, the novel presents the unequal human costs of modernization, particularly for the women of Braz, São Paulo's immigrant factory district. With an ensemble of more than fifty characters, the work targets the economic and cultural elites, including the literary modernists, and an unmindful and self-interested middle class, including bourgeois feminists. All are complicit in the economic and sexual exploitation of the proletariat, embodied primarily in the female textile workers of Braz. The novel's theatrical structure, vanguard visual clips, estranging imagery, and telegraphic phrases construct an instantaneous portrait of its social world that is mordantly satirical, brutally direct, comic, and tragic.

The novel plots the trajectories of key characters: Corina, a sweatshop seamstress who is impregnated and abandoned by her middle-class lover, dismissed from her job and evicted from her home, imprisoned after her syphilitic child is stillborn, and forced into prostitution; Eleanora, a social-climbing Normal School student from the lower middle class who marries the upper-class artist-intellectual Alfredo Rocha but loses interest and pursues women lovers; Otavia, a textile-factory worker and dedicated Communist Party organizer who catalyzes Alfredo's leftist conversion and becomes his lover; Rosinha Lituana, Otavia's immigrant coworker and fellow organizer who faces imprisonment and deportation; Alfredo Rocha, Eleanora's husband, who searches for political commitment through Otavia and Rosinha but is denounced by the party as a Trotskyite; and Pepe, Otavia's rejected petit bourgeois suitor who, in revenge, informs for the party, turns in Rosinha Lituana, and later serves as Corina's pimp. Of the growing criticism on this novel, Besse highlights its Marxist perspective, Jackson its primitivist aesthetic à la Oswald and Tarsila, and others its dominant focus on women.[27] Primarily through a Bakhtinian analysis of its heteroglossic discourse, Hilary Owen has demonstrated ties between the work's modernist aesthetic and its critique of orthodox Marxism's "closed systems of difference" through an exposure of the gender, class, and race tensions marking character interactions (Owen, 84). I share Owen's views of the novel's emergent feminism and deconstruction of the ideology that it cites. Anticipating recent inquiries into the complexities of Brazilian modernism's ideological and political affiliations,[28] the novel challenges the movement's claims to radicalism through the perspective of a modernist insider.

The novel is also pivotal for Galvão's critique of the performance culture and literary world that cast her into musedom, and she deploys theatre and performance strategies for that critique. Building on her portrait of the artist as spy in *O album,* here Galvão creates an authorial persona whose most radical move is a de facto refusal to perform, that is, the claim to see critically while she herself remains unseen. The work's theatrical structure and style are fundamental for this perspective and the fly-on-the-wall authorial presence. While the narrator speaks as a dispassionate insider in the fictional world and occasionally interjects comments in character conversations, this anonymous voice never assumes a bodied form. In the novel's narrative economy of scene and summary, the narrator's voice often speaks in stage directions, clipped descriptors that set the scene, for example of a workers' meeting: "A table, an old tablecloth. A water jug, cups. A faulty bell. The directorate" (24; EKDJ, 22). Such syntax, common to a particular mode of vanguard fiction, creates the rhetorical scenario of a speaker addressing an audience in the "real time" present of a play's performance, a stage manager who introduces dialogue about to unfold. Most striking is the predominance of synecdoche for populating these scenes. Thus an item of clothing, a dab of makeup, a bodily gesture, or a fragment converge in a human scenario, as in this urban evocation: "On the crowded street, blond heads, frizzy heads, simple skirts" (13; EKDJ, 13); or in this morning-after-the-party account: "A small red slipper without a sole is abandoned in the gutter. A shoeless foot is cut on the slivers of a milk bottle. A dark girl goes hopping to reach the black door. The last kick at a rag ball" (5; EKDJ, 8–9). Through the chaining of scenic nodules, this narration anticipates Brechtian form and creates a reader experience analogous to sitting in a theatre for a play or film. But the reiteration of gestures, body parts, or costume as the synecdoche of choice underscores the performative quality of the novel's human interaction. As in a live performance, these summon the "kinesthetic imagination" (to recall Joseph Roach's term) of the reader-spectator who must draw on the cultural contexts of gesture and attire to connect the dots.

As I have argued in the introduction, by definition synecdoche, as a surrogate for the whole, is fundamentally performative, signaling its own substitution for what will not be seen. Roach defines performance itself as a process of substitution or "surrogation" that "stands for an elusive entity that it is not but that it must vainly aspire both to embody and to replace" (3). Galvão's stylistic choice of synecdoche, then, is key for the work's construction of a fictional world shaped by performative display, a feature to which I shall return. But while the narrator's stage directions imbue the novel with a matter-of-fact air, the work's shifts in perspective produce more intricate effects, as rapid-fire dialogue combined with free indirect discourse generate focalization swings that constantly reposition the reader's ideological perspective. This visual vacillation emulates the audience relocations effected not only when a play's characters alternate speaking onstage but also when the performance evokes offstage worlds diegetically through dialogue or sounds.[29] Again, what one does not see is as important as what one sees. In *Parque industrial* this dance between the visible and invisible frames diverse takes on class and gender from the same event. In a representative scene, Alfredo Rocha arrives at the Braz Normal School to pick up Eleanora in his fancy car. While readers initially witness this scene through the envious glances of Eleanora's classmates (from varied class backgrounds) who watch the car pull away, we, too, are then whisked away and experience the world inside the car alternately through Eleanora's desire—she "shivers at the male touch"—and through Alfredo's emergent political consciousness as he contemplates a "starving multitude" through the windshield (32–33; EKDJ, 29).

This vertiginous shuffle of perspectives invests the authorial persona with a fly-on-the-wall quality that the narrator's periodic anonymous appearances reinforce. As in a play, no narrator provides identifying markers for clips of direct discourse. Instead the reader must determine who is speaking by "watching" the scene, attending to the "stage directions" and the context. Periodically a presence surfaces that is neither character-bound nor continuous with the dialogue, the telltale intrusion of an outsider. An elite literary soiree seen from the wall evokes a critical, unidentified observer who is at once integral to this artistic scene: "From the main wall, a tragic, eyeless Chirico spies the nude shoulder that Patou undressed from the hostess's gown" (38; EKDJ, 32–33). In a comparably festive gathering of bourgeois feminists whose conversational banalities alternate with their celebration of literate women's suffrage, an unidentified interloper inquires, "And women workers?" (89; EKDJ, 69)

These shifts keep *Parque industrial* readers on their toes, for in seeking to pin down the work's ideological spin, one must attend to who is speaking—or watching—and from where. For those who watch, there is always something that is not there. Thus the work's theatricality reinforces other negations of orthodoxy, such as in the interplay between literate culture and orality that Owen illuminates. The narrative rarely preaches directly but instead locates its proselytizing discourse in specific characters. Even when the work's attitude toward such a character is sympathetic, the narrator maintains a distance, as in a reference to Otavia's readings as propaganda, a label that challenges the truth claims of any discourse to which it is applied. In highlighting power relations, moreover, the novel portrays the multiple settings where they unfold— for example the streetcar—as heterogeneous in class, race, gender, or ideological orientation. None of these categories unilaterally determines a character's situation, as the novel unpacks the identity communities it constructs. Thus not all working-class women address their oppression in the same way. The subjugation experienced by the proletarian Corina, for example, is exacerbated at work by her mulatto identity and at home by the gender politics of a working-class enclave that castigates her sexuality. Corina has little interest in the Communist Party's relevance to her life when Otavia and Rosinha Lituana recruit her. Shifting class settings, the narrator reveals the fragile petit bourgeois status achieved by Eleanora, whose father supplements his meager white-collar salary with odd jobs and whose mother, herself raised in the kitchen of an elite home, now has her own black maid.

Most revealing of the work's insertion of an authorial "spy" in its ideological midst is the portrayal of the Communist Party as a mixed bag of origins, motives, and intentions. Thus a regional labor union brings together not only women and men of all ages and colors but also "All mentalities. Aware. Unaware. Informers. . . . Revolters. Anarchists. Infiltrators" (23–24; EKDJ, 21). Galvão's ambivalence toward the party takes shape in the handling of Rocha, the convert bourgeois intellectual whom the party denounces as a Trotskyite but whom the narration handles with care. Thus Otavia, as a committed party organizer and Alfredo's lover who has promoted his conversion, "freezes" and rests her head on her knees when he is accused. Although she eventually supports his accusers, the narrator highlights the "pained energy" that charges Otavia's action (132; EKDJ, 104).

Parque industrial, then, constructs a narrator we never see who simultaneously inhabits a world and spies on it. This authorial persona's most brilliant act of critical espionage is to turn the defining mode of that world against itself. Thus Galvão deploys the theatrical to expose a vast performative world, and a novel dominated by dramatic scenes both mimics and confronts a multiclass proclivity for making the scene. Beyond the novel's dominant focus on women's worlds—the women's restroom, the seamstress's sweatshop, the Normal School, the birthing house, the women's prison, the middle-class parlor, and the brothel—its singular attention to performance culture ties Galvão's critique of São Paulo society to her own experience as a muse and literary modernist. While Galvão's journalistic columns render this performance culture the product of bourgeois society's education of women, in *Parque industrial* these practices encompass all classes through scenarios that place women in particular on exhibit: Normal School students flaunting or concealing their appearance, elite *paulistas* promenading on fashionable streets, dancing women in *garçonnieres,* working women grieving for carnival's lost illusions, and masquerading prostitutes in high-class brothels. The novel also paints bourgeois feminism and literary culture as avid participants in the grand show. One scene depicts a meeting in a high-class *garçonniere* of "emancipated" intellectual women and feminists who ostensibly gather to celebrate women's suffrage but instead drink cocktails and chatter about their hairdressers and the challenge of finding good help (88–89; EKDJ, 68–70). Similarly, a gathering of literary modernists at the soiree of Dona Finoca, an "old patroness of new arts," displays caviar-eating and champagne-drinking "novices" who swap partners and show off nude shoulders or topaz cufflinks on their "fists of silk" (38; EKDJ, 33).

Two motifs in this scene, fashion and sexuality, anchor the exploitations of *paulista* performance culture in the grand masquerade of dress, an inspired choice for highlighting changing gender and class relations. As Hahner points out, during these years industrialized dressmaking often constituted women's labor for women consumers in São Paulo: "A dozen women might spend their days hunched over long tables in dark, airless rooms, producing the luxury garments in which elite ladies promenaded on the Avenida Central, attended receptions, or frequented theaters and tea salons" (93). But the fashion motif also epitomizes changing gender and class relationships of modernity and constitutes a finely honed barometer of what Besse terms the "demise of patriarchalism" and consequent "restructuring of patriarchy" in response to modernization (*Restructuring Patriarchy*, 12–37). Besse argues that changes in clothing confection embody the shifts from productive to consumptive activities in Brazilian households beginning in the late nineteenth century. Prior to the early twentieth century, women produced most clothing directly in the households that used it; by the 1920s the retail market had dramatically changed these economies of consumption across class lines. "Those with social ambitions but modest resources," Besse observes, "carefully copied store-bought models in the hope that others would not recognize their clothing as homemade. Those who subsisted on meager budgets treasured any item of store-bought clothing as among their most prized possessions" (*Restructuring Patriarchy*, 19).

Bringing those relationships into focus, the title of the opening chapter of *Parque industrial*—"Looms"—signals the centrality of fashion in the work's social world, and the characters' interaction with clothes embodies the novel's networks of class, gender, and culture. Thus the poor make them, the rich wear them, and modernist poets in trendy salons declaim "How lovely is thy loom!" (7; EKDJ, 10). We should recall here the work of cultural theorist Jennifer Craik, who posits that clothes and bodily demeanor in the modern era construct a "personal *habitus*" (4) that serves both a "tool of self-management" and a "technique of acculturation" into a concrete social world (46, 10).[30] Fashion in *Parque industrial* serves as a key signifier of a character's "personal *habitus*" in relationship to class and gender and offers a "technique of acculturation" from one class to another. The novel portrays almost every character and group through their attire, the announcement of a social position or one to which they aspire. Thus the impoverished Corina often wears the same dress, a waitress "carries her apron like a cross on her back" (130; EKDJ, 102), and the public housing sector is identifiable through its worn clothing hung out to dry. Both Eleanora as elite hostess and Dona Catita, the hostess of the tenement, wear Berta Singerman-style pajamas, ever a favorite Galvão target. Most telling are clothing details that parallel crisis moments in characters' lives. The narrative signals the demise of Eleanora's passion for Alfredo through her aversion to his negligence of dress. He in turn marks his conversion to communism as an "acculturation" to a different class with "well-chosen poor clothes" (115; EKDJ, 91). Alfredo calculates his downward mobility as political engagement, an ideological slumming not so different from the sexual slumming he enacted at carnival in his bourgeois days. But for Corina, who fights starvation, fashion offers a technique of acculturation only to the survival choice of prostitution: "If only she had a decent dress" (143; EKDJ, 112).

Alfonsina Storni, as I have described, also elected fashion as a signifier of gender and class and was particularly interested in dress codes as cultural scripts that might be altered. In the personal *habitus* constructed by fashion, as noted, Craik poses a dynamic relationship between the "prestigious imitation" of "structured and disciplined codes of conduct" and the "license and freedom" of "untrained impulses" in the "way the body is worn" (Craik, 56, 5). Both Storni and Galvão sought greater freedom, but Galvão insisted more categorically that fashion was complicit in exploitative codes of conduct across class and gender lines. Thus in *Parque industrial* fashion serves not only as a signifier of a character's socioeconomic mobility but also as the axis for character movement through the fictionalized urban world. Fashion casts a relational net that nobody escapes. The only outlet from the compulsory class and gender relations fashion performs is the refusal to play the clothing game at all. Thus the party organizer Otavia dresses simply and supposedly without artifice. Her resistance to fashion recalls a single fashion column Galvão published in *O homem do povo* in which she criticized expensive clothes modeled on European trends and lobbied for utilitarian and no-fuss attire ("A tezoura popular," 2).

This notion that one could locate oneself *outside* the tangled web of social interactions embodied in fashion recalls Galvão's conception of sexuality without theatrics in "A mulher do povo," an image she reiter-ated and undermined in *Parque industrial*. Engaging in sex comprises one of the characters' principal activities. But as in the news sheet, Galvão's portrayal of the eroticism she celebrates is ambivalent. In a feminist spirit, *Parque industrial* affirms women's ownership of their sexual desires, such as when Otavia rejects a proposal and affirms she will join "the man that [her] body cries out for" without the hypocrisy of marriage (47; EKDJ, 39). Time and again, moreover, the work emphasizes inconsistencies of gender and class that determine the negative outcomes of sexual desire. Exploitation marks almost every sexual connection in *Parque industrial*: characters are raped, unwillingly seduced, impregnated, abandoned, and sexually harassed on the job; they offer up their bodies for momentary escape, survival, and upward mobility; they exact political revenge for sexual rejection. Undermining the idealized working class of Galvão's col-umns, here proletarian characters in their drive to move up mimic bour-geois double standards.

The inclusion of same-sex encounters in this grand masquerade as-signs a Pyrrhic equality to homosexuals, portrayed as every bit as deca-dent, hypocritical, and bourgeois as any other inhabitants of the urban landscape. At no time does Galvão imply, as had Cuba's Rodríguez Acosta, that same-sex relationships might offer an alternative to patriarchal pair-ings.[31] Only the budding bond between Otavia and Alfredo reiterates Galvão's conception of sexuality without theatre. Thus Otavia eschews coyness and undresses for her lover "purely" (131; EKDJ, 103). While the novel filters this notion of artifice-free sex through Otavia, surrounding ironies suggest that, unlike her character, Galvão does not reveal herself without contrivance. Thus while Otavia imagines "pure" proletarian sex, her lover's impertinent query at a party meeting—"Is cunnilingus imperi-alism?" (128; EKDJ, 101)—leads to his expulsion, a move the novel poses as problematic.[32] If the couple's love scene posits a classless sexuality out-side bourgeois patriarchy, the novel's casting of countless working-class characters in the city's sexual theatre undercuts the utopian gesture.

The truly seditious element of Otavia and Alberto's coupling is its radical claim to privacy. Theirs is the least *visible* sexual liaison in the novel. Gaps in the account of their encounter shut out the audience in a novel that repeatedly flashes it with brief exposures to its characters' most private moments. In a performance culture marked by the tyranni-cal economy of seeing and being seen, privacy, which the novel constructs as the opportunity to act without an audience, is at a premium. Many of the work's spatial sites embody tension between private and public, locales where characters must perform private acts in settings that, if not completely public, are not especially private: a maternity ward, a prison, a brothel, a housing project, the factory's public restroom for workers. As the semiprivate but essentially public space where young women gather as the story opens, these dirty latrines provide the only "joyful minute[s] stolen from slave labor" (8; EKDJ, 10). Here worker women gather to talk, out of sight from bosses and men. But as one woman straddles a toilet, beatings on the door forewarn that this world with no private spaces is grounded in an economy of display, ready or not. Two of the novel's most poignant moments emphasize that this perpetual summons to *be* in public when one would rather be private binds women across class lines. Thus the petit bourgeois living room offers no more privacy than a public stage.

Eleanora—her body bruised from her first sexual act (forced, the novel suggests)—returns home silenced and disillusioned only to discover that she is "obliged to declaim for those present a ballad full of noises by the Paulista poet Pirotti Laqua" (34, 36; EKDJ, 30, 31). Abandoned by both her working-class family and her elite lover when she becomes pregnant, Corina is jailed for the infanticide of her syphilitic, stillborn infant. Lying on a mat in her filthy prison cell, she seeks solace in the excitement of her own beautiful body.[33] But an audience invades even this private moment, as a freckle-faced guard watches through the bars (75; EKDJ, 60).

Corina's heart-rending masturbation scene recalls the more successful claim to privacy enacted by Galvão in *O album*, through the self-absorbed nude with her back to the viewer. This pose tantalizes readers but also maps a measure of reserve around what the spectator is not permitted to see. But of course Galvão had already made this clear in her celebrated municipal performance as the modernist muse. Running to the back of the stage, turning around, and opening and closing her cape enacted a dance of advance and retreat between exhibitionism and distance. Hailed (in the Althusserian sense) to perform as modernist muse, Galvão protected what would not be shown while turning the critical looking toward the viewer. Her self-portrait of the artist as unseen observer in *O album*—a dynamic New Woman who soars so as to spy on those below—reinforced this claim for privacy in a culture of display, an unexpected investiture of new meaning, to paraphrase Judith Butler, in the script Galvão was compelled to cite as an entrée to the literary world. Less the machinations of a mystery woman than an authorizing claim to anonymity, Galvão's countless pseudonyms enact a comparable petition for privacy, a refusal to perform. Above all, as the spying narrator of *Parque industrial,* even as she exposed them to readers Galvão lobbied on her women characters' behalf for the same right not to be seen that she had set aside for herself.

This advocacy constitutes the novel's most important act of feminist camaraderie by a writer who often kept her distance.[34] Even as she attacked the frivolity of such bourgeois characters as Eleanora from the perspective of political orthodoxy, Galvão evidenced compassion for the losses Eleanora accrues as a woman. Similarly, although the novel does not romanticize connections between women who seek legitimacy and social power through liaisons with men or exploit one another across class lines, it does portray efforts at female friendship that mirror the primary focus on the plight of women. This predominance of womanhood underscores the feminist component of Galvão's intellectual agenda. *Parque industrial* portrays this female majority as an invasion comparable to Galvão's own critical ambush of *antropofagia*. Thus again, women's spaces ground much of the novel's action, and in heterogeneous rallies or meetings the work showcases the interventions and thoughts of women. Galvão's "A mulher do povo" columns, signed "Pagu," take up relatively little space, while under the guise of her multiple pen names, her actual contributions to the news sheet overflowed those boundaries. And although the initial scene of women's camaraderie in *Parque industrial* is a latrine block previously assigned to men, overlaying the men's writings on the wall with their own conversations—a palimpsest of gender (ex)change—the women in the bathroom signal Galvão's occupation of her novel in the name of its women.

A "LADY SHOT AND PAINTED" OR A DISGUISING WOMAN?

When Galvão began writing again after her release from prison in 1940, her feminism, though more subdued, did not disappear. As a critic she did not showcase women writers, but although she consistently admired Oswald, she cast women, not men, as intellectual mentors. Rosa Luxembourg's impact on her politics resonates in character names in her novels: the organizer Rosinha Lituana in *Parque industrial* and Rosa, the savvy protagonist of *A famosa revista* (1945), by Galvão and Geraldo Ferraz. But the single person she named unequivocally as an intellectual guide was Tarsila do Amaral, the acclaimed painter who brought her into the *antropofagia* fold in 1928. Twenty-two years later Galvão designated Tarsila as the role model for modern Brazilian women of her generation. Her persona and cultural presence, Galvão proposed, offered the first case of "mental emancipation" among São Paulo women (*Pagu vida-obra,* 203). Beyond her "superior comprehension," Galvão highlighted her intelligence open to *pesquisa* (or inquiry), an activity that for Galvão measured intellectual worth. Moreover, what the *paulista* painter had succeeded in emancipating herself *from,* Galvão indicated, was the very performance culture targeted by Galvão's feminist critique. Thus she praised Tarsila for maintaining her intellect amid the pretentious salon culture she inhabited. Even more germane to her own intellectual persona was Galvão's observation that Tarsila, ever the leading lady, maintained a reserve of privacy and worked hard "*not to be perceived*" (*Pagu vida-obra,* 203; my emphasis).

This ebb and flow of display and reserve ascribed to Tarsila reiterates the feminist avowal of privacy that marked Galvão's self-portrait. The pursuit of privacy also guides *A famosa revista,* enacted through the protagonists' will to escape the tyrannical gaze of any totalizing institution. Combining vanguard structures, lyric prose, and existential themes, this novel presents the Communist Party's "famous" magazine as a metaphor for the authoritarianism of both the party and the fascistic Estado Novo. Rosa, the female lead, writes for the *revista* to protest state dictatorship, but as a party organ, the magazine mirrors the fascist regime through its reach into characters' lives. Jackson points to the novel's futuristic portrayal of the *revista*'s vast surveillance system ("Alienation and Ideology," 298, 300), and in a similar vein Luiz Fernando Valente proposes that in its "specter of a disciplinary society" the work anticipates Foucault (33).[35]

Precisely in this "disciplinary" portrayal of the fictional world, *A famosa revista* expands on the feminist quest in *Parque industrial* for the private. Here the journal's surveillance mechanisms scrutinize intimate relations; the novel also highlights sexual harassment of women on the job, hypocrisies of bourgeois marriage, and inequities of punishment dispensed to men and women for sexual activity. Rosa and her coworker Tribli are stronger than any women characters in *Parque industrial.* Manifesting Galvão's hope of female collaboration, they team up to resist the *revista*'s tyranny. Anticipated by the Otavia-Alfredo alliance in *Parque industrial,* the second novel expands the feminist take on relationships through its unconventional heterosexual couple. Although romance and sex do enter the mix, Rosa and her mate, Mosci, are primarily intellectual and political collaborators, a model also evoked by Wiesse and Rivas Mercado.

The characters' resistance to the *revista*'s watchful eye reiterates Galvão's pursuit of critical viewing while remaining unseen. As in *Parque industrial,* theatrical structures reinforce this interplay. These include, as

Jackson points out, dramatic and musical terms that designate the work's seven major parts (298) as well as the multiple scenes comprising the lengthy section "As cem páginas da revista" and theatrical terminology that titles some episodes. Just as the theatrics of Galvão's earlier writing portrayed the artist as (unseen) spy on São Paulo's culture of display, here Rosa and Tribli defy the *revista*'s surveillance with counterespionage. Jackson's designation of this section of the novel as a "drama of detective fiction" ("Alienation and Ideology," 300) is particularly apt. At the same time that she wrote A *famosa revista* with Ferraz, Galvão published, under the name King Shelter, nine pulp fiction mystery stories in the Rio de Janeiro magazine *Detetive*.

Composed for a broader audience than her experimental novels, Galvão's mystery fiction offers intriguing counterpoints to her other work. The readability of these stylized stories evidences her mastery of the genre's conventions and clichés.[36] But the stories' singular features call to mind Galvão's broader intellectual project and literary persona. Several mine performance venues as their settings, including an international open-air Greek theatre festival in provincial France, nightclub scenarios in Prohibition-era Chicago, and a traveling variety show complete with animal acts, dwarfs, a cobra man, and a bearded lady. The stories revel in sumptuous details of a theatrical ambiance and in the sensuous displays of numerous performing women—actresses, a veiled dancer, a torch singer, and a circus ballerina—whose roles range from victim to victimizer to willing and unwitting accomplices for perpetrators and those who root them out. In the context of Galvão's critical views, these stories relax and enjoy the pleasures of performance that she herself had embraced in her youthful days. At the same time, the women on exhibit form an unpredictable lot whose common experience is the underestimation by others of their physical strength, mental acuity, and capacity for evil as much as for good.

What better genre than a mystery to feature the kind of inquiry that Galvão proclaimed the source of art's power and to highlight, once again, the economy of visibility and the unseen. Galvão's detective alter ego, the first-person narrator, makes an explicit reference to this epistemological mode by contrasting the "perspicacity" and knowledge of psychology that inform a true detective's inquiry with the dependence on denunciation by informants that marks garden-variety police work (*Safra macabra*, 187). Although various detectives populate the stories (with such self-parodying names as Red Flaningan, Hit Hammer, and Hope Hone), the narrator is speaking in this case to Cassira A. Ducrot, the most developed detective character, who reappears in several stories as a Parisian "Sherlock" (*Safra macabra,* 109). The narrator of these particular stories is, as Galvão Ferraz points out, a kind of Watson to Ducrot's Sherlock (8). Most telling is this sidekick's invisibility, a private eye/I voice that only occasionally reveals its own presence but maintains an eagle perspective on events. Metafictional moves in "O dinheiro dos mutilados" (The amputees' fund), which develops this relationship, link its narrator to Galvão's authorial presence. Working in Paris, the sidekick-narrator self-identifies as Mr. King Shelter—Galvão's pseudonym for these stories—and notes that he writes plots for *Detective,* the name of the Rio magazine in which Galvão published her work. Here a female counterpart to Shelter (and instigator of the murder), Violeta Cottot, is credited with writing "the most perfect contemporary detective stories" for the magazine *Delinquents,* under the pseudonym "Mossidora" (which calls to mind Galvão's pen name "Mara Lobo") (*Safra macabra,* 107). Violeta's friendship with the suicidal modern poet Paul Crevel evokes the surrealist René Crevel, whom Galvão knew in Paris and who ended his own life. Among the story's pointed references to the dynamic between these two mystery writers' lives and their writing, moreover, the narrator observes that Violeta must adjust her character portrayals to her editor's and readers' demands. This doubling of the narrator-writer-detective into more than one character recalls the shifting guises of Galvão's authorial persona in earlier work. The reference to a mixed bag of writing styles and motives—Galvão was writing pulp fiction and a hermetic novel at the same time—manifests the challenges for a professional journalist who aspires to be a literary author and Galvão's enduring ambivalence toward the audiences she provoked but still sought to reach. Although her own novels were not particularly accessible to average readers, *A famosa revista* takes the totalitarian *revista* leaders to serious task for ensuring that their constituents "understand nothing" (177).

Galvão's detective fiction sends readers on epistemological odysseys that it solves. But typically the tales' teller tantalizes us with fleeting appearances while maintaining an inviolable zone of reserve. Ferraz characterized his wife after her death as somebody who never sought publicity but always attracted it ("Patrícia Galvão," 263), an affirmation difficult to square with her youthful exhibitionism unless one heeds the mixed signals of a performing woman well aware of the price of the show. Noting them, one is then not at all surprised to hear her son declare that the Galvão he knew "detested being called Pagu" (Galvão Ferraz, Introduction, 3). Such mature rejoinders to youthful identities are particularly understandable when political betrayal, imprisonment, and torture truncate one's youth. But this rejection of a name also confirms Galvão's distance from the cultural roles bestowed on her and reasserts her claim to a zone of mobility—cultural, political, and intellectual—that they did not allow.

Galvão's most poignant rejection of this compulsory casting is the poem "Natureza morta" (Still life or, more literally, "Dead nature"). In this 1948 lyric of existential despair, the speaker describes herself "hanging from the wall" and "made into a portrait" by those who have run a nail through her heart so that she cannot move, "stretched out on the canvas like a pile of rotting fruit" (*Pagu vida-obra,* 169). Although those responsible for the hanging have left her eyes and fingers free, these too are immobile as she struggles to write. This imagery may be a response to Oswald's 1937 theatrical projection of revolution onto the dismembered body of a dead woman in his play *A morta* or to Galvão's endurance of torture during the same years. But this self-framing of the speaker in a portrait not of her own making also calls to mind Mary Ann Caws's apt term for the vanguards' objectification of women as "ladies shot and painted."[37] As always, Galvão's gesture was two-edged, for even as her lyric alter ego hung from a wall, she controlled what would not be seen, in this case the identity of the author. The poem appeared in the *Diário de São Paulo* under the pseudonym Solange Sohl, identified only as an *estreante,* an artist making a debut. This moniker and accompanying descriptions of the poet's "intense dramatism" and "engagement with the future" (*Pagu vida-obra,* 169) evoke Galvão's powerful dramatic debut nineteen years earlier as the outrageous modernist muse. Ironically, this poem provoked more muse-ifying, as students at the University of São Paulo sought to meet this female *poéte maudit,* and Augusto de Campos, not knowing the author, wrote a long poem inspired by and dedicated to the female speaker of "Natureza morta." According to Ferraz, Galvão spread the word that the name was a pseudonym for "a young woman who [did] not want her name to appear" and asked that the anonymity it enclosed be respected ("Quem foi Solange Sohl," 174). Solange Sohl's true identity did not come out until after her death. The chilling poem of an immobilized woman on display and the quest to pin her down further that it unleashed both underscore that, even as Patrícia Galvão acknowledged the wages of the cultural scripts she performed, for a woman writer committed to gender equity, social justice, and intellectual freedom, the resolve to choose her own name endured.

notes

INTRODUCTION

1. On social motherhood see Miller (Chapter 4).

2. Parker and Sedgwick are referring to the "oblique intersection" of "performativity," based on J. L. Austin's work on performative speech acts, and performance as a "loose cluster of theatrical practices, relations, and traditions" (1).

3. Although countless critics draw on Bakhtin to highlight dialogic qualities in poetry, he argued that poetry is far less dialogic than prose (*Dialogic Imagination,* 284–288).

4. In his exegesis of Bourdieu's *Outline of a Theory of Practice,* Jenkins argues that for Bourdieu, "only insofar as one does things is it possible to know things" (69).

5. See the introduction and Chapter 2 of my *Latin American Vanguards.*

6. Marchant argues similarly that early women cultural critics (including Ocampo) "chose the act of writing as a way to intervene in the public realm" (1).

7. On male bonding in *Don Segundo Sombra* see Leland, who calls it an "obstreperously masculine book" (127).

8. See Irwin (Chapter 1).

9. See my *Latin American Vanguards* (Chapter 1).

10. Suleiman, too, highlights the gendering of modernity and the avant-gardes.

11. See Mastronardi (206) on these competitions.

12. See Irwin (Chapter 3), Balderston, and Sheridan.

13. *Caras y caretas* and other magazines did portray Storni as a writer and public figure.

14. See Kirkpatrick's *Dissonant Legacy of Modernismo* (6–7) and Molloy's introduction to Part 2 of *Women's Writing in Latin America* (109).

15. While *advertencia* also means foreword, as in the Onís and Fornoff translation, my choice of the alternate "warning" underscores the tone and content of the novel's opening.

16. Here my own translation coincides with my point more than the Onís and Fornoff version does.

17. See my "Teresa de la Parra and the Avant-Gardes."

18. See my "¿De quién es esta historia?"

19. Garrels argues that the editor–Mamá Blanca relationship implies a feminist aesthetic of collaboration in opposition to a masculinist model of individual achievement (*Las grietas de la ternura,* 132–136). Molloy sees it as highlighting "the conspiratorial female pact" that permeates Parra's writing (Foreword, xiv).

20. Drawing on Foucault, Roach employs the concept of a genealogy of performance to focus on disparities between history, discursively transmitted, and memory, publicly enacted by bodies bearing its consequences (25–27).

21. Molloy proposes Parra's oblique textual articulation of a lesbian identity.

22. Reedy consistently argues that Portal was a feminist throughout her career, while Miller refers to her antifeminism (101–102).

23. Chilean Nobel laureate Gabriela Mistral was a contemporary to Parra, Ocampo, and Storni and an international figure. Although recent criticism reveals an unconventional complexity to her work and authorial persona not previously recognized, she did not engage in the performative interaction with self-consciously innovative literary culture that typifies the women in this study. Among others not included, Loynaz, particularly in the novel *Jardín,* written in the 1930s but not published until 1951, produced some of the best vanguard writing by a Latin American woman. But Loynaz avoided Havana's lively avant-garde literary scene completely, a fact that, regrettably, given her provocative portrayal of a modern woman in *Jardín,* made her a less apt choice for this study.

CHAPTER 1

1. I draw biographical information from Delgado, Phillips, and Nalé Roxlo. Delgado's biography is the most complete source.

2. Storni's radical farces appeared the same year as the completed version of Huidobro's *Altazor* (1931) and her innovative poetry of *Mundo de siete pozos* (1934) just two years after Oliverio Girondo's *Espantapájaros (al alcance de todos)*.

3. Storni's biographers, particularly Delgado and Phillips, detail her theatre background.

4. Between her theatrical tour and her entrance to Normal School, Storni wrote her first play, which was neither staged nor published.

5. See Kirkpatrick's "Alfonsina Storni as 'Tao Lao'" and "The Journalism of Alfonsina Storni." Phillips, too, suggests that Storni adopted roles in Buenos Aires literary society (60), and Nalé Roxlo notes the mobility of her public personality (45).

6. See, for example, García Velloso's manual, *Piedras preciosas*.

7. Kirkpatrick demonstrates the importance of fashion in Storni's journalism and her exploration of gender in that venue. I address its centrality as a

motif in all of Storni's work and its intersection with books as a metaphor for cultural scripting.

8. Kirkpatrick has argued that these essays and Storni's journalistic fiction often drew on melodrama ("Alfonsina Storni as 'Tao Lao,'" 135, 144), a style that obscured the analytical depth of her writing.

9. Similarly, in "La costurerita a domicilio," a seamstress's dreams of social ascendancy materialize in a preference for a male body attired in an elegant tie and exuding cologne rather than the bloodied hands and disagreeable aura of the loyal butcher who courts her (*Nosotras,* 112).

10. Storni lamented an unequal burden placed on the working class by prescriptive mourning fashion (*Nosotras,* 64).

11. Consider the young women who emulate fashion models on Calle Florida in "Las damitas crepusculares" (*Nosotras,* 104) or the "eternal imitator" who impersonates not only the heroines of her favorite novels but also the hairstyles, intonations, pet phrases, and handwriting of her peers in "La impersonal" (*Nosotras,* 109).

12. See "Estafador casi mujer" (n.a.), Carlos Alberto Silva's "Las amazonas," and "Una tribu en que mandan las mujeres" (n.a.), respectively in *Caras y caretas* 29:1455 (August 21, 1926), 30:1524 (December 17, 1927), and 31:1553 (July 21, 1928), all unpaginated.

13. Storni's preface to *Poemas de amor* (1926) described "simple phrases of states of love" that do not pretend to be a "literary work" (n.pag.).

14. See my description of a *Caras y caretas* review of a woman's poetry in this book's introduction.

15. In *Nosotras* see Storni's "Las mujeres que trabajan" (105–108) and "A propósito de las incapacidades relativas de la mujer" (83–91).

16. See Storni's "La mujer como novelista" (159–162) and "El amor y la mujer" (129–132) in *Nosotras*.

17. Masiello observes that the competition between these women relates to their social roles as readers (*Between Civilization and Barbarism,* 191).

18. Phillips argues that Márgara is Storni's alter ego (64–65).

19. See *Homenaje a Buenos Aires en el cuarto centenario de su fundación* (n.a).

20. See Storni's "Siglo XX," in which the poetic speaker, a "woman of the twentieth century," decries the idle futility of her own bourgeois life and calls on workers to tear it down and assuage her guilt (*Obra poética completa,* 240).

CHAPTER 2

1. Molloy, in "The Theatrics of Reading: Body and Book in Victoria Ocampo" (*At Face Value,* 55–75), has given the greatest prior attention to the role of theatricality in her self-figuration, particularly through the metonymy

of body and books. I address the connections between Ocampo's performance experience, *testimonio* aesthetics, and intellectual self-portrait.

2. *Sur* had a brief hiatus in 1934–1935.

3. See Molloy, for example (*At Face Value*, 63).

4. Greenberg makes a compelling case for tensions between public and private in Ocampo's autobiography. While not disagreeing, I see continuity among the facets of Ocampo's work and life, forged through her performance experience.

5. King argues that Ocampo had "little to do with the literary effervescence of the 1920s" and that her writing of the 1920s and lectures for Amigos del Arte differed from the "polemical tone and youthful euphoria of other young writers" (33). By contrast, Masiello underscores the "logic of modernity" in Ocampo's writing but proposes that the "heterogeneity" of her persona and perspective constitutes an oppositional response to the avant-gardes (*Between Civilization and Barbarism*, 162, 158).

6. I draw information about Ocampo's life and performance experience from her own *Autobiografía*, Meyer's *Victoria Ocampo*, Maria Esther Vásquez, and Castilho and Felgine.

7. During the 1920s Ocampo met Borges, his sister, the painter Norah Borges, Pablo Rojas Paz, Brandan Carrafa, and Eduardo Mallea.

8. Ortega y Gasset dwelt at length on Ocampo's "feminine" and "delicious" presence in *De Francesca a Beatrice* (Epilogue, 133–134). Ángel de Estrada, as noted, cast her personal allusions in the essay as indecent exposure (quoted in Ocampo, *Autobiografía*, 3:106).

9. Here again I depart from King's excellent study of *Sur*, as he emphasizes the differences between Ocampo and the vanguard generation. On the innovative lexical, morphosyntactic, and linguistic idiosyncrasies in Ocampo's writing see Ombil.

10. *Revista oral,* organized by the Peruvian expatriate poet Alberto Hidalgo, consisted of sixteen ribald gatherings or "issues" from 1926 to 1927.

11. See Ocampo's tour of Buenos Aires architecture, "Sobre un mal de esta ciudad" (*Domingos*, 153–167).

12. Consider the scarecrow-like structure that Oliverio Girondo carried through the streets of Buenos Aires to advertise his *Espantapájaros (al alcance de todos)*.

13. Ocampo later parted with the couple because of their conservative turn.

14. See Hausman on Ocampo's writing on Woolf.

15. On these women's role in Anglo-European modernism see Benstock.

16. See Miller (Chapter 4).

17. Throughout her autobiography, Ocampo underscored that the standard education of a man of her class was denied her, and she described ongoing battles with her parents about permissible readings.

18. The director Osvald Bonet recalled Ocampo's presence at a rehearsal in the Parisian Odeón theatre: "She would follow silently the laborious repetitions of the actors, their struggles to find themselves in the character. She would not intervene in the work of the rehearsal, but the next day . . . she would send me a short outline with her impressions" (n.a., *Testimonios sobre Victoria Ocampo,* 36). Ocampo followed modern dramatic developments throughout her life, such as the work of Eugene Ionesco and of Dylan Thomas, sections of whose *Under Milkwood* she translated.

19. See Meyer (*Victoria Ocampo,* 186) and Ombil (71).

20. Optimio counters one of Atrabilis's pronouncements with, "All of that is true, but it is also false" (Ocampo, *La laguna,* 51).

21. See Molloy (*At Face Value*) and Greenberg.

22. In a vein remarkably similar to Bakhtin's, Ocampo wrote about studying anatomy: "A part of me seemed to disconnect itself from me and become strange to me, suspicious; a distance was born between us. It was I and it wasn't I" (*Autobiografía,* 1:151–152).

23. In making this argument, Ocampo cited a similar idea in Jacinto Benavente's play *Los intereses creados.*

24. Ocampo's portrait of Anna de Noailles, for example, shifts when the poet responds to her cue: "now she has begun her loquacious and voluble chat and . . . it is a new Anna de Noailles who, for me, enters the scene" ("Sobre dos poetas," 17).

25. Drawing on Bakhtin, Meyer demonstrates the theatrical and dialogic quality of Ocampo's letters, the site for "communicating with oneself and with an Other" ("Letters and Lines," 235).

26. See Guiñazú on Ocampo's construction of "readers as characters in the books they read" (131) and their connection with Woolf's common reader.

27. Ocampo eventually dubbed *De Francesca a Beatrice* her "*Baedeker* of *The Divine Comedy*" (*Autobiografía,* 3:105). The German printer Karl Baedeker published popular guidebooks in the nineteenth century; his name subsequently became synonymous with the genre.

28. These are titles of two Ocampo *testimonios.*

29. In interpreting Ocampo's "margin" as a position from which to read rather than as social marginality, I diverge somewhat from Meyer's conclusion that Ocampo envisioned herself writing from the margins in keeping with the feminine tradition conceptualized by Sidonie Smith that challenges hegemonic discourse from outside. In my reading, Ocampo imagines herself intervening directly in intellectual debates. But my argument that Ocampo conceived the margin as a site of mobility concurs with Meyer's proposal that marginality challenges unitary authority (Meyer, "Reciprocal Reflections," 110–111). In highlighting the ambiguity of Ocampo's self-assigned position, from which she could enter and exit the scenario of ideas, I concur in part with Guiñazú.

30. We should recall here the poet Gabriela Mistral's legitimization of her public persona through the performance of the teacher role.

31. See Guiñazú.

32. For Ocampo's first inquiry into cultural hierarchies see "Babel" (*Testimonios,* 1:43–52).

33. Ocampo also apparently distanced herself from Storni. Gabriela Mistral criticized her for not supporting a fellow woman writer. A bewildered Ocampo excused herself on the grounds that they seldom crossed paths (*Testimonios,* 3:171–181).

CHAPTER 3

1. The house on Calle Tronador appears in *Adán Buenosayres,* Leopoldo Marechal's *roman à clef,* and is represented with a sense of refuge that parallels the Borges poem in a contrast between "the intimacy" of the house and the "indiscretion of external eyes" (quoted in Miguel, 13).

2. While other women sometimes joined the group's gatherings, Lange was the only one to enjoy enduring membership as a writer.

3. Magda Portal was the other woman included in the landmark collection.

4. Perhaps because autobiographical elements weave through Lange's literary work, particularly *Cuadernos de infancia,* her own writing constitutes the primary source for biographer Miguel. Supplemented by occasional interviews, particularly with Nóbile, and recollections from Martín Fierro members or others who knew her, Lange's own impressionistic accounts comprise most of what is known about her life.

5. Domínguez argues that Lange negotiated her public (literary) and private (family) spheres through two different voices, one trapped in the familial world of her fiction, the other ensnared in the performative guises she assumed in the literary world (32). With an analogous dichotomy, Masiello affirms that Lange's fiction constitutes a retreat "into a world of the imagination with a closed and private subjectivity" that resists the power of nation and state and contrasts with her less effective role as *damisela* in the public literary world (*Between Civilization and Barbarism,* 147, 154). Lindstrom offers a similar contrast between Lange's written, artistic production and her "paraliterary activities" (136).

6. Here I expand on Molloy's affirmation of continuity between Lange's public performances and those she executed through writing (*At Face Value,* 126–136) and take it in a new direction.

7. Here I agree with Domínguez's argument that in Lange's prose, "the position from which the family is narrated is an ambiguous one, invoking both distance and engagement, spying and interpretation, participation and detachment" (39).

8. On this projection in European modernism see Felski's Chapter 2.

9. Lange and Girondo married in 1943.

10. Sarlo's characterization of the public Lange is distinctive in highlighting the "child-woman" quality that Lange embodied among the early *ultraístas* and the familial nature of her relationship to them (*Una modernidad periférica,* 70–83).

11. The poem "Norah Lange" by Córdova Iturburu appeared in 1924 in *Martín Fierro* and portrayed an enigmatic figure conjured up by her mysterious name (Sarlo, *Martín Fierro,* 49).

12. Borges's cousin Guillermo Juan Borges was the son of Lange's mother's sister.

13. Lange changed the spelling of her name from Nora to Norah.

14. Muschietti highlights Borges's linkage of Lange with Buenos Aires geography, observing that he depicted her as "one more element of the suburban landscape" (91).

15. On the vanguards' link of originality with origins see Krauss.

16. In a review that appeared in *Síntesis,* Borges insisted that this "supposed novel" was actually Lange's third book of poetry, not prose (quoted in Miguel, 127–128). But while the prose's imagery resembles Lange's verse, the storytelling conventions and epistolary frame organize the material into a short novel.

17. Masiello draws on this critical review by Ramón Doll to support her contention that Lange constructed a project of verbal resistance to the norms of gender, history, and nation that the review embodied (*Between Civilization and Barbarism,* 155–156).

18. The timing of *Voz de la vida* also encourages a semiautobiographical reading of the relationship between Lange and Girondo, particularly as their first meeting in 1926 and their developing friendship were interrupted soon thereafter by his European travels until his return to Buenos Aires in 1932.

19. During the 1920s, however, Lange was not allowed to go out at night in Buenos Aires (Nóbile, 13).

20. A copy of this photograph appears in Miguel (n.pag.), although she does not identify its source.

21. Molloy highlights the "removal from referential reality" of *Cuadernos de infancia* that undermines its potential as a foundational fiction (*At Face Value,* 129), and Masiello, expanding on Molloy's observation, argues that in both poetry and prose, Lange created a voice unencumbered by time and place (*Between Civilization and Barbarism,* 149).

22. Lindstrom calls Lange's *discursos* "anti-logical" (135); Miguel calls them "pataphysical" (in an allusion to Alfred Jarry; 169); Molloy calls them "macaronic" (evoking the tradition of Menippean satire) and their site of delivery a "Dadaist banquet" (*At Face Value,* 127).

23. My source for this characterization of the literary anatomy is Frye's well-known exposition (308–312).

24. These include writers Amado Villar, Evar Méndez, Pablo Rojas Paz, Samuel Eichelbaum, Rafael Alberti, and Marta Brunet and painters and sculptors Rafael Crespo, Toño Salazar, and María Carmen Portela.

25. Lange described this careful process in a 1968 interview (Nóbile, 20).

26. Molloy has translated excerpts from *Cuadernos de infancia* under the title *Childhood Copybooks*. See *Women's Writing in Latin America*, edited by Castro-Klarén, Molloy, and Sarlo (152–156).

27. Domínguez reads *Cuadernos*, along with Lange's subsequent novels, as a composite "macro" text and novel of apprenticeship.

28. On the singularities of the novel of apprenticeship among women writers see Abel, Hirsch, and Langland's *The Voyage In*, in particular the introduction and Roskowski's piece in that volume. On gender in the Spanish American *Bildungsroman* see Kushigian.

29. Here I differ with Domínguez's argument that Lange's disguises constituted an "attractive and amusing repetition of a gender" (44) and concur with Butler that no reiteration is a mere replica (23, 28).

30. Domínguez suggests that the shift to this world contrasts with the unconventional women protagonists of *Voz de la vida* and *45 días y 30 marineros* and results from reviews of her work (such as Doll's) that sought to police Lange's resistance to thematic and rhetorical standards for women's writing (33).

31. On the rooftop acts of *Cuadernos de infancia* Molloy observes: "This ritualistic performance . . . surely prefigures the adult Lange's nonsensical *discursos*" (*At Face Value*, 135).

32. Masiello sees the uncanny in Lange's work as the emergence of a "feminine grotesque" (*Between Civilization and Barbarism*, 153).

33. Lange's later prose works also include authorial figures and the scene of writing.

CHAPTER 4

1. For years, uncertainty surrounded Campobello's dates of birth and death, the former because of her own shifting reports, the latter because of her mysterious disappearance in the mid-1980s and apparent demise reportedly through malignant neglect or foul play at the hands of the guardians who wanted her worldly goods (in particular artwork by muralist José Clemente Orozco created for dance projects). See García.

2. Segura quotes this account from the report of a dancer who as a schoolgirl participated in the *30-30* (23).

3. On Campobello's contributions to Mexican dance see Tortajada Quiroz's *Danza y poder*, Segura, and Tibol. On Gloria and Nellie's ties to the cultural politics of the period see Calle.

4. Here I use Ortega y Gasset's familiar characterization of modern writing (25).

5. I am referring to Artaud's 1936 journey to Chihuahua, recorded in *A Voyage to the Land of the Tarahumara* (1945). Campobello reported having advised Artaud during his journey, drawing on her knowledge of the region (Carballo, 412).

6. My biographical account draws on Matthews's biography, García, and Nickel.

7. See Tortajada Quiroz's *Danza y poder* (51–131) on the changes in name and leadership undergone by the Escuela Nacional de Danza.

8. Segura argues that Gloria was the better dancer of the two.

9. Tortajada Quiroz notes Campobello's propensity for control and difficult relationships with coworkers and students (*Danza y poder*, 87–131).

10. Segura portrays Campobello's sister, by contrast, as the more self-effacing, "feminine," and talented of the two.

11. See Segura (33) and Carballo (413).

12. See Collado on the efforts of Mexico City's affluent classes to control their daughters' contact with the dance culture of the 1920s and provide respectable alternatives to clubs and theatres deemed too seedy.

13. On Miss Carroll's Girls see Segura (12–13), Matthews's biography (52–54), and Tortajada Quiroz ("Danza de mujer," 88–89). Matthews documents the presence of Miss Carroll's Girls in "discreet" ads (53).

14. Matthews (52) and Tortajada ("Danza de mujer," 88) note the link between female emancipation and dance in Noriega Hope's article.

15. Molloy, too, notes the distinction, explaining that she focuses on the "dynamics of posing" (rather than "the self containment of isolated gestures") and on how a sequence of posing creates a narrative ("Politics of Posing," 148). Here I focus on the difference between performance and posing in showcasing and undermining norms.

16. On the construction of masculinity and emergence of gay male writers in Mexican cultural life of the period see Irwin, Sheridan, and Balderston.

17. Consider the *estridentista* writer Arqueles Vela's short fiction *La Señorita Etc.,* first published in 1925.

18. Although in the preface to *Mis libros* and her 1960 interview with Carballo she alluded to works in progress and although she disseminated articles on dance in the Departamento de Bellas Artes, *Mis libros* was her last significant publication.

19. Jaime Torres Bodet's *La educación sentimental* (1929) is a prime example.

20. Calle builds a strong case for Guzmán's influence on changes of style and characterization of the mother between *Cartucho* and *Las manos de mamá,* arguing that while the former portrays a more virile, autonomous woman, the latter presents a more traditional, feminine character.

21. See Schneider's *Fragua y gesta* and Tortajada Quiroz's *Danza y poder* (61–62).

22. Fernández de Castro, Campobello's Cuban host, and List Arzubide, freshly returned from the Soviet Union, introduced her to Mayakovsky.

23. See Fernández de Castro on Campobello's visit and work (*Barraca de Feria*, 93–100).

24. Although I draw on the later edition of *Yo, por Francisca* published in *Mis libros*, the extant poems from the first edition, published in Fitts, demonstrate a comparable propensity for short verses in vertical display.

25. An earlier version of "Juego," translated by Langston Hughes, appeared in Fitts (212–214).

26. The early version of "Yo" appears under the title "Juego" in Campobello's *Mis libros*, where the title "Yo" is reassigned to the poem with the opening verse "They say that I am brusque."

27. See Felski's Chapter 2.

28. Meyer reads this ambivalence as a dynamic between "self-revelation" and "self-concealment" typical of an "adolescent female dilemma" ("Divided against Herself," 52). While not disagreeing, I see the youthful persona as a pose, an interpretation consistent with Matthews's confirmation that Campobello was actually born in 1900 and was, therefore, twenty-nine when *Yo, por Francisca* appeared.

29. In connection with Campobello's doll "who cannot eat honey," consider Storni's ironic celebration of the "sugar" constituting her identity as a *poetisa* (Chapter 1 of this volume).

30. On *Cartucho*'s reception in its time see Nickel (124–125).

31. On *Cartucho* as testimonial narrative see Meyer's "Dialogics of Testimony." On its narrative voice see also Cázares and Parle.

32. Here I diverge from Calle and Strickland Nájera, who highlight differences between editions of *Cartucho*.

33. Castro Leal's introductory comment on the "natural tenderness" of Campobello's "childlike" perspective of the Revolution illustrates the persistence of such cultural scripts even in narrative scenarios that belie them (Campobello, *Cartucho*, 923).

34. In Latin American autobiography of the nineteenth century, childhood constitutes, according to Molloy, "one of the most expressive silences" (*At Face Value*, 6).

35. I use my own literal translation of this section in order to preserve the conditional verb phrase *haría un resoplido de general*, which is essential for my point.

36. Although Strickland Nájera argues that there are fewer uses of *yo creo* in the later edition of *Cartucho* (62), in fact each instance of it in the 1931 edition reappears in the later editions, which also include several more instances of the phrase.

37. Campobello's vehement insistence on her work's originality in *Mis libros* contrasts with List Arzubide's suggestion years later that he had transformed

her "disordered papers" into publishable material (García, 28), an assertion illuminating the necessity of the vehemence.

38. Calle develops this view.

39. See Richards (Chapter 3) and Oyarzún.

40. Campobello and her sister Gloria, the coauthor, expressed comparable essentialism in *Ritmos indígenas de México,* which argues that body movements are racial characteristics and that certain groups possess an "expressive primitivism" (14). Similarly, in the interview with Carballo, Nellie Campobello referred to the "humble majesty" of the Indians' poverty (Carballo, 412). Tortajada Quiroz in *Danza y poder* writes that Campobello's racism manifested itself in condescension toward people of color in the dance school (99, 126). At the same time, Campobello identified with indigenous groups when she argued that their alleged preference for bodily over verbal communication characterized marginalized people who communicated through body language what "they would not have dared say in another manner"(*Ritmos indígenas,* 13–14).

41. Here I prefer my own translation for "rimando . . . pasos" to Matthews's "stepping in rhythm" (IM, 125).

42. On international modernism's machine-woman see Huyssen (65–81).

CHAPTER 5

1. Lyons writes that in performance "the unity provided by the continuity of the presence of the actor/character tends to obscure the collision of readings that precedes the performance" (126).

2. As Danny Anderson sums up in a book in progress on the culture of reading in Mexico, epithets assigned to Rivas Mercado include Vasconcelos's prediction that she would have become one of Latin America's top women writers (Vasconcelos, 1079) and José Emilio Pachecho's more recent portrayal of her as Mexico's first emancipated woman (Pacheco, 108). Martínez-Zalce examines how myths surrounding Rivas Mercado overshadow serious consideration of her writing.

3. The following caption appears below a photo of Rivas Mercado that accompanies Novo's piece for *El universal ilustrado:* "Antonieta Rivas Mercado, the soul of the company of intellectuals that created the 'Teatro de Ulises,' the night of its public debut with the work 'Simili' by Roger Marx in the Teatro Fábregas" (Novo, 21).

4. Rivas Mercado also funded the publication of Andrés Henestrosa's *Los hombres que dispersó la danza* (1929).

5. Bradu seeks to "reintegrate the tensions" that characterized Rivas Mercado's life and work (10). Other biographical sources include Schneider's introductory study to the *Obras completas,* Rojas Rosillo, Henestrosa, and Blair's fictionalized version of her life story. Robles focuses on the relationship of Rivas Mercado's work to the Vasconcelos campaign; Granillo Vázquez

examines her work in the context of a Mexican feminine tradition of maternity; and Gliemmo addresses the role of writing in her cultural activity.

6. The Asociación Mexicana de Críticos de Teatro regularly awards an Antonieta Rivas Mercado recognition prize for the dissemination of theatre.

7. These include Carlos Saura's 1983 film *Antonieta;* the dramatic works *El destierro* by Juan Tovar (1975) and *Antonieta: Soledad y esplendor* by Salvador Lemis (1996); the novelized biography *A la sombra del Ángel* (1995) by Kathryn Skidmore Blair; the poem "S/T" by Cuban poet Ernesto Adrián Mozón; the painting "Los Milagros Rojos de Rivas Mercado" (1999) by Esperanza Gama; and the 1998 "coreodrama" *Antonieta Rivas Mercado, la antorcha hija del ángel* by Gladiola Orozco, performed at Mexico City's Palacio de Bellas Artes. Artistic depictions of Rivas Mercado during her lifetime included paintings by Diego Rivera and photographs by Tina Modotti.

8. See Collado on Mexico City dance clubs in the 1920s.

9. On Rivas Mercado's Parisian theatrical experiences see also Schneider's *Fragua y gesta* (17).

10. On the collaborative work style and informal atmosphere of the Teatro de Ulises see Mendoza-López (30–32) and Schneider's *Fragua y gesta* (11–64).

11. One contemporary reviewer wrote: "I believe that a goodly number of those lead actresses who tour the world followed by applause and admiration would have a difficult time surpassing Antonieta Rivas Mercado" (Dalevuelta, 67).

12. Although Schmidhuber attributes the theatrical adaptation of *Los de abajo* exclusively to Rivas Mercado (79), Schneider says she collaborated with José Luis Ituarte (Schneider, *Obras completas,* 25), which is confirmed by her own epistolary references (*Obras completas,* 403) and those of Azuela (*Epistolario*). An anonymous explanatory note accompanying the first published edition of the dramatic version states: "in 1929 a dramatic arrangement of *Los de abajo* was staged at the Teatro Hidalgo, a version elaborated without the author's intervention" (Azuela, *Teatro,* 11). For his part, Azuela explained that the arrangement was Ituarte's work and the source of its official failure (due to the latter's relative lack of knowledge of the Mexican context) and the "plastic presentation" of the staging was the work of Rivas Mercado, whom he congratulated as well for the "artistic success" of the piece (Azuela, *Epistolario,* 150, 157). Azuela also mentioned a failed performance in Los Angeles (*Epistolario,* 168) and documented negotiations for the play's translation into English and a staging by the Theatre Guild, although, following the Los Angeles failure, he himself carried out a dramatic version and a friend translated it into English (*Epistolario,* 180).

13. Rivas Mercado's meetings with Lorca took place in New York in October and November 1929 within the Hispanic circle at Columbia University that included Federico and Harriet de Onís, Fernando de los Ríos, and Dámaso Alonso. She spoke of "profound community" with Lorca (*Obras completas,* 390) and planned collaboration. In response to a Theatre Guild request for

contemporary Spanish and Spanish American work, Lorca was to give her two unpublished plays for translation. Lorca's correspondence testifies positively to these meetings with his "great friend" (García Lorca, 82). In his Lorca biography, Gibson notes Rivas Mercado's opinion that Lorca's theatre surpassed his poetry (277), and her own comment to Rodríguez Lozano confirms this with the judgment that Lorca's theatre was the most important existing contribution to modern theatre (*Obras completas,* 406).

14. According to a letter to Rodríguez Lozano written from New York, Rivas Mercado also wrote a critical study of Mexican popular theatre traditions (*Obras completas,* 395). Blair's novel on Rivas Mercado refers to her "Street Performers of Mexico" published in the little-known periodical *Latin America Speaks* (Blair, 527).

15. In a November 1929 letter, Rivas Mercado commented on a Theatre Guild production of *Karl and Anna,* praising its two "surreal" acts and denigrating the "worst realism" of its third one (*Obras completas,* 397). This would have been the play by the German playwright Leonhard Frank staged in October 1929 and esteemed in guild annals as one of that season's failures (Nadel, 100).

16. Rivas Mercado reported having attended readings of Lorca's *Los títeres de Cachiporra,* which was not staged until 1937 nor published until 1949, and *Los amores de Don Perimplín, Belisa en su jardín: Aleluya erótica* (first staged in 1933). Given that in 1929 these pieces were as yet unpublished, it is likely that they would be the ones that Rivas Mercado indicated Lorca was going to give her for translation. It is also possible that Lorca gave her information on *El público,* conceived during Lorca's New York period and written (though not completed) in Havana in 1930 (Gibson, 294; Edwards, 60).

17. Bradu describes in detail Rivas Mercado's presence at the Teatro de Ulises soirees (108).

18. Holquist's succinct phrasing sums up Bakhtin's dramatic conception of self and other in the essay "Author and Hero in Aesthetic Activity" from *Art and Answerability.* Here Bakhtin moves from a concept of the subject as the "leading actor" in his own life to the fundamental role of outside perspectives in the self's constitution (Bakhtin, *Art and Answerability,* 32).

19. Schmidhuber affirms that this play is a pioneer of Mexican testimonial theatre (125). Rivas Mercado's *Un drama* also anticipates the investigations of historical truth in contemporary plays by Vicente Leñero and Sabina Berman.

20. Here I diverge from Franco's account of Rivas Mercado's "ventriloquism of a nationalist discourse" in the chronicle from which "she herself is conspicuously absent" (112–115). While not denying that she reiterated discourses surrounding her, I focus instead on the potential for resignification implicit in any performative reiteration of dominant discourse and the agency of the ventriloquist who authors and chooses the voice selected for a particular performance. Through those choices, Rivas Mercado is fully present in her own writing.

21. Bradu suggests that Rivas Mercado elaborated opposite versions of her actions and intentions for Rodríguez Lozano and Vasconcelos (184).

22. The source of this repeated critical allusion is Rivas Mercado's own epistolary affirmation to Rodríguez Lozano: "I consider myself absolutely incapable of tracing a dividing line between my spirit and my body, because I love, when I love, completely" (*Obras completas,* 369). Drawing on this declaration, Skirius (176–189), Bradu (122–124 and 187–188), and Franco (117–121) investigate the tension between her private and public life embodied in her oscillating relationships with Rodríguez Lozano and Vasconcelos.

23. In the United States, Rivas Mercado wrote, women were already state governors and senators (*Obras completas,* 323).

24. In the campaign chronicle she constructed a comparable *arielista* opposition when she contrasted Yankee materialism to Mexican spiritualism (*Obras completas,* 90).

25. "La mujer mexicana" was initially presented to a non-Mexican audience in *El Sol de Madrid* in 1928, which could account in part for the title's implicit homogeneity.

26. Bradu, for example, cites "Páginas arrancadas" as a personal account of Rivas Mercado's marriage (65–66), and Franco, while affirming its fictional status, uses the story as a source of information on her attitudes toward marriage (113).

27. See Irwin (152–186) and Balderston.

28. On the verbal pyrotechnics of the young *vasconcelistas* see Skirius.

29. Rivas Mercado's struggle between commitment and reflection also emerges in the fact that she envisioned the Vasconcelos campaign chronicle as exercises in "objectification and precision" (*Obras completas,* 443), a work that is actually her most politically engaged and that Franco aptly describes as "a nationalist discourse in which Vasconcelos is the hero and redeemer" (112). But as Rivas Mercado described the differences between the chronicle and the novel, by "objectification" she meant the exposition of facts from a single and clear point of view, whereas novelizing required what she described as the more interesting activity of creating facts from multiple perspectives (*Obras completas,* 443).

30. Specifically, Rivas Mercado's character Plekanoff asks: "Who in their countries until now has had the courage to act, to penetrate first, forcing the virginity of their soul" (*Obras completas,* 282).

31. The character Malo's first novel, *Círculo,* bears a title that Rivas Mercado had planned for a novel of her own, and the letter from Dorantes that beckons him home to Mexico intimates that he might, like Rivas Mercado, chronicle a campaign.

32. The apt epithet *prosa de intensidades* was coined by Ruy Sánchez to characterize the work of José Martínez Sotomayor, in particular *La rueca de aire,* a novella that he associates with the lyrical prose of the Contemporáneos writers (Ruy Sánchez, 23–29).

1. Jose Enrique Rodó, the Uruguayan author of *Ariel* (1900), pillow book to a generation of Latin American writers, remarked in a letter to Varona that the character Próspero, whose lecture to his students constitutes the essay, might well have been modeled on Varona himself. Portions of this letter appeared in the monthly *Social* and are reproduced in Cairo (88–89).

2. In her analysis of the professions of eighteen Cuban feminist leaders of the period, Stoner observes that seven, the largest single number, were journalists, poets, or novelists (83).

3. Although Masiello sees a greater coherence between the journal's political and aesthetic proposals than does Cairo, she, too, highlights an emerging conception of the intellectual as a privileged "arbiter of art and social life" (Masiello, "Rethinking Neocolonial Esthetics," 28).

4. In titling one of her *Bohemia* columns "Homenaje a Mariblanca de Cuba," Rodríguez Acosta observed that Mañach had assigned her this popular nickname ("Homenaje," 17).

5. My biographical summary draws on the *Diccionario de literatura cubana* (2:931), Carrera (157–171), Stoner (89–97), and Sabas Alomá's own columns for *Bohemia* and *Carteles*.

6. Sabas Alomá supported the Cuban Revolution and received a 1966 journalism award for the best work on the *zafra* (cane harvest).

7. The other woman signer was María Villar Buceta, a poet and prose writer who left public cultural life and became a librarian. While many vanguard groups constituted themselves through a manifesto, the Grupo Minorista's "Declaración" of June 1927 appeared almost four years after many of its signers had begun meeting regularly. The manifesto was followed by a gradual dissolution into smaller groups, as some members (Alejo Carpentier, Ichaso, Mañach, and Juan Marinello, joined by the Spaniard Martí Casanovas) founded the *Revista de avance,* a more predominantly artistic journal than the Minorista periodical *Social,* and others turned to politics and journalism. See Cairo on the ideological alliances and tensions between art and politics marking Minorista history.

8. Characterizing the women as "audacious," Mañach, in his chronicle of the group's "sabbatical lunches," played down the presence of Sabas Alomá and Graziela Garbalosa, calling them "women of this and that" (23). But the group's most assiduous chronicler, Emilio Roig de Leuchsenring, numbered Sabas Alomá as a founding, regular member (34), and Mañach himself later named her "Mariblanca de Cuba" and engaged her in debate.

9. See Fernández de Castro's "Positivos ix—Mariblanca Sabas Alomá."

10. In length and style, Magda Portal's "Andamios de vida" and *El nuevo poema y su orientación hacia una estética económica* constitute critical essays more than manifestos. While the painter Tarsila do Amaral played a key role in the 1928 "Manifiesto antropófago" published in the inaugural issue of Brazil's

Revista de antropofagia, Oswald de Andrade and literary tradition attributed authorship to him.

11. On the vanguards' performance manifesto see my *Latin American Vanguards* (Chapter 1). Mário de Andrade's "As enfibraturas do Ipiranga" (1922), among others, creates an artistic assemblage on the grand scale of Sabas Alomá's imaginary congress.

12. The brief 1928 Havana stay of Magda Portal and Serafín Delmar was critical for Sabas Alomá's alliance with this network.

13. With the adjective "oriental" Sabas Alomá highlights her origins in Santiago.

14. My analysis of Sabas Alomá's journalism is based on the full run of the columns she published in *Bohemia* (1927–1930) and *Carteles* (1928–1933) and a few additional pieces published in *Social.*

15. On journalism's stylistic shifts and interaction with literary discourse see González (Chapter 5).

16. Sabas Alomá admired the propensity of Jean Cocteau's dramatic monologue *The Human Voice* to generate spectator "intelligence and sensibility" for imagining the absent character it evokes. She saw Cocteau performed by Berta Singerman, whose work she extolled in "Algo más que recitar" (24).

17. An example in Sabas Alomá's time is Delmira Agustini, whose murder by her ex-husband shaped the critical reception of her poetry.

18. See, respectively, Sabas Alomá's "Figuras del ayer glorioso" (48), "¡Tampa cubanísima!"(12, 56), and "A las mujeres mexicanas"(20). Bayamo, the birthplace of Sabas Alomá's father, has long been cited as the birthplace of Cuban independence and the namesake of the national anthem, *Himno Bayamés.* Noting her mother's devotion to Martí, in "¡Tampa cubanísima!" on the Florida city's Cuban ties and community, Sabas Alomá included a photo of herself and a retired eighty-four-year-old tobacco worker on the steps of the Martínez Ibor factory, where the worker had heard Martí speak. Davies argues that from 1900 to 1935, the relationship of Cuban women writers to Cuban nationalism was predominantly oppositional (34). While not disagreeing, I focus here on performative negotiation of discursive norms rather than outright resistance to them.

19. See Sabas Alomá's "Guajira y pobre."

20. See Sabas Alomá's "Figuras del ayer glorioso" (17), "El indio inmóvil" (18), and "Elia, Francisco, Guayabal" (44).

21. During the years of Sabas Alomá's *Carteles* columns, for example, her Minorista colleague Roig de Leuchsenring also published a weekly column but included no photographs and only rare verbal self-portraits.

22. In Sabas Alomá's *Feminismo* see "Pepillitos y Garzonas" (95–100), "Feminismo contra garzonismo" (101–105), and "Génesis económica del garzonismo" (106–113). Rodríguez Acosta herself, notwithstanding her matter-of-fact inclusion of homosexual characters in her fiction, also once portrayed

lesbianism as a "deviation" provoked by a corrupt social and economic system (*La tragedia social*, 17).

23. See Sabas Alomá's "Algo sobre nudismo."

24. I use "miniworld" to render Sabas Alomá's colloquial "mundillo."

25. Cairo documents a publicized debate between Mañach and Rubén Martínez de Villena on the boundaries between art and politics, with Mañach favoring a sharper division between the two (175–182).

26. Although I have not succeeded in locating Mañach's remarks to which Sabas Alomá refers, her extensive quotations enable a reconstruction of the exchange.

27. This debate between Sabas Alomá and Mañach resembles in kind the polemical exchange between Mañach and Martínez Villena.

28. News of the arrests that included Rodríguez Acosta appeared in *Bohemia* ("Nuestra protesta") on January 11, 1931. See Stoner (116–118) on feminist leadership in protests surrounding this murder and Jongh's "Feminismo y periodismo en la Cuba republicana" (9–10) on Rodríguez Acosta's participation.

29. My biographical summary draws on the *Diccionario de literatura cubana* (2:908), Gay Calbo, Jongh, Menéndez ("*Garzonas y feministas*," 97–102), and Rodríguez Acosta's interview with Berta A. de Martínez Márquez and her own columns.

30. Rodríguez Acosta's early literary work included the prose impressions *Evocaciones,* the 1925 play *La ilusa,* and the travelogue *Apuntes de mi viaje a Isla de Pinos* (1926).

31. Rodríguez Acosta's other novels include *Dolientes* (1931), *En la noche del mundo* (1940), *La dama del arcón* (1949), and *Hágase la luz* (1953). She also published *Algunos cuentos* (1957), which incorporated stories published in periodicals during the 1920s and 1930s, chronicles of her European travels during the 1930s, *Europa era así* (1941), and, beyond essays noted in this chapter, *La muerte pura de Martí* (1955).

32. On the Minorista collective novel see Nieves.

33. Titled "La importancia de un teléfono," Rodríguez Acosta's contribution to this collective project appeared in the April 1927 issue of *Social*. In the June 1927 issue, the Minorista literary editor, Roig de Leuchsenring, noted that the project had been abandoned because its topic of adultery generated too much repetition.

34. Rodríguez Acosta's first story titled "Agonía," to which I refer here, appeared in *Bohemia* in 1929. She published a different story with the same title in her 1957 collection, *Algunos cuentos*. She identified this second narrative as previously unpublished (*Algunos cuentos,* 15).

35. See, respectively, Rodríguez Acosta's "Exigencias de la vida moderna," "El postulado de la ciencia," and "Más allá."

36. See also Rodríguez Acosta's "Anticipándonos a la vida futura."

37. Similarly, Rodríguez Acosta's "La alameda de Paula" offers a first-person version of the third-person account of the character Lucrecia's experiences in *Dolientes,* and her "Carta caída de una gaveta" rehearses a comparable episode in the novel.

38. In Rodríguez Acosta's *La vida manda,* the character Fonseca says that Gertrudis is a "modern woman" but not up-to-the-moment; she is instead a "tragic symbol" of the transition from one epoch to another (144). In a review of the novel published shortly after its publication, Bertot referred to the character as a "woman of transition" (11).

39. See Benstock on the literary midwifery of women intellectuals in European and American modernism.

40. See Rodríguez Acosta's "El derecho de amar" (13), "El ritual en nuestra vida" (19), and "Feminismo efectivo" (10).

41. On the "as if" condition of performance see Blau's *Eye of Prey* (164) and Turner.

42. Rodríguez Acosta's *Sonata interrumpida,* however, has received recent attention. See Jongh's "Constructing Gender and Author(ity)" and Montero's Chapter 2.

CHAPTER 7

1. Portal's reviewer was Nicanor Delafuente, the work, her *El nuevo poema y su orientación hacia una estética económica.*

2. On Peruvian feminism of the 1920s see Miller (Chapter 4) and Guardia (Chapter 5).

3. Other innovative Peruvian magazines with an *indigenista* orientation include *Poliedro* (Lima, 1926), *Boletín Titikaka* (Puno, 1926–1930), and *Chirapu* (Arequipa, 1928).

4. See Denegri.

5. The collection *Constancia del ser* included unpublished work from the 1920s and 1930s, selections from her poetry collections *Una esperanza i el mar* (1927) and *Costa sur* (1944), her story collection *El derecho de matar* (1926), co-authored with Serafín Delmar, and more recent poems.

6. To preserve the reading of Mariátegui's metaphors fundamental to my argument, I use my own translations of the *7 ensayos* rather than published versions.

7. My biographical synopsis draws on Portal's "Yo soy Magda Portal," Miller, Chaney, Reedy's groundbreaking biography and articles, and my own interview with her in July 1983.

8. See the entry on Portal in Toro Montalvo. That contemporaries recalled bodily details about Portal from the early 1920s is as revealing of their times as is of our own the fact that a 1996 literary history would incorporate them.

9. Portal alluded to her 1923 refusal of the poetry award in my 1983 interview, and Herrera described it in 1935 (22). For details see Reedy's biography (59–64).

10. Portal explained in 1978 that while she sought to instruct APRA women in political thought, Haya de la Torre advised them on how to be wives and mothers ("Yo soy Magda Portal," 216).

11. Flórez casts Mariátegui's incipient feminism in stronger terms than I do. While I agree that he perceived its radical potential, his writing also manifests the gender stereotypes of his time.

12. Reedy examines Kollontai's impact on Portal's work and draws personal and political parallels between them (*Magda Portal,* 172–177). Miller contends that Portal was not an original thinker and that her ideas were "part of the received political wisdom" of Latin America in the 1930s (102).

13. Historical perspectives on Portal include Miller (101–103), Chaney (92, 95, 123), and Guardia (81–84). Literary critics highlighting the role of Portal's politics in her art include Reedy's articles and biography, Arrington, and Grunfeld. Akin to my own approach, Smith reads Portal's poetry and politics as an example of women's relationship to the vanguards.

14. Reedy affirms that the unsigned artwork accompanying "Fantasía" was by Peruvian surrealist poet César Moro and notes its style resembling the work of Aubrey Beardsley, well known at the time in Latin America (*Magda Portal,* 44).

15. Portal was briefly married to Federico Bolaños and subsequently sustained a long-term relationship with his brother, Reynaldo (Serafim Delmar), father of her daughter, Gloria.

16. Hispanists have long used the term "postmodernist" to designated Spanish American poetry no longer adhering to *modernista* conventions but not yet embracing the avant-gardes. *Flechas* also included material by writers of a previous generation, Manuel González Prada, Ventura García Calderón, and the younger, more innovative José María Eguren and Abraham Valdelomar.

17. Other magazines of Peru's vanguards included the two issues of *Guerrilla* (1926), edited by Blanca Luz Brum Parra del Riego; *Boletín Titikaka* (1926–1930), edited in Puno by the brothers Gamaliel Churata (born Arturo Peralta) and Alejandro Peralta; *Poliedro* (August–December 1926), edited by Armando Bazán, youthful companion and first biographer of Mariátegui; and *Chirapu* (January–July 1928), edited in Arequipa by Antero Peralta Vásquez.

18. The Peruvian writers published in the *Trampolín, Hangar, rascacielos, TIMONEL* series included the Peralta brothers and Brum and the poets Carlos Oquendo de Amat, author of the experimental *5 metros de poemas* (1927); Alberto Hidalgo, creator of literary *simplismo;* César Alfredo Miró; and Julián Petrovick.

19. On Latin American writers who challenged the title or intent of Ortega y Gasset's landmark essay see my *Latin American Vanguards* (21–27).

20. See Arrington and Reedy's biography (120–121, 140–146).

21. See my "Mariátegui's Aesthetic Thought."

22. This description resembles the "decadence" Mariátegui ascribed to some variants of the new art in his key essay "Arte, Revolución, y Decadencia" (*Obras completas,* 6:18–22).

23. On the role of the Tristán biography in Portal's construction of a "foremother" for her Marxist-feminist position see Schlau (Chapter 4).

24. Portal wrote: "There were few women in those groups: Blanca Luz Brum, Ángela Ramos, Mariátegui's wife, I, and others who would arrive spontaneously. Women, in reality, did not visit Mariátegui much" ("Yo soy Magda Portal," 213). Curiously, Portal makes no mention of Wiesse, the woman who wrote most extensively for *Amauta.*

25. Wiesse recognized her class benefits and other women's hardships, as in her column "La página femenina" in *Mundial* (April 1921).

26. Wiesse's story "El forastero" receives brief attention from Pratt (63–64); Aldrich discusses two of her works in his study of the Peruvian short story (71–74); McBride includes some Wiesse stories in her dissertation on Andean women writers; Bustamante Moscoso mentions Wiesse in her article on intellectual women of Mariátegui's generation; and Flórez addresses her role in *Amauta.*

27. Signed J. A. H., a performance review of Wiesse's play *El lazo* appeared in *Variedades* on April 3, 1920.

28. Such racist stereotypes were common in Wiesse's time. Mariátegui, for one, while discussing Peruvian *mestizaje* made unfortunate references to blacks who, he argued, brought their "sensuality," "superstition," and "primitivism" to Peru. (*Obras completas,* 2:342).

29. See also Wiesse's "Poetas americanos modernos," in which she translated poems by Alan Seeger.

30. See Wiesse's "La página femenina" in *Mundial,* numbers 60 (June 17, 1921) and 52 (April 22, 1921), respectively (n.pag.).

31. See, respectively, Wiesse's "La página femenina" in *Mundial* (1921) numbers 55 (May 13), 61 (June 24), 49 (April 1), 47 (March 18), 52 (April 29); "Señales de nuestro tiempo" in *Amauta* 1.4 (1926): 11–12; and "La página femenina" in *Mundial* (1921), number 58 (June 3). These issues of *Mundial* have no pagination. Wiesse used the pseudonym "Myriam" in much of her journalism.

32. See Wiesse's "La página femenina" in *Mundial* 50 (April 8, 1921): n.pag.

33. On the importance of the maternal in Latin American women's narrative see Castro-Klarén.

34. On the singularities of the women's *Bildungsroman,* including the association of adolescence with loss see the collection by Abel, Hirsch, and Langland. See Kushigian on gender issues in the Spanish American *Bildungsroman.*

35. See also Wiesse's "Literatura femenina (fragmentos de un ensayo)."

36. Although Wiesse's "Infancia" on her childhood summers in Lausanne expresses nostalgia for Peru as her maternal homeland, it also recalls her subversive readings (*Paul et Virginie* at age ten) and her invention of imaginary characters ("Infancia," 28).

CHAPTER 8

1. Literary historiography distinguishes between Brazilian *modernismo,* a twentieth-century vanguard literary movement originating in the early 1920s and corresponding in its first decade to Spanish American *vanguardias* or avant-gardes, and Spanish American *modernismo,* a late-nineteenth- and early-twentieth-century movement that preceded and is distinct from the vanguards.

2. In keeping with the practice throughout this book to avoid the mythologizing nicknames these women acquired, I do not refer to Galvão as Pagu. Although widely used, according to her son, she affirmed that she detested the name (Galvão Ferraz, 3).

3. The drawing and comments appeared in *Para todos* in 1929 and are reproduced in *Pagu vida-obra* (303). *Pagu vida-obra* is an anthology of some of Galvão's writing and of critical and biographical material about her, edited by Augusto de Campos. Bloch, Besse ("Pagu"), and Jackson (Afterword) also link images of Galvão to the *antropofagia* aesthetic.

4. My description of Galvão's extravagant performance is taken from the testimony (*depoimento* in Portuguese) that Pedro de Oliveira Ribeiro Netto and Franciso Luis de Almeida Sales gave at the São Paulo Museu da Imagem e do Som on May 10, 1978, reproduced in part in the anthology *Pagu vida-obra* (270–274).

5. Scholarship on Galvão also includes Campos, Daniel, Marshall, Owen, Risério, Unruh, and Valente. *Eternamente Pagú* (1988), a full-length film, was directed by Norma Bengell, the short documentary *Eh Pagu, eh!* (1982) by Ivor Branco, and a short video *Pagu—livre na imaginação, no espaço, e no tempo* (1999), based on the script by Lucía Maria Teixeira Furlani, by Rudá de Andrade and Marcelo Giovanni Tassara.

6. My biographical sources on Galvão include Besse, Campos, Risério, Ferraz, Galvão Ferraz, Jackson, and Teixeira Furlani. (Besse and Jackson draw on Campos and Risério as well.)

7. See Jackson's "Alienation and Ideology" (301). Jackson cites a party pamphlet, *Contra o Trotskismo,* that notes Galvão's "scandalous attitudes of a sexual degenerate" (303). Galvão herself detailed her tumultuous party history in *Verdade e liberdade,* a segment of which appears in *Pagu vida-obra* (186–189).

8. Galvão's literary criticism appeared primarily in literary supplements to dailies in São Paulo and the nearby city of Santos.

9. Galvão's younger son, Geraldo Galvão Ferraz, collected, edited, and introduced the volume of her detective fiction.

10. This photo of Galvão and its caption are reproduced in *Pagu vida-obra* (295).

11. Oswald's plays of the 1930s include *O homem e o cavalo, A morta,* and *O rei da vela.*

12. Carvalho's "Theatro antigo e o moderno" appeared in *O homem do povo,* and Oswald wrote *O homem e o cavalo* for Carvalho's *Teatro de experiência.* See Toledo on Carvalho's work with Oswald and the modernists.

13. George notes the EAD's fundamental importance for modern theatre in São Paulo (35).

14. Campos notes the vanguard-theatre link in Galvão's criticism (*"Pagu,"* 223).

15. Galvão's *O album,* given to Tarsila and discovered in her nephew's library in the 1970s, resembles Galvão's drawings for the *Revista de antropofagia.* Both Campos and Risério underscore the compositions' hybridity as to genre; Campos notes that the texts cannot be defined as either poetry or design but lie somewhere in between ("Pagu: Amadora de artes," 31), and Risério notes that they lie between poetry and prose (18).

16. In citing prose poem-scenes of *O album,* I use the roman numerals from Galvão's text.

17. At the bottom of this scene, the numbers "IXV" appear in Galvão's own handwriting. In the sequence, scenes 1 through 11 are correctly numbered, scenes 12 through 15 are misnumbered, respectively, as XIII, IXV, XV, and again IXV. With XVI, the text resumes the sequential numbering previously maintained until scene 12.

18. When asked by the author of this piece to name people she admired, Galvão's first response was Tarsila; she later added "With Tarsila, I become romantic. I'd give her my last drop of blood. As an artist I admire only her superiority" (*Pagu vida-obra,* 60). I am not arguing that Galvão had a sexual tie with Tarsila, only that she represented the painter as an object of desire in *O album.*

19. Galvão's representations of race reiterated stereotypes of her time, particularly in sexual insinuations, seen in *O album* in the sexualized black maid of the protagonist's family (58) and in the stereotypically beautiful *mulata* Corina in *Parque industrial.*

20. "La gran artista de la declamación Berta Singerman" (n.a., *Repertorio americano,* 1927) presents favorable judgments on Singerman's art from Ramón del Valle Inclán, Manuel Machado, Juan Ramón Jiménez, and Alejo Carpentier, among others.

21. Galvão cites Havelock Ellis, for example, in "Saibam ser maricons" (2).

22. In the subtitle to their edition of Nogueira Cobra's work, Susan Quinlan

and Peggy Sharpe designate her and Aldazira Bittencourt, whose novel is also included, as "two forgotten modernists."

23. For a discerning study of women's novels on sexual morality and marriage see Rago's "A subjetividade feminina."

24. See Rago's "Sexualidade e identidade."

25. Galvão was not alone in her heterocentrism. In the *Revista de antropofagia,* under the pseudonym Cabo Machado, Oswald cast aspersions on the masculinity of modernist leader Mário de Andrade, a homosexual, calling him "our Miss São Paulo, translated into the masculine" ("Os tres sargentos," 6). On the implications of this episode for the cultural history of homosexuality in Brazil see Green.

26. On Moura see also Hahner (83–84, 136–137, and 152–155) and Besse (*Restructuring Patriarchy,* 179–180).

27. Critical studies focusing primarily on *Parque industrial* include Jackson's afterword, Marshall, Owen, and Daniel.

28. Consider, for example, Johnson's "Brazilian Modernism" and "Dynamics of the Brazilian Literary Field."

29. See Issacharoff for the distinction between mimetic (onstage) and diegetic (imagined, often offstage) space in a play performance.

30. See my treatment of Craik's work in Chapter 1 (74–75).

31. In *Lusosex* (xxiv), Quinlan and Arenas note Galvão's treatment of same-sex desire in *Parque industrial* among her contemporaries who did the same. But in writing published after *O album,* Galvão's take on the topic was ambivalent and problematic.

32. These scenes from *Parque industrial* ironically presage the party's expulsion of Galvão in 1937, when, as I have noted, it accused her both of Trotskyism and sexual degeneracy.

33. This portrayal of Corina in *Parque industrial* as the beautiful, sexy *mulata* typifies Galvão's ascription to the racial stereotypes weaving through the primitivism of *antropofagia* and the international vanguards as well. See Owen (71–72).

34. Here I diverge from two scholars with whom I otherwise concur. Noting that for Galvão class and gender were inseparable, Valente argues that in *Parque industrial* she "rejects any possibility of a feminine solidarity soaring over class differences" (30). Besse notes that with the exception of Galvão's own writing and a contribution from her sister, the anthology *Pagu vida-obra* contains all male voices, a fact, she argues, that underscores Galvão's "alienation from female culture and the difficulty (or disinterest) she had in finding female allies" (*Restructuring Patriarchy,* 247). While I agree that Galvão moved in cultural worlds inhabited primarily by men and that her interest in women's fate constituted only one component of her cultural politics, the quest for solidarity among women was an important feature of her writing of the 1930s.

35. Jackson compares the novel's depiction of existential alienation to Dostoyevsky, Kafka, and Sartre and draws parallels in its portrayal of totalitarianism with Kafka's *Der Prozess* and *Das Schloss* and Huxley's *Brave New World* ("Alienation and Ideology," 300).

36. In his introduction to the 1998 collection of Galvão's detective stories, Galvão Ferraz traces the publication of international mystery fiction in Brazil and notes the multiple influences on Galvão, including, among her favorite authors, Georges Simenon and Maurice Leblanc, as well as popular writers such as Baroness of Orczy, Gaston Leroux, and Edgar Wallace. He also notes her distaste for Ellery Queen's writing (Galvão Ferraz, Introduction, 8).

37. See Caws and Kuenzli.

references

Abel, Elizabeth, Marianne Hirsch, and Elizabeth Langland, eds. *The Voyage In: Fictions of Female Development.* Hanover, New Hampshire: University Press of New England, 1983.

Aldrich, Earl M., Jr. *The Modern Short Story in Peru.* Madison: University of Wisconsin Press, 1966.

Alonso, Carlos. *The Burden of Modernity: The Rhetoric of Cultural Discourse in Latin America.* New York: Oxford University Press, 1998.

Althusser, Louis. *Lenin and Philosophy and Other Essays.* New York: Monthly Review, 1971.

Anderson, Danny J. "Cultural Conversation and Constructions of Reality: Mexican Narrative and Literary Theories after 1968." *Siglo XX/20th Century* 8, no. 1–2 (1990–1991): 11–30.

Andrade, Oswald de. *Obras completas.* 10 vols. Rio de Janeiro: Civilização Brasileira, 1970–1974.

———. "Os tres sargentos." *Revista de antropofagia* (2d series) no. 5 (March 14, 1929): 6.

Arlt, Roberto. *Obra completa.* 3 vols. Buenos Aires: Sur, 1981–1991.

Arrington, Melvin S., Jr. "Magda Portal, Vanguard Critic." In *Reinterpreting the Spanish American Essay,* ed. Doris Meyer, 148–156. Austin: University of Texas Press, 1995.

Arriola Grande, Mauricio. *Diccionario literario del Perú.* 2d ed. Lima: Universo, 1983.

Austin, J. L. *How to Do Things with Words.* 2d ed. Cambridge: Harvard University Press, 1978.

Azuela, Mariano. *Epistolario y archivo.* Mexico City: Universidad Nacional Autónoma de México, 1969.

———. *Teatro. Los de abajo. El buho en la noche. Del llano hermanos, S. en C.* Mexico City: Botas, 1938.

Bakhtin, M. M. *Art and Answerability: Early Philosophical Essays by M. M. Bakhtin,* ed. Michael Holquist and Vadim Liapunov. Trans. Vadim Liapunov. Austin: University of Texas Press, 1990.

———. *The Dialogic Imagination: Four Essays,* ed. Michael Holquist and trans. Caryl Emerson and Michael Holquist. Austin: University of Texas Press. 1981.

———. "Discourse Typology in Prose." In *Twentieth Century Literary Theory,* ed. Vassilis Lambropoulos and David Neal and trans. Richard Balthazar and I. R. Titunik, 285–303. Albany: State University of New York Press, 1987.

Balderston, Daniel. "Poetry, Revolution, Homophobia: Polemics from the Mexican Revolution." In *Hispanism and Homosexualities,* ed. Sylvia Molloy and Robert McKee Irwin, 57–75.

Bary, Leslie. "The Tropical Modernist as Literary Cannibal: Cultural Identity in Oswald de Andrade." *Chasqui* 20, no. 2 (November 1991): 10–19.

Benstock, Shari. *Women of the Left Bank: Paris, 1900–1940.* Austin: University of Texas Press, 1986.

Berman, Marshall. *All That Is Solid Melts into Air: The Experience of Modernity.* New York: Viking Penguin, 1988.

Bernhardt, Sarah. *The Art of the Theatre.* Trans. H. J. Stenning. London: Geoffrey Bless, 1924.

Bertot, Lorié. "Ofelia Rodríguez Acosta, frente a la nueva ética sexual." *Bohemia* 21, no. 49 (December 7, 1929): 11–12.

Besse, Susan. "Pagu: Patrícia Galvão—Rebel." *The Human Condition in Latin America,* ed. William H. Beezley and Judith Ewell, 103–117. Wilmington, Delaware: Scholarly Resources, 1987.

———. *Restructuring Patriarchy: The Modernization of Gender Inequality in Brazil, 1914–1940.* Chapel Hill: University of North Carolina Press, 1996.

Blair, Kathryn S. *A la sombra del Ángel.* Trans. Leonor Tejada. Mexico City: Alianza, 1995.

Blau, Herbert. *The Eye of Prey: Subversions of the Postmodern.* Bloomington: Indiana University Press, 1987.

———. *To All Appearances: Ideology and Performance.* New York: Routledge, 1992.

Bloch, Jayne H. "Patrícia Galvão: The Struggle Against Conformity." *Latin American Literary Review* 14, no. 27 (January–June 1986): 188–201.

Bopp, Raul. "Coco." In *Pagu vida-obra,* ed. Augusto de Campos. São Paulo: Brasiliense, 1982.

Borges, Jorge Luis. *Obras completas.* Vol. 1. Barcelona: Emecé, 1996.

———. Prologue to *La calle de la tarde,* by Norah Lange, 5–8. Buenos Aires: J. Samet, 1925.

Bourdieu, Pierre. *The Rules of Art: Genesis and Structure of the Literary Field.* Trans. Susan Emanuel. Stanford: Stanford University Press, 1992.

Bradu, Fabienne. *Antonieta (1900–1931).* Mexico City: Fondo de Cultura Económica, 1991.

Brown, John Russell, ed. *The Oxford Illustrated History of Theatre.* Oxford, England: Oxford University Press, 1995.

Bustamante Moscoso, Cecilia. "Intelectuales peruanas de la generación de José Carlos Mariátegui (III)." *La insignia* (June 22, 2002), *http://www.lainsignia. org/2002/junio/cul_044.htm.*

Butler, Judith. "Critically Queer." *GLQ: A Journal of Lesbian and Gay Studies* 1, no. 1 (1993): 17–32.

Cairo, Ana. *El grupo minorista y su tiempo.* Havana: Ciencias Sociales, 1978.

Calinescu, Matei. *Five Faces of Modernity.* Durham, North Carolina: Duke University Press, 1987.

Calle, Sophie de la. " 'De libélula en mariposa': Nación, identidad y cultura en la posrevolución (1920–1940). Un estudio de la danza y narrativa de Nellie Campobello." Ph.D. diss. University of Maryland, 1998.

Campobello, Nellie. *Cartucho. Relatos de la lucha en el norte de México.* In *La novela de la Revolución Mexicano,* ed. Antonio Castro Leal, 921–968. Mexico City: Aguilar, 1965. Trans. Doris Meyer in *Cartucho and My Mother's Hands* (Austin: University of Texas Press, 1988).

———. *Las manos de mamá.* In *La novela de la Revolución Mexicana,* ed. Antonio Castro Leal, 969–989. Mexico City: Aguilar, 1965. Trans. Irene Matthews under the title *My Mother's Hands* in *Cartucho and My Mother's Hands* (Austin: University to Texas Press, 1988).

———. *Mis libros.* Mexico City: Cia. General de Ediciones, 1960.

———. "8 poemas de mujer." *Revista de la Habana* 4 (October, November, December 1930): 133–139.

———. *Tres poemas.* Mexico City: Cia. General de Ediciones, 1957.

Campobello, Nellie, and Gloria Campobello. *Ritmos indígenas de México.* Mexico City: Oficina Editora Popular, 1941.

Campos, Augusto de. "Pagu: Amadora de artes." In *Pagu vida-obra,* ed. Augusto de Campos, 30–35. São Paulo: Brasiliense, 1982.

———. "Roteiro de uma vida-obra." In *Pagu vida-obra,* ed. Augusto de Campos, 319–347. São Paulo: Brasiliense, 1982.

———, ed. *Pagu vida-obra.* São Paulo: Brasiliense, 1982.

Carballo, Emmanuel. *Protagonistas de la literatura mexicana.* 3d ed. Mexico City: Ermitaño, 1989.

Carlson, Marvin. *Performance: A Critical Introduction.* New York: Routledge, 1996.

Carrera, Julieta. *La mujer en América escribe* . . . . Mexico City: Alonso, 1956.

Carvalho, Flávio de. "Theatro antigo e o moderno." *O homem do povo* 1, no. 3 (March 31, 1931): 4.

Castilho, Laura Ayerza de, and Odile Felgine. *Victoria Ocampo.* Trans. Roser Berdagué. Barcelona: Circe, 1993.

Castro-Klarén, Sara. Introduction to *Women's Writing in Latin America: An Anthology,* ed. Sara Castro-Klarén, Sylvia Molloy, and Beatriz Sarlo, 3–26. Boulder, Colorado: Westview, 1991.

Castro-Klarén, Sara, Sylvia Molloy, and Beatriz Sarlo, eds. *Women's Writing in Latin America: An Anthology.* Boulder, Colorado: Westview, 1991.

Caws, Mary Ann. "Ladies Shot and Painted: Female Embodiment in Surrealist Art." In *The Female Body in Western Culture,* ed. Susan Rubin Suleiman, 262–287. Cambridge: Harvard University Press, 1986.

Cázares H., Laura. "El narrador en la novelas de Nellie Campobello: *Cartucho* y *Las manos de mamá.*" In *Mujer y literatura mexicana y chicana: Culturas en contacto,* ed. Aralia López González, 159–169. Tijuana, Mexico: Colegio de la Frontera Norte, 1988.

Chaney, Elsa M. *Supermadre: Women in Politics in Latin America.* Austin: University of Texas Press, 1979.

Collado, María del Carmen. "Vida social y tiempo libre de la clase alta capitalina en los tempranos años veinte." *Historias* 28 (April–September 1992): 101–126.

Craik, Jennifer. *The Face of Fashion: Cultural Studies in Fashion.* New York: Routledge, 1994.

Dalevuelta, Jacobo. "El Teatro de Ulises." *El universal ilustrado* 11, no. 557 (January 12, 1928): 27, 67.

Daniel, Mary L. "Life in the Textile Factory: Two 1933 Perspectives." *Luso-Brazilian Review* 31, no. 2 (winter 1994): 97–113.

Davies, Catherine. *A Place in the Sun? Women Writers in Twentieth-Century Cuba.* London: Zed, 1997.

"Declaración del Grupo Minorista." *Social* (June 1927): 7.

Delafuente, Nicanor. Review of *El nuevo poema y su orientación hacia una estética económica,* by Magda Portal. *Amauta* 3:24 (1929): 102.

Delgado, Josefina. *Alfonsina Storni: Una biografía esencial.* Revised edition. Buenos Aires: Planeta, 2001.

Denegri, Francesca. *El abanico y la cigarrera: La primera generación de mujeres ilustradas en el Perú.* Lima: Instituto de Estudios Peruanos, 1996.

Diccionario de la literatura cubana. Instituto de Literatura y Lingüística de la Academia de Ciencias de Cuba. 2 vols. Havana: Letras Cubanas, 1984.

Doll, Ramón. *Ensayos y críticas.* Buenos Aires: Doll, 1929.

Domínguez, Laura. "Literary Constructions and Gender Performance in the Novels of Norah Lange." In *Latin American Women's Writing: Feminist Readings in Theory and Crisis,* ed. Amy Brooksbank Jones and Catherine Davies, 30–45. Oxford, England: Clarendon, 1996.

Duarte, Eduardo de Assis. "Eficácia e limites do discurso ideológico em *Parque industrial,* de Patrícia Galvão." *Suplemento literario Minas Gerais* 1105 (September 3, 1988): 6–7.

Edwards, Gwynne. *Lorca: The Theatre beneath the Sand.* London: Marion Boyars, 1980.

El Joven Telémaco. "'El Peregrino' y 'Orfeo' en el Teatro de Ulises." *El universal ilustrado* 11, no. 568 (March 29, 1928): 5, 65.

Elmore, Peter. "La ciudad enferma: 'Lima la horrible', de Sebastián Salazar Bondy." In *Mundos interiores: Lima 1850–1950,* ed. Aldo H. Panfichi and

Felipe Portocarrero S., 289–313. Lima: Centro de Investigación, Universidad del Pacífico, 1995.

"En marcha." *Flechas* 1, no. 2 (November 13, 1924): 1–2.

Felski, Rita. *The Gender of Modernity.* Cambridge: Harvard University Press, 1995.

Fernández de Castro, José Antonio. *Barraca de Feria (18 ensayos y 1 estreno).* Havana: Jesús Montero, 1933.

———. "Positivos ix—Mariblanca Sabas Alomá." *Social* (June 1930): 15.

Ferraz, Geraldo. "Patrícia Galvão militante do ideal." In *Pagu vida-obra,* ed. Augusto de Campos, 261–264. São Paulo: Brasiliense, 1982.

———. "Quem foi Solange Sohl." In *Pagu vida-obra,* ed. Augusto de Campos, 174–175. São Paulo: Brasiliense, 1982.

Fitts, Dudley, ed. *Anthology of Contemporary Latin-American Poetry.* Norfolk, Connecticut: New Directions, 1942.

Flórez, Nélida. "La Mujer Amauta: Presencia de la mujer en la obra de José Carlos Mariátegui." *Anuario Mariateguiano* 7, no. 7 (1995): 135–157.

Font Saldaña, J. "Mariblanca Sabas Alomá." *Índice* 2:18 (September 13, 1930): 291.

Franco, Jean. *Plotting Women: Gender and Representation in Mexico.* New York: Columbia University Press, 1989.

Fraser, Howard M. *Magazines and Masks: Caras y Caretas as a Reflection of Buenos Aires, 1898–1908.* Tempe: Arizona State University Center for Latin American Studies, 1987.

Frye, Northrop. *Anatomy of Criticism: Four Essays.* Princeton: Princeton University Press, 1971.

Galvão, Patrícia. *O album de Pagu: Nacimento vida paixão e morte.* In *Pagu vida-obra,* ed. Augusto de Campos, 41–59. São Paulo: Brasiliense, 1982.

———. "Cinema sexual." *O homem do povo* 1, no. 7 (April 9, 1931): 2.

———. "Freud e o cinema." *O homem do povo* 1, no. 5 (April 4, 1931): 4.

———. "Liga de trompas cathólicas." *O homem do povo* 1, no. 5 (April 4, 1931): 2.

———. "Maltus além." *O homem do povo* 1, no. 1 (March 27, 1931): 2.

———. "Mulher mulher." *O homem do povo* 1, no. 1 (March 27, 1931): 2.

———. "Normalinhas." *O homem do povo* 1, no. 8 (April 13, 1931): 2.

———. "As óperas faladas de Berta." *O homem do povo* 1, no. 1 (March 27, 1931): 4.

———. "O retiro sexual." *O homem do povo* 1, no. 3 (March 31, 1931): 2.

———. *Pagu vida-obra.* Ed. Augusto de Campos. São Paulo: Brasiliense, 1982.

———. *Parque industrial.* São Paulo: Alternativa, 1981. Ed. and trans. Elizabeth Jackson and K. David Jackson under the title *Industrial Park* (Omaha: University of Nebraska Press, 1993).

———. *Safra macabra: Contos policiais.* Ed. Geraldo Galvão Ferraz. Rio de Janeiro: José Olympio, 1998.

———. "Saibam ser maricons." *O homem do povo* 1, no. 6 (April 7, 1931): 2.

———. "A tezoura popular." *O homem do povo* 1, no. 2 (March 28, 1931): 2.

Galvão, Patrícia, and Geraldo Ferraz. *Dois romances.* Rio de Janeiro: José Olympio, 1959.

Galvão Ferraz, Geraldo. "Cronologia de Patrícia Galvão." *Safra macabra: Contos policiais,* by Patrícia Galvão, ed. Geraldo Galvão Ferraz, 10–15. Rio de Janeiro: José Olympio, 1998.

———. Introduction to "A *pulp fiction* de Patrícia Galvão." *Safra macabra: Contos policiais,* by Patrícia Galvão, ed. Geraldo Galvão Ferraz, 3–9. Rio de Janeiro: José Olympio, 1998.

———, ed. *Safra macabra: Contos policiais,* by Patrícia Galvão. Rio de Janeiro: José Olympio, 1998.

García, Clara Guadalupe. *Nellie Campobello: El caso Campobello.* Mexico City: Aguilar, León y Cal, 2000.

García Lorca, Federico. "Federico García Lorca escribe a su familia desde Nueva York y la Habana (1929–1930)." *Poesía. Revista Ilustrada de Información Poética* 23–24 (1986).

García Velloso, Enrique. *Piedras preciosas.* Buenos Aires: Novela Semanal, 1922.

Garrels, Elizabeth. *Las grietas de la ternura: Nueva lectura de Teresa de la Parra.* Caracas: Monte Ávila, 1985.

———. "*Piedra Azul,* or the Colonial Paradise of Women." In *Mama Blanca's Memoirs,* by Teresa de la Parra, trans. Harriet de Onís and Frederick H. Fornoff, 136–150. Critical edition. Pittsburgh: University of Pittsburgh Press, 1993.

Gay Calbo, Enrique. "Ofelia Rodríguez Acosta." *Revista de la Habana* 1, no. 1 (January–March 1930): 347–360.

George, David. *The Modern Brazilian Stage.* Austin: University of Texas Press, 1992.

Gibson, Ian. *Federico García Lorca: A Life.* London: Faber and Faber, 1989.

Gide, André. *The School for Wives.* Trans. Dorothy Bussy. New York: A. A. Knopf, 1929.

Gliemmo, Graciela. "Antonieta en su escritura." *Feminaria literaria* 2 (1992): 4–7.

Girondo, Oliverio. *Espantapájaros (al alcance de todos).* Buenos Aires: Proa, 1932.

Giusti, Roberto F. *Literatura y vida.* Buenos Aires: Nosotros, 1939.

Glenn, Susan. *Female Spectacle: The Theatrical Roots of Modern Feminism.* Cambridge: Harvard University Press, 2000.

González, Aníbal. *Journalism and the Development of Spanish American Narrative.* Cambridge: Cambridge University Press, 1993.

González Lanuza, Eduardo. *Aquelarre*. Buenos Aires: Samet, 1927.

Granillo Vásquez, Lilia. "La abnegación maternal, sustrato fundamental de la cultura femenina en México." In *Identidades y nacionalismos: Una perspectiva interdisciplinaria,* coord. Granillo Vásquez, 195–255. Mexico City: Gernika, 1993.

Green, James N. "Challenging National Heroes and Myths: Male Homosexuality and Brazilian History." *Estudios interdisciplinarios de América Latina y el Caribe* 12, no. 1 (January–June 2001): 61–78.

Greenberg, Janet. "A Question of Blood: The Conflict of Sex and Class in the Autobiografía of Victoria Ocampo." In *Women, Culture, and Politics in Latin America,* ed. Seminar on Feminism and Culture in Latin America, 130–150. Berkeley: University of California Press, 1990.

Grunfeld, Mihai. "Voces femeninas de la vanguardia: El compromiso de Magda Portal." *Revista de crítica literaria latinoamericana* 26, no. 51 (2000): 67–82.

Guardia, Sara Beatriz. *Mujeres peruanas: El otro lado de la historia*. Lima: Humboldt, 1985.

Guiñazú, María Cristina Arambel. "'Babel' and *De Francesca a Beatrice:* Two Founding Essays by Victoria Ocampo." In *Reinterpreting the Spanish American Essay,* ed. Doris Meyer, 125–134. Austin: University of Texas Press, 1995.

Hahner, June. *Emancipating the Female Sex: The Struggle for Women's Rights in Brazil, 1950–1940.* Durham, North Carolina: Duke University Press, 1990.

Hammergren, Lena. "The Re-turn of the Flâneuse." In *Corporealities: Dancing, Knowledge, Culture and Power,* ed. Susan Leigh Foster, 53–69. New York: Routledge 1996.

Hausman, Bernice L. "Words Between Women: Victoria Ocampo and Virginia Woolf." In *In the Feminine Mode,* ed. Noël Valis and Carol Meier, 204–226. Lewisburg: Bucknell University Press, 1990.

Henestrosa, Andrés. *María Antonieta Rivas Mercado*. Mexico City: Porrúa, 1999.

Herrera, Oscar. "Magda Portal." *Claridad* 294 (October 1935): 22.

Hidalgo, Alberto, Vicente Huidobro, and Jorge Luis Borges. *Índice de la nueva poesía hispanoamericana*. Buenos Aires: El Inca, 1926.

Holquist, Michael. *Dialogism: Bakhtin and His World*. New York: Routledge, 1990.

Homenaje a Buenos Aires en el cuarto centenario de su fundación. Buenos Aires: Municipalidad de Buenos Aires, 1936.

Huyssen, Andreas. *After the Great Divide: Modernism, Mass Culture, Postmodernism.* Bloomington: Indiana University Press, 1986.

Hymes, Robert. *Way and Byway: Taoism, Local Religion, and Models of Divinity in Sung and Modern China*. Berkeley: University of California Press, 2002.

Ibarra, Néstor. *La nueva poesía argentina: Ensayo crítico sobre el ultraísmo, 1921–1929.* Buenos Aires: Molinari, 1930.

Irwin, Robert McKee. *Mexican Masculinities.* Minneapolis: University of Minnesota Press, 2003.

Issacharoff, Michael. "Space and Reference in Drama." *Poetics Today* 2, no. 3 (spring 1981): 211–224.

J. A. H. "'El lazo', comedia de María Wiesse." *Variedades* 7, no. 631 (April 3, 1920): 325–326.

Jackson, K. David. Afterword to *Industrial Park,* by Patrícia Galvão, ed. and trans. Elizabeth and K. David Jackson, 115–153. Lincoln: University of Nebraska Press.

———. "Alienation and Ideology in *A famosa revista* (1945)." *Hispania* 74, no. 2 (May 1991): 298–304.

———. "Patrícia Galvão and Brazilian Social Realism of the 1930s." *Proceedings of the Pacific Northwest Council on Foreign Language* 28 (1977): 95–98.

Jenkins, Richard. *Pierre Bourdieu.* New York: Routledge, 1992.

Jiménez, Juan Ramón, ed. *La poesía cubana en 1936.* Havana: Institución Hispanocubana de Cultura, 1937.

Johnson, Randal. "Brazilian Modernism: An Idea Out of Place?" In *Modernism and Its Margins: Reinscribing Cultural Modernity from Spain and Latin America,* ed. Anthony L. Geist and José B. Monleón, 186–214. New York: Garland, 1999.

———. "The Dynamics of the Brazilian Literary Field: 1930–1945." *Luso-Brazilian Review* 31, no. 2 (winter 1994): 5–22.

Jongh, Elena M. de. "Constructing Gender and Author(ity): Ofelia Rodríguez Acosta's *Sonata interrumpida.*" In *Studies in Honor of Gilberto Paolini,* ed. Mercedes Vidal Tibbits, 441–447. Newark, Delaware: Juan de la Cuesta, 1996.

———. "Feminismo y periodismo en la Cuba republicana: Ofelia Rodríguez Acosta y la campaña feminista de *Bohemia*" (1930–1932). *Confluencia* 11, no. 1 (fall 1995): 3–12.

———. "Gender and Controversy: Cuban Novelist Ofelia Rodríguez Acosta." *SECOLAS Annals* 23 (March 1992): 23–35.

Kaminsky, Amy. "Essay, Gender, and *Mestizaje:* Victoria Ocampo and Gabriela Mistral." In *The Politics of the Essay: Feminist Perspectives,* ed. Ruth-Ellen Boetscher Joeres and Elizabeth Mittman, 113–130. Bloomington: Indiana University Press, 1993.

King, John. Sur: *A Study of the Argentine Literary Journal and Its Role in the Development of a Culture.* Cambridge, England: Cambridge University Press, 1986.

Kirkpatrick, Gwen. "Alfonsina Storni as 'Tao Lao': The Confessional 'I' and the Roving Eye." In *Reinterpreting the Spanish American Essay,* ed. Doris Meyer, 135–147. Austin: University of Texas Press, 1995.

——. *The Dissonant Legacy of Modernismo: Lugones, Herrera y Reissig, and the Voices of Modern Spanish American Poetry*. Berkeley: University of California Press, 1989.

——. "The Journalism of Alfonsina Storni: A New Approach to Women's History in Argentina." In *Women, Culture, and Politics in Latin America,* ed. Seminar on Feminism and Culture in Latin America, 105–129. Berkeley: University of California Press, 1990.

Krauss, Rosalind E. *The Originality of the Avant-Garde and Other Modernist Myths*. Cambridge: Massachusetts Institute of Technology Press, 1985.

Kuenzli, Rudolf. "Surrealism and Misogyny." In *Surrealism and Women,* ed. Mary Ann Caws, Rudolf Kuenzli, and Gwen Raaberg, 17–31. Cambridge: Massachusetts Institute of Technology Press, 1993.

Kushigian, Julia A. *Reconstructing Childhood: Strategies of Reading for Culture and Gender in the Spanish American Bildungsroman*. Lewisburg: Bucknell University Press, 2003.

"La fiesta de la planta." *Amauta* 1, no. 6 (1927): 33–34.

"La gran artista de la declamación Berta Singerman." *Repertorio americano* 14, no. 8 (February 26, 1927): 120, 122.

Lange, Norah. *La calle de la tarde*. Buenos Aires: Samet, 1925.

——. *Cuadernos de infancia*. Buenos Aires: Domingo Viau, 1937.

——. *Estimados cóngeres*. Buenos Aires: Losada, 1968.

——. *45 días y 30 marineros*. Buenos Aires: Tor, 1933.

——. *El rumbo de la rosa*. Buenos Aires: Proa, 1930.

——. *Voz de la vida*. Buenos Aires: Proa, 1927.

Latcham, Ricardo A. "Crónica literaria." In *Constancia del ser,* by Magda Portal, 217–220. Lima: Villanueva, 1965.

Lavrin, Asunción. *Women, Feminism, and Social Change in Argentina, Chile, and Uruguay, 1890–1940*. Lincoln: University of Nebraska Press, 1995.

Leland, Christopher Towne. *The Last Happy Men: The Generation of 1922, Fiction, and the Argentine Reality*. Syracuse, New York: Syracuse University Press, 1986.

Lemaître, Louis Antoine. *Mujer ingeniosa: Vida de Teresa de la Parra*. Madrid: La Muralla, 1987.

Lindstrom, Naomi. "Norah Lange: Presencia desmonumentalizadora y femenina en la vanguardia argentina." *Crítica hispánica* 5, no. 2 (1983): 131–148.

Liscano, Juan. "Testimony." In *Mama Blanca's Memoirs,* by Teresa de la Parra, trans. Harriet de Onís and Frederick H. Fornoff, 119–126. Critical edition. Pittsburgh: University of Pittsburgh Press, 1993.

Lorca, Federico García. See García Lorca, Federico.

Ludmer, Josefina. "Tretas del débil." In *La sartén por el mango,* ed. Patricia González and Eliana Ortega, 47–54. Rio Piedras, Puerto Rico: Huracán, 1984.

Lyons, Charles. "Beckett, Shakespeare, and the Making of Theory." In *Around the Absurd: Essays on Modern and Postmodern Drama,* ed. Enoch Brater and Ruby Cohn, 91–127. Ann Arbor: University of Michigan Press, 1990.

Macías, Anna. *Against All Odds: The Feminist Movement in Mexico to 1940.* Westport, Connecticut: Greenwood, 1982.

Magdaleno, Mauricio. *Las palabras perdidas.* Mexico City: Fondo de Cultura Económica, 1956.

Mañach, Jorge. "Los minoristas sabáticos eschuchan al gran Titta." *Social* (February 1924): 23.

Marchant, Elizabeth. *Critical Acts: Latin American Women and Cultural Criticism.* Gainesville: University Press of Florida, 1999.

Margueritte, Victor. *La Garçonne.* Paris: Flammarion, 1922.

Mariátegui, José Carlos. Vols. 2, 6, and 14 of *Obras completas de José Carlos Mariátegui.* 20 vols. Lima: Amauta, 1982, 1983, and 1982.

Marshall, Todd. "Marxist Feminism in Brazil." *Romance Notes* 36, no. 3 (spring 1996): 283–292.

Martínez Márquez, Berta A. de. "Mariblanca." *Bohemia* 22, no. 17 (April 27, 1930): 42, 57.

———. "Ofelia Rodríguez Acosta: La novelista que venció a la mujer." *Bohemia* 22, no. 16 (April 20, 1930): 9.

Martínez-Zalce, Graciela. "Antonieta Rivas Mercado y Concha Urquiza: Donde la leyenda rebasó al lenguaje." *Iztapalpa* 15, no. 37 (July–December 1995): 25–36.

Masiello, Francine. *Between Civilization and Barbarism: Women, Nation, and Literary Culture in Modern Argentina.* Lincoln: University of Nebraska Press, 1992.

———. *Lenguaje e ideología: Las escuelas argentinas de vanguardia.* Buenos Aires: Hachette, 1986.

———. "Rethinking Neocolonial Esthetics: Literature, Politics, and Intellectual Community in Cuba's *Revista de avance*." *Latin American Research Review* 28, no. 2 (1993): 3–31.

———. "Women, State, and Family in Latin American Literature of the 1920s." In *Women, Culture, and Politics in Latin America,* ed. Seminar on Feminism and Culture in Latin America, 27–47. Berkeley: University of California Press, 1990.

Mastronardi, Carlos. *Memorias de un provinciano.* Buenos Aires: Ediciones Culturales Argentinas, 1967.

Matthews, Irene. *Nellie Campobello: La centaura del norte.* Mexico City: Aguilar, León y Cal, 1997.

McBride, Mary Bridget. "Prefeminist Discourse in Short Fiction by Andean Women Writers." Ph.D. diss., University of Texas, 1995.

Mendoza-López, Margarita. *Primeros renovadores del teatro en México, 1928–1941.* Mexico City: Instituto Mexicano de Seguro Social, 1985.

Menéndez, Nina. "*Garzonas y feministas* in Cuban Women's Writing of the 1920s: *La vida manda* by Ofelia Rodríguez Acosta." In *Sex and Sexuality in Latin America,* ed. Daniel Balderston and Donna J. Guy, 174–189. New York: New York University Press, 1997.

———. "No Woman Is an Island: Cuban Women's Fiction in the 1920s and 30s." Ph.D. diss. Stanford University, 1993.

Meyer, Doris. "The Dialogics of Testimony: Autobiography as Shared Experience in Nellie Campobello's *Cartucho.*" In *Latin American Women's Writing: Feminist Readings in Theory and Crisis,* ed. Amy Brooksbank Jones and Catherine Davies, 46–65. Oxford: Clarendon, 1996.

———. "Divided Against Herself: The Early Poetry of Nellie Campobello." *Revista de Estudios Hispánicos* 20, no. 2 (May 1986): 51–63.

———. "Letters and Lines of Correspondence in the Essays of Victoria Ocampo." *Revista Interamericana de Bibliografía* 42, no. 2 (1992): 233–240.

———. "Reciprocal Reflections: Specular Discourse and the Self-Authorizing Venture." In *Reinterpreting the Spanish American Essay: Women Writers of the 19th and 20th Centuries,* ed. Doris Meyer, 102–114. Austin: University of Texas Press, 1995.

———. *Victoria Ocampo. Against the Wind and the Tide.* Austin: University of Texas Press, 1990.

Meyer, Doris, ed. *Reinterpreting the Spanish American Essay: Women Writers of the 19th and 20th Centuries.* Austin: University of Texas Press, 1995.

Mignolo, Walter. "La figura del poeta en la lírica de vanguardia." *Revista iberoamericana* 48, no. 118–119 (January–June 1982): 131–148.

Miguel, María Esther de. *Norah Lange: Una biografía.* Buenos Aires: Planeta, 1991.

Miller, Francesca. *Latin American Women and the Search for Social Justice.* Hanover, New Hampshire: University Press of New England, 1991.

Mistral, Gabriela. *Gabriela piensa en . . . .* Santiago, Chile: Andrés Bello, 1978.

Molloy, Sylvia. *At Face Value: Autobiographical Writing in Spanish America.* Cambridge, England: Cambridge University Press, 1991.

———. "Disappearing Acts: Reading Lesbian in Teresa de la Parra." In *¿Entiendes? Queer Readings, Hispanic Writings,* ed. Emilie L. Bergmann and Paul Julian Smith, 230–256. Durham, North Carolina: Duke University Press, 1995.

———. Foreword to *Mama Blanca's Memoirs,* by Teresa de la Parra, trans. Harriet de Onís and Frederick H. Fornoff, xi–xiv. Pittsburgh: University of Pittsburgh Press, 1993.

———. Introduction to Part 2 of *Women's Writing in Latin America,* ed. Sara Castro-Klarén, Sylvia Molloy, and Beatriz Sarlo, 107–124. Boulder, Colorado: Westview, 1991.

————. "The Politics of Posing." In *Hispanisms and Homosexualities,* ed. Sylvia Molloy and Robert McKee Irwin, 141–160. Durham, North Carolina: Duke University Press, 1998.

Molloy, Sylvia, and Robert McKee Irwin, eds. *Hispanisms and Homosexualities.* Durham, North Carolina: Duke University Press, 1998.

Montaldo, Graciela, ed. *Yrigoyen entre Borges y Arlt.* Vol. 7 of *Historia Social de la literatura argentina.* Buenos Aires: Contrapunto, 1989.

Montero, Susana A. *La narrativa femenina cubana 1923–1958.* Havana: Academia, 1989.

Montesano Delchi, Arturo. Review of *El Santo de la Higuera,* by Victoria Gukovsky. *Nosotros* 25, no. 72 (1931): 92–93.

Monvel, María. *Poetisas de América.* Santiago, Chile: Nacimiento, 1929.

Moura, Maria Lacerda de. *A mulher é uma degenerada.* 3d ed. Rio de Janeiro: Civilização Brasileira, 1932.

Muschietti, Delfina. "Las mujeres que escriben: Aquel reino anhelado, el reino del amor." *Nuevo Texto Crítico* 2, no. 4 (1989): 79–102.

Nadel, Norman. *A Pictorial History of the Theatre Guild.* New York: Crown, 1969.

Nalé Roxlo, Conrado. *Genio y figura de Alfonsina Storni.* Buenos Aires: Editorial Universitario de Buenos Aires, 1964.

Newman, Kathleen. "The Modernization of Femininity in Argentina, 1916–1926." In *Women, Culture, and Politics in Latin America,* ed. Seminar on Feminism and Culture in Latin America, 74–89. Berkeley: University of California Press, 1990.

Nickel, Catherine. "Nellie Campobello." In *Spanish American Women Writers: A Bio-Bibliographical Source Book,* ed. Diane E. Marting, 112–217. New York: Greenwood, 1990.

Nieves, Dolores. "Fantoches 1926: Una novela vanguardista." *Universidad de la Habana* 239 (September–December 1990): 23–39.

Nóbile, Beatriz de. *Palabras con Norah Lange.* Buenos Aires: Carlos Pérez, 1968.

Noriega Hope, Carlos. "El ballet como un nuevo sentido educacional." *El universal ilustrado* (June 16, 1927): 32–33.

Novo, Salvador. "Como se fundó y que significa el Teatro de Ulises." *El universal ilustrado* 12, no. 575 (May 17, 1928): 21, 62.

"Nuestra protesta." *Bohemia* 23, no. 2 (January 11, 1931): 15.

Ocampo, Victoria. *Autobiografía.* 6 vols. Buenos Aires: Sur, 1980–1984.

————. *De Francesca a Beatrice.* 2d ed. Madrid: Revista de Occidente, 1928.

————. *Domingos en Hyde Park.* Buenos Aires: Sur, 1946.

————. "El hombre que murió." *Sur* 2 (1932): 7–56.

————. *La laguna de los nenúfares.* Buenos Aires: Sur, 1982.

————. "Ramón Gómez de la Serna." *Sur* 1 (1931): 205–270.

————. "Sobre dos poetas de Francia." *Sur* 4 (1934): 7–68.

———. *Testimonios.* Vol. 1. Madrid: Revista de Occidente, 1935.

———. *Testimonios.* Vol. 2. Buenos Aires: Sur, 1941.

———. *Testimonios.* Vol. 3. Buenos Aires: Sudamericana, 1946.

Oliveira, Emanuelle. "O falocentrismo e seus descontentes: Por uma leitura feminista da antropofagia." *Nuevo texto crítico* 12, no. 23–24 (January–December 1999): 261–272.

Ombil, Alba. *Frente y perfil de Victoria Ocampo.* Buenos Aires: Sur, 1980.

Ortega y Gasset, José. *The Dehumanization of Art and Other Essays on Art, Culture, and Literature.* Trans. Helen Weyl. Princeton: Princeton University Press, 1968.

———. Epilogue to *De Francesca a Beatrice* by Victoria Ocampo, 133–181. 2d ed. Madrid: Revista de Occidente, 1928.

Osorio T., Nelson. *La formación de la vanguardia literaria en Venezuela.* Caracas: Academia Nacional de la Historia, 1985.

Owen, Hilary. "Discardable Discourses in Patrícia Galvão's *Parque Industrial.*" In *Brazilian Feminisms,* ed. Solange Ribeiro de Oliveira and Judith Still, 68–84. Nottingham: University of Nottingham, 1999.

Oyarzún, Kemy. "Identidad femenina, genealogía mítica, historia: *Las manos de mama.*" In *Sin imágenes falsas, sin falsos espejos: Narradoras mexicanas del Siglo XX,* coord. by Aralia López González, 51–75. Mexico City: Colegio de México, 1995.

Pacheco, José Emilio. Review of *Las palabras perdidas, Cartas a Manuel Rodríguez Lozano,* by Antonieta Rivas Mercado. *Eco: Revista de la Cultura de Occidente* 31, no. 187 (May 1977): 107–111.

"Pagu." *Para todos* (July 27, 1929): 21.

Panfichi, Aldo H., and Felipe Portocarrero S., eds. *Mundos interiores: Lima 1850–1950.* Lima: Centro de Investigación, Universidad del Pacífico, 1995.

Parker, Andrew, and Eve Kosofsky Sedgwick. *Performativity and Performance.* New York: Routledge, 1995.

Parle, Dennis J. "Narrative Style and Technique in Nellie Campobello's *Cartucho.*" *Kentucky Romance Quarterly* 32, no. 2 (1985): 201–211.

Parra, Teresa de la. *Las memorias de Mamá Blanca.* Madrid: Archivos, 1988. Trans. Harriet de Onís and Frederick H. Fornoff under the title *Mama Blanca's Memoirs,* critical edition (Pittsburgh: University of Pittsburgh Press, 1993).

———. *Obra (narrativa-ensayos-cartas).* Caracas: Ayacucho, 1982.

———. *Obra escogida.* 2 vols. Caracas: Monte Ávila, 1992.

———. *Obras completas.* Caracas: Arte, 1965.

Pérez Firmat, Gustavo. *Idle Fictions: The Hispanic Vanguard Novel, 1926–1934.* Durham, North Carolina: Duke University Press, 1982.

Phillips, Rachel. *Alfonsina Storni: From Poetess to Poet.* London: Tamesis, 1975.

Picchia, Paulo Menotti del. "Arte Moderna." in *Vanguarda européia e modernismo brasileiro,* ed. Gilberto Mendonça Teles, 287–293. Rio de Janeiro: Vozes, 1976.

Pineta, Alberto. *Verde memoria.* Buenos Aires: Antonio Zamora, 1962.

Poniatowska, Elena. *Las siete cabritas.* Mexico City: Era, 2000.

Portal, Magda. "Andamios de vida." *Amauta* 1, no. 5 (January 1927): 12.

———. "Carlos Montenegro, 'El renuevo y otros cuentos.'" *Amauta* 23 (May 1929): 100–102.

———. "Círculos de violeta." *Amauta* 1, no. 3 (November 1926): 1.

———. *Constancia del ser.* Lima: Villanueva, 1965.

———. *Una esperanza i el mar.* Lima: Minerva, 1927.

———. (Tula Soavani) "Fantasía." *Mundial* 3, no. 115 (July 28, 1922): n.pag.

———. *Flora Tristán, precursora.* Lima: Páginas Libres, 1945.

———. (Tula Soavani) "El fracaso." *Mundial* 4, no. 167 (July 27, 1923): n.pag.

———. *Hacia la mujer nueva: El Aprismo y la mujer.* Lima: Cooperativa Aprista Atahualpa, 1933.

———. "Los libros de la revolución mexicana: 'Lecturas populares' de Esperanza Velásquez Bringas." *Amauta* 11 (January 1928): 41.

———. (Tula Soavani) "Mujer." *Mundial* 2, no. 36 (January 1, 1921): n.pag.

———. *El nuevo poema i su orientación hacia una estética económica.* Mexico City: APRA, 1928.

———. Personal interview. August 22, 1983.

———. "Réplica de Magda Portal." *Amauta* 2, no. 7 (March 1927): 28.

———. "Rol de la mujer revolucionaria: El voto femenino." *Repertorio americano* 22, no. 21 (June 6, 1931): 332, 336.

———. *La trampa.* Lima: Raíz, 1956.

———. (Tula Soavani) "Violetas." *Mundial* 1, no. 6 (May 28, 1920): n. pag.

———. "Yo soy Magda Portal." In *Ser mujer en el Perú,* ed. Esther Andradi and Ana María Portugal, 209–232. Lima: Ediciones Mujer y Autonomía, 1978.

Pratt, Mary Louise. "Women, Literature, and National Brotherhood." In *Women, Culture, and Politics in Latin America,* ed. Seminar on Feminism and Culture in Latin America, 48–73. Berkeley: University of California Press, 1990.

"Prólogo-manifiesto." *Flechas* 1, no. 1 (October 23, 1924): 1–2.

Quinlan, Susan C., and Fernando Arenas. *Lusosex: Gender and Sexuality in the Portuguese Speaking World.* Minneapolis: University of Minnesota Press, 2002.

Quinlan, Susan C., and Peggy Sharpe. *Visões do passado, previsões do futuro: Duas modernistas esquecidas.* Goias, Brazil: Universidade Federal de Goiás, 1996.

Rago, Margareth. "Sexualidade e identidade na historiografia brasileira dos anos vinte e trinta." *Estudios interdisciplinarios de América Latina y el Caribe* 12, no. 1 (January–June 2001): 39–60.

————. "A subjetividade feminina entre o desejo e a norma: Moral sexual e cultura literária feminina no Brasil, 1900-1932." *Revista brasileira de história* 15, no. 28 (1995): 28–44.

Rama, Ángel. *La ciudad letrada*. Hanover, New Hampshire: Ediciones del Norte, 1984.

"Rama frágil." Review of *Rama frágil* by María Luisa Carnelli. *Caras y caretas* 29, no. 1431 (March 6, 1926): n.pag.

Ramos, Ángela. *Una vida sin tregua*. 2 vols. Lima: Minerva, 1990.

Rebagliati, Edgardo. Review of *José María Córdoba* by María Wiesse. *Mundial* 5, no. 230 (October 10, 1924): n.pag.

Reedy, Daniel R. "Aspects of the Feminist Movement in Peruvian Letters and Politics." In *The Place of Literature in Interdisciplinary Approaches,* ed. Eugene R. Huck, 53–64. Carrollton, Georgia: Thomasson, 1975.

————. *Magda Portal: La pasionaria peruana*. Lima: Flora Tristán, 2000.

————. "Magda Portal: Peru's Voice of Social Protest." *Revista de estudios hispánicos* 4, no. 1 (1970): 85–97.

————. "*La trampa:* Génesis de una novela política." *Texto/contexto en la literatura iberoamericana*. Proceedings of the XIX Congreso del Instituto Internacional de Literatura Iberoamericana, ed. Keith McDuffie and Alfred Roggiano, 299–306. Madrid: Artes Gráficas Benzal, 1980.

Reyes, Alfonso. *Vocaciones de América: Antología*. Ed. Victor Díaz Arciniega. Mexico City: Fondo de Cultura Económica, 1989.

Richards, Judith C. "Revolting Developments: Gender, Revolution, and the *Bildungsroman* in Contemporary Mexican Women's Fiction." Ph.D. diss., University of Kansas, 1994.

Risério, Antonio. "Pagu: Vida-obra, obravida, vida." In *Pagu vida-obra,* ed. Augusto de Campos, 19–30. São Paulo: Brasiliense, 1982.

Rivas Mercado, Antonieta. *Obras completas de Antonieta Rivas Mercado*. Ed. Luis Mario Schneider. Mexico City: Oasis, 1987.

Roach, Joseph. *Cities of the Dead: Circum-Atlantic Performance*. New York: Columbia University Press, 1996.

Robles, Martha. *La sombra fugitiva: Escritoras de la cultura nacional*. Mexico City: Universidad Nacional Autónoma de México, 1985.

Rodríguez Acosta, Ofelia. "Agonía." *Bohemia* 21, no. 30 (July 28, 1929): 38–39.

————. "La Alameda de Paula." *Bohemia* 21, no. 15 (April 14, 1929): 33, 54.

————. *Algunos cuentos (De ayer y de hoy)*. Mexico City: B. Costa-Amic, 1957.

————. "Anticipándonos a la vida futura." *Bohemia* 22, no. 42 (October 19, 1930): 13.

———. "El carácter y la personalidad en la mujer." *Revista de la Habana* 1, no. 1 (January–March 1930): 313–315.

———. "Carta caída de una gaveta." *Bohemia* 21, no. 36 (September 8, 1929): 9, 65.

———. "Concepto del patriotismo." *Bohemia* 22, no. 43 (October 26, 1930): 17.

———. "El derecho de amar." *Bohemia* 24, no. 21 (May 22, 1932): 13.

———. *Dolientes*. Havana: Hermes, 1931.

———. "Doscientos años atrás." *Bohemia* 21, no. 3 (January 20, 1929): 30–31, 58.

———. *En la noche del mundo*. Havana: La Verónica, 1940.

———. "Exigencias de la vida moderna." *Bohemia* 23, no. 4 (March 22, 1931): 28.

———. "Feminismo efectivo." *Bohemia* 22, no. 21 (May 25, 1930): 10.

———. "Feminismo teórico y feminismo práctico." *Bohemia* 22, no. 2 (January 12, 1930): 9.

———. "El gobierno de las mujeres." *Bohemia* 24, no. 23 (June 5, 1932): 13.

———. "Homenaje a Mariblanca de Cuba." *Bohemia* 22, no. 27 (July 6, 1930): 17.

———. "La importancia de un teléfono." *Social* (April 1927): 33, 69, 72.

———. "La intelectual feminista y la feminista no intelectual." *Revista de la Habana* 1, no. 1 (January–March 1930): 75–79.

———. "La lepra social." *Bohemia* 24, no. 5 (January 31, 1932): 11.

———. "Más allá." *Bohemia* 23, no. 21 (September 20, 1931): 17.

———. "Mujeres de cabaret." *Social* (February 1930): 45, 90.

———. "Por los fueros de la cultura." *Bohemia* 23, no. 16 (June 14, 1931): 21.

———. "El postulado de la ciencia." *Bohemia* 22, no. 40 (October 5, 1930): 19.

———. "La propia ruta." *Bohemia* 24, no. 22 (May 29, 1932): 13.

———. "La raza humana." *Bohemia* 24, no. 29 (July 17, 1932): 17.

———. "El ritual en nuestra vida." *Bohemia* 21, no. 41 (October 13, 1929): 19.

———. "Sobre la manera de producir del novelista." *Revista de la Habana* 2, no. 3 (June 1930): 253–257.

———. *Sonata interrumpida*. Mexico City: Minerva, 1943.

———. *La tragedia social de la mujer: Conferencia*. Havana: Genesis, 1932.

———. *La vida manda*. 2d ed. Madrid: Rubén Darío, 1930.

Roig de Leuchsenring, Emilio. "Nuestros colaboradores los Minoristas." *Social* (January 1926): 34.

Rojas Rosillo, Isaac. Prologue to *87 Cartas de amor y otros papeles,* by Antonieta Rivas Mercado, ed. Isaac Rojas Rosillo, 9–17. Xalapa, Mexico: Biblioteca Universidad Veracruzana, 1980.

Russ, Joanna. *How to Suppress Women's Writing*. Austin: University of Texas Press, 1983.

Ruy Sánchez, Alberto. Prologue to vol. 1 of *Trama de vientos: Cuentos y relatos completos,* by José Martínez Sotomayor, 9–29. Mexico City: Colección Biblioteca, 1987.

Sabas Alomá, Mariblanca. "A la emancipación por la cultura." *Carteles* 15, no. 23 (June 8, 1930): 16, 67–68.

———. "A las mujeres mexicanas." *Carteles* 18, no. 14 (April 3, 1932): 20.

———. "Ah! . . . si fuera así!" *Carteles* 14, no. 3 (August 18, 1929): 16, 48.

———. "Algo más que recitar." *Carteles* 19, no. 19 (May 7, 1933): 24, 44.

———. "Algo sobre nudismo." *Carteles* 17, no. 36 (November 8, 1931): 42.

———. "Ana Abril Toro de Torres, honra del magisterio cubano." *Carteles* 12, no. 45 (November 4, 1928): 26, 38, 43.

———. "Como queremos que nos quieran." *Carteles* 18, no. 34 (August 21, 1932): 44.

———. "De mi humilde soberbia." *Carteles* 17, no. 34 (October 25, 1931): 28.

———. "Elia, Francisco, Guayabal." *Carteles* 18, no. 51 (December 18, 1932): 32, 44.

———. "Una entrevista con Carlos Montenegro." *Carteles* 12, no. 39 (September 23, 1928): 14, 45.

———. "Feminidad." *Carteles* 17, no. 3 (May 31, 1931): 28, 44–45.

———. *Feminismo: Cuestiones sociales—crítica literaria.* Havana: Hermes, 1930.

———. "Figuras del ayer glorioso." *Carteles* 11, no. 21 (May 20, 1928): 17–18, 48.

———. "Guajira y pobre," *Carteles* 14, no. 34 (August 25, 1929): 16, 64.

———. "Ida Mola, novelista y argumentista cubana." *Carteles* 18, no. 19 (May 8, 1932): 40, 47.

———. "El indio inmóvil." *Carteles* 16, no. 37 (September 14, 1930): 18, 56.

———. "Letras a Mañach." *Carteles* 17, no. 31 (October 4, 1931): 16.

———. "Un libro; una mujer; un carácter." *Carteles* 18.36 (September 4, 1932): 44.

———. "Literatura femenina: 'Cuentos', de Hortensia de Varela." *Carteles* 18, no. 39 (September 25, 1932): 28, 45.

———. "Lyceum. Una entrevista con su presidente, Bertha A. de Martínez Márquez." *Carteles* 13, no. 10 (March 10, 1929): 26, 40.

———. "Maledicencia tradicional." *Carteles* 19, no. 22 (May 28, 1933): 32.

———. "¡Me parece muy bien!" *Carteles* 17, no. 22 (August 2, 1931): 18, 70.

———. "Un muchacho de hoy." *Carteles* 17, no. 27 (September 6, 1931): 16.

———. "La moral del seudónimo." *Carteles* 13, no. 4 (January 27, 1929): 16, 43.

———. "Nuestra Gabriela." *Carteles* 17, no. 19 (July 12, 1931): 18, 58.

———. "Ofelia Rodríguez Acosta, la originalidad de las ideas, y yo." *Carteles* 12, no. 40 (September 30, 1928): 20, 40, 43.

————. "Palabras a la mujer dominicana." *Carteles* 17, no. 33 (October 18, 1931): 28, 48.

————. "Un pie sentimental para un retrato." *Carteles* 18, no. 46 (November 13, 1932): 28.

————. "Poema de la mujer aviadora que quiere atravesar el Atlántico." *Repertorio americano* 16, no. 14 (April 14, 1928): 218.

————. "Poema en cinco aristas y una llama." *Social* (October 1932): 10.

————. "Poema en si bemol." *Social* (July 1928): 34.

————. "Primer congreso de poetas de vanguardia." In *Manifiestos, proclamas y polémicas de la vanguardia literaria hispanoamericana,* ed. Nelson Osorio, 321–325. Caracas: Ayacucho, 1988.

————. "Regino Pedroso poeta proletario." *Carteles* 19, no. 15 (April 9, 1933): 40.

————. *La rémora.* Havana: El Siglo XX, 1921.

————. "Los siete puñales." *Carteles* 17, no. 8 (April 26, 1931): 26, 64

————. "¡Tampa cubanísima!" *Carteles* 13, no. 26 (June 30, 1929): 12, 56.

————. "El terrible caso de Ruth Kinsey." *Carteles* 15, no. 24 (June 15, 1930): 18, 47.

————. "Vanguardismo." *Repertorio americano* 16, no. 23 (June 16, 1928): 359.

Sarlo, Beatriz. *Una modernidad periférica: Buenos Aires, 1920 y 1930.* Buenos Aires: Nueva Visión, 1988.

————, ed. *Martín Fierro 1924–1927.* Buenos Aires: Carlos Pérez, 1969.

Schechner, Richard. *Between Theater and Anthropology.* Philadelphia: University of Pennsylvania Press, 1985.

————. *Performance Theory.* Revised edition, New York: Routledge, 1988.

Schlau, Stacey. *Spanish American Women's Use of the Word: Colonial Through Contemporary Narratives.* Tucson: University of Arizona Press, 2001.

Schmidhuber, Guillermo. *El teatro mexicano en cierne, 1922–1938.* New York: Peter Lang, 1992.

Schneider, Luis Mario. *Fragua y gesta del teatro experimental en México: Teatro de Ulises. Escolares del teatro. Teatro de Orientación.* Mexico City: Universidad Nacional Autónoma de México, 1995.

————, ed. *Obras completas de Antonieta Rivas Mercado.* Mexico City: Oasis, 1981.

Scott, Joan. "Experience." In *Feminists Theorize the Political,* ed. Judith Butler and Joan Scott, 22–40. New York: Routledge, 1992.

Segura, Felipe. *Gloria Campobello: La primera ballerina de México.* Mexico City: Instituto Nacional de Bellas Artes, 1991.

Seminar on Feminism and Culture in Latin America, ed. *Women, Culture, and Politics in Latin America.* Berkeley: University of California Press, 1990.

Sheridan, Guillermo. *México en 1932: La polémica nacionalista.* Mexico City: Fondo de Cultura Económica, 1999.

Skirius, John. *José Vasconcelos y la cruzada de 1929*. Trans. Félix Blanco. Mexico City: Siglo Veintiuno, 1978.

Smith, Anna Deavere. *Talk to Me: Listening between the Lines*. New York: Random House, 2000.

Smith, Myriam. "Re-Thinking the Vanguardia: The Poetry and Politics of Magda Portal." Ph.D. diss., University of California, Santa Barbara, 2000.

Sofovich de Gómez de la Serna, Luisa. "Retrato con pelo dorado." In *Páginas escogidas de Norah Lange,* ed. Beatriz de Nóbile, 136–148. Buenos Aires: Kapelusz, 1972.

Sommer, Doris. "Mirror, Mirror, in Mother's Room: Watch Us While We Tell and Groom." In *Mama Blanca's Memoirs,* by Teresa de la Parra, trans. Harriet de Onís and Frederick H. Fornoff, 162–183. Critical edition. Pittsburgh: University of Pittsburgh Press, 1993.

———. *Proceed with Caution, When Engaged by Minority Writing in the Americas*. Cambridge: Harvard University Press, 1999.

Soravilla, Lesbia. *El dolor de vivir*. Havana: n.p., 1932.

States, Bert. "Performance as Metaphor." *Theatre Journal* 48 (1996): 1–26.

Stoner, K. Lynn. *From the House to the Streets: The Cuban Woman's Movement for Legal Reform, 1898–1940*. Durham, North Carolina: Duke University Press, 1991.

Storni, Alfonsina. "Algunas líneas." *La Nota* 2, no. 66 (November 11, 1916): 1307–1308.

———. *Antología poética*. 6th ed. Buenos Aires: Espasa-Calpe, 1943.

———. "Autodemolición." *Repertorio americano* 20, no. 21 (June 7, 1930): 329, 331.

———. "Derechos civíles femeninos." *La Nota* 5, no. 210 (August 22, 1919): 877–878.

———. "La fina crueldad." *La Nota* 2, no. 69 (December 2, 1916): 1365–1366.

———. "Niñas." *Nuestra Revista* 4, no. 45 (March 1924): 56–59.

———. *Nosotras . . . y la piel: Selección de ensayos de Alfonsina Storni*. Comp. Mariela Méndez, Graciela Queirolo, and Alicia Salomone. Buenos Aires: Alfaguara, 1998.

———. *Obra poética completa*. Buenos Aires: Meridión, 1961.

———. *Obras escogidas: Teatro*. Buenos Aires: Sociedad Editora Latina Americana, 1984.

———. *Poemas de amor*. Buenos Aires: Nosotros, 1926.

Strickland Nájera, Valeska. "La obra de Nellie Campobello." Ph.D. diss., Northwestern University, 1980.

Suleiman, Susan Rubin. *Subversive Intent: Gender, Politics, and the Avant-Garde*. Cambridge: Harvard University Press, 1990.

Teixeira Furlani, Lúcia Maria. *Pagu—Patrícia Galvão livre na imaginação, no espaço, e no tempo.* Santos, Brazil: Editora da Universidade Santa Cecília dos Bandeirantes, 1989.

Testimonios sobre Victoria Ocampo. Buenos Aires: n.p., 1962.

Tibol, Raquel. *Pasos en la danza mexicana.* Mexico City: Difusión Cultural, Universidad Nacional Autónoma de México, 1982.

Toledo, J. *Flávio de Carvalho: O comedor de emoções.* São Paulo: Brasiliense, 1994.

Toro Montalvo, César. Vol. 11 of *Historia de la literatura peruana.* 13 vols. Lima: AFA Editores, 1996.

Tortajada Quiroz, Margarita. "Danza de mujer: el nacionalismo revolucionario de Nellie Campobello." *El cotidiano* 84 (July–August 1997): 87–94.

———. *Danza y poder.* Mexico City: INBA, 1995.

Turner, Victor. "Frame, Flow and Reflection: Ritual Drama as Public Liminality." In *Performance in Postmodern Culture,* ed. Michel Benamou and Charles Caramello, 35–55. Milwaukee: University of Wisconsin-Milwaukee Center for Twentieth Century Studies, 1977.

Unruh, Vicky. "Las ágiles musas de la modernidad: Patrícia Galvão y Norah Lange." *Revista iberoamericana* 64, no. 182–183 (January–June 1998): 271–286.

———. "¿De quién es esta historia? La narrativa de vanguardias en Latinoamérica." In *Naciendo el hombre nuevo . . . Fundir la literatura, artes y vida como práctica de vanguardias en el Mundo Ibérico,* ed. Hans Wentzlaff Eggebert, 249–265. Frankfurt am Main, Germany: Vervuert Verlag, 1999.

———. *Latin American Vanguards: The Art of Contentious Encounters.* Berkeley: University of California Press, 1994.

———. "Mariátegui's Aesthetic Thought: A Critical Reading of the Avant-Gardes." *Latin American Research Review* 24, no. 3 (1989): 45–69.

———. "Teresa de la Parra and the Avant-Gardes: An Equivocal Encounter with Literary Culture." In *Todo ese fuego: Homenaje a Merlin Forster,* ed. Mara García and Douglas Weatherford, 65–79. Universidad Autónoma de Tlaxcala, 1999.

Urquieta, Miguel Ángel. "César Atahualpa Rodríguez." *Libros y revistas* 1, no. 6 (December 1926): 4.

———. "Izquierdismo y seudoizquierdismo artísticos." *Amauta* 2, no. 7 (March 1927): 25–27.

Valente, Luiz Fernando. "Canonizando Pagu." *Letras de hoje* 33, no. 3 (September 1998): 27–38.

Varona, Enrique José. "Feminismo." *Revista de avance* 2, no. 15 (November 15, 1927): 64.

Vasconcelos, José. *El desastre. El proconsulado.* Vol. 2 of *Memorias.* Mexico City: Fondo de Cultura Económica, 1982.

Vásquez, Maria Esther. *Victoria Ocampo*. Buenos Aires: Planeta, 1991.

Villaurrutia, Xavier. *Obras*. Mexico City: Fondo de Cultura Económica, 1953.

Weininger, Otto. *Sex and Character*. Authorized translation. New York: William Heinemann and G. P. Putnam's Sons, 1906.

Wiesse, María. "Algunos apuntes sobre literatura femenina (fragmentos de un ensayo)." *Variedades* 7, no. 633 (April 17, 1920): n.pag.

———. "El alma americana." *Variedades* 7 (July 7, 1920): 11–12.

———. *Croquis de viaje*. Lima: Rosay, 1924.

———. "El hechizo." *Mundial* 2, no. 55 (May 13, 1921): n.pag.

———. *La hermana mayor. El modistón*. Lima: Centro Editorial 1918.

———. *La huachafita (ensayo de novela limeña)*. Lima: Lux, 1927.

———. "Infancia." *Amauta* 3, no. 16 (July 1928): 28.

———. *José Carlos Mariátegui: Etapas de su vida*. Vol. 10 of *Obras completas de José Carlos Mariátegui*. Lima: Amauta, 1982.

———. *José María Córdova (1799–1829) ensayo biográfico*. Lima: Voce d'Italia, 1924.

———. *José Sabogal: El artista y el hombre*. Lima: n.p., 1967.

———. "Literatura femenina (fragmentos de un ensayo)." *Variedades* 7, no. 635 (May 1, 1920): 437–438.

———. "Notas sobre algunos films." *Amauta* 4, no. 26 (September–October 1929): 99–100.

———. "900." *Amauta* 3, no. 13 (March 1928): 43–44.

———. *Nueve relatos*. Lima: n.p., 1933.

———. "La página femenina." *Mundial* 47 (March 18, 1921), 49 (April 1, 1921), 50 (April 8, 1921), 52 (April 22, 1921), 55 (May 13, 1921), 58 (June 3, 1921), 60 (June 17, 1921), 61 (June 24, 1921), n.pag.

———. "Pequeñas prosas." *Amauta* 3, no. 15 (June 1928): 29.

———. "Poetas americanos modernos." *Variedades* 7 (July 7, 1920): n.pag.

———. *Quipus: Relatos peruanos para niños*. Lima: La Voce d'Italia, 1936.

———. *La romántica vida de Mariano Melgar*. Lima: Club del Libro Peruano, 1938.

———. *Rosario: Historia de una niña*. Lima: Lux, 1929.

———. "San Francisco de Asís y nuestro siglo." *Amauta* 1, no. 2 (October 1926): 3.

———. "Señales de nuestro tiempo." *Amauta* 1, no. 4 (December 1926): 11–12.

———. *Vida del Perú y su pueblo; ensayo*. Lima: n.p., 1958.

Wiesse, María, ed. *Antología de la poesía amorosa peruana*. Lima: Hora del Hombre, 1946.

Williams, Raymond. *Keywords: A Vocabulary of Culture and Society*. Revised edition. New York: Oxford University Press, 1985.

gender, 37, 41, 63–64; and language, 41, 86, 93, 121–122; and performance, 52, 88, 112; and women, 161, 181
Boedo group, 9, 32, 55
Bohemia (periodical), 2, 135, 138, 143, 146, 153, 236nn4,5, 237n14, 238nn28,34
Bombal, María Luisa, 29
Bopp, Raul, 195–198
Borges, Jorge Luis, 9, 49, 72–77, 91, 228nn14,16
Bourdieu, Pierre, 7–8, 35
Bradu, Fabienne, 117, 120, 127, 132, 232n5, 234n17, 235n21,22
Brecht, Bertolt, 40, 200
Brum, Blanca Luz, 29, 140, 148, 166
Bürger, Peter, 200
Burgos, Carmen de, 148
Burke, Kenneth, 7
Butler, Judith, 4, 8, 35, 63, 84, 145, 171, 179, 216

Cabrera, Lydia, 29
Cairo, Ana, 136, 140, 150, 236, 238n25
Campobello, Nellie: and androgyny, 93, 101–103, 108, 113; and art of living, 93–94, 100; authochthonous forms, 95, 112, 232n40; and authorial persona, 93, 98, 101–102, 106; and avant-gardes, 100–103, 106, 111; biography, 94–95; and the body, 92, 99–103, 109–112, 232n40; and dance, 28, 92–100, 112, 199, 229n3; and fashion, 95, 104; and feminism, 104, 112; and gender, 96–98, 103–104, 108; and journalism, 100, 105; and *machismo*, 96–97; and *mexicanidad*, 93–98, 103, 115; and Miss Carroll's Girls, 94–105; and modernity, 100–104, 113; and the New Woman, 96–98,

101–103, 110–113; and performance, 92–95, 114; and pose, 92–94, 97–99, 102–113, 231n28; and theatre, 94, 100; and writing, 92–94, 98–105, 108–110, 113. Works: *Apuntes . . .*, 113–114; *Ballet de masas 30–30*, 92, 108; *Cartucho*, 92–93, 99–114, 203, 230–231, 231nn33,36; "Collar," 101; "8 poemas de mujer," 99, 102, 105–108, 111; "Juego," 101; *Las manos de mamá*, 93, 99, 105, 110–113, 230n20; "Mi pobre grandeza," 102; *Mis libros*, 92–93, 98–105, 110–114, 230n18, 231nn24,26,37; *Ritmos indígenas . . .*, 95, 113; "Tenacidad," 102; *Tres poemas*, 99; *Yo, por Francisca*, 93–95, 99–102, 231n24
Campos, Augusto de, 221, 243n15
Caras y caretas (periodical), 1, 11–13, 39, 45, 222n13
Carlson, Marvin, 3
Carpentier, Alejo, 9, 100, 136, 140, 163
Carteles (periodical), 2, 135–138, 143–149, 236n5, 237nn14,21
Castillo Ledón, Amalia de, 29
Contemporáneos (periodical), 117
Contemporáneos group, 11–12, 25, 93–94, 100, 117, 129–134
Craik, Jennifer, 35, 213–214
Cruz, Sor Juana Inés de la, 37, 48, 125
Culture: body, 111; 85; concept of, 6; and fashion, 31, 123; and gender, 123, 128, 137; intellectual, 41, 136; literary, 2, 4, 7–10, 13–14, 16–17, 19–21, 22, 24–25, 27–29, 42, 49, 54, 56, 65, 70, 72, 74, 76, 82, 98, 100, 107, 136–137, 150, 152, 157–158, 160, 162–167, 173, 184, 188,

173, 183–185, 189, 193, 241nn25,30,31,32

Nación, La (periodical), 49–50, 55, 62, 168
Nelken, Margarita, 23, 125
Newman, Kathleen, 23
New Woman, the: and *Amauta,* 170; and androgyny, 41; Aprista, 172; Argentine, 12–15, 28, 45; as consumer, 2, 15, 48; and Mariátegui, 166; masculine, 131–133, 207; and media, 15, 48, 98, 138, 171; and *modernismo* (Spanish American), 15, 158; and modernity, 10; and performance, 5, 87, 133, 137, 161, 184, 191; and the professional writer, 14, 20; U.S. models of, 25, 116; and writing, 2, 4
Noailles, Anna de, 58, 63, 78, 226n24
Nogueira Cobra, Ercília, 29, 206
Nosotros (periodical), 12, 32, 49
Nosotros group, 31, 33, 55
Novo, Salvador, 16, 140

Ocampo, Victoria: and art of living, 55; and avant-gardes, 53–56, 225nn5,9; biography, 53–55; and the body, 63–64, 224n1, 226n22; and the city, 56–57; and Dante, 55, 58, 63–64, 66–69; and dialogue, 59–67, 226n25; and feminism, 58, 70–71; and gender, 27, 54–59, 71; as guide, 68–69; and the intellectual, 53–58, 66–67, 70; and mass culture, 57, 70; and modernity, 67, 225n5; and the New Woman, 56, 66; and performance, 52–53, 56, 60–66, 225nn1,4; and the reader, 56, 66–68, 226n26; and Storni, 54, 70–71, 76, 227n33; and *Sur,*

53, 100; and *testimonio,* 52–55, 60–69; and theatre, 60–61, 226n1; and women, 57–58, 68–69; and writing, 53–60, 63, 66–71, 225n9, 226n29. Works: *Autobiografía,* 52, 54–56, 63–64, 66–69; *Domingos . . . ,* 66; *De Francesca a Beatrice,* 55–67, 225n8; *La laguna . . . ,* 52–55, 61–64, 68; *Testimonios,* 58–59, 62–66, 227n33
Oliveira, Emanuelle, 202
Orozco, José Clemente, 100, 114
Ortega y Gasset, José, 58, 64–66, 70, 165, 176; 225n8, 240n19
Owen, Hilary, 209, 211

Para todos (periodical), 2, 195, 199, 204, 242n3
Parker, Andrew, 3, 222n2
Parra, Teresa de la, 26, 27, 28, 148, 149, 223nn19,21; and avant-gardes, 22; and feminism, 21; and modern women, 22; and performance, 21. Works: *Ifigenia . . . ,* 17–20; *Las memorias de Mamá Blanca,* 17–22
Pérez Firmat, Gustavo, 14
Performance: and art of living, 3–9, 162; and the body, 5, 52, 88, 112; concepts of, 3–9, 210; and culture, 4–9, 27, 118, 146–147, 167, 184, 196–197, 205, 212, 215, 218; and feminism, 155, 159; and gender, 33, 59, 96; and the New Woman, 4–5, 15, 21, 87, 146–147, 161, 170, 184, 193; and *poetisa* role, 31, 33, 43; and posing, 97, 230n15; and rehearsal, 40–41; and theatre, 4–6, 28, 34, 198–201, 207, 209–210, 212, 219; theory, 3–9; and the woman writer, 2, 9, 19, 27, 33, 39, 200; and women, 15–16, 41, 76–77,

Variedades (periodical), 2, 166–167, 183–185, 189, 241n27
Varona, Enrique José, 135
Vasconcelos, José, 94–95, 115–116, 124
Villaurrutia, Xavier, 101, 117–119, 124

Weininger, Otto, 58, 124
Wiesse, María: and Amauta, 26, 100, 166, 183, 184; and authorial persona, 184, 187, 189, 192; and avant-gardes, 165–167, 188–191; biography, 183–184; and fashion, 184, 190; and feminism, 165–167, 184, 187, 190–192; and film, 167, 183; and gender, 167, 185–187, 190–191; and the intellectual, 166, 183–184, 187, 192; and journalism, 167, 185, 188–190; and Mariátegui, 188, 192; and masculinity, 185, 192; and modernity, 187–189, 194; and performance, 184; and Portal, 164, 183–184, 187–193; and the reader, 186, 190; and Sabogal, 192; and women, 28, 166, 184–190; and writing, 184–188, 192–193. Works: Antología de . . . , 188; Croquis de viaje, 185–189, 192; "El forastero," 189, 241n26; "El hechizo," 193; La hermana mayor, 184, 189–190; La huachafita, 184, 190; "Infancia," 192, 242n36; El lazo, 184; José Sabogal . . . , 193; "Levedades," 189, 241n24; El modistón, 184; Nueve relatos, 189; "La página femenina," 189, 241nn25,30,31,32; Quipus . . . , 188; La romántica vida . . . , 188; Rosario . . . , 184, 190–192; Vida del Perú . . . , 188
Wilde, Oscar, 45, 181, 189
Woman writer, the: aesthetic strategies of, 19; and androgyny, 162; and avant-gardes, 2, 73, 153; and the Contemporáneos, 130, 134; and fashion, 30, 41; and feminism, 135, 147, 153; and Mariátegui, 166, 177; in México, 98; and modernity, 188; and modernization, 188, 204; and performance, 1, 2, 27; professional, 66; role of, 41, 56
Writing: and the Contemporáneos, 130, 134; and fashion, 30–31, 41; and gender, 12, 31; and literature, 150; and masculinity, 11, 97; and motherhood, 125; and the New Woman, 2–6; and self-portrayal, 138, 168; and voice, 53
Woolf, Virginia, 56–59, 70–71

Milton Keynes UK
Ingram Content Group UK Ltd.
UKHW011442031123
431797UK00012B/158